NAZIS OF COPLEY SQUARE

NAZIS

OF COPLEY SQUARE

THE FORGOTTEN STORY
OF THE CHRISTIAN FRONT

CHARLES R. GALLAGHER

Harvard University Press

Cambridge, Massachusetts & London, England

First Harvard University Press paperback edition, 2023
First printing

Publication of this book has been supported through the generous provisions of the
Maurice and Lula Bradley Smith Memorial Fund.

Library of Congress Cataloging-in-Publication Data
Names: Gallagher, Charles R., 1965– author.
Title: Nazis of Copley Square : the forgotten story of the Christian Front /
  Charles R. Gallagher.
Description: Cambridge, Massachusetts : Harvard University Press, 2021. |
  Includes bibliographical references and index.
Identifiers: LCCN 2020055096 | ISBN 9780674983717 (cloth) |
  ISBN 9780674293878 (pbk.)
Subjects: LCSH: Coughlin, Charles E. (Charles Edward), 1891–1979. | Christian Front.
  | Fascism and the Catholic Church—United States—History—20th century. |
  Nazis—United States—History—20th century. | Anti-communist movements—
  United States—History—20th century. | Christianity and antisemitism—
  United States—History—20th century.
Classification: LCC BX1397 .G345 2021 | DDC 940.53 / 73088282—dc23
LC record available at https://lccn.loc.gov/2020055096

To the memory of Joseph G. Gallagher

CONTENTS

NAZIS OF COPLEY SQUARE

Introduction

IN THE SUMMER OF 1939, FATHER CHARLES EDWARD COUGHLIN, famed "Radio Priest" of Detroit, Michigan, called for the creation of a Christian Front. He hoped the group would act as a counterpoise to the Popular Front, adopted by the Seventh World Congress of the Communist International in 1935 and ostensibly aimed at reconciling revolutionary objectives with a commitment to democracy. As far as Coughlin was concerned, this was merely sleight of hand—a "nefarious . . . endeavor to Sovietize America" wearing "the false mask of liberalism." In his broadcasts and his publications, Coughlin pushed his millions of followers to reject atheistic Communism in the name of Christ and country, and he saw a Christian Front as the key means of resistance.[1]

Coughlin is familiar to readers of US history, especially those who have hoped to understand the influence of the far right on modern American politics. Less well known are the men and women who fought to make the dream of a Christian Front a reality. This book tells their story. They were American Catholics, led by now-forgotten lay acolytes like John F. Cassidy of New York and Francis P. Moran of Boston. The people who formed the Christian Front saw themselves as the advance guard in a holy war against Communists and Jews—groups whom they perceived as one and the same, under the rubric of what scholars have called Judeo-Bolshevism. This is also a story of how Catholics came to embrace anti-Semitic violence as theologically permissible. Along the way, the work of the Christian Front became embroiled with that of President Franklin Roosevelt, Prime Minister Winston Churchill, and the top brass of the Third Reich. There were terrorist plots in New York and Nazi spies in Boston. And there were priests. At its heart, the story of the Christian Front is one of priests who drew upon some of the most vibrant theological movements of the Catholic Church and used them to justify evil.[2]

Priests provided political cover, theological leadership, and ecclesiastic approval for the far-right Christian Front movement. Although the front was a lay organization, priest advisers enabled its growth and prosperity, whether by promoting the front's mission or by defending its members against their critics. When fronters got into trouble with the law, priests were there to rationalize and downplay their actions. Coughlin, the most famous priest of the 1930s, was the spiritual leader of the front, but he did not work alone. Fathers Edward Lodge Curran of Brooklyn and Edward F. Brophy of Queens both dedicated their energies to building up the Christian Front in New York and Boston from 1938 to 1945. The Jesuit Michael Ahern of Boston played a key role in preserving the front when it was under threat.

The details of the Christian Front receive little attention from historians. Its origins and genuinely Catholic philosophy have gone unexplored, as has the role of the Boston front during World War II, when Francis Moran knowingly served as a Nazi agent whose purpose was to propagandize on behalf of American neutrality—a task he took up in the name of Christ and the Church, not in the name of Hitler or the German volk. Even the front's most notorious moment occupies hardly more than a footnote in the larger histories of the American right and the American Catholic Church: the 1940 sedition trial of John Cassidy and a small group of his New York fronters, who attempted to incite a revolution. Their goal was to install in the United States a temporary dictatorship that would eliminate Communists and Jews.

But the Christian Front was well known in the United States in its own time. The news coverage was voluminous, and the radio broadcasts were constant. Front rallies routinely attracted thousands of attendees. Governors, mayors, and police commissioners both loathed and courted the front. Joseph Goebbels, the commander-in-chief of Nazi propaganda, toasted Moran. British intelligence worked hard to take the front down; there is reason to believe Soviet spies also tried. A raft of US law enforcement and intelligence joined in the effort. The FBI's Christian Front file amounts to 2,500 pages, equaling its file on Martin Luther King Jr. and the Southern Christian Leadership Conference. By sheer quantity of paper, the Christian Front investigation was one of the three largest the bureau ever undertook.

In 1940, when fronters were on trial, US Catholic leadership swept the organization's deeds under the rug. But not only their deeds: what mattered above all to the front's clerical protectors was that the defendants' views never be associated with sincere Catholicism. Remarkably, prosecutors participated in this project, demanding that the front's revolutionary action had nothing to do with religion. Yet everything the front did, in New York and Boston, had everything to do with religion. The front propounded the myth of Judeo-Bolshevism because its pious working-class membership, radicalized by priests and charismatic laypeople, understood Communism to be a Jewish-led plot against Christianity. Fronters believed firmly in the deicide, the idea that Jews had killed Christ, and their leaders moved them from this age-old position toward a distinctly modern and violent blend of anti-Semitism and anti-Communism.

The paramilitarism for which the New York fronters were indicted reflected more than a simple excess of zeal. So did the explosion in Boston, in 1943, of police-abetted anti-Semitic street gangs inspired by the front. The front and its followers were acting on their true conviction. At the foundation of this conviction lay what I call theological anti-Communism, a novel doctrine blessed by the highest reaches of the Vatican, albeit the hierarchy never used this term. The Vatican approved the idea that Christians everywhere were linked spiritually and indeed physically in a single body engaged in a divinely ordained conflict with Communism. And because fronters understood Communism to be a Jewish plot, they extended the Vatican's blessing to incorporate anti-Semitism, sacralizing their war on Jews.

This was not a war for capitalism. Fronters were not laissez-faire libertarians but rather populists with many socialistic preferences. They agitated for fairness under a system they called Christian economics, which meant business opportunities for everyday Christians, welfare for Christians in need, and redistribution from Jews to Christians. They were often anti-union, but because unions were perceived as infected by Communism. Some American far-rightists were "pro-business," but the front often took aim at corporate barons. Coughlin despised Roosevelt and the New Deal but also championed Social Security.

The fronters were also not engaged in a war for America, although their avowed patriotism was not false, either. To the extent that they saw the

United States as an expression of Christian values, they were passionate Americans. They were also covetous of their constitutional rights, especially the right of free speech, which they mistook as a guarantee against not only government censorship but also private sanction. Yet the fronters had little interest in democracy and no loyalty to the United States as such—only to their vision of the United States as a Christian nation.

From its first days to its last, the front served one master: religious faith. Its leaders preached hate, praised and worked for Hitler, and engaged in violence because they understood these actions as fulfilling the requirements of Catholic dogma.

Forgetting the Front

With rare exceptions, students of American politics and religion have ignored the Christian Front. Historian Rick Perlstein has argued that organizations like the front tend to go missing from accounts of the twentieth century because they reflect the "political surrealism of the paranoid fringe." In other words, the likes of the front were so ridiculous, irrational, and utopian—and so far from the centers of influence—that they were presumed irrelevant in the broad sweep of history. *Nazis of Copley Square*, a reference to the Boston neighborhood where Moran had his headquarters, bears out Perlstein's insight. The seditious plot of which the New York front was accused was so absurd that hardly anyone could believe Cassidy was serious, even when the evidence was plain to see. The fronters had collected rifles and probably also two military-grade machine guns. They had built pipe bombs and assembled plans to deploy their ordnance. But fewer than twenty men were active in the scheme, and twenty men cannot overthrow the US government.[3]

But, as Perlstein also has argued, "the 'far right' was never that far from the American mainstream." Our story bears out this insight as well. The front's narrowly targeted economic populism looks similar to that which Donald Trump promoted during his 2016 election campaign. The front possessed settled ideas on issues such as free speech, isolationism, globalism, pronatalism, and religious liberty—constants of American politics. The front was also a dominant force in mainstream institutions: in New York and Boston, the police were rife with fronters and front sympathizers. Both Moran and Cassidy, alongside some journalists who investigated them, knew the front could count on the police. Cassidy and the New Yorkers also made inroads in the National

Guard. And if the front itself never achieved the scale that Coughlin hoped for—he anticipated millions of members, coast to coast—the Radio Priest himself spread the front's message far and wide. He was one of the most popular broadcasters of his day, and his newspaper, *Social Justice*, was widely read.

The front also was considerably more tied into establishment politics and media than one might expect of the paranoid fringe. Moran was chummy with James Michael Curley, who served multiple terms as a US congressman, mayor of Boston, and governor of Massachusetts. At one point House Speaker John W. McCormick, a US representative from Boston, protected Moran from possible incarceration under wartime custodial detention laws. Cassidy was a press darling who could get a quote in the *New York Times* seemingly whenever he felt like it. When Cassidy was on trial, top-ranking members of the US Catholic hierarchy petitioned the Justice Department and FBI Director J. Edgar Hoover on his behalf. *Time* magazine ran interference for Cassidy during the trial.

Alongside political historians, theologians and historians of religion also have underestimated the Christian Front. These scholars have failed to parse the theological claims of the front and of Christian extremists generally. The thinking seems to be that we can either take claims of religious motivation at face value or simply discount such claims as false and then look no further— that nothing is gained in knowing the details. It is especially easy to embrace such incuriosity when it comes to the front. In its most public moment, during the federal trial in New York, both the Catholic hierarchy and the US government agreed that the front was not a religious organization. Thus the tendency with respect to the Christian Front has been to view the organization as one of an endless range of American anti-Communist groups, albeit a group that disingenuously claimed the mantle of Christianity. In fact the front's Christianity was not disingenuous, and the exact nature of its Christianity is essential to understanding its mission and the choices its leaders made. If historians wish to shed light on the American religious right, they will have to become exegetes.

Taking the Christianity of the Christian Front seriously demands that we step outside the grand narrative of American Catholic history. This is the narrative of assimilation: of a constant process of Roman Catholic incorporation into the American democratic project. Broadly, this narrative sees American Catholics transforming from a small, persecuted minority in the eighteenth century into a politically empowered bloc by the late nineteenth century, and by the mid-twentieth century entering the halls of power in Washington. Catholics beat back the discrimination of the Know-Nothings and the KKK and, during World War I, fought bravely on the battlefield, proving their patriotism and their loyalty. Under President Roosevelt, Catholics occupied cabinet-level appointments and other high administrative positions. From there came the ascendence of the Kennedys, a slew of Supreme Court justices, and another Catholic president, Joe Biden.

These civic notables are merely the most visible expression of a less celebrated, but perhaps more important, trend. Catholics have successfully pursued what every immigrant group seeks: standing as ordinary citizens. Delighting in motherhood and apple pie, Catholics fully embraced not just the American creed but also the American state. As Steve Rosswurm put it in *The FBI and the Catholic Church, 1935–1962*, a book that does not address the Christian Front, there solidified at mid-century a "friendly convergence of values between the US government, the FBI, and American Catholics." One needs no theological analysis to understand this historical trajectory of uninterrupted Americanization.[4]

And yet, along the way, the Christian Front, a group of ardent Catholics influenced by priests, attempted to overthrow the US government. St. Thomas Aquinas described sedition as "a special sin, having something in common with war and strife."[5] But here was Cassidy, the leader of the seditionists, clasping his Rosary beads while being hauled off to his jail cell. The Christian Front smashes the simplistic Americanist historical narrative and challenges us to think more deeply about what exactly constitutes Catholic values as they relate to the political sphere. In this book we will take up that challenge, for the actions of the Christian Front were every bit a result of their values, and their values were Catholic through and through.

A Matter of Faith

The rejection of Aquinas and of American law speaks to the importance of theology in understanding what the Christian Front did. Catholicism changed during the twentieth century, as Catholics, guided by their Church, learned to pledge their loyalty to each other even when doing so collided with their obligations to their political communities.

Two authentic Roman Catholic values that dominated Catholic life from the 1920s to 1950s played key roles in catalyzing the Christian Front. One was the theology of the Mystical Body of Christ; the other was the doctrine of Catholic Action. Combined with the anti-Semitism latent in the story of the deicide, these were the intellectual taproots of the Christian Front and major sources of its popular appeal. Most US Catholics would have been exposed to these concepts through sermons, the Catholic press, parish life, and social activism. Mystical Body theology and Catholic Action drove the missionary outlook of lay and ordained Catholics alike. These values were loadbearing pillars of Catholic practice in the mid-twentieth century, so that even the front's Catholic critics—and there were many—could not contest the organization's sources in their shared faith.

I discuss Mystical Body theology in more detail later in the text, but its central tenet is that everyone baptized as a Christian shares the same physio-spiritual being. The whole of Christianity is said to constitute a divine body, with Christ the head. The effect of this theology during the period of its influence was centrifugal, pressing far-flung Catholics into a felt communion with each other and with Christians of other denominations, as long as those denominations practiced baptism. In practical terms, this made for a new-found sense of solidarity among Catholics. If Christians were hurting elsewhere, Catholics were enjoined to feel their brothers' and sisters' pain.

And pain they felt. Beginning in the 1920s, Christians became the targets of systematic political persecution by leftist regimes. The first of these struggles was in Russia, in the wake of the October Revolution of 1919, when the outcast dissident Vladimir Lenin returned to lead the Bolsheviks into power. What followed was a bloody civil war pitting the Red Army against the White Russians, who fought for the restoration of the tsar. Horrifying stories routinely reached the ears of European and American Christians: Russian Orthodox priests were being tortured and killed by Bolsheviks unless they recanted their Christian faith and adopted the new state line.

For leaders of the emerging American Christian right, the Russian Civil War was a holy war. Major Protestant right wingers such as Elizabeth Dilling of the Mothers' Movement, George Deatherage of the American Nationalist Confederation, and William Dudley Pelley of the Silver Shirts visited Russia during the civil war. In the 1930s they flitted on the edges of the Christian Front movement, sometimes lending public support, sometimes providing encouragement behind the scenes. More importantly, they emerged from their experience of the Russian conflict with a new Christian theology of war. Bolshevism had become an enemy to Christians everywhere.[6]

Catholics, too, felt the fires of holy war in Russia. Coughlin frequently noted the depredations committed by the Soviets against the Mystical Body, claiming that Lenin and his successors were responsible for murdering millions of Christians in the name of Bolshevism. Indeed, not just Bolshevism but Judeo-Bolshevism. Every member of the Christian Front saw the myth of Judeo-Bolshevism as true. The Judeo-Bolshevist idea alleged that, because (secular) Jews held so many positions in Lenin's original soviets, it was axiomatic that Leninist Communism was a product of global Judaism—which was already suspicious, owing to the deicide. For those on the far right, Lenin, who had some Jewish ancestry, had militarized the benign economic ruminations of Marx, also a Jew, for the purpose of installing an atheistic absolutism. Jews had killed the earthly body of Christ before. Now, under the guise of Bolshevism, Jews were persisting in that most horrifying sin by killing Christ's Mystical Body as well.

In Coughlin's view, the holy war reached new heights in Spain, where in the mid-1930s a left-wing government associated with the Popular Front persecuted Catholics. Coughlin and many other Catholics lined up behind the opposed forces of General Francisco Franco. Franco's Catholic supporters abroad acknowledged his own atrocities but viewed them as justified in defense of the Mystical Body. Among these foreign Francoists was Arnold Lunn, a British Catholic convert and evangelist who originated the idea of a Christian Front to protect Christians from their Communist enemies. Lunn recruited elite Catholics to argue his case to the Vatican. Soon enough Eugenio Cardinal Pacelli—the Vatican's secretary of state, soon to become Pope Pius XII—was endorsing the idea of a Christian Front.

Lunn and Pacelli did not promote the Judeo-Bolshevist myth, but, in the American context, Judeo-Bolshevism became intertwined with a specifically Christian anti-Communism. The 1930s saw a flowering of American ecumenism as right-wing Protestants and Catholics joined hands in opposition to Judeo-Bolshevism and the defense of Christians. Given that Catholic doctrine at this time officially embraced the deicide, it was all too easy for Fathers Coughlin, Curran, and Brophy to nurture a Christian Front committed above all to eradicating the Judeo-Bolshevist enemy.

It is impossible to overemphasize the stakes in the minds of these Catholic leaders. As historian Sandrine Sanos put it, the phantom of Judeo-Bolshevism "infused their apocalyptic vision of a nation and culture being undone."[7] Cassidy and Moran shared that vision. It hardly needs saying that, as committed Catholics of their era, they were devoted to the Mystical Body. And as acolytes of Father Coughlin, the consummate hunter of Judeo-Bolshevists, they were certain that defending the Mystical Body against Communism necessitated combatting Jews. Cassidy would attempt to do so directly, through force of arms. "It was not we, the defendants, who were on trial," Cassidy wrote of the 1940 Christian Front trial. "It was the Mystical Body of Christ." Cassidy and his supporters "ventured forth into the streets of Brooklyn to defend the Mystical Body of Christ against the Marxian forces there assembled to defeat Her."[8]

Moran, who was more cerebral than Cassidy and who saw how the government came down on the New York front, took a different approach. For Moran, Mystical Body theology became a justification for cooperating with Nazis. When a Nazi SS officer and consul named Herbert Scholz came to Boston to undertake espionage under the cover of diplomacy, Moran became his agent. An ex-seminarian and talented organizer, Moran would become deeply involved in Nazi propaganda and antiwar efforts, including counter-recruitment, morale sabotage, and German-directed activism on behalf of federal legislation that—unbeknownst to its American sponsors—could have hamstrung the US Army during the war. Moran sought to keep the United States out of what he derided as a Jewish and British war with the Axis or at least to ensure that the United States, if it did participate, did so from a position of disadvantage.

It is not incidental that Moran, Cassidy, Coughlin, Curran, and Brophy—along with many of their enablers in government and the American Catholic hierarchy—were of Irish descent. Their primary motivations were religious, but they also felt powerful animus toward the British owing to centuries of Irish suffering on the orders of the Crown and Parliament. Both Moran and Cassidy, but Moran especially, cultivated a heavily Irish American following. As the center of Irish American life and political power, Boston was fertile ground for cultivating a principled opposition to Britain's war.

For it cannot be said that Moran lacked principles. He often lied and contradicted himself, but he was consistent in pursuing what he believed were the right ends on behalf of the Mystical Body. Moran opposed Britain's war because it was a war for the benefit of Jews, the enemy of Christ and the Church. And he worked for Scholz not because he was a committed proponent of Nazi ideas but rather because the Nazis were fighting both Jews and Communists. The Fascist relationship with Christianity was complex, but

Moran, like many other Christians of his time, believed that, between Fascism and Communism, the choice was obvious.

Having said that, as the war dragged on, Moran did become Nazi-like in his views. The early Moran was a savvy anti-Semite, who toed the Coughlinite line: the problem was not necessarily Jews, but rather secular Jews, who were equated with Bolsheviks. What drove Moran toward the Nazis' genocidal position was a combination of Scholz's tutelage and the opposition the Christian Front eventually faced in Boston. Scholz was a flawless Nazi. He almost literally had a doctorate in anti-Semitism, having completed his dissertation under a premier Nazi professor whose goal was the eradication of Jewish influence from German philosophy. Just about every decision Scholz made in his adult life was geared toward advancement in the Nazi Party and service to Hitler's government. At least before the end of the war.

But even more influential in Moran's radicalization was Frances Sweeney. Another Irish Catholic from Boston, Sweeney followed her faith along an anti-Fascist path. For Moran and other Coughlinites, every inch of the Mystical Body was baptized, which meant that solidarity ended with Christians. But Sweeney understood *human* solidarity as an imperative of Catholicism. That vision led her to contest Moran's anti-Semitism by means of a brilliant scheme that exposed his work as a Nazi propagandist—work that continued even after Germany and the United States had declared war on each other.

Yet Sweeney's success was marked by two profound ironies. First, her efforts wound up emboldening Moran. In response to Sweeney's revelations, the Boston Police, acting on the impulse of a publicity-seeking commissioner, illegally shut Moran down, violating his civil rights and forcing him underground. From his place outside the public eye, Moran stewed in his own grievances, further developing his anti-Semitism. Second, Sweeney was also a foreign agent. Her efforts were funded, entirely without her knowledge, by British intelligence. In the lead-up to the war and during it, Boston was overrun with spooks.

It is entirely understandable that it would be a lay Catholic like Sweeney, rather than an ordained priest, who would become the Christian Front's chief antagonist. Alongside Mystical Body theology, a second principle, Catholic Action, shielded the front from official Church criticism. Catholic Action was described by Pope Pius XI as "participation by the laity in the hierarchical apostolate."[9] Or, as one San Francisco parishioner explained to his coreligionists in 1938, "Catholic Action opens up a new world for the zeal of the faithful, a new world wherein they can share in the Apostolate of the Church and cooperate with their pastors and priests in spreading the Kingdom of Christ in individual souls, in families and in society." Cooperation between lay Catholics and their priests, bishops, and nuns united the faithful in shared activity under the aegis of the papacy. Catholic Action could be anything, as long as a priest—or, better still, a bishop—condoned it. From organizing a parish Bible study to creating a parish-linked organization, Catholic Action gave significance to almost any work of Catholic corporate endeavor in 1930s and 1940s America.

As historian William Issel has pointed out, Catholic Action also created a new concept: the "Priesthood of the Layman." Cassidy and Moran stretched this idea to its limits, as they cast their Christian Front work as Catholic Action. Yet the gambit succeeded. Clerics like the Jesuit editor of *America* magazine claimed, "In its origin, the Christian Front was one of several religious groups dedicated to Catholic Action." The priestly sanction that the front received from the likes of Coughlin, Curran, Brophy, and Ahern meant that the Church, in a sense, owned everything the front did. Thus when the US government came after Cassidy, many Catholics did not see the feds as putting down an insurrection. Rather, they were disrupting the internal work of the Roman Catholic Church. For his part, Moran was always careful to emphasize that he led a religious organization, not a political one. Doing so assured him the constitutional protections of religious freedom. But this was not just an expedient posture: Moran was a deeply religious person with considerable theological knowledge. He was the ideal representation of the lay priest. He was also thoroughly committed to Catholic Action, as were his followers. The Archdiocese of Boston never put its stamp of approval on the Christian Front, but as far as Moran's followers knew, their meetings with him were extensions of parish life. Ahern and others felt similarly.[10]

The elimination of the Christian Front from historical memory owes something to the eventual withdrawal of Catholic Action and Mystical Body theology. As prominent as these two principles were in the 1930s and 1940s, virtually no one remembers them today. "Mystical Body of Christ theology was, even beyond the 1920s, roaring," theologian Timothy R. Gabrielli has written, "but by 1970 . . . it had virtually disappeared from Catholic discourse." Moral theologian Charles Curran has posited that by the time the Second Ecumenical Council of the Vatican (Vatican II) closed in 1965, the "shift away from the primacy of the hierarchy" had doomed Catholic Action. If lay Catholics could claim to do the work of the Church without hierarchical approval, there was no longer a place for the clerically linked culture of Catholic Action. Thus the "social glue" that held the Christian Front together, to use Émile Durkheim's phrase, dissolved. With Catholic Action and Mystical Body theology both distant memories, Catholics today lack the intellectual grounding to make sense of the Christian Front.[11]

A final religious theme that runs through the book concerns an observation about the Christian Front made by the Protestant theologian Paul Tillich. In "Catholicism and Anti-Judaism," an unpublished 1940 manuscript hitherto unknown to historians, Tillich warned against a "type of clerical anti-Semitism [that] uses the methods of Fascism for its purposes." Tillich noted that "this is the type of Father Coughlin and the 'Christian Front.'" Tillich worried that the clerical element embedded within the ostensibly lay Christian Front would push American Catholics toward the Fascist anti-Semitism that was taking over Europe. Tillich knew that anti-Judaism had a long-standing place in Catholicism, via the deicide. But anti-Judaism was not the same as Fascist anti-Semitism. Anti-Judaism was a theology, which saw Jews as suspect but redeemable; a Jew could become a Christian and thereby join the Mystical Body. But Fascist anti-Semitism was racial. On this view, Jews were permanently tainted by virtue of some intrinsic quality; nothing could save them. As Tillich saw it, the Christian Front was a vehicle for transitioning Catholic anti-Judaism into racial anti-Semitism, via the conduit of the Judeo-Bolshevist fantasy. The Christian Front's priests embraced that fantasy, which saw Judeo-Bolshevism as a feature of secular Jews specifically. There was not much distance between this view and a view that Jews were intrinsically and irredeemably enemies of Christianity. The logic is inexorable: if, after stripping away the Jewish faith, one is left with a Jewish enemy, then there is something essential to the person that makes him or her an enemy. Whether the Christian Front would actually lead American Catholics toward racial anti-Semitism had everything to do with the activity of its priests, Tillich thought. In this he was prescient.[12]

Resonances and Futures

Readers will note many echoes from this history in the time elapsed since. One of the major themes of *Nazis of Copley Square* is the surveillance of Americans by their government, a matter of ongoing concern. Five US law enforcement and intelligence agencies, as many as three foreign intelligence services, and multiple Jewish American organizations kept tabs on the Christian Front. So did a large number of journalists. This was an astonishing outlay of national and international resources—all for the observation of a purported religious organization. The staggering quantity of surveillance resulted in a rich set of sources that provides much for the historian to work with. Yet such detail comes at a cost to the surveillance subject. Some Americans know this firsthand because their political activities were monitored by state agents; their places of work, worship, and meeting were infiltrated; and their communications were tapped. There was an opportunity for the wider public to take stock of such encroachments after the attacks of September 11, 2001, particularly as Americans were made aware of the George W. Bush administration's domestic spying activities. Surveillance targets, often Muslims, disclosed their own experience, and alarmed individuals with security clearances, like the defense contractor Edward Snowden, shared inside information. Yet awareness did not lead to fundamental reform, and public debate on the issue eventually ceased.

Surveillance is a double-edged sword if ever there was one. It can reveal criminality, but it can also undermine people's liberty, and past incidents continue to haunt our politics. Consider that the intense surveillance of Coughlin became a defense of Donald Trump during the 2019 House Judiciary Committee hearings concerning impeachment. Representative Ken Buck of Colorado brought up President Roosevelt's surveillance of Coughlin to suggest that President Trump's attempt to withhold congressionally allocated funds from Ukraine in exchange for a Ukrainian promise to investigate his political opponent, Joe Biden, was not without precedent and therefore was not impeachable. There is something to be said for the comparison: the two presidents did not use precisely the same means, but both sought to undermine their political adversaries by diverting official resources. As becomes clear throughout this book, and as others have noted, President Roosevelt was an avid scrutinizer of his political enemies, who used the official resources of the government to investigate and undermine those who disagreed with his preferred policies, especially when it came to prodding the United States into the war.[13]

My focus is less on the political surveillance of Father Coughlin—amply covered elsewhere—than on the surveillance of Moran. As an operative for Scholz, Moran was an unregistered foreign agent. Like Michael Flynn,

Trump's campaign aide and national security advisor, Moran bumped up against the Foreign Agents Registration Act, which was passed in 1938 with the goal of rooting out American Nazis. Moran definitely broke that law; Flynn was given an opportunity to retroactively comply, after his own breach was revealed. Trump's 2016 campaign manager Paul Manafort was accused of violating FARA and certainly did so, though he accepted a plea bargain that eschewed the charge. The FARA investigations of Flynn, Manafort, and Moran were legitimate, but other surveillance of Moran was not. Some of the scrutiny Moran faced was politically motivated and violated his constitutional rights. Hence J. Edgar Hoover's many outraged missives to the Boston FBI. Hoover sought for years to pin a charge on Moran, but local agents could find nothing other than an American expressing controversial opinions. The FBI director was, to use a contemporary phrase, on a "fishing expedition." This despite the fact that Moran actually had broken laws. The trouble for the FBI was that it never found out about his liaison with Scholz.

The FBI's history of overreach has become a source of suspicion across the American political spectrum. The bureau's excesses, especially under Hoover, have marred the credibility of federal investigations into political activists, perhaps permanently. Racial justice and worker's rights advocates point to surveillance of civil rights, American Indian, labor, Puerto Rican, and Mexican American activists, among others. Meanwhile conservatives point to surveillance of Coughlin and to the Great Sedition Trial, in which the federal government in the 1940s attempted unsuccessfully to prosecute thirty American right-wingers as Nazi spies but could produce no evidence of crimes. That case plays a bit part in *Nazis of Copley Square*. If contemporary conservatives knew about Moran, they would probably look to his story as well. When former FBI director Robert Mueller undertook his inquiry into Trump's campaign over allegations that his advisors were doing the bidding of Russian agents, it was inevitable that partisans would bring up the FBI's checkered past— regardless of the factual differences between Mueller's investigation and those historical investigations that justifiably anger Americans to this day.[14]

Mueller was also investigating Russian meddling in US political affairs, another parallel with the history related in *Nazis of Copley Square*. The chapters that follow disclose previously undetected Nazi and British intelligence operations run against US citizens on American soil. The consequences, intended and unintended, of these illegal operations were considerable. It is my contention that the British operation led directly to the anti-Semitic violence that beset the city of Boston in 1943. There is also reason to believe that John Franklin Carter, a member of Roosevelt's inner circle who urged Moran's summary incarceration, was a Soviet spy, who understood that Moran's antiwar activities conflicted with Soviet war interests. Likewise the British knew that Moran's pro-neutrality campaign conflicted with their own war interests. The British prosecuted a massive spy operation in the United States in an effort to sway public opinion concerning the war. There is further reason to believe that these British operations enjoyed Roosevelt's tacit approval, suggesting that the president allowed foreign agents to pursue illegal activities in the United States in order to move the country to his preferred interventionist position. It seems that obtaining political advantage by courting foreign subterfuge is not so unusual as some Americans would like to believe. We need not, as a result of acknowledging this historical truth, force ourselves to condone behavior we consider to be wrong. But we might be humbled and induced to consider what sort of social and legal change might be necessary to ensure a politics that better comports with our values.

Finally, examination of the Christian Front reveals many uncomfortable constants and evolutions in the history of American far-right politics. The political rhetoric of the Christian Front feels remarkably contemporary. Fronters were adept at cloaking their anti-Semitism in a shroud of deniability knit from terms such as "globalism" and "international bankers." They redbaited liberals incessantly, adding pages to a playbook that fell out of favor somewhat after the collapse of the Soviet Union but which has since been restored to popularity. Front spokespersons complained constantly of what has lately been termed "cancelation," an effort on their part to change the subject of debate from their claims to their rights. Indeed, changing the subject may have been their favorite fallacy: they dismissed the suffering of Jews by pointing to the suffering of Christians and avoided discussing Hitler's atrocities by instead emphasizing those of Stalin. And Coughlin and Moran especially were masterful manipulators of human-rights language. At the dawn of the human-rights era, they recognized that they could inoculate themselves from criticism and could win support by claiming to be victims of discrimination. Perhaps more distressingly, their appreciation of human rights was genuine and inspired their economic populism, which might impel us to consider the limits of human-rights ideas. In so many ways, right-wing politics has come back around to the Christian Front style, with economic populism replacing free-market dogma and the embrace of victimhood status supplanting—or perhaps augmenting—denials of minority persecution.

At the same time, we must avoid generalizing too greatly the rhetoric and ideology of the Christian Front and thereby losing sight of its uniqueness. The Front arose in a particular moment. As the historian Oscar Handlin noted in 1975, "Between 1910 and 1940, anti-Semitism developed to a point at which it threatened to alter the whole character of American society." During the 1930s "at least four million, and perhaps as many as ten million Americans enlisted in such organizations as the Ku Klux Klan, the Silver Shirts, and the Christian Front." Handlin feared that, unless rigorously examined, such groups would simply be "slotted under a common rubric with other manifestations of hostility, disagreement, or approval." If that happened, we would "understand little about their appearance, or ultimate disappearance."[15] I argue that Handlin's fear came to pass. The front became just another manifestation of some easily refuted tendency toward intolerance. This failure to reckon with what was distinctive about the front has been a boon to those who would perpetuate its mission, which still percolates close to the surface of mainstream America. We are worse off for having forgotten the Christian Front and so stand to gain by placing its remarkable story in full view.

CHAPTER 1

The Idea of a Christian Front

THE GUESTS HAD JUST BEEN SEATED FOR DINNER WHEN THE TELE-phone rang in the hall of Major General Smedley Butler's suburban Phila-delphia mansion. The general excused himself; he planned to be brief. But when he picked up the phone, he was instantly suspicious. Recognizing the voice on the other end, Butler signaled to one of his guests, a newspaper ed-itor, to scurry upstairs to another phone and secretly listen in on the call. "Smedley," the voice crackled, "would you be willing to head an armed force of men . . . to proceed to Mexico and overthrow the Mexican government?"[1]

It was Father Coughlin on the line, the Radio Priest with tens of millions of listeners. The Mexican government was "picking on the Catholic Church," Coughlin explained, and President Lázaro Cárdenas "had kidnapped the Archbishop" of Mexico City. Coughlin indicated that he had financial backing, men, and arms. All he needed was someone to lead the troops. Butler had fought in World War I and the Mexican Revolution, but by August 1935, when Coughlin called, the general had hung up his spurs. He also knew that to join an unofficial expedition to overthrow the Mexican government "amounted to treason." Butler later explained that he instructed Coughlin to back off: if Coughlin "started such a movement, the President of the United States would assemble a militia" and put a stop to it. The priest reportedly then told the general not to worry about President Roosevelt, because the fighters "would take care of him on the way down." Butler, one of the most decorated Marines in history, was thunderstruck. "It seemed to be Coughlin's intention to start an armed revolution in the United States," Butler worried.[2]

A few weeks later Coughlin had another exchange with a general, but this conversation was conspicuously public. The matter at hand was the Nye-Sweeney bill, then under debate in Congress. If passed into law, the legislation would give Congress sole authority to issue currency and would create "peoples' banks" in each state, replacing the Federal Reserve. Coughlin believed the state-controlled peoples' banks would alleviate the problem of "Jewish gold" hoarded by "Shylocks" and instead emphasize what he called "Gentile silver." General Hugh S. Johnson, head of the New Deal's National Recovery Administration, was having none of it. He pushed back at Coughlin, arguing that the priest's support for the Nye-Sweeney bill was a function of religious intolerance and racism, not banking sense. Addressing Coughlin directly on the radio, Johnson argued that "both you and Adolf" had proposed policies "as alike as peas in a pod" and warned that Coughlin "could become a *Reichsfuehrer*." Coughlin responded that Johnson had "out-Stalined Stalin" by presiding over an increasingly "Communistic" National Recovery Administration.[3]

In 1935 no Roman Catholic priest in America had ever been publicly compared to Hitler, and no American public servant had ever been publicly compared to Stalin. The idea of a Roman Catholic priest urging the overthrow of a foreign government was as fantastic as it was incomprehensible. In these two episodes, Coughlin announced, in rough form, the central commitments of what would become the Christian Front in the United States: anti-Communism and anti-Semitism. Coughlin had been preaching these values in sermons, on the radio, and in writing for some time, but the mid-1930s was an inflection point—the period when sometimes-inchoate and contradictory commitments began to coalesce into an ideology that could drive an armed revolutionary movement in the United States.

That is what the Christian Front became in 1939, but it did not start out that way. Indeed, it did not start in the United States at all but rather in Spain. In 1936 brewing tensions exploded into civil war between the left-wing government and Fascists under the command of General Francisco Franco. The suffering of some Catholics at the hands of the government inspired outrage from the likes of Coughlin, but also from a man whom has history has largely ignored: Arnold Lunn, a British Catholic convert who covered the war as a reporter and went on to develop the idea of the Christian Front.

To Lunn, the Christian Front was a necessary reaction to the depredations of the civil war. Lunn's key ideas included Christian militancy and what later became known as ecumenical anti-Communism, whereby Christians of all denominations would join together in defending each other from the onslaught of godless leftists under Moscow's command. In just two years or so, Lunn's ideas would cross seas and oceans, penetrating the Vatican and the United States. Adherents such as Coughlin refit the Christian Front concept to suit their purposes, a subject I discuss in detail in the next chapter. Nonetheless, Lunn would leave an enduring mark. His focus on the persecution of Catholics in Spain galvanized activists for years to come, as did his certainty that Christians were under violent attack from the mortal adversary of Communism. Lunn and key supporters argued that Christians had to defend themselves, if necessary using force, lest the "reds" wipe them off the map.

Coughlin was already a militant when he heard the call of the Christian Front, but the clarity of Lunn's thesis, and the sanction it won from the Vatican, changed the game. In 1935 Coughlin dreamed of a Catholic army to unseat a Mexican government perceived as an enemy of the cloth, but he was still far more a provocateur than an organizer. That much seems clear in his absurd, doomed outreach to General Butler. By 1939, having embraced the idea of a Christian Front, Coughlin was armed with new ideas and rallying cries—ideas and cries around which he could muster men eager for battle.

Ecumenism and Anti-Communism: The Birth of a Global Movement

Father Coughlin was an agile political barnstormer. Over the course of the 1930s, he reached out to the working class and campaigned for the relatively novel ideal of human rights even as his anti-Semitism deepened. He also vacillated between Catholic militancy and engagement through normal political channels. Thus in 1934, a year before his failed effort to recruit General butler to lead a paramilitary expedition, Coughlin announced the creation of his National Union for Social Justice (NUSJ), which was running populist, anti-Roosevelt candidates for office two years later.

If the NUSJ was neither militant nor overly activist, some critics were nonetheless skeptical, fearing that Coughlin's politics pointed inevitably toward violent, authoritarian ends. For instance, William E. Dodd, the US ambassador to Germany from 1933 to 1937, was convinced that the NUSJ was nefarious, seeing in it "the germs of Fascism." The NUSJ's advocacy of consolidating all American union activity under the Department of Labor smacked Dodd as nothing more than the establishment of a "Nazi-like labor front in America." "The program of Hitler," Dodd warned, "resembles in many respects the program inaugurated by Father Coughlin's Union for Social Justice."[4] But what was clear to Dodd was muddled in the minds of others. Roman Catholic and Jewish leaders in the United States struggled to figure out Coughlin's relationship to Fascism, Nazism, Communism, and American political life. This was new territory: an immigrant church had its first celebrity priest, and he blurred the lines between sacred theology and profane politics. Coughlin's political ideas were quasireligious, sometimes comical, and sometimes penetrating.

Coughlin's efforts were indeed hard to add up, given his vacillation between militancy and political activism, a ministry of the soul and absorption in worldly matters. But there was a thread connecting it all. Between 1935 and 1938, Coughlin sought in secret to foster a Christian arm for the sword of the spirit—a sword that could be brought to bear against the incursions of global Communism. Communism, Coughlin believed, was an evil nurtured and foisted upon the world by Jews. Communism in his time was becoming more and more the enemy of Christians, its allegedly exterminationist tendency having infected not just revolutionary Russia but also overwhelmingly Catholic countries such as Mexico and Spain.

Coughlin was hardly alone in his concern for global Christianity in the face of "godless" Communism. A major influence on Coughlin proved to be the British Catholic Arnold Lunn. The two sympathized with each other's writings on the Spanish Civil War and would meet secretly in 1940. Like Coughlin, Lunn became incensed by atrocities committed against Catholics by Spain's left-wing government, known as the Popular Front. During the height of the civil war, Lunn reported to Coughlin that hundreds of Spanish churches "had been totally destroyed" by the "Red bombers" of the Popular Front government. "A victorious Red Loyalist government," Lunn warned, "means to destroy religion once and for all on the Spanish peninsula." Lunn also expressed to Coughlin his displeasure with left-leaning American Catholics, who showed a "pious refusal to grow indignant over the butcherings by the Reds and their destruction of religion."[5]

Unlike Coughlin, Lunn went beyond the American Catholic scene and called out Protestants as well. From his perch as a visiting professor of apologetics at Notre Dame in Indiana, Lunn excoriated Protestants who seemingly did not care about the considerable suffering of Spanish Catholics—more than 6,000 priests, nuns, and others in the employ of the Church were executed by the government's firing squads. "When we find Protestants traveling around our country as the guests of militant atheists who have murdered thousands of priests and nuns," Lunn wrote in early 1938, "we begin to wonder whether these Protestants think of Catholics as fellow Christians."[6] Statements like these caught Coughlin's attention, helping him envision the conceptual framework for an anti-Communist Christian militancy responsive especially to the persecution of Catholics.

Lunn's own views were the product of an exciting and multifaceted life of overlapping commitments to flesh and spirit. Born in Madras in 1888 to the medical doctor and English Methodist missionary Henry Lunn, Arnold Lunn spent his youth at the Harrow school and Oxford, with stints in the Swiss Alps. He established the Alpine Ski Club, was the founding editor of a publication aimed at skiers, and in 1922 introduced the modern slalom course into the world of downhill skiing. A cultural elite and a Methodist who seemed most enthusiastic about playing outdoors, Lunn was, as one observer noted, "peculiarly outfitted to rank in the [Catholic] Church Militant."[7]

There are, however, signs in Lunn's background that point to his later militant awakening. Although Lunn's conversion to Roman Catholicism in 1933 put him doctrinally at odds with his father Henry, the younger Lunn shared his father's missionary spirit and capacious sense that Christians should cooperate across lines of sect. While working in India from 1886 to 1888, Henry rankled the sensibilities of the Methodist leadership, arguing that "missionaries should spend more time helping the lower castes and Untouchables" in order to "lift degraded man nearer God and nearer Heaven."[8] Likewise Arnold's militancy reflected his sense of responsibility for the world as it is—for humanity, in addition to the divine. When Henry's missionary service in India ended, he began a tourism business, which he connected to Christian ecumenism by promoting travel to the growing circuit of ecumenical conferences being held at fashionable European resorts. Later Arnold would take advantage of his father's company to bring together Christian leaders to discuss the situation in Spain and the need for cross-denominational opposition to Communism.

When the Spanish Civil War broke out in July 1936, Arnold Lunn sped to the scene to report on the conflict. Spain would become the proving ground for Lunn's Catholicism. Like many British Catholics who were paying attention to

Spain, Lunn viewed the war as a contest between the Church, championed by General Franco and his Nationalists, and what Lunn called the "militant, anticlerical Communism" of the Popular Front, also known as the Republicans or Loyalists. Some American Catholics felt similarly. Lunn became a sort of spokesperson for English-speaking Catholics sympathetic with Franco. Lunn was under no illusions about Franco's authoritarian intentions, but, as far as Lunn was concerned, the Republicans had come to power illegitimately and were no more enamored of democracy. The war was nothing but a stark choice between "an authoritarian government which would [either] protect [or] persecute Christianity."[9]

With the zeal of a recent convert, Lunn cast the Spanish conflict as a holy war. "On Palm Sunday, 1937," he wrote, "I stood on a tower near Madrid and saw the churches in which the Red Lamp had been extinguished by the Red Fury." (The red lamp refers to the vigil light placed in church sanctuaries, indicating the presence of the divine.) Lamenting Christian suffering in Spain, Lunn was convinced that the streets of Madrid would each become a latter-day Via Dolorosa, the path Jesus walked through Jerusalem en route to the crucifixion. But Lunn also "thanked God for the fact that the Catholic pulse still beat in the arteries of Madrid," and the Nationalists, whatever their flaws, were on the right side spiritually, "fighting the battle of Christian civilization."

The profound sense of duty Lunn felt for his Spanish coreligionists inspired the writings—largely ignored by scholars—that introduced the concept of a Christian Front. It was Lunn's small 1937 book *Spain and the Christian Front* that put forward the Christian Front as the Popular Front's politico-theological opposite. The stakes could not be higher, Lunn argued: the Popular Front, directed from Moscow, was trying to exterminate Catholics. "By means of Red terror," the Popular Front "murders and terrorizes any moderates into submission," he wrote. Church burnings and executions of priests and nuns, atrocities that were especially pronounced in Madrid and the Basque country, proved the point. Yet, wary of the Nationalists' own extreme violence, the Holy See refused to endorse either side politically. "Priests have an odd reactionary bias against people who want to kill them," Lunn wrote in a wry moment.[10]

Critically, it was not only the Vatican Lunn hoped to convince, because the Christian Front was to be more than a geopolitical counterpoise to Spain's Popular Front. Lunn pitched his work primarily to lay Americans and British who could build a popular, unifying, and durable movement—not a one-off political statement or alliance against a particular political rival. The Christian Front would respond to the Popular Front, but it would also, and more grandly, catalyze ecumenism, bringing together Christians across denominations and across the world in a cohesive spiritual and political project. Once reunited socially and theologically under the aegis of the Christian Front, Protestants and Catholics would battle against their shared enemy: global Communism.

The common ground on which Lunn would unite Christians was a theological one, marked above all by persecution. The persecution of Catholics by Communists was of a piece with the persecution Saints Augustine and John Chrysostom had discussed in writings that resonated across denominational boundaries. Lunn also tied Catholic persecution to the crucifixion, a site of solidarity for all Christians. Through Christo-centrism—attention to the figure of Christ and his suffering—the Christian Front would bring diverse Christians back to the basics on which they all agreed.[11]

Lunn's embryonic Christian Front was perhaps the first instance of ecumenical anti-Communism, a term Richard Hofstadter used in 1965 to describe the postwar affiliation between Catholic McCarthyites and American Evangelical anti-Communists, who were mainly Baptists. These groups joined hands on the basis of a number of interests, but a shared sense of persecution was key among them, as McCarthy's backers crossed denominational lines in their perception that Communism threatened Christians of every stripe. Ecumenical anti-Communism as practiced by Lunn was not only new, it was also novel in that it broke with expectations: usually religious persecution turns the members of a group inward, creating a siege mentality within the religion itself. But Lunn argued that Communist persecutions of Spanish Catholics should have turned Catholics outward and brought other Christians to their aid. As Lunn put it, "When they are attacked or persecuted by atheists," authentic Christians "instinctively align themselves with Christians of other communions." He urged Protestants not to "pass by on the other side like the Levite in the parable" but rather to heighten "the bond which unites them with Catholics."[12]

In December 1937, a month after publishing *Spain and the Christian Front*, Lunn had his first opportunity to test the appeal of his message, during a lecture at Boston College on the topic of "a united Spanish front." The environment at Boston College was a friendly one, as the Jesuits who ran the school were predisposed against Communism. But what Lunn said in Boston had little to do with ecumenism, in spite of its centrality to his vision. Instead he marked out the battlefield by encouraging antipathy toward the Spanish Republicans and sympathy for the Catholics they persecuted. "Whenever Communists gained control in Spain," Lunn argued, "terrorism followed." He assailed the Popular Front for "destruction of church property and the burning of priests and nuns and the mass murder of the faithful." "The Loyalists aren't loyal at all," Lunn said, "unless it's to Russia and Communism." He also scored "pinkish professors and newspapers" for supposedly justifying the ruin of church property.[13] The introduction of the Christian Front in Boston, a city that would later be the movement's epicenter, might have attended to the possibilities of Christian ecumenism. Instead that introduction was freighted with fear and intolerance.

If Boston College welcomed Lunn, England seemed determined to push him away. Lunn was baffled by English Protestant leaders, who remained unwilling to make statements in support of Spanish Catholics. Indeed, many English Protestant leaders were backing the Loyalists. "I have cudgeled my brains in vain to find the explanation of their support of the so-called Government of Spain," Lunn wrote. Could it be that the church of Lunn's father did "not regard the Catholic Church as a branch of Christianity"—that the English clergy did not accept "professing Roman Catholics as entitled to the rights enjoyed by the rest of mankind"?[14] Perhaps fear and anger worked at Boston College, but if Lunn was to attract support closer to home, he would have to redouble his ecumenical outreach. Arnold and his father Henry would work together on that project, taking advantage of Henry's travel business.

At about the time of Arnold's conversion in 1933, Henry devised a new offering, an upscale and exclusive package tour. He called it the Hellenic Travelers Club. The club consisted of two- or three-week summer cruises to Greece and the Aegean Islands, aboard a yacht hosting eminent scholars and writers. These intellectuals, who traveled for free, were expected to mingle and converse with the well-heeled paying customers. One sailing included the novelist Hugh Walpole, the journalist and poet Vita Sackville-West, and her husband the historian and politician Harold Nicolson. William Butler Yeats joined another cruise, along with fellow poet Lennox Robinson. These luminaries might also present short lectures, and, as Walpole recalled, "in the evening Sir Henry Lunn delivered an appropriate sermon."[15] (Henry was named a knight bachelor in 1910.)

In February and March 1938, rather than sermonizing, Henry used his Hellenic Travelers Club to bring Catholics and Protestants together on the issue of Communism. With Arnold's prompting, Henry invited Catholic and Protestant dignitaries to his yacht to discuss mutual "efforts which are called for by the campaign against religion and the propagation of Godlessness by Russian Soviet Communism." Putting out to sea, the horizon sinking in the background, Henry believed that his gathering was the first since the Reformation at which Catholics and Protestants joined in confronting a theological issue.[16]

The guests included four Anglican bishops, one Methodist bishop, one Catholic bishop, two lords, an earl, a viscount, two laywomen, and one Jesuit priest. The Protestant cleric most in agreement with the Lunns' proposal for a Christian Front was W. R. Inge, the dean of London's famed St. Paul's Cathedral. Fuming about the "massacres and outrages" in Spain, Inge compared Communism to a "disease." He claimed that in areas of Spain controlled by Loyalists, "no religious services have been possible" for over a year. "The issue is perfectly clear," Inge impressed upon the assembled, "the enemy . . . is [the] anti-Christ in person." Inge asked his fellow Protestants to "close ranks as far as we can" with Catholics. He was not ready to achieve total theological harmony, noting that "reunion is far away." But exigency called at least for an alliance. "In this battle we may surely all fight together," he concluded in militaristic terms that previewed the language Christian Fronters in the United States would soon adopt as they recruited men eager to do violence.[17]

Arthur Hinsley, the Cardinal Archbishop of Westminster, joined Inge in supporting "a United Christian Front against the worldwide anti-Christian onslaught." Anti-Communism as a motivator for ecumenism made sense to Hinsley. "There have been in the past misunderstandings and faults of manner on both sides," he allowed, referring to Catholics and Protestants, "but the realization of a common peril is drawing Christians together in practical sympathy." To Arnold Lunn, comments like Hinsley's were a balm. Lunn's conversion to Roman Catholicism had erected a barrier between himself and his devout Methodist father, yet here was a cardinal endorsing reconciliation. The effort to ground ecumenism in anti-Communism was of great personal meaning to the Lunns, becoming a shared passion of father and son. Arnold would go on to write glowingly about his father's efforts to create a Christian Front.[18]

Not everyone aboard ship was friendly to the proposition of a Christian Front. Lord Willoughby Hyett Dickinson, leader of the World Alliance for

International Friendship, was wary of the militarism built into the concept. "It was during the Great War that the term front" came into use, Dickinson noted. "Pictures still fill the minds of millions with ghastly memories and nightmares." He insisted that any strain of militarism be expunged. "If we are to speak of a Christian Front we must be careful lest we associate it too directly with the process of fighting." Dickinson approved of Lunn's organizational idea and of ecumenism, but he made clear that "Christians need not use machine guns."[19]

Another onboard critic was the Jesuit priest Martin D'Arcy. On paper, D'Arcy seemed a likely partner: the Master of Campion Hall, Oxford—the first Roman Catholic college established at Oxford since the Reformation—D'Arcy was strongly anti-Communist. In the late 1950s, he would publish *Communism and Christianity*, in which he made plain that the two systems were "as opposed as earth to heaven" because Communism "denied the grace and transcendence," of God. D'Arcy was also Arnold Lunn's close friend and had administered his first Holy Communion.[20]

Yet D'Arcy objected to the very core of the Christian Front thesis. "A Catholic is not bound to take the side of Franco in the Spanish Civil War," D'Arcy urged the Hellenic Travelers Club. This was so because the fight carried on by the Church Militant had nothing to do with politics. Rather, "the fight is principally an interior one fought by each individual against himself," D'Arcy held. He also rejected the notion that a Christian Front movement was necessary from an ecumenical standpoint: "Already, I believe the threat of the barbarians has served to unite Christians," he said. Finally, in an ominous foreshadowing, D'Arcy cut to a more basic concern. "A single idea can create fanaticism," he warned.[21]

·   ·   ·

The cruises had mixed results, winning the Lunns support among some influential thinkers and churchmen while alienating others. Exactly what sentiments emerged among the paying guests is impossible to say. We can, however, be confident in the success of the Lunns' other key project of persuasion, this one decidedly more important than intellectual courtship on the high seas.

Rather than poets and priests, the second project was directed at the top of the Roman Catholic hierarchy. Outreach to the Vatican began in late summer 1937, when Henry Lunn commissioned Captain Archibald Henry Maule Ramsay, a Conservative member of Parliament, to approach the Holy See in an effort to get the pope's blessing for a "united Christian Front against the Communists in Spain." Ramsay was a fierce ally, appalled by the Loyalist attacks on Roman Catholics in Spain and a strong supporter of Franco. Indeed, Ramsay may have been a more apt forerunner of the Christian Front in practice than the Lunns were, as he not only supported ecumenical anti-Communism, avant la lettre, but also proved to be a strident anti-Semite. In the years after his initial involvement with the Lunns, Ramsay gave speeches to Britain's Nazi-aligned Nordic League and earned the praise of Fascist journals. Later he founded the Right Club, a group of high-powered British politicians and business magnates who spurned Jews. Ramsay also was a confidant of Tyler Kent, a twenty-nine-year-old cipher clerk at the US Embassy in London and fellow anti-Semite, who became a cause célèbre on the American and British far right after he was arrested for espionage in 1940, stripped of diplomatic immunity, secretly tried and convicted, and sentenced to a seven-year prison term in the United Kingdom. Kent's supporters on both sides of the Atlantic argued that he was framed by the Roosevelt administration, which they alleged was controlled by Jews.[22]

But before Ramsay dove headfirst into anti-Semitism, he was an anti-Communist attracted to the idea of a unified Christian bulwark against the Soviets and their perceived agents—like the Spanish Loyalists. In his initial outreach to the Vatican—a letter to Monsignor Paschal Robinson, the Holy See's Apostolic Delegate to Ireland—Ramsay described "the British Churches cooperating with the Roman Catholic Church with a view to presenting a United Christian Front against the Red Menace to Christianity." Ramsay's letter noted that 6,000 clergy, nuns, and others working in the Church had "been murdered by the Reds," constituting a "Spanish tragedy" that was "threatened and inspired by Moscow."[23] The letter's appeal was limited to the situation in Spain, which perhaps was attractive to the Vatican, enabling it to consider an incremental step toward anti-Communist ecumenism—a less drastic position than later, overtly violent incarnations of the Christian Front would adopt. In any case, the Holy See was intrigued, and its Secretariat of State began preparing a reply.

A draft reply to Ramsay, completed in early October 1937, indicates the Holy See's high level of interest. The draft offered "commendation for such initiatives" as were carried out by the Lunns' Committee for a United Christian

Front, which was said to be "on the same path" as the Holy See itself. The draft also announced support for the front's "specific mission."[24] Indeed, the Vatican had already begun sacralizing anti-Communism; the draft recommends that Ramsay examine the previous month's encyclical *Ingravescentibus malis*, in which Pope Pius XI encouraged "evangelic wisdom" as a repellent to "the execrable theories of the Communists."[25] Both the encyclical and the draft letter affirm that the Vatican saw anti-Communism as theologically justified.

There is no indication that the draft letter was ever sent to Ramsay. Giuseppe Cardinal Pizzardo, the secretary for Extraordinary Ecclesiastical Affairs, asked Paschal Robinson for guidance on the response, but Robinson demurred.[26] Robinson promised Pizzardo a report on Ramsay's Christian Front committee, but the available evidence suggests that no such report ever arrived. We also do not know if Eugenio Cardinal Pacelli, the Holy See's secretary of state and future Pope Pius XII, saw Ramsay's original plea.

Yet Pacelli soon adopted the Christian Front idea in no uncertain terms. "Cardinal Pacelli Urges United Christian Front to Fight Foes of Church," one headline blared after the cardinal announced his position at the 34th International Eucharistic Congress, which gathered in Hungary in early June 1938. Pacelli's speech was addressed to an audience of 150,000 at Budapest's Heroes' Square, and from there to the rest of the world. The pope had sent Pacelli to Budapest as papal legate *a latere*, a special designation signaling that Pacelli's message was important for both believers and diplomats. The speech was controversial, with some interpreting it as an expression of Vatican support for the Nazis and for the Hungarian National Socialist Party, both of which premised their appeals on anti-Communism. Was Pacelli signaling support for Nazism's anti-Communism, or was he unveiling a distinctive Catholic anti-Communism? Whatever the case, his ninety-minute address perfectly captured the Lunn thesis.

Pacelli proposed an ecumenical Christian Front as an effort to save not just Catholicism but indeed the "Christian creed" from a "godless Army." Pacelli warned that "the Godless strive to proscribe Christ" and to "destroy churches in their efforts to substitute a travesty upon the gospel for true Christianity." For many who heard the speech or read excerpts, the image of destroyed churches undoubtedly inspired thoughts of the conflict in Spain. "Threatened by atheistic Communism, all nations should unite," Pacelli urged, without distinguishing Catholic and Protestant countries. "The militant Godless are face to face with us . . . shaking the clenched fist of [the] anti-Christ against everything we hold most sacred."[27] It was as if Pacelli had lifted Ramsay's letter and broadcast its contents in Budapest.

There is no evidence that Arnold Lunn was aware of Pacelli's Budapest speech. Had he been, surely the convert Lunn would not have minded the Holy See's appropriation of his ecumenical anti-Communist agenda. And, one way or the other, Pacelli's endorsement of the Christian Front concept reached powerful figures who would carry the Christian Front idea forward. On that score, it is almost certain that Father Coughlin absorbed Pacelli's words. In a strange and stunning development, earlier in the year Coughlin declined an invitation by the Vatican to speak alongside Pacelli at the Budapest Eucharistic Congress.[28] But on June 20, less than three weeks after Pacelli's speech, Coughlin's newspaper, *Social Justice*, featured a giant photograph of Pope Pius XI and, in large type underneath, "The Christian Front." Father Coughlin added his own spin, though, attacking Communism as the work of Judeo-Bolshevists. Coughlin's Christian Front would align itself against "non-Christians," a term understood by Catholics as anti-Semitic code.[29]

In Coughlin's hands, the Christian Front became something other than Arnold Lunn and probably Pacelli intended. Coughlin dropped the element of ecumenism, preferring his Christian Front to be exclusively Catholic. Coughlin did apparently share Lunn's Christo-centrism, but the Detroit priest saw this theology as a way of appealing specifically to Catholics. And while Coughlin's incorporation of anti-Semitism—veiled at first, later overt—was aligned with Ramsay, neither the Lunns nor the Catholic Church pressed the Judeo-Bolshevist myth.[30]

That said, a key area of overlap between Coughlin's and Lunn's Christian Fronts was militancy. "It is gratifying to learn that so many are interested in making arrangements for the establishment of platoons," Coughlin wrote in his June 20 reflection entitled "From the Tower." Eerily prophetic, the Detroit priest signaled that his Christian Front "platoons" could be deployed on a "not far distant [day]—perhaps a matter of two years." Coughlin did not, in June 1938, immediately set about recruiting an armed group under the name of the Christian Front, but he shared Lunn's conviction that Catholics were engaged in a literal war with Communism, with their bodies on the line. As Lunn put it in a December 1938 diary entry, "Unless Catholics can be stirred up to militancy, then they are going to get it in the neck." The solution was "a crusading and militant spirit," although Lunn did not specify what exactly this would look like.[31] Coughlin thought in the same terms. He had been searching for a Catholic militant option against worldwide Communism since 1935, when he called up Smedley Butler and asked him to lead a strike force in Mexico. Cardinal Pacelli, apparently drawing on the ideas of Ramsay and the Lunns, crystallized the philosophy underlying that militant option, and Coughlin took Pacelli's sanction to heart. Hatched in Spain, explored in Boston, improved on the Aegean, refined in the Vatican, and announced from Budapest, Lunn's Christian Front matured rapidly. In 1939 it would flower under the care of Coughlin and fresh recruits in New York City.

CHAPTER 2

Soldiers for the Body of Christ

AFTER THE ELECTION OF 1936, FATHER COUGHLIN FADED FROM minds of the political class. Franklin Roosevelt, the priest's chief enemy, had won reelection in a landslide, ceding just eight electoral votes and carrying the popular vote by a huge margin. But the British, at least, were not so sure that Coughlin was in retreat. In April 1938 the British Library of Information, a New York arm of the Foreign Office, assembled a detailed report on Coughlin's activities. "Recently . . . he has regained some influence," the report noted. Coughlin still had millions of radio listeners and, after just two years on news-stands, the circulation of *Social Justice* had grown to 350,000. After Coughlin encouraged his followers to protest President Roosevelt's 1937 Judicial Reorgani-zation Act—the so-called court-packing bill—Congress received 233,000 tele-grams, and the bill was voted down. "While Father Coughlin cannot be given by any means all of the responsibility for this defeat, his influence was clearly considerable," the report read. Isaiah Berlin, then a twenty-nine-year-old clerk for the British Information Services, scribbled his own views on the report's cover letter, before the findings made their way to the British embassy in Wash-ington. "He is indeed a dangerous and irresponsible element in the American scene," the future philosopher wrote.[1]

Another outsider to the United States, also one of the esteemed thinkers of the twentieth century, felt similarly. Expelled from Germany by the Nazis in 1933, the Protestant theologian Paul Tillich had, as he put it, "the honor to be the first non-Jewish professor dismissed from a German university." He then accepted a position at Union Theological Seminary in New York. From his refuge in Manhattan, Tillich watched as right-wing politics gained traction in New York and the wider American scene. What alarmed him was not just that Christians, especially Catholics, were embracing militancy but also that their targets included Jews. Even worse, the impetus for anti-Semitism was theological, and the oracles of Jew hatred were Catholic priests.[2]

Tillich explained his apprehensions in "Catholicism and Anti-Judaism," a wide-ranging essay written around 1940. A keen observer of Christian-Jewish relations, Tillich was hardly naïve about Catholic anti-Judaism, but he saw something else in the politics of American Catholic militancy: anti-Semitism. Anti-Judaism encompassed discrimination against Jews on religious grounds, but anti-Judaism easily slipped into anti-Semitism—discrimination against Jews on the basis of race. "The soil of all anti-Semitism is anti-Judaism," Tillich wrote. Observing "no *basic* difference between Europe and America," Tillich realized that American Catholics might welcome Fascism and its attendant anti-Semitism.

That potential was being unleashed by the Church hierarchy itself. Tillich decried "the Fascist type of clerical anti-Semitism," which was "the type of Father Coughlin and the 'Christian Front.'" The leadership of priests was distressing for at least two reasons. First, history showed that priests represented the "officer class" of the Church, capable of spurring laypeople to odious action. By way of example, Tillich argued that the Dreyfus affair, in which a French Jewish military officer was wrongly convicted of treason, would have made no headway without the direction of Jesuits.

Second, and perhaps more important, priestly anti-Semitism gave Catholics sanction to adopt Nazi ideas in spite of Pope Pius XI's expressed view that Hitler was promoting a pagan heresy. "Hitler as an anti-Semitic pagan Fascist could not be accepted" by the Catholic faithful, Tillich argued. But "Hitler as an anti-Judaistic Catholic Fascist could be accepted." At risk, then, were not just individual Jews but also the sort of society in which Jews could be secure. This "reactionary type of clerical anti-Semitism," Tillich feared, would end up "destroying the liberal-democratic world to which the Jews as equals belong."[3] American democracy itself was imperiled by the movement from anti-Judaism to anti-Semitism, a movement of laypeople led by clerics.

Tillich's concerns were well placed. The "dangerous and irresponsible element" that Isaiah Berlin feared was plainly coalescing in New York, in the form of an anti-Semitic anti-Communism elevated in the name of Christianity. Thus the combination of religiously imbued anti-Semitism and anti-Communism that marked the Christian Front was obvious as well in an event held at the Commodore Hotel in Manhattan on October 30, 1938. Dubbed a Pro-American Rally, the occasion featured Elizabeth Dilling, best-selling author of 1934's *The Red Network: A 'Who's Who' and Handbook of Radicalism for Patriots.* Dilling railed against the supposedly radical leftist activities of Mayor Fiorello LaGuardia and mocked First Lady Eleanor Roosevelt and her fellow "comrats." Dilling was well known as a religious speaker and throughout the 1930s made the rounds of Bible conventions and Christian-sponsored lectures. Under the banner of Americanness, the rally seamlessly integrated Dilling's Christian anti-Communism with Fascist anti-Semitism, exemplified by the screening of a short film showing "the swastika . . . and a picture of Adolf Hitler and Benito Mussolini [who] were applauded (and hissed)," according to a *New York Times* report. Fritz Kuhn, leader of the German American Bund, a US Nazi organization, looked on from the audience along "with two uniformed members of the bund."[4]

The Pro-American Rally was organized by Allen Alderson Zoll, executive vice president of a murky organization known as the American Federation Against Communism. Zoll perfectly embodied the amalgamation of anti-Semitism and anti-Communism. By his own proud admission, his group's main goal was to infiltrate "agents" into meetings of the Communist Party of the United States of America and disrupt the organization. And the responsibility for Communism lay, of course, with Jews. A short while after the rally, Zoll found himself in Washington, testifying to a Senate subcommittee about the horrifying prospect that Harvard law professor Felix Frankfurter might soon have a seat on the Supreme Court. "The Jew has been fostering movements that are subversive to our government," Zoll told the senators.[5]

For Zoll, a believer in the myth of Judeo-Bolshevism, anti-Communism necessitated Jew hatred. Father Edward Lodge Curran, a Roman Catholic priest who spoke at the Commodore Hotel rally, shared Zoll's views on Judeo-Bolshevism. Curran's International Catholic Truth Society used a word—truth—that Catholics recognize as a reference to the Gospel message of Jesus Christ. Yet Curran's was the gospel of anti-Communism. Curran fused theology and politics, creating a distortion that went unnoticed. Speaking to the crowd of 2,000 at the October 1938 rally, he warned that Communism, not Nazism, was the new "twentieth century paganism," a statement that gave Nazism theological sanction while configuring Communism as a heresy.[6]

In the 1930s Curran was one of the most educated priests in the United States. A member of the New York Bar, he held an MA from Columbia, a PhD from Fordham, and an LLM from Brooklyn Law School. He was a tremendous speaker and a presence on any podium. He would also go on to become the "shadow theologian" of the Christian Front. Always lurking in the background, he stood ready to lend expert theological and legal advice to the front's public-facing leaders. Curran was extremely shrewd, as evidenced by one of the few occasions on which he spoke publicly. In July 1939 Curran became the only priest ever to substitute for Father Coughlin as the host of his weekly radio show, after Elliott Roosevelt, the president's son, suggested censoring Coughlin for his anti-Semitism. Coughlin did not want to have a political shouting match with the president's son, so Curran appeared with a retort to the White House as clever as it was twisted. "Let him call Moses an anti-Semite," Curran countered, "since Moses pleaded with the tribes of Israel and Judah to follow him." By 1942 Curran was known to US intelligence officials as "Father Coughlin's Eastern echo."[7] This was just the kind of man Tillich had warned about: a Catholic priest who would draw on fears of Communism to shepherd the faithful from anti-Judaism to anti-Semitism.

Zoll's anti-Communist rally had an ecumenical bent, as evidenced by one of its scheduled speeches: an invocation delivered by the pastor of Manhattan's Marble Collegiate Church, the Reverend Norman Vincent Peale.[8] A bespectacled forty-year-old who liked to drape himself in academic robes, Peale was accustomed to praying in public spaces with large multitudes. Two weeks earlier, with a giant American flag in the background, he presided over an Easter morning service at Central Park attended by a crowd of ten thousand and broadcast nationwide. How Peale, a Reformed Church in America pastor, got roped into what the *Daily Worker* called a "Rally of Fascists" is a mystery, but Peale was himself notably pro-capitalist and so may have been impressed by the anti-Communist roster of speakers.[9]

Peale was also given to bouts of militancy, and the idea of ecumenism appealed to him. "We must consecrate ourselves in militant religion," he argued in a 1939 keynote speech at a Christian ecumenical conference in upstate New York. "The only cohesive force in the world is religion," he noted, echoing the Lunns. Peale urged his listeners not to give up hope, even as war clouds gathered in Europe. "The game is not up by a good deal, for Christ is with us. . . . The center around which all warring nations can gather."[10] This was just one example of Peale's hallmark optimism. The author of *The Power of*

Positive Thinking would go on to become a celebrated American spiritual guru, the intellectual north star of a materialistic Christianity that celebrates the accretion of wealth as a marker of God's love.

Peale was never a far-right figure. His inclusion alongside Curran and Dilling may have been a play for mainstream appeal. After all, if Zoll had fringe ideas, he was also intent on spreading them into the center of society. His invitation to testify before the Senate demonstrates that he achieved some success in this regard. Today Peale is the only member of this motley crew whom the wider American public has heard of. The rest have been consigned to the dark corners of history's closest, occasionally trotted out as "cranks who salved their 'status anxiety' with conspiracy theories and bizarre panaceas."[11] But such dismissals belie the truth that, in the late 1930s, the likes of Curran and Dilling had substantial impact in society. Dilling exemplified the layperson of faith who understood Communism as a threat to Christianity writ large. Other members of the faithful, Catholic and Protestant, could look to her for a charismatic articulation of their own views. And Curran and his ilk provided the clerical leadership that Catholics in particular needed to turn their sentiments into militant action. It was Curran and other priests who sacralized anti-Communism and anti-Semitism, casting the fight against the Judeo-Bolshevist menace as a theological necessity. That was just the kind of inspiration a Christian Front would need, if one should ever come to fruition.

Still, the question remained: How? How would the Christian Front materialize? What form would it take? Who would lead it, and who would serve? Would it be a source of militant action, or just militant rhetoric? There was already rhetoric to spare; the Pro-American Rally signaled as much. But none of its orators would ever plan an uprising, point a gun, or set a bomb. None of them ever claimed membership in any Christian Front, although Curran would be there behind the scenes. By early 1939 someone would emerge to harvest the crop planted at events like the Pro-American Rally. His name, even more distant from contemporary recognition than those of Dilling and Curran, was John F. Cassidy.

From Idea to Reality

Cassidy was radicalized, appropriately enough, by Father Coughlin. Specifically, Cassidy was radicalized by the criticism directed at Coughlin for an extraordinary broadcast he delivered on November 20, 1938.

"Thousands of people must have been jolted out of their chairs," Coughlin biographer Charles Tull wrote. In "Persecution—Jewish and Christian," broadcast just a week and a half after Kristallnacht, "the Detroit priest actually proceeded to explain the Nazi persecution of the Jews as a defense mechanism against Communism."[12] Nearly a hundred German Jews were murdered during Kristallnacht, more than 250 synagogues were desecrated and burned, and nearly 7,000 Jewish-owned businesses were vandalized. By the time Father Coughlin delivered his speech, Nazi authorities had rounded up more than 30,000 people and sent them to concentration camps for the "crime" of being Jewish.

But none of this moved Coughlin to sympathy. What did was the plight of Christians in Russia, Mexico, and Spain, which, according to Coughlin, "the Jewish gentleman who controlled the radio in the press" refused to report. Like Arnold Lunn, Coughlin found his grievance claim in the apparent widespread disinterest in Catholic suffering. But instead of using that grievance to foster a seemingly positive venture such as ecumenism, Coughlin castigated the silent. He engaged in what some today call "what-aboutism": Jews were being oppressed, yes, but what about Catholics? A master manipulator of the media, he aimed to snatch away airtime from discussion of the Jewish persecution and steer attention to Catholic persecution under Communism. For Coughlin, Kristallnacht was an opportunity to talk about the real victims: Roman Catholics, who in the decades since the Russian Revolution had been placed under the thumb of "Jewish Communists," with nary a word of protest from America's Jews, politicians, or ecclesiastics.

Coughlin's speech was an outrageous defense of Nazi atrocities. But to his followers, it was an impassioned plea for cosmic justice. "Witness the price that Christians have paid to uphold their religion against those who were anti-religionists," Coughlin begged, "to uphold their Christ against those who were anti-Christ, to uphold their patriotism, their nationalism, against those who were unpatriotic and international." As Bernard Duffy and Halford Ryan note, Coughlin's speech was unusually effective in melding religious discourse and political critique. His "social and economic views were persuasively argued alongside and even within his religious and doctrinal message."[13]

The speech has received a great deal of scholarly attention, but it may be the fifteen minutes afterward that most stimulated the audience. This portion of the broadcast—less noted in the voluminous Coughlin literature—was occupied by a prayer. After justifying the Nazi persecution of Jews, Coughlin delivered a version of the most recognizable exhortation of the entire Christian canon, galvanizing to Catholics and Protestants alike: the Lord's Prayer. "Our Father who art in Heaven," he began, as lilting organ music played in the background. At first there was nothing conceivably controversial in these rhythms and cadences. But then, between lines, Coughlin interspersed political nuggets. "Instead of gifts to the afflicted in distant lands," Coughlin prayed, "our ships carry cargoes of debt." "Forgive us our sins," he continued, interjecting that "for too long we have been loud in our praise for those who preach the Gospel of Hate." Finally, Coughlin's growing tilt toward Catholic militancy came to the fore. "Thy kingdom come; Thy will be done," he implored, "God give us power, give us courage, courage even unto death oh God, to marshal our forces, to battle for thy will."[14] The organ music drifted to a stop, followed by a reflective pause heard across crackling radios from coast to coast.

Coughlin's speech and prayer spoke to the existential struggle his followers already perceived between Communism and Catholicism, if not Christianity as a whole. But the general public, and many in his Coughlin's church, were aghast at his willingness to blame German Jews for the catastrophe visited on them. In light of his incendiary words, Coughlin's broadcaster in New York, WMCA, demanded that he clear his speeches with programmers before going on air. When he refused, the station dropped him. Coughlin's supporters saw WMCA's rebuke as a violation of his First Amendment rights, an overheated allegation given that the station, not the government, took him off the air. In any case, from the perspective of his fans, rejection by WMCA proved Coughlin's point: Catholics like him were persecuted by "non-Christians."[15]

The WMCA incident was a key step on the road to a living, breathing Christian Front. Coughlin's removal from the station's roster won him much clerical sympathy—James Keeling, a priest from St. Francis of Assisi parish in the Bronx, thought that the WMCA affair "was a dark cloud with a silver lining," since "people have become aroused to the fact that [their] liberty is endangered." A Paulist priest, Reverend James Carnell, defended Coughlin, saying that the "Communist government in Russia has murdered Christians and destroyed Catholic churches." But more important was the lay reaction. In New York the Irish-American Progressive League and the Christian-American Committee Against Communism (CACAC) held a joint meeting to urge other radio stations to keep Father Coughlin on the air. For CACAC, Father Coughlin was "the one voice that America needs to stop Communism."[16]

The only lay Catholic New Yorker to defend Coughlin in the press was the leader of CACAC: John Cassidy.

•   •   •

Anti-Communism gave direction to Cassidy's life. Before there was CACAC, there was little more than the frustration of a rudderless young man. Thereafter, he would go on to become one of the Christian Front's national leaders and its first field general, promoting and planning terrorist activities in New York. Cassidy's iteration of the front was the genuine article. The Lunns had their committee, exploring the idea of a Christian Front as an ecumenical bulwark against Communism. The Vatican pressed that same agenda. Father Coughlin urged another agenda under the same name—anti-Communist, certainly, but also anti-Semitic and dispensing with ecumenism. It was Coughlin's variation on the Christian Front that Cassidy, joined by other far-right New York Catholics, made real.

Eventually Cassidy and his Christian Front would generate one of the largest files in the FBI's history. At first, though, Cassidy hoped to be the one writing such files, not their subject. On January 20, 1935, Cassidy applied for a position at the FBI's New York Field Office. This was the last-gasp job search of an overeducated, unemployed twenty-four-year-old amid the gloom of the Great Depression. Cassidy had finished two years of law school at Fordham University, completed an LLB at St. John's University Law School in Queens, and then failed the bar exam twice. So he set his sights on becoming one of J. Edgar Hoover's famed G-men, whom he most likely had heard about through movies, magazines, and comics. At the time, the FBI was rebranding itself as "a super police force to check the growth of organized crime"—heroes fighting evil and defending America through force of law and arms.[17] A career like that was probably seductive to Cassidy, who understood himself as a patriot and who saw the world in binary terms: there were good guys, bad guys, and no shades of gray. Yet it was a short distance from enthusiasm to desperation. On his FBI application, Cassidy stated that he would "accept the lowest entrance salary" and that he hoped to hear from the bureau within the week.[18]

The FBI did not reciprocate Cassidy's interest. Hoover's men were fully aware of the "fantasy identification" that drew men like Cassidy. The special agent who drew up Cassidy's psychological profile found the eager applicant "an insipid personality" of "limited ability, lacking in initiative." Almost with disgust, the agent noted that Cassidy was just five feet seven and a half inches tall and "wears a small waxed mustache." Indeed, Cassidy "made an unfavorable impression" and had no observable "qualifications that might be useful" to the bureau.[19]

Arguably Cassidy was a better fit for the FBI than agents were willing to admit. He was in important ways not so different from J. Edgar Hoover, diagnosed by biographer Athan Theoharis with "authoritarian character disorder," latent sadism, compulsive personality characteristics. Although he always denied the nickname publicly, he became known to his followers as "the little Führer." The FBI's Christian Front file recalls a telling occasion in Narrowsburg, New York. Front members were dining together casually when Cassidy entered the room; they "immediately arose, clicked their heels together, and greeted Cassidy in a typical Nazi salute with upraised arms."[20]

Cassidy had authoritarian views to go along with his authoritarian personality—anything was acceptable, even brutal dictatorship, if it served as an obstacle to leftism. As Cassidy saw it, Nazism and Fascism were "the only forces that could stop Communism." The Popular Front's claim that Communism was the protector of democracy was simply a lie, Cassidy thought; the world was riven between two antidemocratic tendencies, and a moral person had to choose between them. "The majority of organizations in New York fighting 'isms' concentrate all of their efforts on Fascism and Nazism," he complained, when in fact "Communism was the real menace to the nation." The idea of securing democracy, whatever its substantive results, did not motivate him.

Alongside anti-Communism, Cassidy embraced anti-Semitism. In an ominous warning, he told the members of CACAC that "in their fight against Communism they must expect the cry of 'anti-Semitism' whenever they attack Communist leaders." This was deft rhetoric, hardening followers against the logic of their own Judeo-Bolshevist myth-making and steeling them for battle in the arena of public opinion. What better way to deflect charges of anti-Semitism than to determine a priori that they could not be leveled in good faith?

Cassidy was everything Father Coughlin had dreamed of. Cassidy was, first and foremost, militant—and not in a metaphorical sense. "Communism in America has formerly been a battle of words," he exclaimed in November 1938, "but now has become a battle of militant action." When Cassidy thundered that "only a Christian front will defeat Communism," he was mating firmly the concept of a Christian Front with actual battle.[21] His Christian Front was not a roundabout form of Christian ecumenism. In Cassidy's mind, the concept melded paramilitarism and Catholicism, specifically. Indeed, Cassidy's Christian Front grew out of CACAC, a Catholic group that had been tottering on the edge of violence since its founding. So obvious was CACAC's combativeness that police were detailed to the group's inaugural meeting to prevent a riot.

Brooklyn's Flatbush neighborhood, where CACAC emerged, was a hotbed not just of Catholic anti-Communism but also anti-Semitism. A case in point was Floyd A. Carridi, the grandstanding president of the Flatbush Anti-Communist League (FACL). "If the Jews in America don't watch out," Carridi announced just as the news of Kristallnacht emerged from Europe, "they will get the same treatment they got in Germany. I will lead the move against them, and we have guns." An ACLU report distilled the FACL to its essence: "It can be said without fear that a major purpose [of the group] is to foster anti-Semitism." Carridi routinely urged violence, once telling the audience at an outdoor Flatbush meeting that the platform he was standing on could be dismantled in about ten seconds and its parts used for bludgeons.[22]

Between Cassidy and Carridi, what was happening in Flatbush and all over Brooklyn was the merger of the Judeo-Bolshevist myth and a Roman Catholicism already suspicious of Jews. This was decidedly a spiritual and intellectual transformation: when they weren't throwing punches or shouting fighting words, the speakers at these street meetings came across as deeply theological. "When Christ walked down the street with his cross on his back, dressed in tatters," Carridi bellowed in a November 1938 speech, "they spat upon him and mocked him the same way they do it to you when you try to oppose Christian-baiting at a Communist meeting." From Carridi's perspective, it was important that Catholics see Christ in themselves, because this was the justification of their militancy. "They are trying to put you on the Cross," Carridi said of Communists. "You possess the same human nature that Christ possessed," he continued. "Christ rolled up his sleeves and he took out a whip and went around the temple with it . . . you can do everything that your leader, Christ did." An ACLU report indicates that Carridi's theological hollering was met with great applause. Cassidy spoke during the same meeting. "I am a Catholic," he exclaimed. "My pledge—my heart to Rome—my body to America—my soul to God!"[23]

Father Coughlin shined his light on Cassidy rather than Carridi. Carridi's star may have dimmed when he was arrested by New York Police officers in October of 1938, whereas Cassidy appealed to Coughlin due to his public loyalty during the WMCA episode, his level of education, and his semiprofessional credentials. It is not clear precisely when Father Coughlin decided to formally commit to creating an organization called the Christian Front, but it was not much before March 1939, when Marcel Honore, the organization's nominal president, placed Cassidy in charge of the front's Brooklyn unit. Cassidy's coming-out party took place on March 9, when he arranged for a screening of the movie *Spain in Arms*. "A film 'made in Spain, not Hollywood,'" the producers claimed, would show "the International Brigade in action, burning churches and looting." Cassidy designed Christian Front insignia for the occasion and screened the film through July.[24]

Using authentic shots from the Spanish Civil War, "the film showed alleged shooting of a statue of Christ" by firing squad, "desecration of church figures, burning of sacred vestments, and the destruction of churches." As one filmgoer noted, these scenes "made the blood of the audience boil pretty highly." The appearance on screen of the hammer and sickle "drew loud boos." When Loyalist soldiers showed up in the film, an audience member jeered, "Tell Abie and Cohen to come back to Union Square!" The film was "a valuable emotionalizing agent," the anonymous observer wrote. "The average and sub-average individual" can "be emotionalized a great deal more from a visual instead of a verbal presentation."[25]

Cassidy also showed *Golgotha*, a film about the Crucifixion. Another anonymous observer stereotyped the audience as "a family affair" full of "women with rumps grown oversized through childbearing, children by the dozen, laboring men, red-faced, thick-wristed, and leather necked." It was "a coarse crowd, very coarse, and most of them impressionable, fanatic, religious . . . all of them bloodthirsty for Jewish blood." The audience seemed mesmerized by the "gory, miserable sickening sight of Christ carrying the cross."

Golgotha expressed the core messages of the Christian Front. *Golgotha* was a *religious* film with political messaging, much as the Christian Front viewed anti-Communism as a religious imperative—a papal imperative, even—that would be realized in the political realm. Cassidy, alongside theological mentors such as Coughlin and Curran, was filtering true Catholic teachings and biblical texts through the lens of a particular style of political activism. But this was not a matter as simple as distorting true Catholic teaching. Rather, the Christian Front appropriated true Catholic teachings and left them intact while grafting their own view of Catholic activism on those teachings. "I daresay they have been faithful to the Biblical text," the *Golgotha*-screening observer noted. The distortion lay in interpretations and additions inserted by the Christian Front and the propagandists it relied on.

The anonymous reporter's review of *Golgotha* contained several examples, including Pontius Pilate greeting the on-screen crowd with what looked to be a Nazi salute. More significant was the crucifixion scene, which generated the strongest audience reaction. On the screen, "As the mob clamored for the crucifixion of Christ many a fist shot out in what was intended to be a parallel to the Communist salute." The raised, clenched fist thus took on an "anti-God" symbolism. "Note the strategy," the observer wrote. "Jewish people almost 2,000 years ago shooting out their fists, just as today they are accused of being behind the Communist movement." The result was a novel and twisted religious belief, albeit one that had roots in long-standing Catholic anti-Judaism: "Jews—Communist Jews—crucified Christ. Jews—Communist Jews—are today trying to crucify Christianity." Here was the old story of Jews as Christ killers transformed by, and into, the Judeo-Bolshevist myth. "It is no laughing matter with these people," the observer concluded. "They believe it heart and soul."

After *Golgotha* ended, the stage was turned over to Joseph E. McWilliams, leader of the Christian Mobilizers, a Christian Front–adjacent group in New York that shared the front's militancy. "I heard the voice of our Savior in this film tonight," he said softly and reverently to the assembled. "I was reminded of another voice—in Royal Oak," the Detroit suburb where Father Coughlin was based. As the applause died down, McWilliams made the comparison explicit. Father Coughlin's was "a voice which today is being persecuted as was the voice of Christ."[26]

In comparing Father Coughlin to Jesus Christ, McWilliams was making a play for leadership of the Christian Front. A formidable speaker, if rather bombastic, McWilliams was also a well-organized activist. His Christian Mobilizers were picking up recruits throughout the spring of 1939, and he counted Father Edward Brophy, a so-called philosopher of the Christian Front, as a friend and supporter.[27] But the front's designated leaders—Honore and Walter Ogden, the group's first secretary-treasurer—were skittish about McWilliams. Not only did they keep him out of leadership, they even denied him membership. In December 1939, some months after McWilliams arrived in New York, Ogden pointed him out to the FBI. It was, Ogden said, McWilliams's connections to the Ku Klux Klan in Texas that made him unfit for membership in the Christian Front. However, it is more likely that McWilliams was rebuffed because his Christian Mobilizers were tainted with lawbreaking—two of the group's leaders had been convicted of inciting riots the previous summer. Both Ogden and Coughlin wanted to avoid any association with criminals, and they feared that their fledgling Christian Front would be swallowed up by the more publicly belligerent Mobilizers. Ogden described the McWilliams organization as "a very dangerous group of individuals and undoubtedly very pro-German."[28]

Of course, another possibility is that Cassidy simply did not want the competition from McWilliams. From early on, though Honore and Ogden were officially in charge, it was clear that Cassidy was Coughlin's general in New York, and he was not the kind of man to accept a challenge from the likes of McWilliams. Many who have written about the Christian Front view Cassidy as an interloper who bullied his way into leadership, bowling over the unsuspecting Ogden and Honore. But an official Christian Front letter signed by Ogden makes clear that he and Cassidy carried on a close working relationship from the group's earliest days and that Cassidy's authority was accepted by the front's nominal leadership. Postmarked February 16, 1939, Ogden's letter affirmed that Cassidy would be the membership recruiter for the Christian Front and that Cassidy's approval was necessary before a membership application could proceed upward to Ogden. As secretary-treasurer, Ogden officially welcomed recruits into the Christian Front, but the talent-spotting and gate-keeping were done by Cassidy. And Cassidy was good at his job. The FBI noticed that the Christian Front was growing "by leaps and bounds" all over New York in the spring of 1939. According to the bureau, membership numbers in New York City reached "3,000 to 4,000" by the summer. Cassidy was not Ogden's rival but rather a respected colleague, and by late summer the Brooklyn activist had severed ties with CACAC so that he could focus exclusively on the Christian Front. Cassidy was building the organization and, in the process, gaining the religious and social relevance he coveted.[29]

The actual membership tally of 1939 is impossible to confirm. Historian Daniel McInerney has estimated that "Christian Front membership peaked at 1,200," a number that seems unlikely since an investigation by the New York City Mayor's Office concluded that there were "more than one thousand" front members just in the New York Police Department. At the high end, an unsigned and unverified report from the American Jewish Committee claimed there were more than 38,000 fronters in the New York area alone. "Organizers have been sent throughout the Atlantic seaboard," the report warned. Ogden confirmed the 38,000 number to the FBI. Whatever the case may be, the FBI put the figure at a tenth of that, while scholars are left to make educated guesses. Cassidy outfoxed the FBI—and posterity—by hiding all the Christian Front's membership applications.[30]

Cassidy's caution notwithstanding, the front must not be confused with a secret society. Its leaders were well known and made no efforts to shroud their identities; indeed, they were proud to announce themselves. Individual members were also expected to carry an official Christian Front identification card showing their photograph, while a second photograph was kept in the front's files. As with most everything related to the Christian Front, transparency had a religious purpose. Since 1810 American bishops had banned membership in secret societies, prohibiting the reception of the sacraments by any Catholic who joined organizations with oaths of secrecy, such as the Masons. Membership transparency thus reconciled the Christian Front with Roman Catholic canon law. The front took pains to clarify its position, stating in one of its first explanatory pamphlets that it was "neither a Political Party nor a Secret Society."[31]

In any event, the front was committed to growth and the publicity needed to achieve it. At one point Coughlin wrote in *Social Justice* that he hoped to expand the "national membership of the organization to 5 million before the summer and fall of 1940." Coughlin, himself a massively popular public presence, made sure to promote Cassidy's leading role to the world. According to the FBI's December 1939 report on the front, in July of that year, "Cassidy visited Father Charles E. Coughlin in Detroit, Michigan, and represented that he (Cassidy) was the National Director of the Christian Front"; Coughlin apparently agreed, or at least associated Cassidy with the front's ongoing success. "God bless John Cassidy and the Christian Front," Coughlin declared in an amplified telephone call to a "wildly enthusiastic" crowd of 6,000 at an open-air meeting in Philadelphia on July 14.[32]

Syndicated columnist Dorothy Thompson captured the importance of the moment when she wrote that Coughlin "conveyed upon Mr. Cassidy the blessings of Almighty God." Cassidy was now a Levite in the order of the Christian Front. Newly ordained in his semipriestly capacity, Cassidy wasted no time in advancing the front to its next stage of militancy. "There is no law under the Constitution which prohibits a man from owning a gun," Cassidy told the crowd in Philadelphia, "and there is no law that prohibits a man from belonging to a defensive organization." Yet, by Cassidy's own admission, the front was not interested in defense. "We must not wait until the Communists act," he told his followers. "We ourselves must take the initial step."[33]

A Theological Call to Arms

Cassidy's gun-talk in Philadelphia was a kind of opening salvo. A few more months would pass before the Christian Front actually began taking up arms. But only two weeks separated Cassidy's speech from another by Father Coughlin, announcing the front's theology of violence.

On July 30, 1939, Coughlin broadcast "The Popular Front vs the Christian Front."[34] After revving up the engine of grievance with a discussion of a recent dust-up between himself and Mayor LaGuardia, Coughlin turned to the Spanish Civil War, the conflict foremost on the minds of the Lunns, the Vatican, and other forces popularizing the idea of a Christian Front. Spain's Popular Front had tried to "tear down the cross and massacre Christians in the name of democracy," Coughlin explained, but Franco saved the day. "There came a Franco. And when Franco came, there came the dissolution of your lost, diabolical cause," Coughlin said. "And who composed Franco's forces? I will tell you. It was the Christian Front." Just as Franco's Christian Front had saved Spain, so Coughlin's Christian Front would save America. "The Christian Front is no longer a dream," he accurately noted, it "grows stronger, and more determined."

Echoing Cassidy's prophylactic rhetoric against charges of anti-Semitism, Coughlin assured listeners that members of the Christian Front could expect nothing but hardship and persecution—but this made them Christlike: "Though the modern scribes and Pharisees will term you 'Fascist'; though they will accuse you of stirring up the multitudes; though they maintain you consort with sinners—be they Nazi or anti-Semitic or what-not—were not more scurrilous epithets than these hurled at Jesus Christ?" Thus the way of the Christian Front would be the way of the cross. "If you are assailed or assaulted, be mindful that when He was spat upon, condemned, stripped of His garments and lashed at the pillar of injustice, He suffered patiently."

At a first listen, it may be difficult to hear the call to arms in Coughlin's oratory. Even when he pointed out that "the Crusaders of old were Christians when they repulsed the Mohammedan hordes," he could have been speaking metaphorically, arguing for a militancy of head and heart that stopped short of combat. But many Catholics of the time would have recognized in Coughlin's words a theology not only permitting violence but compelling it. The strongest clue lay in his invocation of the Mystical Body of Christ. "Christianity does not teach that the Mystical Body of Christ shall submit to the body of Satan," Coughlin said.

How does announcing an ontological threat to the Body of Christ constitute incitement in the here and now? To answer that question, we have to look back to two major organizing principles of Roman Catholicism in the 1930s and 1940s. These were, first, the theology of the Mystical Body of Christ and, second, the ecclesiology of Catholic Action—an official exhortation from the Church that sacralized laypeople's social missions. These principles are no longer valid parts of Catholic doctrine—Mystical Body theology was dropped in the 1960s, by the Second Vatican Council—but when Father Coughlin called on them, they were dominant features of everyday life for American Catholics. Catholic leaders who did not share Coughlin's enthusiasm for anti-Communism would have been loath to contest his doctrines, based, as they were, in sound theological precepts. For the same reason, lay Catholics would have been highly susceptible to his message.[35]

Mystical Body theology piqued the interest of Pauline scholars between 1900 and 1920, then took off among the Catholic public in the 1930s.[36] The power of the theology lay in its emphasis on the Church as a spiritual union forming the body of Christ. Through their participation in the sacraments—especially baptism—and their shared convictions, all Catholics constituted together the incarnation of Christ himself. Precisely why Mystical Body theology became such a powerful force when it did is hard to say with certainty, although one can immediately appreciate why such a vision, implying both human community and oneness with the divine, might offer emotional and spiritual nourishment to seekers. Historian Sally Dwyer-McNulty insightfully suggests that the changing technology of media was also key to Mystical Body theology's popularity: improved distribution transformed Catholic diocesan media into a national mass media, introducing Catholics across the United States to each other and to Catholic life globally. The result was a sense of connection to something larger than one's parish or diocese. Furthermore, cheaper photography and printing meant this media could be "image-rich" and therefore depict Catholicism in the world, inspiring a sense of the weight and physicality of the Church.[37] The Church was no longer an abstract entity or voice from on high: any Catholic could literally see its presence, a presence of which he or she was a part.

Mystical Body theology had important implications for political action, as the exiled German political philosopher Eric Voegelin explained in a 1940 essay on Nazi race theory. Voegelin was concerned that Mystical Body theology supplied a number of symbols that easily slipped into Nazi ideology. He also focused on the transnational cohesion Mystical Body theology encouraged under the heading of *homonoia*, or like-mindedness. The "fraternal sentiment between the members of a symbolic group" gave Mystical Body theology its centripetal force, drawing Catholics inward toward unity. That sentiment left Christian Front members in Brooklyn painfully concerned about the welfare of their coreligionists in Spain—or, potentially, in any corner of the world. *Painfully* concerned—not intellectually. To be Catholic was not just to be particularly aware of the persecution of other Catholics but also to feel that persecution oneself.[38]

Father Coughlin came under the sway of Mystical Body theology well before he turned its symbols and doctrines into a justification for violence. He was also far from alone in seeing the potential for militancy within Mystical Body theology, a point worth keeping in mind as we try to grasp the breadth of ideological support for his mission. For example, in August 1938 John F. Noll, the bishop of Fort Wayne, Indiana, took to the pages of Coughlin's *Social Justice* to argue that Pope Pius XI had encouraged Catholics to join a United Christian Front, which meant serving "as soldiers in the world-wide army of Christ as members of his Mystical Body."[39]

Of course, there was, as Voegelin noted, a "tension between the body symbol and the social reality." Organizations like the Christian Front salved that tension. They bridged the gap between symbol and social reality, spreading the ethos of global Christian unity and arguing that this ethos should govern action. The Christian Front was bold in its outreach on behalf of an activated Mystical Body theology. For instance, when the shooting war in Europe began in September 1939, the front put out an open letter to General George Marshall, chief of staff of the US Army, ghostwritten by Cassidy. Marshall was "the one man . . . who in the event of war, [would] be charged with the responsibility of conscripting an army to go across the seas and murder our innocent Brothers-in-Christ," Cassidy explained. "We, General, are Christians who believe in the Social Order ordained by Jesus Christ," he continued. "Ours is a spiritual cause based on the Christian concept of the immortality of the soul. ALL MEN are our brothers in Christ." Expressing the transnational nature of the Mystical Body, the letter concluded, "we will not murder them"—Europe's Christians—"on any pretense that internationalism may invent."[40]

Here Cassidy was engaged in a bit of hyperbole. If Mystical Body theology required pacificism toward fellow Christians, it did not imply the brotherhood of *all* men. Part of the danger of Mystical Body theology lay in its exclusivity. "Baptism constitutes our 'naturalization' into the Mystical Body of Christ," Monsignor Fulton Sheen, a major figure of twentieth-century American Catholicism, wrote in 1935. Those who were not baptized were not of the body. Sheen, who joined Coughlin in projecting his ministry through radio and later television, made sure that his followers knew the limits of their spiritual community, which were also the limits of the Mystical Body. Coughlin explicitly translated spiritual into political limits. As he indicated in his "call to arms," a Christian Front inspired by Mystical Body theology was to array itself against "the forces of the Jew, Karl Marx."[41]

The role of baptism in Mystical Body theology enabled precise theological lines of demarcation between Catholics and Jews, and the conflation of Jews and Communists ensured that Jews would be targets of the anti-Communist crusade.[42] What the likes of Coughlin and Cassidy—and Cardinal Pacelli—were creating was a *theological anti-Communism*. Others have analyzed the Christian Front differently, as an agent of anti-Communist anti-Semitism, but this interpretation reduces the Christian Front to just another manufacturer of the Judeo-Bolshevist myth. The Christian Front did promote that myth, but so did non-Christians, Christians with nondoctrinal motivations, and Christians with doctrinal motivations unrelated to those of the front. To grasp what the front was and why it was so dangerous, we must attend to what made it distinctive: not the combination of anti-Communism and anti-Semitism but rather the fulsome embrace of mainstream Catholicism. The front was on a specifically Catholic mission inspired by teachings at the heart of the Catholic canon—teachings elaborated by ordained and respected clerics like Coughlin, Curran, and Sheen.[43]

While the Christian Front used the rhetoric of resistance and defense—defending the body of Christ from Judeo-Bolshevist assailants—its platform was decidedly aggressive. Coughlin and the Christian Front recruited men who would be soldiers in a "platoon." For instance, local organizers in Lowell, Massachusetts, mustered "Social Justice Platoons" to fight for Father Coughlin. Notably, the front's theology encouraged Catholics to try to convert Jews, a matter of concern to Tillich and a marker of the ambition built into this more-than-defensive tendency.[44]

By late 1939 fronters were following in the footsteps of Hitler. Records of a September 1939 Christian Front meeting in New York note a comment from member Joe Leveque, who said "he would like to see the blood of Jews thrown over all the streets in America; that he wished to see Jewish blood stream all over the streets of America." Nazi successes in the early weeks of World War II did nothing to protect Spanish Catholics, but they did leave fronters jubilant. "We Christians, especially Catholics, should exterminate the Jews just like Hitler did in Germany and is now doing in Poland," Leveque concluded.[45]

.   .   .

If Mystical Body theology motivated the substance of the Christian Front's mission, Catholic Action protected the group from those within the Church who might have preferred that Coughlin, Cassidy, and their followers would disappear. Pope Pius XI defined Catholic Action as "the participation of the laity in the apostolate of the hierarchy." In the eyes of the Church, Catholic Action included all of the social work of the institution, and the work of the institution included organized action receiving clerical approval. If lay Catholics took on a social project with the blessing of their local priest or bishop, that was Catholic Action. As Fulton Sheen put it, Catholic Action was "a *participation* in the organic life of the Church. . . . Meaningless apart from the hierarchy."[46]

Catholic Action gave cover to the Christian Front whenever it faced controversy and even when it was seen as threatening to national security. Most bishops found dealing with the Christian Front perplexing precisely because, as a lay organization guided by Roman Catholic priests such as Coughlin and Curran, it was a definitive example of Catholic Action. Tillich was right to be skeptical that this lay-clerical nexus would remain untainted by anti-Semitism. A lay group had only to receive the support of an anti-Semitic priest in order to obtain official sanction for its project.

As a form of social mission responsive to the interests of lay Catholics, Catholic Action was bound to reflect the politics of the day. Thus, while not intrinsically focused on Communism, Catholic Action was a haven for anti-Communist efforts, and the whole program of Catholic Action began to be described as anti-Communist after 1940.[47] Clearly Catholic Action proponents at least paid close attention to Communist activities and learned from them, in the process redefining a religious practice as a political act. For instance, one popular handbook, printed in six editions in the 1940s alone, suggested that young Catholics create Catholic Action "cells," mimicking the Communist cell structure. "Each morning cell members stand with Christ at the reenactment of His death and resurrection," the handbook directed. When "cell members stand so intimately at the renewal of their redemption" they bring Catholic Action "into all social relationships."[48]

Catholic Action was an important companion to Mystical Body theology in that both emphasized corporate, univocal efforts. Setting aside the fact that not all Catholics were anti-Communist, when an anti-Communist Catholic Action group undertook its work, it did so in the name of the whole Mystical Body. This was truly a dangerous situation, for all the reasons that Tillich identified. There was no way the Church hierarchy could intervene against the sort of fanaticism that Tillich and Martin D'Arcy warned about when that fanaticism belonged to the entire Church.

Also like Mystical Body theology, Catholic Action carried a martial undertone. "The Holy Spirit has come," popular Jesuit pamphleteer Daniel J. Lord wrote in 1936, "and soldiers have been consecrated to warfare under Christ, the Captain." "A great summons has gone forth," Father Lord cried out, and those who "took up the standard of the Cross" were "to be soldiers, not in name only, but in fact and heroism, under the command of their captains, the bishops." Lord viewed Catholic Action not as a movement but rather "a sacrament."[49] With such a dubious mixture of ecclesiology and theology in place, Christian Front operatives in New York began to organize their own "sacramental cells."

The pledge Cassidy wrote for new Christian Front recruits is a masterful melding of anti-Communism, Mystical Body theology, and the imperatives of Catholic Action. The pledge even incorporated a loophole allowing anti-Semitism. "I pledge myself to combat all attacks on the Christian Social Order," each new recruit repeated, "even if by doing so, I may erroneously be branded 'intolerant.' . . . I promise to work by both word and action for the destruction of Communism in America." Chillingly, recruits also promised "to cooperate with those, who labor for the preservation of our American Republic, and if need be to defend it by force of arms." Finally, in a grand gesture of faith, the recruit grasped a crucifix "as a symbol of willingness to devote all the energies of mind and all strength of endurance to the cause of Christ and Country."[50]

Fired up by Cassidy's and Coughlin's calls, and certain of the rightness of Catholic Action on behalf of the Mystical Body, a New York Christian Front recruit made the first move toward paramilitarism all on his own. In mid-August 1939 Corporal Claus Gunther Ernecke of the 101st Cavalry of New York's National Guard approached the leader of his troop's machine gun platoon, Sergeant Henry Fischer. Speaking in a thick German accent, Ernecke asked Fischer if he would consider "instructing a group in the use of the Browning machine gun." Fischer was rendered speechless by his fellow soldier's request—the Browning was a serious weapon, a .30 caliber air-cooled machine gun that could shoot between 400 and 1,500 rounds per minute at a range of up to 1,500 yards. The astonished Sergeant Fischer wanted to know a little more about the "group" Ernecke intended him to train. All Ernecke would say was that it "was an organization formed to combat Communism" and that "he was very enthusiastic about the organization." Ernecke later admitted the group was Cassidy's Christian Front—"a more progressive organization" than all the other patriotic groups.[51]

The Christian Front had come a long way. No longer a vision of ecumenical anti-Communism in service of protecting Christians from persecution, it was now a Catholic-only organization whose "purpose . . . was to combat Communism and to eradicate Jews from public life." So concluded FBI agent Peter Wacks, who investigated the Ernecke-Fischer exchange. The Christian Front as realized by Cassidy was far from defensive—it was "progressive," as Ernecke put it, the kind of group that sought high-powered weapons whose only use was in killing people. Agent Wacks wrote that the Christian Front "allegedly . . . owns machine guns and rifles" and "allegedly secured 15,000 rounds of ammunition."[52] Back on the Lunns' cruise, Lord Dickinson had been adamant that "Christians need not use machine guns." Inspired by mainstream Catholic teaching and urged on by priests, the men who joined the Christian Front had other ideas.

CHAPTER 3

Terror in the Name of Christ

THE HEYDAY OF THE CHRISTIAN FRONT IN NEW YORK WOULD prove brief. The group began consolidating under Cassidy's leadership in fall 1938 and took off as a recruiting juggernaut in spring and summer 1939. Its paramilitary training then began in earnest. But by the winter of 1940, its most aggressive members were under federal indictment on charges of seditious conspiracy and weapons theft. The prosecution became a matter of great intrigue, with the mainstream press, Catholic publications, and undercover journalists providing intensive coverage. Then, after the trial ended in July, the front was barely heard from again.

For those who bother to remember the front, this is the arc of its existence. Although the trial was a disaster for the government, securing not a single conviction, it was clear that the front was under FBI surveillance, making further paramilitary activities impossible. Thereafter the Christian Front receded into the dim corners of history. While figures like Father Coughlin continue to engage the interest of scholars and a public seeking to understand the development of the US Christian right and of far-right politics globally, the front itself was too ephemeral to find purchase in any wider narrative.

Yet this simple story of a rapid rise and equally rapid fall is lacking for all sorts of reasons. Most basically, as a matter of brute historical fact, the front did not disappear. After the trial, the front remained a part of community life in Brooklyn, albeit there is no evidence of additional conspiracies or large-scale violence. But the front would go on to become a major player in Boston, as discussed in later chapters. The persistence of the front was enabled by the failure of the trial but not only by that. The front also received protection from the highest reaches of the US Catholic hierarchy, which sought both to downplay the group's violence and anti-Semitism and to distinguish the indicted men from the Church and its teachings. This is the genesis of another mistaken narrative: historians acknowledge that the government bungled the case but have not ascertained the role of the Church in safeguarding the defendants. Even as priests threw their influence behind the front, and even as the front's public meetings welcomed crowds of thousands for Christian revivals and lessons in Catholic theology, the Church was successful in convincing the public that Cassidy's fight had nothing to do with religion. The Church, along with defense lawyers, also excised anti-Semitism from the front's mission. The men on trial were to be understood only as patriotic anti-Communists. Remarkably, even the prosecution spread this message, doing its part to ensure that devotional matters had no presence in the trial and that the defendants appeared as sympathetically as possible.

Indeed, it was not only anti-Semitism, Catholic theology, and the involvement of Catholic priests that were erased from the trial. The front's lawyers and public-relations managers, including its clerical apologists, also deemphasized the group's revolutionary intentions. As we will see, in late 1939 the Christian Front became committed to the overthrow of the US government. Their strategy was to bomb Communist and Jewish institutions in order to incite an uprising among these groups, which were, according to the Judeo-Bolshevist idea, one and the same. Then the conspirators would lead the National Guard in suppressing the rebellion and install themselves as the heroic leaders of an America renewed. But neither the public nor, frankly, prosecutors could wrap their heads around the idea that seventeen men could take over the United States. The notion was so laughable that the sedition charge was hard to take seriously, and the jury agreed. Thus, far from bringing the Christian Front to an end, the trial absolved the group and absolved the Church that had inspired, empowered, and protected it. After a few months of rapt attention, America forgot all about the Christian Front.

A Revolutionary Front

The first Christian Front firearms training session took place as early as July 1939, at a property owned by a friend of Cassidy's near Hazleton,

Pennsylvania. Cassidy and several others would "hold rifle practice for several hours, sometimes standing up, sometimes lying down." They shot on Sunday morning, too, after members of the group had gone "into Hazleton [for] Catholic church."[1]

It was only a few weeks after this initial foray into paramilitary training that the front tried to graduate from rifles to machine guns. In August Claus Ernecke first approached Sergeant Henry Fischer, and when that failed turned to a second machine gunner. Denis Healy was as an engineer on the New York Central Railroad and another Browning operator in New York's National Guard. He accepted Ernecke's entreaty and then went straight to the FBI. Immediately, FBI Assistant Director Edward Tamm and Special Agent in Charge for New York City P. E. Foxworth enlisted Healy to infiltrate the Christian Front. Agent Peter Wacks would directly supervise Healy's spy mission.

Healy's early reports portray a deeply religious organization committed to violence against Jews and Communists, but not yet to revolution. At Healy's first Christian Front meeting, a mysterious soldier of fortune named William Bishop "discussed the principles of the Talmud" for an hour and a half and explained why Jews had always been "subjected to bitter criticism." Thereafter the group took "instructions on military tactics." Finally the meeting turned to planning. Macklin Boettger, one of the New York Christian Front's top organizers, proposed bombing the offices of the *Jewish Daily Forward* and the Communist newspaper the *Daily Worker*. "Boettger suggested to [Healy] that he should obtain a supply of dynamite from the warehouse of the New York Central Railroad." Boettger's idea was that "the dynamite could be thrown through an open window in the plant of the *Daily Worker*" while fronters acting as lookouts would help the bombers make their getaway in a waiting car. Boettger also recommended having "an individual dressed in the uniform of a New York City policeman . . . direct traffic at the nearest intersection in order to aid their escape."[2]

A greenhorn informant procuring dynamite was too much for Agent Wacks to allow, so he told Healy "to inform Boettger that he couldn't secure the material." But Boettger's enthusiasm was undampened. He "replied that he did not need dynamite to do the job, but could use black powder and a lead pipe if necessary." When some Christian Front members expressed alarm, Boettger scolded them. "The police couldn't prove anything unless they caught him actually 'throwing the Goddam pipe.'" The worry was not that the front might kill people, but that its members would be caught in the act.[3]

Boettger directed what was known variously as the Sports Club, Country Gentlemen, or Action Committee—a layer of camouflage for the increasing militarization of the movement. In July 1939 Father Coughlin described the Sports Club as "an athletic division headed by a competent director" and as a "gun club." It was perfectly acceptable that the Sports Club be a matter of public knowledge, but its mission was another story. "It was desired to keep the activities of the Sports Club very secretive," Healy told his FBI handlers. "The primary purpose of the Sports Clubs and the Country Gentlemen," Healy reported, "is to train men with executive ability, who in turn will be able to direct the affairs of the Christian Front not only from a political point of view, but from a military angle as well."[4]

A military requires discipline, but the men of the Christian Front could be a rough bunch. "The meeting wound up in four separate fistfights," an anonymous reporter wrote of a September 20, 1939, Christian Front meeting in the Crown Heights section of Brooklyn. Cries of "Jew dogs—we'll wipe up the streets with you" and "wait till Hitler comes here" filled the air. Catcalls alluded to FDR as "Rabbi Rosenfeld." Such sentiments were of course encouraged by the front, but Cassidy could not be satisfied with mere brawlers, so he and fellow front leaders developed methods for recruiting men with military backgrounds and for instilling order. The application forms he drew up had sections for "military record" and "rank," so that he and Boettger could pick the members best suited for paramilitary service. The front also arranged for a kind of uniform. As Albert Parry, writing for the liberal newsletter the *Hour,* reported. "Military caps with the letters CF on one side and the sign of the cross on the other were sold to members." Aside from imparting a whiff of military discipline, the hats served a public-relations purpose. Ever careful to project itself as a defensive organization with nothing to hide, the front marketed the hats as a means of identification. The caps would also ensure that fronters were recognizable to authorities "in New York, Boston, Philadelphia, and other cities" when the Communist revolution broke out.[5]

Cassidy also developed a Christian Front salute, of which he was clearly proud. Like the front itself, the salute seamlessly combined political and religious symbolism. "The right hand is extended as in the Nazi salute," Cassidy explained to reporters, "but whereas the Nazis extend the whole hand, Christian Fronters extend only the index and middle fingers," which "represented Christ and country." The gesture resembled the "V for victory" sign that would become popular after America entered the war, but with a twist:

the third and middle fingers were clamped down by the thumb. "The bent third and little fingers represent Communism and atheism," suppressed under the thumb "of Christian Front principles."[6]

On October 21 Healy saw firsthand how the Christian Front paramilitary functioned in practice. The FBI informant joined Cassidy and eight others in Narrowsburg, New York, where they honed their marksmanship and drilled maneuvers. Outfitted with 30-06 Springfield and Lee-Enfield rifles, the group "engaged in firearms practice, shooting at silhouette targets at a distance of approximately 100 yards." As Agent Wacks noted in his report, the training in "military tactics" also "consisted of military rushes of fifteen to twenty yards at which time the men would fall to a prone position and fire their rifles." The fronters were undeterred by "a very heavy rainstorm which made the ground very wet and soggy," indicating "the zeal and enthusiasm which the group possess." Bishop reinforced the point in an undated letter to Cassidy from a firing range near Rowlesburg, West Virginia. "It's raining today," Bishop wrote, "but the Browning Light Machine guns are rattling on the side of the mountain range. Rain can't stop us."[7]

While members of the Sports Clubs trained for offensive maneuvers and pondered the destructive potential of pipe bombs, they remained invested in religious piety and Mystical Body theology. These constituted both the public face shrouding secret paramilitary efforts and the motivation underlying those efforts. A report from the December 19 Christian Front meeting held on East 138th Street noted that the gathering "started off with the Lord's Prayer, and some religious stuff enunciated by David Ahearne, of the de La Salle Brothers," a mainstream Catholic education organization that continues to operate the world over. Then "the people crossed themselves." Arthur Derounian, the investigative journalist who observed the meeting, wrote that the discussion was "immersed in ecclesiastical dopage." Brother Ahearne, who "swears by everything the church stands for," conflated America and the cross. "Inside his coat he had a special pocket for a large cross," Derounian reported, "he lifted the cross as [a hypnotist] would a watch." Ahearne "kept pointing it toward the flag reciting, 'For God and for Country.'" He made clear that "he would be willing to die" for those ends, "as all those present should" be willing. Findings from the Jewish War Veterans suggest this event was fairly typical. The veterans noticed a pattern: during street meetings of the Christian Front, which featured public exhortations to violence, no priests appeared alongside the speakers; when indoor meetings were held "practically all of the speakers appear . . . on the same platform with priests . . . so . . . the audiences believe they have the sanction of the hierarchy."[8]

At this point, December 1939, Cassidy and his men were beginning to think of themselves as religious revolutionaries. Historians debate such claims, asking whether Fascism could ever be a revolutionary movement, given its constitutive opposition to a political left self-described as revolutionary. By contrast the Italian Fascist theorist Giovanni Gentile took revolutionary aims seriously, and lately some scholars have characterized Fascism as a "revolutionary fusion of deviant Marxism and radical nationalism." David Schoenbaum views the Nazis as authors of "a social revolution," transferring wealth and power from Weimar elites—in particular, Jewish civil servants—to middle-class German Christians.[9] Members of the Christian Front had more or less the same perspective as other right-wing revolutionaries seeking "liberation" from Jews and Communists. "When we overthrow the government," Bishop explained in November 1939, "we will take all the gold that is in the Federal Reserve Banks . . . controlled and operated by twelve Jew banks, and redistribute it among the people."[10]

The immediate cause of the front's lurch toward anti-government violence was President Roosevelt's successful effort to repeal the Neutrality Act of 1937. On November 4, 1939, Roosevelt and his congressional backers prevailed over isolationist opponents and lifted the arms embargo on belligerents in the war in Europe. Until this point, the United States could not supply weapons and other military equipment either to Germany or any of the states fighting it and its allies. But Roosevelt's novel program, known as cash and carry, enabled American firms to do just that. Technically, the new law allowed US businesses to sell to any of the parties at war, but the terms of the legislation meant that, effectively, only Britain and France, which had not yet fallen to the Germans, would benefit. The move incensed Cassidy and Bishop, who were outwardly, and genuinely, isolationist while also being privately pro-Nazi. They also saw Roosevelt's effort not only as a move toward war but also, correctly, as a lifeline to Great Britain. The US government was now supporting the enemies of Fascism, which the front considered a valuable bulwark against Communism. Even worse, Washington was throwing its weight behind the British, a repellant act in Irish-American circles. Revulsion toward Great Britain was a key part of the front's recruitment toolkit, as I discuss in later chapters.[11]

Reflecting on the repeal of the Neutrality Act, Cassidy "stated that he personally believes someone should 'knock off' about a dozen of the Congressmen" who voted for repeal "just to show them that the Christian Front means business." If Congress did not "take a different attitude and adopt different policies . . . the United States undoubtedly would have a revolution," Cassidy asserted. Bishop argued that fronters "might as well be killed over here carrying on a program of sabotage" rather "than going to some foreign country and fighting a war . . . promoted by the Jewish bankers in the United States." Claus Ernecke was panicked by all the revolutionary talk. "If the God damn FBI ever hears of it, they will have us all in jail and we would be of no use to the movement . . . because men behind bars cannot blow up railroad bridges." The FBI did hear of it, of course. Each of these statements is from a December 1, 1939, report compiled by Agent Wacks from Healy's observations.[12]

The revolution was to start with a bombing campaign. On December 6 Boettger, Bishop, and two other fronters, John Viebrock and National Guard Captain John T. Prout, Jr., met at Denis Healy's house for a conversation "as to the proper method of preparing or manufacturing bombs." Bishop brought four tin cans to the meeting "for demonstration purposes." He explained that "the smaller of the two cans should be inserted into the larger can" and cement poured between the two cans. "This type of bomb," he stated, "although it did not possess killing power, could do great damage to property." Bishop had tested his homemade bombs, exploding one under a billboard. "It blew the billboard to pieces," he recalled gleefully. When Boettger suggested using brass pipes instead of cement-lined cans, Bishop objected. "That is just what we do not want . . . something that will fly to pieces at the time of the explosion." What Bishop wanted was "just enough to smash a window out, and if possible set the thing on fire." That is because the bombing campaign was not intended to destroy a target but rather to terrorize Communists and Jews, inciting them to revolution. Cassidy, Bishop, and other planners hoped the bombings would provide a trigger for a "temporary dictatorship" of the United States under a military officer amenable to the Christian Front.[13]

One week after the meeting, Healy went to Boettger's home in Brooklyn to inspect the front's ordnance. Healy was shown precisely which cans would be placed inside the cement-lined bombs. The interior fitting was made of "ordinary Campbell's soup cans reinforced on both ends with pieces of steel and filled with black powder to which was attached a fuse." Bishop also showed Healy 7,000 rounds of loose 30-06 rifle ammunition along with "several fully loaded machine gun belts." Bishop further indicated that the bombs "would be used sometime subsequent to the first of the year." The pace of action had ramped up immensely.[14]

By the first week of January 1940, Viebrock, who now was claiming to be codirector of the Christian Front along with Cassidy, overruled both Bishop's and Boettger's objections to the use of pipe bombs. The FBI's sources immediately informed Hoover, who on January 4 was advised that Bishop had just returned from a trip to West Virginia "with some caps and dynamite fuses."[15] On January 10, with eight other fronters attending, Viebrock provided a spine-chilling course on how to make a pipe bomb. His expertise was evident in the detailed notes Healy compiled.

> Viebrock stated that, in order to make a bomb out of a piece of pipe, he would take a length of pipe approximately one foot long and screw a cap on one end, that, after attaching to the end of the pipe, he would fill it with powder; that he would allow a space of approximately one inch on the open end of the pipe, at which he would insert a piece of cardboard the same size as the inside of the pipe and press it down against the powder already inserted in the pipe. He would then attach a cap to the other end of the pipe and force a tin cylinder through a hole in that cap down into the pipe until it punctured the cardboard covering the powder; that he would then insert a fuse through the tin cylinder until the fuse had gone into contact with the powder in the pipe; that he would press the edges of the tin together, so that the fuse would not fall out.

Viebrock thought "this type of bomb would probably be one of the most dangerous bombs that he could manufacture," although he could make it still more deadly "by cutting a ring around the pipe at small intervals with a plumber's cutter." This would cause "bits of the pipe to fly under the force of the explosion in all directions." Viebrock was proud of the idea, which "was patterned after the hand grenade used in Army warfare."[16]

Gone were the previous month's discussions about "killing power" and the ethical distinctions between the destruction of people and the destruction of property. Just two days later, on January 12, the FBI secretly recorded Viebrock telling an unnamed source that the front would have more drills in Hazleton on January 20, and this time "twenty bombs would be available for firearms training." In addition, Viebrock deposited fuses with the unnamed source. Simultaneously the Sports Club "designated its youngest member to case the *Daily Worker.*"

At this point, the FBI had heard enough. Given the heightened firearm and bomb-making activity, E. J. Connelley, assistant director of the FBI's New York office, "thought the US Attorney should be contacted" immediately "in connection with warrants." Connelley believed that if Cassidy and Bishop ran another paramilitary training session, they could explode and expend most of their bombs and ammunition, leaving less evidence for the government to build a case. Hoover greenlighted the warrants that very day, as did the Justice Department's Alexander Holtzaff, a special assistant to the US attorney general.[17]

Judge Grover Moscowitz of the Eastern District of New York issued arrest warrants for Cassidy and sixteen others on January 13. "G-Men swooped down," the United Press reported, and seized "arms, ammunition and bombs." The FBI found fifteen partially made bombs, eighteen canisters of cordite powder, assorted rifles, and 750 rounds of Browning light machine gun ammunition. Agents also confiscated four mortar detonator cartridges and seven "cans of cordite powder for firing three-inch [Mark I] Stokes trench mortars." Later FBI scientists realized that the mortar ammunition was not cordite but rather the nitrostarch compound designed by the Army Chemical Warfare Division. This was the same explosive the US Army used in hand grenades.[18]

The arrests took place overnight. When booked, Bishop was wearing a "crucifix blessed by Father Coughlin" and a medal of St. Rita, patron saint of impossible causes. Bishop claimed to be a Protestant. For his part, Cassidy arrived at the jail with a rifle bullet in his shirt pocket. When asked why he had it, he responded that "he carried [it] as a symbol." Languishing in his cell at the Federal House of Detention on West 11th Street, Cassidy told a reporter he was "not guilty of anything but Christian-American self-defense." Speaking to another reporter, he explained, "All I can say is—Long live Christ the King!—Down with Communism!—Be sure and put that in."[19]

Cassidy's retort to the justice system was steeped in the transnational language of Christian anti-Communism, the gist of Mystical Body theology as it was practiced in the 1930s and 1940s. "Long live Christ the King" were the exact words shouted by Father Miguel Agustín Pro, the Mexican Jesuit executed by firing squad at the hands of the collectivist government of Plutarco Elías Calles in 1927. Mexican Catholics chanted the same words during their public protests against the government throughout the Cristero War of 1926–1929. The phrase became a rallying cry for US Catholic anti-Communists in the 1930s and into the Cold War. The crypt of Father Coughlin's Shrine of the Little Flower in Royal Oak, Michigan, was and remains dedicated to Father Pro.

Sedition, Insanity, or Patriotism?

The US justice system came at Cassidy and his men full bore, with two extremely serious charges. The first was an indictment for conspiracy to "overthrow, put down, and destroy by force the Government of the United States"—a conviction could have meant many years behind bars. Such a charge would be difficult to prove, though, so prosecutors might have paired it with an additional indictment that would virtually guarantee a guilty finding on at least one count. The obvious choice was weapons possession, but Hoover suggested the more legally potent—and less easily proven—charge of weapons theft. At his press conference announcing the arrests, Hoover asserted that "elaborate plans had been made" by the Christian Front "for the theft of armament for revolutionary use from National Guard arsenals." Behind the scenes, President Roosevelt appeared equally convinced. In the cover note on a memo to his new attorney general, Robert Jackson, Roosevelt listed several topics he wanted the Justice Department to prioritize. One of these was "Cassidy & Co. Tried to Penetrate the US Armed Forces." The government set bail at $50,000 (just shy of $1 million in 2020 dollars) for each alleged conspirator, another sign of prosecutors' belief in the gravity of the case.[20]

From the moment of his arrest, Cassidy pushed two themes in his defense. First, he argued that the Christian Front was never so great a threat as prosecutors claimed. He hewed to this position for the rest of his days, mocking the FBI in a 1995 interview for its handling of his supposedly harmless band. "They had a truck full of special agents with machine guns pointing at us," Cassidy scoffed to the *New York Times* fifty-five years after his arrest. Second, he claimed that the Christian Front was nothing more than a group of patriotic citizens concerned about Communism, which placed them among the majority of Americans. He denied revolutionary intentions and left the group's anti-Semitism unaddressed. At no point after his arrest did Cassidy publicly connect his anti-Communism to the Judeo-Bolshevist conspiracy theory. Both defenses would gain the tacit support of the Catholic hierarchy.[21]

From the perspective of the historian with access to the FBI's records and the full range of reporting on the Christian Front, these defenses seem faulty to say the least. But in 1940 Americans were disposed to Cassidy's position.

Two days after the arrests, the United Press followed up with a front-page story reporting that "public opinion was inclined to dismiss as fantastic the alleged plot." Caught off guard, Hoover famously and hyperbolically argued at a press conference that "it took only twenty-three men to overthrow Russia." He told reporters that, "among its early acts of terrorism, the Christian Front planned to bring about the complete eradication of all Jews, seize all railroads, public utilities, power and water plants, and all other forms of communication and transportation."[22] Hoover was simply repeating for the public what his informants were reporting, including Bishop's own statements. Yet the plot officials were describing was too much for the public to take seriously. By April United Press was reporting on the Christian Front's "playful plot."[23]

If Americans could not believe the front actually intended to carry out revolutionary violence or had the capacity to do so, this was in part because Catholic leaders used their considerable influence to de-emphasize the sedition charge. About two weeks after the arrests, Morris Ernst, a respected liberal lawyer and close friend of President Roosevelt's, arranged for "some of the Catholic Hierarchy" to meet with O. John Rogge, an assistant attorney general and head of the Justice Department's Criminal Division. The main purpose of the gathering was "discussing the Christian Front case." It was extraordinary for a federal prosecutor to consult with parties having a vested interest in the outcome of an ongoing case. On top of that, it seems the Catholic hierarchs prepared a letter for Roosevelt, which they hoped Ernst would transmit on their behalf. There is no evidence that the letter ever reached Roosevelt, but the archived draft makes clear the clergy's position that the detainees had done essentially nothing wrong. Arguing that Cassidy and his followers were "earnest Americans misled by demagogic appeals to race hatred" and men who "harbored no seditious sentiments toward our country," the clergy asked Roosevelt to extend "every possible consideration to the members of the Christian Front." The letter makes no mention of who misled these earnest Americans, which is to say that the Church did not admit that its own doctrines and priests were in any way responsible. The Church leaders did not suggest that Cassidy and his crew were entirely blameless but asked "that justice may be tempered with mercy" and that the men "may be allowed to return to their respective homes and occupations."[24]

Meanwhile Monsignor Maurice Sheehy of the Catholic University of America, a regular correspondent with President Roosevelt, wrote directly to Hoover. The monsignor portrayed the Christian Front as an anomaly in

American history, a deviation from the constant trajectory of American Catholic patriotism. "The Christian Front," Sheehy wrote, "is, as I see it, about fifty per cent anti-Semitism, thirty per cent anti-Rooseveltism, and twenty per cent infantile exhibitionism." Sheehy was keen to underscore that the Christian Front was in no sense a product of Roman Catholicism itself. Ever protective of his church, Sheehy was at a loss to explain how a bout of "infantile exhibitionism" could generate such paramilitarism. [25]

Catholic media spread much the same message, both distancing the men from the Church and suggesting that they were merely crackpots, as hapless as they were deluded. *America*, the widely read Jesuit magazine, characterized the detainees as "a few psychopathic cases who need straightjackets," "nerve-ridden enthusiasts made violent by dark brooding," and "dupes." In other words, not only were the alleged plotters obviously incapable of carrying out the plan the government described, but they also represented no one besides themselves. The magazine did not attempt to describe who exactly had duped these fools: the likes of Coughlin, Brophy, and Curran—all respected, if not uncontroversial, priests steeped in mainstream Catholic theology. The liberal New York Catholic journal *Commonweal* was unusual in blaming Coughlin's "powerful propaganda" and even went so far as to call out Catholics generally. But the publication described the plotters as "hypnotized men," suggesting they bore little moral responsibility, if any. *Time* referenced the *Commonweal* editorial but kept only the hypnotized men, erasing the journal's courageous stand against the sources of extremism within the Church itself. Politicians also played their part. "I don't think the United States Government is in much danger from eighteen [*sic*] guys like these," New York City Mayor Fiorello La Guardia scoffed.[26]

We should be careful not to presume that the elite Catholic defense of the suspects reflected sympathy with their views and actions—whether their actual views and actions or those imputed by the men's backers. After all, neither bishops nor magazine writers argued the wisdom of collecting guns and bombs for a war with Communists, much less for revolutionary violence. Rather, many Catholics turned to the crackpot theory because it was essential that the plotters be dissociated from the larger community of believers, subject as it was to constant suspicion. In the 1930s Catholics were finally integrating into American society at a rapid pace, but even as Roosevelt stocked his cabinet with Catholics, distrust remained. For instance, between 1915 to 1930, the Ku Klux Klan—then an organization enjoying widespread credibility—routinely accused Catholics of subversiveness. This despite the hard work Catholics had done in reconciling their religion with democracy and the American experiment. Now the same Catholics who had proven their patriotism by serving in the Great War were beset by a group of Christ-loving coreligionists charged with sedition. Catholics did whitewash the Christian Front plot, but as a function of fear more than support.

For their part, historians have looked at the Christian Front case from a number of angles. Scholars have always been skeptical of the front's capacity to carry through with their plans. Some historians have viewed the roundup of the fronters as evidence that President Roosevelt was using a politicized FBI to eliminate opposition. Donald Warren, who has written the most scientific study of Father Coughlin, describes a quite sinister plot to "start an uprising that would destroy Jewish-owned newspapers and stores and blow up bridges, utilities, docks, and railroad stations in the New York City area."[27]

But for Cassidy and his followers, this was only half of the plan. In order to understand Cassidy's motivations accurately, we must place ourselves within the realm of what historian Rick Perlstein has called the "political surrealism of the paranoid fringe." Cassidy genuinely saw international Communism as an existential threat to Roman Catholicism. Both the news of the day and the timeless doctrine were seemingly unequivocal on this point. So Cassidy devised a two-part strategy combining assaults intended to inspire a Jewish and Communist uprising, followed by a Christian front–led counterattack.[28]

Warren correctly describes the first half of the plan, which was a kind of false-flag operation. Cassidy aimed to use small cordite bombs to inflict property damage at the New York Customs House, utilities throughout the city, and Jewish-owned businesses. The simultaneous bombings would provoke terror, with the bonus of victimizing Jews. Christian Front operatives throughout New York City would then spread the word that the bombings were the work of the Communist Party of the United States, sowing a revolutionary fever among Communists. The second half of the plan saw the Christian Front directing a counterattack. As John Viebrock put it, according to FBI records, "Instead of waiting for the Communists to start a revolution, and then stepping in to quell it," the fronters "would incite the Jewish and Communist elements to revolution and then step in and take over."[29] The theory was that, with bombs exploding all over New York City, New York Governor Herbert Lehman would call out the National Guard to put down the Communist insurrection. It was William Bishop's role to turn the National Guard into an organization that would "become so permeated with the ideals of the Christian Front that . . . in case of emergency," they would "take orders from . . . the Christian Front, rather than the officers of the National Guard."[30]

This explains the closeness between the front and the guard as Cassidy recruited operatives and set them to training. It is no accident that three of the men arrested were active-duty Guardsmen of the New York 165th Infantry Regiment. These included Captain Prout, who was removed from duty upon arrest and whose name would be attached to the 1940 court case, *USA v. John Prout, Jr., et al.* An additional four of the alleged plotters had been members of the Guard "at some time."[31] The front's Sports Club spent months developing combat skills that would enable them to fight alongside the guard specifically. If all went according to plan, the front and the guard would be in lockstep against the godless Communists.

The idea of working with the National Guard came naturally to Cassidy, who, in his heart of hearts, was less a revolutionary than a counterrevolutionary—at least as he saw the matter. He had long believed that there was "an imminent danger of a revolution in the United States . . . having studied revolutions in other countries . . . where police departments, arsenals, utilities, and transportation" were the first targets of Communist forces. Cassidy "felt that he, as a patriotic citizen, should do something about it, and not wait until it started." This calculus complicated the prosecution because, as the unemployed Brooklyn lawyer argued, "he did not intend to commit any overt act" but rather to "start thinking about it, and try to get . . . all men possible on their toes to start a counter-revolution." By law, sedition required an overt act.

Cassidy was also suggesting that Christian Front could not have been seditious because its aim was to safeguard America, which the group saw as a Christian nation. Cassidy believed that while others, including too many Christians, were ignoring Communists—and, worse still, protecting Communists by protecting Jews—the members of the Christian Front were uniquely willing to put their lives on the line at a moment of national peril. The front may have used revolutionary means, including violence and the imposition of a temporary dictatorship. But its goal was to then reestablish American democracy, understood as Christian in character and free of Jewish and Communist influence.

When Cassidy explained his plan to Walter Ogden, who had been the Christian Front's first secretary, Ogden "thought that his idea was crazy."[32] Ogden was right; there was no way realistically that the plan would work. But historians have unfortunately taken the improbability of Cassidy's effort as an excuse to downplay and ignore the front. Yes, Cassidy's group was the paranoid fringe. But, as Perlstein argues, that is precisely where we must look to understand the development of far-right politics that have had substantial impact on American life. The fringe, after all, may also be the avant-garde—the leading edge of a mass movement.

The Prosecution Unravels

When the government put forward the weapons-theft charge, prosecutors already knew that their case was on shaky ground. The source of the bad news was one Herbert Cox, of Wilmington, Delaware. While reading his hometown newspaper, Cox saw a photo of the weapons cache the FBI had seized from the Christian Front. "One thing about it struck me very forcibly," Cox wrote to Hoover on January 15, 1940. All of the guns in the photo were of a type that could be readily "obtained through the office of the Director of Civilian Marksmanship of the US War Department, via the NRA."[33] Perhaps surprisingly, Hoover read the unsolicited letter from an unknown private citizen. The FBI director came away stunned. He wrote a pro forma acknowledgment to Cox and asked Deputy Director Tamm to look into the matter.

It turned out that Cox was spot on. Since 1903, an obscure section of the US Army Code allowed civilian members of the National Rifle Association to purchase military-grade weaponry and ammunition directly from the War Department. "It appears," Tamm wrote matter-of-factly to Hoover, "that a civilian through this organization may purchase not only rifles, but accessories and appendages . . . as well as ammunition, ammunition components, and military targets." An NRA member need only send their membership card to the War Department, along with an order slip and a small payment, and a Lee-Enfield rifle would be sent for pickup to the National Guard armory nearest the applicant. For an additional $1.35 fee, the armory could ship the rifle directly to the buyer's home. Tamm concluded that an Enfield rifle could "be purchased through this medium for $7.50," about $135 in 2020 dollars.[34]

Cordite, too, could be had this way, and Bishop and Cassidy knew it—even if Hoover and Tamm did not. The front had used the NRA rule to acquire their rifles, ammunition, and cordite legally. Bishop had also made use of squib fuses, designed for fireworks, which he bought at a hardware store in

West Virginia. The government still put forward the weapons charge, but it was clear at the time that the sedition charge would have to carry the day.

Yet Hoover and Tamm appear to have known that the sedition charge also was unlikely to prevail in court. At 4:05 A.M. on January 14, while the arrests were underway, Clyde Tolson, the FBI's assistant director, telephoned Tamm and related something he, Tolson, had heard from Hoover. While the Christian Front investigation was unfolding, the director had reminisced about an obscure 1920 case involving "the Elareta Society of Buffalo, New York," in which a court held that the seditious conspiracy statute "did not apply because there was no overt act." This case evidently reminded Hoover of the front's, a bad sign for the government's position.[35]

To fit Cassidy's actions to the seditious conspiracy charge, the prosecution would have to twist the facts of the case. In a January 17, 1940, memo, FBI agents did just that, arguing that the paramilitary sections of the Christian Front had "devoted themselves to intensive firearms training and the study of military tactics . . . to be used . . . in an attempt to overthrow the existing Government." Unfortunately the government's own witness, Denis Healy, undercut this assessment in the press, laying out for reporters in exact detail the strategy of false-flag bombings, incitement, and defensive counterattack. "The ultimate objective was to incite the Jews to riot and then revolution, and then have a counter revolution," he explained. At the trial, Cassidy and the others would be able to deny truthfully much of what the prosecution would throw at them.[36]

As if these evidentiary and charging problems were not enough, prosecutors arguably brought more difficulties on themselves by indicting the wrong people. Harold Kennedy, the US attorney for Brooklyn, insisted on prosecuting all seventeen of the arrested Christian Front members on the seditious conspiracy charge. But a source in the Justice Department told journalist Gardner Jackson that department lawyers thought that charge "applied only to four or five," of the defendants and that "several of the men should not have been indicted" at all. Jackson's contact also did not view any of Kennedy's assistant US attorneys as "particularly competent" and questioned their "ability to pick a proper jury." The Associated Press reported that government prosecutors "would seek to obtain an all-Protestant jury," meaning that there would be no Jewish people passing judgment on the fronters. As it turns out, the jury was not entirely Protestant, but nor did it include any Jewish New Yorkers.[37]

A jury comprising exclusively Brooklyn residents was impaneled on April 4, 1940, and the trial proceeded for almost three months. On the stand Cassidy disputed the premise of the indictment, claiming that the Christian Front never intended to overthrow the government. It was Communists who wished to overthrow the government, and it was the front that sought to protect the government from the Communists. Cassidy claimed he knew nothing about bomb-making, blaming any such activities on William Bishop. Denis Healy, the informant and the government's star witness, collapsed on the witness stand after four days of testimony and had to be rushed to a doctor. While in the witness box, Healy admitted that he and his wife had invited fronters into their home and plied them with alcohol while asking them about their plans for revolution. The credibility of any revolutionary talk was badly marred by the compromised state of the speakers. Perhaps even worse, in the course of the trial it became clear that the FBI had paid large sums of money to Healy, who had requested compensation on the grounds that he would "incur considerable expense in his endeavors to assist the Bureau." This secret payment scheme undercut Wacks's testimony to the effect that Healy was simply a citizen doing his patriotic duty. On top of all this, due to the NRA rule, no charges were filed concerning the rifles and ammunition. And the Browning light machine guns, alluded to in letters and interviews, were nowhere to be found, further undermining the allegation that the fronters had stolen weapons owned by the US armed forces.[38]

The jury deliberated for six days. "Mrs. Helen Titus, foreperson of the jurors, said that all eleven members of the jury were in favor of acquittal for all after the first day," but one member held out.[39] Ultimately, on June 24, nine of the defendants were acquitted and charges were dropped against five more, although the possibility of a retrial remained in their cases. This came after two defendants had their charges dismissed entirely. That makes sixteen of seventeen not guilty. The seventeenth defendant did not live to see the verdict. Less than ten days into the trial, Claus Ernecke, who had tried to recruit a machine gun instructor, was found hanging dead in the cellar of an apartment building two blocks from his home. Quoting "medical authorities," the New York Times reported that "Ernecke must have been very anxious to die, as he had to lift his feet from the floor and hold them up after he fastened the noose around a steam pipe and put his neck in it." Ernecke's lawyer claimed that his client had been kidnapped and murdered on the way to the courthouse. There was no investigation.[40]

"There was great joy when the decisions were announced," according to an unidentified observer from the Communist Party of the United States, who was present for the reading of the verdict. "Much kissing and backslapping and handshaking among the spectators and defendants." US Attorney Kennedy "congratulated Cassidy and said, 'You got a fair shake of the dice, didn't you?'" Hoover seethed. Cassidy asked for his guns back.[41] On the night of June 28, 1940, Cassidy and Father Brophy took to the stage at Prospect Hall in Brooklyn to celebrate the triumph. Brophy, ecstatic, congratulated Cassidy and the rest of the "Brooklyn boys." Then, after a dramatic pause, Brophy made an announcement: "There is one matter connected to the jury in this case that hasn't been disclosed up to this moment, but I think it's safe to tell you now. I refer to Mrs. Helen Titus, foreman of the jury. You may be interested to know that she is my first cousin." As it turns out, Titus also was related by marriage to Leo Healy (no relation to FBI informant Denis Healy), the attorney who represented the defendants.[42]

Losing Their Religion

The inclusion at trial of a conflicted juror was not the only ethically questionable dimension of the proceedings against the Christian Front plotters. The case of USA v. Prout also witnessed a curious effort by both the prosecution and the defense to eliminate from the courtroom any discussion of religion. This effort involved clear coordination between defense lawyers and high-ranking members of the Catholic clergy as well as possible collusion between clergy and the prosecutor. It seems that both lawyers in the case, prosecutor Kennedy and Leo Healy on behalf of the accused, were arguing for the defense—the defense of the Catholic Church. For the front, secularizing the trial was good strategy, but for the prosecution, doing so made little sense. The result was smoother sailing for the defense and the solidification in the public mind that the Church and its teachings had nothing to do with the terrorist activities of which the defendants were accused.

An extraordinary, and heretofore unexamined, July 25, 1940, letter from Hoover to Attorney General Robert Jackson partially explained what happened on the side of the prosecution. Hoover told Jackson that he "had just received information from a confidential source" indicating that Kennedy, "as soon as he was advised of the facts in this case," made an appointment to see Bishop Thomas Molloy of the Diocese of Brooklyn. Molloy was a public

and private supporter of Cassidy's movement, leading historian Leonard Dinnerstein to dub Molloy "the Bishop of the Christian Front." Hoover's confidential source was certain that "Kennedy and Bishop Molloy held a conference in the Bishop's office, at which time the Reverend Edward Lodge Curran
was present." The idea that a US attorney would meet with a bishop and priest
having well-known connections to the men he was prosecuting was disturbing,
to say the least.[43]

Exactly what transpired at this meeting is unknown, but when the trial
began on April 4, Kennedy used his opening statement to set some ground
rules that must have been music to Molloy's and Curran's ears. "The Christian Front is not on trial," Kennedy made clear, "neither is race or religion
on trial here." Furthermore, "it makes no difference to what race or religion
these defendants belong . . . or what race or religion may be brought up in
controversy during the trial."[44] Treating the seventeen Christian Front defendants as though they were driven purely by nonreligious impulses meant
Roman Catholicism would be left unsullied. At the same time, there would
be no place at the trial for an inquiry into the front itself, its anti-Semitism,
or its sources in mainstream Catholic doctrine. Thus the prosecutor effectively opened his trial by sympathizing with the defendants and ensuring that
others would, too. Instead of portraying the fronters as revolutionary religious
zealots and anti-Semites, Kennedy told the jury that Cassidy and his crew were
simply anti-Communists, a position that Americans overwhelmingly associated with patriotism and even civic duty.

For Cassidy and his followers, religion of course made every difference. In
their minds, they acted exclusively as their religion compelled them. But Leo
Healy, a fine lawyer and former judge, knew not to turn down a prosecutor
peddling gifts. Delinking religion from the case reduced the sense that the
defendants were fanatics. They were energetic, to be sure, but the jury would
never have to hear about the frightful sources of Christian paramilitarism:
the myth of Judeo-Bolshevism, clerical anti-Semitism, religious anti-Judaism,
Mystical Body of Christ theology, Catholic Action, and priestly shadow leadership. Any of these matters might have upset a juror, perhaps especially the
esoteric mystery of Catholic doctrine, which had never inspired friendly
thoughts among the average American Protestant.

Even before the trial was underway, some observers worried that the government was imposing on the case a secular cast that belied the truth of the
defendant's motivations and downplayed the danger of the front. On Feb-

ruary 20 Maurice Rosenblatt, a behind-the-scenes-lobbyist who years later would be instrumental in engineering the censure of Senator Joseph Mc-Carthy, wrote to reporter Gardner Jackson that the Justice Department's Rogge "had no appreciation of the 'local situation'" in Brooklyn—"the political and popular tides in the community." Rosenblatt pointed out that "letters are pouring in to the [Justice] Department from Jews and Catholics," a clear sign that, among the public, "the issue seems to be boiling down to a religious one." If prosecutors thought that they could promote popular harmony by stifling discussion of the front and of the defendants' religious motivations, they were fooling themselves. "It is in the community where these cases are won and lost," Rosenblatt noted.[45]

The courtroom became a kind of hermetic bubble, which even the obvious could not penetrate. "The same gang that crucified Christ are at it again," one hawker of *Social Justice* hollered outside the Federal Building in Brooklyn as the trial started, "they are trying to convict seventeen innocent Christian boys." Whatever Kennedy might have thought, Catholics outside the courtroom saw a crucifixion underway. That much was clear as well to Arthur Derounian, the investigative journalist. As the case went to trial, Derounian was deeply disturbed by prosecutors' bizarre insistence that the Christian Front was not a religious organization. "The fight here is between the Catholic Church and those who are seeking to check the anti-Semitic activities of the Church," Derounian wrote in a February 4 memo. "It'll be a dirty, dirty, dirty, fight."[46]

Had Kennedy consulted Derounian, the prosecutor would perhaps have learned a great deal about what the front really stood for, to say nothing of its inseverability from religion. For four years, Derounian ingratiated himself with Christian Front leadership and attended their meetings under deep cover, sometimes at great peril to himself. He wrote his February 4 memo after joining a meeting of the Christian Front at Prospect Hall in Brooklyn, the epicenter of Cassidy's activity. "The place was jammed," he recorded, "about 65% Irish, and a lot of Protestants too." He estimated that "2,500 men, women, and children packed the hall." They had not come to hear political speeches: "this was in a sense a religious revival meeting," Derounian noted. "It had deeply religious implications." These were the implications of Mystical Body theology, specifically. Derounian remarked that the meeting seemed like "a magnificent demonstration of solidarity and friendliness." A "we are all friends here" attitude prevailed. "Faith—the Catholic faith bound these people together. A powerful, strong bond." On top of that, and equally important, "98% of those present were convinced that the seventeen were framed by the Jews, and that the Jews would get theirs in the long run." As he left Prospect Hall, Derounian could not escape the feeling that the front was engaged in "a religious fight, I tell you—the most vicious and damnable in the world."[47]

Six weeks later, while the trial was in full swing, Derounian infiltrated another Christian Front meeting—this one held under the name of the Christian Civil Liberties Committee, a pseudonym that likely appeared after the arrests. "Tonight I detected it clearly and unmistakably," he jotted in his notes. "This is a war *for* Christ." Derounian was knocked off his heels when none other than Father Edward Brophy appeared on the stage and "read a lengthy prepared sermon to prove that Jews were the killers of Christ." Brophy read various Bible passages, "tying up the killing at the very end with the effect of a lawyer." One argument that Brophy aimed to quash was that "Christ was put to death not by the Jews, but by the Romans." He argued that "during the entire legal process," surrounding Christ's Passion, "every detail was in complete and continuous control of the Jews." These arguments, from Brophy's recently published book *The Christian Front—Its Justification and Need*, were also the heart of his speech, and the audience was mesmerized. Brophy's logic seemed true: he contended that, because the Gospels did not cite any Roman law that Christ violated, Romans must not have been responsible for his death. This was a specious claim based on a technicality; the Gospels do not the cite Roman law, but other sources do, indicating that Christ was charged under Herodian law with blasphemy against the Temple. But Brophy's case was good enough for the audience that night, and his book was imbibed as a philosophical apologia for the Christian Front. Derounian left the event taking care to ensure that he was not followed.[48]

· · ·

In some ways, Leo Healy's elision of religion was even more stunning than Harold Kennedy's. The same February 4 Christian Front meeting that Derounian called a "religious revival" was also a soapbox for Healy: the attorney and former judge who was representing Cassidy and ten other defendants got up on stage and whipped the audience into a frenzy. When Healy invoked Cassidy's name, the crowd "cheered for a full minute." In fact "they wept,"

Dernounian wrote, "when Judge Healy said Cassidy was saying his Rosary when he saw him in the jug." After "Healy raised his hand in the air, and shouted 'this is a fight for Christ!'" the hall erupted in "delirious emotionalism," with Healy continuing, "I don't have to apologize to anyone for being a Christian!"[49]

This is the same Healy who, about three weeks before the trial began, met with Fathers Curran and Brophy to devise a defense of the fronters as pro-democracy activists utterly disconnected from theological concerns. It was Curran, himself a lawyer, who developed the strategy, which Healy would employ deftly in the courtroom. The central idea was to divorce the defendants from their commitments to the Judeo-Bolshevist myth. As Curran put it, the defense should argue that there were several "fronts," some good and some bad. These included Christian, Jewish, liberal, and Soviet or Communist fronts. With great duplicity, Curran proposed that the Christian and Jewish fronts be presented as though in league. Curran encouraged Healy to stress the humanitarian and philanthropic work of B'nai B'rith and the American Jewish Congress, the better to suggest that the Christian Front wanted to work with Jews and to argue that the Jewish and Christian fronts were alike "in the sense of their aims in preserving Democracy."[50]

The posture was of course a sham. Another attendee at the legal-strategy meeting, Boston Christian Front leader Francis Moran, had spent the previous week pounding home the theory that the American Jewish Congress and B'nai B'rith were Communist organizations. Curran, however, sensed that the prosecution was skittish about portraying the defendants as religious extremists. So he took the opportunity he was given and crafted a defense of patriots committed to democracy, just like the Jewish brothers whom the front in other contexts equated with Communists hellbent on eliminating Christianity from the face of the globe.[51]

Healy did a masterful job presenting Curran's arguments in court. Healy boiled down the defense to a single claim: "Communists wanted to destroy the Christian Front." Healy argued that there were "three fronts," operating in the case. The Christian and Jewish fronts both did good works, noble and charitable actions to better the lives of their fellow Americans. As such, both were enemies of the Communist Front, consisting of "the government of Russia in coordination with the Communist Party of New York State." This was "a very bad front," Healy said, because it stirred up "bigotry and religious discord." The Christian Front did not want to overthrow the United States government. Rather it wanted "to overthrow the Communist Front." With no mention by the prosecution of Cassidy's and the Christian Front's foundational obsession with the Judeo-Bolshevist phantom, the jury was left thinking that the defendants actually believed the words Healy was saying.[52]

In the end, Maurice Rosenblatt's skepticism about Assistant Attorney General Rogge's understanding of the "local situation" proved prescient. If overt anti-Semitism was tough for some Brooklynites to swallow, anti-Communism and appeals to patriotism were considerably easier. As Healy put it squarely to the jury, "The Communists will hail you as heroes if you convict these boys." None of the Brooklynites on the jury wanted that on their consciences. Brooklyn was the epicenter of "radical anti-Communism" in New York, according to the American Jewish Congress. And the Catholic diocesan paper, the *Brooklyn Tablet*, was considered one of the most pro-Coughlin and red-baiting newspapers in the country. These New Yorkers could not afford to be seen as Communist sympathizers.[53]

With the possibly witting assistance of the Justice Department, Healy and Father Curran successfully stripped the Christian front of its poisonous ideology while it was on trial. Healy, with Curran's encouragement, flat-out lied about the beliefs motivating Cassidy and his men, while playing to the fears and prejudices of a jury the prosecution evidently had not bothered to vet. The effects of these lies, as well as the state's whitewashing efforts, were many and durable. Most immediately, Cassidy and his coconspirators went free. They also became heroes in their communities, as well as symbols of Christian martyrdom. Here was a clutch of American patriots, protecting the nation from godless Communists, and their own government wanted them in prison. Cassidy had imbibed the politics of grievance from Father Coughlin, and now he would be a fine symbol of that same grievance.

In the longer term, the erasure of spiritual commitment from the activities of the Christian Front undermined public, journalistic, and scholarly attention to religiously imbued far-right groups. The Christian Front became one of innumerable anti-Communist organizations, a minor example of a much larger tendency overlapping all boundaries of faith. Not only that, but in the verdict of history, the Christian Front was unimportant because it was short-lived. Scholars have argued that "the FBI shut down the Christian Front in 1940" or else "suppressed" the group. Only one scholar, historian Philip Jenkins, has argued that the Christian Front exposes a larger religious impulse in America: a tropism toward terror in the name of Christ. And no one had to wrestle with the fact that the front's fanaticism was a product not of twisted faith but rather of comportment with the faith as practiced and preached the world over. This is not to say that Catholicism was a violent religion in the 1930s and 1940s but instead that it could be interpreted as demanding violent action without undermining its theology. It was so interpreted—by Cassidy, Curran, Brophy, Coughlin, and others. These lay and clerical leaders drew on popular Catholic ideas, ignored the portions of those ideas they did not care for, and combined the result with theories like Judeo-Bolshevism that had no place in any Christian teaching. When the clerical hierarchy saw what happened, they did not urge Catholics to renounce the violent ideology the Christian Front had discovered in Mystical Body theology and Catholic action. Rather, the Church swept the bad news under the rug.[54]

* * *

If Jenkins has been a lonely voice on the Christian Front's role in America's history of right-wing religious violence, then one other scholar, historian Stephen Norwood, has been the lonely voice on the Christian Front's persistence after the summer of 1940. Norwood has argued that the front was as vibrant as ever in 1943. The brew of clerically and doctrinally supported anti-Semitism and anti-Communism was now being quaffed in Boston.[55]

Boston was perhaps an unlikely place for the resurrection of the Christian Front. In the summer of 1939, when the House Un-American Activities Committee asked George Deatherage, the fascist-leaning founder of the American Nationalist Confederation, if he was making headway in organizing a nationwide right-wing clearinghouse, he mumbled, "Well, with the exception of the New England states, which are so blinking stubborn, we can't do anything with them." As far as the FBI's far-right watchers were concerned, Boston was barely a blip on their radar screen. True, when the FBI interviewed Walter Ogden in October 1939, he revealed that "Cassidy made a trip to Boston where he spoke before a mass meeting of the Christian Front." But when pushed, Ogden could tell the bureau little about the Boston unit of the front. It was headed by a fellow named Moran, but Ogden "didn't know Moran's first name or his occupation."[56]

CHAPTER 4

What's the Matter with Me?

AS SOON AS NEWS OF THE CHRISTIAN FRONT ARRESTS IN NEW YORK broke, Francis Moran presented himself at the FBI field office in Boston's Post Office Square. Introducing himself as the "head of the Christian Front in Boston," Moran "wanted to know whether the Bureau was investigating him." He was particularly concerned that the FBI might have infiltrated his speaking engagement the previous day at the Kiwanis Club in Sanford, Maine, where he "struck out at Communist activity in government, and charged that 1500 Communists held key positions in federal service." In the course of the speech, Moran attacked the president and Supreme Court justices and suggested that Secretary of Labor Frances Perkins was a Russian spy.[1]

FBI Special Agent in Charge Virgil Peterson "declined to make any comment" to Moran. Sitting face-to-face, "Peterson treated Moran cordially and courteously but at the same time told him nothing." Moran announced that he planned to speak that night in Somerville, Massachusetts, to a group called the United Minutemen. He asked Peterson if FBI agents were going to cover the meeting. The fact was that Peterson heard of neither Moran nor the Christian Front, and no agents were scheduled to attend.[2]

News reporters seemed more aware of the Christian Front than was the Boston branch of the FBI. After the barrage of headlines out of New York, one Boston reporter simply walked to "the Copley Square Hotel, where the Christian Front headquarters [were] located," inquired at reception, and found that "Mr. Moran was out of town for several days." But even if Special Agent Peterson had known where to look, he would not have found much of interest. Shortly after the New York arrests, investigators from the Boston Police Department's Radical Squad illegally entered Moran's office, swept it, and stole various pieces of "literature." They did not find any guns or bombs, though, nor evidence of violent intent or illegal activity of any kind.[3] The fearsome ordnance of the New York Christian Front occupied front pages everywhere, alongside the latest pithy quote from John Cassidy. There was not a peep from his Boston counterpart, however. Francis Moran was an enigma.

·   ·   ·

The first time Moran attracted public notice, he was being tossed out of a raucous political meeting. On July 20, 1936, the new Coughlin-controlled Union Party held its regional meeting in Worcester, Massachusetts. Father Coughlin himself was routinely visiting the state, to stump for the party he hoped would displace Roosevelt from the White House. Moran, who was the assistant to the Union Party's state supervisor, Myles Hayes, became combative when attendees at the meeting decided to cut ties with Hayes. The *Boston Herald* reported that "Francis P. Moran was escorted from the hall while members shouted, 'throw him out!'"[4]

As a religio-political voice, the radio priest articulated the aspirations and the metaphysic that Moran had been grasping for since his youth. Moran was born on March 10, 1909, on East 3rd Street in South Boston to Patrick and Bridget Moran, immigrants from County Mayo, Ireland. Although they met in Ireland, Patrick and Bridget moved to the United States separately during the later stages of the Irish diaspora, around 1906, and were reacquainted in New Jersey before moving to Boston. Patrick was industrious, taking a sales job for a wholesale grocer and later training and working as a butcher. The family moved three times, on each occasion relocating to more desirable areas. They finally settled in the Dorchester section of Boston in 1920. Francis was the first of his parents' eleven children.[5]

The Boston that Francis Moran was born into was not the helter-skelter world of nineteenth-century Irish immigration. By the time Moran was a teenager, the Boston Irish had a foothold in politics and finance and could wield patronage at will. But the Irish of Boston continued to face discrimination, especially from the city's old-money families, who were largely Protestant. As the Boston Brahmin Arthur Crew Inman put it in 1933, "The worst misfortune which ever happened to the United States was the Irish. They have debased our political life. . . . They have taken all and given nothing in return to our national life save a rotten core. They are parasitical drones."[6] These were common sentiments among the Yankee elite.

Growing up in an Irish enclave, Moran would not have had much exposure to the derision of his social betters, and the world of his youth appears to have been largely peaceful. "Frank was a contemplative sort," a family history noted, "always thinking. More at home with a book than a ball." As a young man, Moran's main choice would be between the sign of the dollar and the sign of the cross—large Irish Catholic families were always in need of the money that business could provide, but those same families often encouraged the "bookish" son to study for the priesthood. Moran's early years were steeped in religion: his mother was "a very pious woman," apt to get her children "down on their knees to say a Rosary." The relatively affluent St. Margaret's Parish in Dorchester was just a ten-minute walk from the Moran household, and "the Church was very much a part of their lives," according to Bridget and Patrick's granddaughter Nancy.[7]

Eventually Francis did in fact pursue the priestly life, but first he attended Boston's High School of Commerce. That choice was in keeping with what we know of Moran's personality. Throughout his life he was lured to money. Before his career as an activist, he worked in insurance, and, with the Christian Front, he labored constantly to turn a buck. All that fundraising ensured he would not have to live on piety alone. Instead of working from a community center or church basement like the rest of the nonprofit world, the nattily dressed Moran set up at the high-end Copley Square Hotel in the heart of downtown. A degree from the school of commerce would have put Moran on the path to wealth that he appears to have craved. In addition, graduates of the school had access to social position. Historically, such aspirations were unthinkable for most working-class Irish Bostonians, but during the era of the Great War, the popular mindset shifted. The Boston Irish rethought their accommodationist view of the Yankee upper-crust, seeking to step out unapologetically as the city's powerbrokers. The inspiration for this cultural shift was, in part, old-country nationalism. After the 1916 Easter Rising in Ireland, resentments curdled in Boston, and the Irish became more antagonistic toward the Brahmin elite.[8] A business education would have put Moran on the road to leadership in a changing city, not to mention life beyond the clannish Dorchester–South Boston nexus.

But while money was a genuine vocation for Moran, so was the priesthood. He stayed at the commercial school for only a year. Given his family's association with St. Margaret's, the Archdiocese of Boston would have been the natural environment for Moran's Catholic schooling and the straightest path to ordination. But he took a different approach, instead entering the Franciscan order. In fall 1923, at age fourteen, Moran traveled to St. Joseph's Seraphic Seminary in Callicoon, New York, to commence his studies. St. Joseph's would provide Moran with formative personal, cultural, and religious experiences, alongside an educational program unlike any available to his neighborhood pals in Boston. Friars taught all of the classes at St. Joseph's, and they did not sacrifice rigor. Former students described "the Callicoon liberal arts program and the philosophical studies" as "genuinely challenging," the seminarians as "scholastically brilliant."[9]

The St. Joseph's campus sat on a promontory over the Delaware River Valley and commanded eighty-five acres. Mottled stone buildings lent a symmetric and subdued beauty to a complex that otherwise might have seemed out of place on the edge of a small Catskills town. The aesthetic of the seminary was Christocentric; a ten-foot tall sculpture of St. Joseph holding the Child Jesus greeted everyone who walked up the front steps. Elsewhere, the "walls were filled with mosaics, statues, candles, and the like." Life at the school was regimented, as one seminarian, apprehensive about rising every day at 5:20 A.M., noted. "The days were filled with Mass, prayer, Stations of the Cross, spiritual reading, recitation of the Rosary while walking around the lake, and visits to the chapel." This made for "a very uniform and scheduled way of life, with lots of surveillance."[10]

There is every reason to believe that Moran had his first encounter with anti-Bolshevism while studying on the hill in Callicoon. The friars, especially younger ones, often preached warnings about creeping Communism and "unions turning red." A former student explained in an interview that "an atmosphere of fairly strong anti-Communist animus" existed among the administration as well. A kind of nonintellectual anti-Communism prevailed: faculty and students did not critique Marxist treatises, but they did focus on Lenin's persecution of Christians and the fear generated by the Red Army's 1920 invasion of Catholic Poland. The cult of Mary, long associated with Catholic anti-Communist impulses, was also strong at the seminary. In addition the school was the site of a certain amount of patriotic fervor, applying an American cast to a religious education that, at least formally, had nothing to do with earthly politics.[11]

At the same time, a subdued German nationalism and more overt German cultural orientation mixed with American and Roman Catholic ideals. Callicoon had been home to German speakers since the 1840s, and the friars who built St. Joseph's were German refugees, driven about by Otto von Bismarck's Kulturkampf against the Catholic church in the 1870s. Many of the friars at St. Joseph's retained their German accents. The thickest belonged to the non-ordained Franciscan brothers. The brothers worked the farm, took care of chores, and had only nonacademic contact with the seminarians. Consequently, the seminarians found the brothers an approachable lot—simple, dedicated men, highly devout. Surrounded by Germans, the students celebrated all the German religious feasts, and German hymns were often sung at Mass. Historian Joseph M. White has called St. Joseph's a place where "mostly Irish ethnics, and mostly German natives" were forced to live together, bypassing the national separation that was becoming common in Catholic parish life as communities divided into Irish, Italian, German, Polish, and other churches.[12]

Moreover, "the seminary," as one student explained, was "ruled by Germanic discipline further stiffened by persecution and exile." The more oppressive aspects of this history were hard to overcome. "Within the political culture of German Catholicism," historian Richard S. Levy has argued, "the Kulturkampf represented an early high-water mark of Catholic Anti-Semitism, since many Catholics accused liberal Jews of supporting Kulturkampf legislation."[13] But Callicoon does not seem to have been the seedbed of Moran's anti-Semitism. There is no evidence of anti-Semitism making its way into the classrooms at St. Joseph's, nor did the school become pro-Nazi when it had the chance. Franciscans exiled by Nazi persecutions supplied the school a second wave of German refugees in the 1920s and 1930s.

But if St. Joseph's did not educate Moran in anti-Semitism, he did receive there a theological understanding of what American Catholics believed about Jews in the 1920s: that they were responsible for deicide. As Monsignor Fulton Sheen later put it, "The Crucifixion was not [just] murder; it was deicide—the worst that sin can do." This view colored the American Catholic psychology of anti-Semitism; until 1965, when the deicide accusation was discredited theologically, most American Catholics believed that Jewish agency lay behind the Crucifixion. It is not hard to see how this anti-Judaism bordering on anti-Semitism fused in some students' minds with the "friendly affection" for German culture and customs inculcated at the school.[14]

Moran flourished in his first years at the seminary. Notably he received a perfect score in arithmetic during the 1924 school year—a singular achievement, since the friars were averse to granting any student a record of perfection. The grade was perhaps a tribute to Moran's training at Commercial High School, although clearly he was not just a math whiz. He also earned A-grades in Latin, English, and German, a language he would retain with fluency all his adult life. He even received an A for "conduct," a testament to his strengths in an area at which few teenage boys excel: asceticism.[15]

During his time as a public figure, Moran never made any comments about his seminary education other than to say he had "once studied for the priesthood." But while he downplayed his experience at St. Joseph's, those years were important in his development, setting him apart from other Christian Front leaders like Cassidy and Floyd Carridi. Moran learned to think theologically, which would make him more influential as a lay leader because he understood the theological lexicon and even Biblical exegesis. He also was trained to inhabit a public persona. From a young age, Moran was witness to powerful religious oration, delivered by men who impressed on him the importance of sharing theological concepts with the laity. This, after all, was the central objective of St. Joseph's: to train students who would, as priests, shepherd the faithful. Moran thus straddled the lay-clerical divide, and that made him especially dangerous once he developed a violent ideology. Recall Paul Tillich, who feared the influence of priests because "the sharp distinction between Catholic anti-Judaism and modern anti-Semitism seems to be contradicted by the fact of clerical anti-Semitism."[16] Men like Moran were perhaps the most threatening of all. Though Moran lacked the doctrinal authority of a priest, he possessed similar charisma and skills and enough theological knowledge to persuade many unordained Catholics. Meanwhile, he never had to negotiate the distance that can accrue between an educated, cloistered priest and a flock beset by the concerns of daily life. Moran was an ecclesiastic without a collar, "one of the boys" while being as well a man of God. The Christian Front would become his movable parish.

As to why Moran wound up a learned layperson rather than a priest, it is impossible to say with certainty. What we know is that after his third year of seminary, in 1925, his pursuit of ordination came to crashing halt. All of Moran's grades for that year were barely passing, and he dropped from the top of his class to the very bottom. Perhaps he fell ill, experienced depression, or rebelled against the severity of seminary life. According to Michael Daly's biography of Father Mychal Judge, the St. Joseph's graduate and New York City Fire Department chaplain who died during the response to the attacks of September 11, 2001, it was not unusual for a friar to tell a student, "You're not doing enough for God." The "notion was to be hard, be tough." In addition, the close of the third year was a major turning point in seminary education, followed by vows of poverty, chastity, and obedience. This prospect, too, may have disillusioned Moran. He swallowed the stigma of failure and left for home.[17]

The years from 1925 to 1930 are largely blank ones in Moran's biography. There are indications that he enrolled at a four-year high school in Boston, but no records prove it. The next time Moran showed up in records of any kind was 1929, when he took a job as a furniture delivery driver for Boston's Jordan Marsh Department Store. An auto accident bounced him from that job in May, but he was soon hired at Sears Roebuck Company only to be let go when the Depression set in during the fall. Yet Moran was able and determined, and he weathered the Depression far better than most. While 20 to 30 percent of Boston's labor force was idle, he was moving up in the world: in March 1930 he secured a job selling insurance for the John Hancock Life Insurance Company, one of the largest and most venerable Boston firms. A slender six-footer with brown hair and blue eyes, Moran cut a fine corporate cloth. He must have been good at the work, too, because in July 1932, at age twenty-three, he was poached by rival company Prudential. He turned them down.[18]

But within a few years, Moran would again be deflected from a promising trajectory. In March 1935 John Hancock fired him "because of poor business," but there was almost certainly more to the dismissal. Specifically, a management shakeup at Hancock put Moran under new leadership in 1935, that of one Albert Meltzer. This was probably the same Albert Meltzer who was active on the executive committee of Boston's Jewish War Veterans organization. According to a private detective who in 1939 investigated Moran on behalf of the New England office of the Anti-Defamation League of B'nai B'rith, Moran's relationship with Meltzer quickly deteriorated. Meltzer apparently considered Moran a "crack pot." The investigator reported that "eventually things got so bad that Moran and Meltzer became involved in a fist fight." Moran was fired soon after the altercation. He had lost the best job he ever had—a job on which he apparently relied to support his father, mother, and ten brothers and sisters.[19]

The investigative report does not clarify the source of the friction between Moran and Meltzer. Meltzer of course would have been pressing Moran to increase his sales, an almost impossible task during the Depression. But the widespread Catholic suspicion of Jews was probably not far from the heart of the matter. Meltzer would have provoked particular misgivings. In the wake of World War I, many US Catholics developed a strong antipathy toward Jewish veterans like Meltzer, whom they deemed cowardly. American Catholics believed their community had proved its patriotism, as indicated by the number of their sons dead on the battlefield. By contrast, Jews who served were more likely to come home. This result is easily explained as an artifact of a small sample size: there were relatively few Jews in the United States and therefore few in the armed forces, so the effects of chance would be more pronounced within that group. But instead of luck, Catholics saw weakness and even treachery. The idea took hold across Catholic life, including in seminaries.[20] The figure of Meltzer would have both challenged and reinforced many of Moran's cognitive constructions about Jews. Jewish war veterans were supposed to be cowards, but more than likely it was Meltzer who bested Moran in their office slugfest. The Jews were responsible for deicide, yet here was Moran, a Christian, subservient to someone whose people had committed "the worst of all sins."

Moran tried to rebound with a job at Boston Mutual Life Insurance, but he was let go within two months. "The reason for the severance of his employment was not stated," an FBI agent later recorded. In spring 1936 Moran was twenty-seven years old and unemployed. It is hard to escape the conclusion that he blamed Jews for his state of crisis, and that his interpretation of his own life story informed his anti-Semitism in years to come. "The Jew is a demoralizer," Moran shouted to a "spellbound" Roxbury audience in December 1940, "a sap-thirsty creature who drains our resources."[21] While other Christian Front leaders focused on Jewish banks, Jewish media, and Judeo-Bolshevism, Moran paired these slanderous abstractions with more concrete grievances. He knew—or thought he knew—from personal experience that the trouble with Jews was not just the banks they owned but also the bank accounts they emptied. His bank account, and those of his fellow Christians. That line of attack resonated with working-class Bostonians who feared for their livelihoods and families.

Evolution of a Radical

Theologically inspired right-wing thought was a balm for Moran, as it was for Cassidy. Driftless, angst-ridden, and indignant at a world that did not appreciate his intelligence and ability, in 1936 Moran found direction in the appeal of Father Coughlin. This was perhaps a homecoming of sorts, as the radio priest had been well received in the Moran household. Moran's mother, Bridget, "thought the world" of Father Coughlin. It is not far-fetched to believe that mother and son listened to Coughlin's Sunday broadcasts together.[22]

Coughlin's speeches reflected on the main question asked by the Franciscans at Callicoon: Are you doing enough for God? For Moran, doing enough for God meant doing something for Coughlin. Moran became a Coughlin political operative as early as 1936. Moran's FBI file indicates that he "had been introduced to Father Coughlin by a Father Duffy, whose name appeared in the columns of *Social Justice* on many occasions." This was probably Bishop John Duffy of Syracuse, New York, whom Coughlin considered "an old, tried, and true friend." In the late 1930s, Duffy joined Coughlin in rejecting a possible partnership with the Soviet Union against the rising Nazi regime, arguing that Americans should refuse to sign up "rather than serve as an ally of a Communistic government and atheistic cabal." Moran, as leader of the Christian Front in Boston, would echo this plea.[23]

According to the FBI, Moran met personally with Father Coughlin during the priest's 1936 visit to Massachusetts. Coughlin eyed the state as one in which his Union Party could have significant political impact and in July "barnstormed across Massachusetts," visiting the "strongly Irish neighborhoods such as Charlestown and South Boston." Indeed, Coughlin enjoyed much support as well as powerful connections in the state. Bostonian Joseph P. Kennedy, patriarch of the Kennedy political dynasty, was chairman of the Securities and Exchange Commission in 1935 when he arranged a meeting between Father Coughlin and President Roosevelt. Massachusetts governor and ardent Democrat James Michael Curley, who was running for the Senate in 1936, did not hesitate to engage Coughlin in a photo opportunity, even as Roosevelt warned that Coughlin's third party could throw votes to the Republicans. For Curley, obtaining the favor of the Detroit priest was electioneering 101. Boston was "the most Coughlinite city in America," Curley thought. "Politicians tripped over one another to be seen with him."[24]

Evidently Moran impressed Coughlin during their face-to-face encounter. This would have been Coughlin's first meeting with one of his eventual henchmen. In 1936 the idea of a Christian Front was a glimmer in Arnold Lunn's eye, and while Coughlin had his own dreams of Catholic militancy, he had no grassroots leaders on his side. It would be nearly three years before either Cassidy or Carridi decided to put in with Coughlin. Indeed, at this point, Coughlin was not entirely sure that men like Cassidy, Carridi, and Moran were the right people to direct his movement. He was focused on big names, reaching out to war heroes like Smedley Butler. An unnamed FBI informant who spoke with Moran reported that, during the Coughlin-Moran meeting, "Father Coughlin mentioned that someone should start an anti-Communist program in Boston" but then paused and ruminated. Presumably Coughlin hoped that a well-known Boston Catholic would carry through with his suggestion. Moran told the informant that he responded to Coughlin's suggestion by staring him in the eye and asking, "What's the matter with me?" Coughlin was delighted, and Moran was soon on board, working with the state supervisor of the Union Party.[25]

By joining the party, Moran was signing up for anti-Communism explicitly and anti-Semitism implicitly. Coughlin's "union" brought together the populism of Francis Townsend—the architect of Social Security, and an official Union Party member as of summer 1936—and the hard-line anti-Communism of Gerald L. K. Smith, a protégé of the late Senator Huey Long. Before he turned to Coughlin, Smith was fanatically devoted to Long and eulogized the Louisiana senator in terms that drew on the Judeo-Bolshevist myth. This was a revealing mix, given that ideas associated with both Long and Townsend were incorporated into the New Deal, yet Coughlin's goal, as he put it, was "to take a Communist out of the chair once occupied by Washington." Evidently what made Roosevelt a Communist in Coughlin's and Smith's eyes was not his redistributive policies but his welcoming of Jews and his unwillingness to grant Christians official favor.[26]

The Union Party, for the first time ever in a presidential election, used anti-Communist rhetoric extensively. "The choice," Coughlin crowed, was between the Union Party with its freedom of worship, constitutional government, and "purified" capitalism, "or the black bread of Communism." Coughlin argued that "the Communistic tendencies of the New Deal" could only be overcome by voting for the Union Party. The party did not incorporate anti-Semitism in its platform, but by 1936 Coughlin had made clear his views: some Jews—"religious Jews," who maintained connection to the God of Israel and their covenant—were to be commended, but the rest had rejected God and taken up Bolshevism as a violent, expansionist substitute for religion. Moran was publicly cryptic about his own anti-Semitic views, first to protect the Union Party and later because he knew that outright anti-Semitism could soil the Christian Front's reputation in some quarters. In 1943 Moran would express to an FBI informant his desire to "get rid of every Jew overnight," as well as his opinion that "returning veterans of World War II will be a large and important factor in eliminating the Jews inasmuch as they will be organized and will not be afraid of handling firearms." But in 1936 Moran stuck to the language of anti-Communism.[27]

To say that the Union Party was crushed in the election would be an understatement. All Union Party candidates for the House and Senate were defeated. The party's presidential candidate, William Lemke, a member of the US House from North Dakota, secured less than a million votes. Still, Lemke pulled 8 percent of the vote in Boston, his fourth-highest metropolitan total. Massachusetts was Lemke's second-best state after Ohio, netting him 118,639 votes. For Moran, an unemployed insurance salesman and political novice, these results were passable, and he managed to retain Father Coughlin's approval. Still, no one would have been surprised had Moran fallen off the political radar after the 1936.[28]

But just as he was about to be eclipsed by history, Moran received a major opportunity. Sybil Holmes, a Republican Massachusetts senator, gave him a public forum in which to parade himself as an authority on the Communist menace. Holmes was the first woman ever to serve in the state senate. A *Boston Daily Globe* profile published two days after her election in 1936 described her "gracious smile and sparkling dark blue eyes," and she magnified her apolitical image by telling the paper, "I didn't plan to be a senator." But Holmes would prove to be a firm ideologue in office. Though she was as junior a senator as could be, in her first term, she chaired the attention-grabbing Special Commission to Investigate Activities within this Commonwealth of Communistic, Fascist, Nazi, and Other Subversive Organizations. That was an ungainly name for a kind of un-American affairs committee within the Massachusetts legislature, and Holmes was an uncompromising spokesperson for the mission. "Members of the Communist Party have been instructed to . . . infiltrate the Democratic Party, the Republican Party, religious and civic groups, and labor unions," she warned in 1938. "We must be on our guard."[29]

In Massachusetts and the Boston area specifically—Holmes represented Brookline, a neighboring town in the heart of the metro area—anti-Communism was good political sense. Holmes's platform won her the support of Boston's Democratic mayor Maurice Tobin, who was as paranoid as she. In Old North Church on Patriots' Day in 1938, Tobin described anti-Communism as "Paul Revere's latest ride" and insisted, "Our peril today is not from sword and gunfire, but from the onward rush of Communism." Politicians in eastern Massachusetts had to win votes in the same communities that, only ten years earlier, had been at aghast at the likes of Nicola Sacco and Bartolomeo Vanzetti, convicted in court for murder and in the public for their left-wing politics. Lurking in the background was the Boston Police Department's Red Squad, a cadre of elite officers trained in the surveillance of political activists—specifically, those of the "revolutionary" stripe. Herbert A. Philbrick, who would become one of the foremost FBI moles in the Communist Party of the United States (CPUSA), began his career as a youth minister at Grace Baptist Church in Somerville, a few miles from Boston. The 1950s television series *I Led 3 Lives*, which glorified anti-Communist espionage, was based on his life. Holmes added more fuel to this already-raging fire.[30]

As a special commission, Holmes's panel was to operate for a fixed period, receive testimony, and publish a report on its findings. Its first day of official business was September 30, 1937. Opening remarks were delivered by a most unexpected speaker, the choice of whom reflected perhaps an inexplicable blunder or maybe an attempt to shock the public: Earl Browder, head of the CPUSA. Browder took the opportunity to disabuse the legislature of the belief that the CPUSA wished to forcefully overthrow the US government. To a "packed audience" in the State House, he outlined a plan "removed from guns or bloodshed" and "pooh-pooed the suggestion of Commission members that Communists would even think of gaining their ends by violence." Communists, Browder explained, believed in "the democratic form of government, the Constitution, the Declaration of Independence, Washington, Lincoln, and Jefferson."

Neither the Holmes commission nor many outside it were moved by Browder, who was never technically a witness and whose remarks did not appear in the commission's final report. Although commissioners found his position difficult to rebut, they were happy to share their own views. Senator Thomas Burke responded to Browder by suggesting that "all who wish to overthrow democracy and American institutions should be put in a ship, towed out into the middle of the Atlantic Ocean, and sunk." Father Coughlin, paying attention from afar, portrayed Browder's statement in a manner exactly at odds with the man's words, declaring in *Social Justice* that "revolution is coming to the United States." The Browder speech injected further tension into a political environment that was already on edge. "The alarmist accuses everybody who disagrees with him as being in the pay of Moscow," Boston University president and Methodist minister David Marsh observed. The city needed to cure its "communisticphobia."[31]

But Holmes was just getting started. Soon she summoned Edward Hunter, the executive secretary of the Industrial Defense Association of Boston, a group that supported manufacturers combating union activity. By 1937 Hunter had gained a reputation as Nazi sympathizer. He also had plenty of experience chatting with legislators on the "subversives" beat. In 1930 he had testified to the Fish Committee, a subcommittee of the US House Special Committee to Investigate Communist Activities in the United States. On that occasion, Hunter claimed to have uncovered "Soviet Sunday Schools," sponsored by the CPUSA in the Massachusetts cities of Worcester, Quincy, and Brockton. "You do not mean schools teaching a form of religion?" Maine Republican John Edward Nelson asked. "Atheism and class hatred are the principal things," Hunter replied. Hunter also told the committee that "Bolshevism in New England is largely under Jewish leadership," as he rattled off the names of twenty-one Jewish men who were leaders of what he deemed Communist-affiliated organizations.[32]

Hunter's visit to the Holmes commission might have mollified the senator's anti-Communist base, smarting over Browder's invitation. But while Browder was speaking freely, Hunter was under subpoena. Anti-Communists saw this as deeply unfair. Furthermore, while Browder was questioned only by legislators, Hunter was questioned by John Spivak, an "expert on Nazism." The hearing proved to be intense and eventually devolved into name-calling. Senator Burke, who seemed genuinely aghast at both Communists and Nazis, accused Hunter of carrying a gun into the hearing, which turned out to be true. Spivak sniped that Hunter was getting direction from Nazis; Hunter shot back that Spivak was in the pay of Communists. The heated exchange was a glimpse into the house of mirrors that wartime Boston would become: in fact both men were guilty as charged. By 1940 Hunter was meeting secretly with Nazi Party officials, and it was revealed in the late 1990s that Spivak was an agent of the KGB and its predecessors.[33]

In April 1938, as the hearings were winding down, the committee received testimony from "a student of Communism." This turned out to be Moran, although nothing in the Holmes archive explains how the senator knew of the former insurance salesman turned political organizer. From his pulpit at the State House, Moran preached with gusto, demanding that the legislature "drive all the rats out of state government." The substance of his remarks is otherwise unknown, as nothing from his testimony appeared in the commission's final report. But Moran got his chance to speak as a professional and an intellectual of public importance. The experience went to his head: in December of that year, when he applied to the Boston Police Department for a permit to carry a pistol, he "described himself as a lecturer" and claimed, no doubt proudly, that "his life had often been threatened."[34]

While Moran's testimony was apparently too banal to earn any attention—unlike Hunter's, which garnered massive notoriety in the press—his appearance before the commission was not lost on Massachusetts politicians, Coughlinites, Communists, and anti-Communists. Indeed, because the hearings were such a disaster for Hunter, Moran found himself in the right place at the right time, the heir-apparent to the very sort of anti-Communist organizing that the commission's "Red Report" implicitly encouraged. Released to the public in June 1938, the report disregarded Browder's opening remarks and insisted that Communists amounted to "a conspiratorial body" that "took orders from a foreign power" with the objective of "replacing American Constitutional Democracy with a dictatorship of the workers." Only 16 of the report's 600 pages were dedicated to "Nazi and Fascistic Activity." Still, for Hunter and the Industrial Defense Association, the damage was done during his testimony. While the organization survived, it was discredited by its Nazi associations, its growth stymied. Hunter was never again a player on the Boston anti-Communist and anti-Semitic scenes. Moran, whose own anti-Semitism was deepening at this time, was ready to fill the vacuum.[35]

A Christian Front in Boston

One of the few people who recognized that a changing of the guard might be underway in the Boston far right was Arthur Derounian, the undercover journalist who infiltrated the Christian Front in New York. On June 14, 1939, Dernounian sent a report to the FBI on Hunter's Industrial Defense Association but added that "there is one other Boston group deserving attention."

This was "the American League for the Defense of Constitutional Rights . . . , headed by Francis P. Moran." Derounian got the organization's name wrong—it was the Committee for the Defense of American Constitutional Rights—but he was correct to note that the group was "definitely a Coughlin unit." Derounian observed that "whenever there is a Coughlin rally, Moran pops up," but, otherwise, both the organization and its leader were hard to pin down. "So far [the group] has no headquarters—it can only be reached by mail by writing to the Copley Square Hotel. Mr. Moran is equally elusive." Moran was "not listed in the telephone directory and no one seems to know how to locate him." To most observers, such a phantom organization would merit little scrutiny. Something told Derounian to be wary of Moran, though. "It is quite possible that he will develop into a more important person than Hunter," Derounian concluded.[36]

The Committee for the Defense of American Constitutional Rights (CDACR) was Moran's bridge to the Christian Front. As CDACR director, he was in a position to fundraise and ask for speaker fees. It was also in this context that he began presenting Communism as a theological issue. In one lecture advertisement, Moran promised to explain why his anti-Communist project was "founded on Christian principles enunciated by Robert Bellarmine," the Catholic Counterreformation thinker who "systematically applied the idea of the Mystical Body of Christ to the Pilgrim community of the church on earth."[37] In another public lecture, Moran argued, "Whereas in New York Communistic doctrines have received much support from state and civic authorities, in Boston, our political leaders are as a rule religiously and patriotically opposed to such an ideology." The idea that public officials in New York supported Communism is difficult to credit, but it is true that, more than in other East Coast cities, Catholics in Boston successfully pressed politicians to treat political questions in moral and religious terms. An example was the Red Report itself, which contained an extensive section on Communism and religion. "Communists remain implacable enemies of all organized religion, whether of the Old or New Testament," the report maintained. "The practice of Marxism-Leninism entails as a basic and absolute fundamental the ultimate destruction of organized religion." Holmes's commission baptized anti-Communism, much as Moran did.[38]

When Moran spoke of New York authorities giving aid and comfort to Communists, he may have had in mind the WMCA affair of late 1938, which was a turning point for Moran as much as it was for Cassidy. No public officials were involved, and no one who was involved was acting in sympathy with Communist ideals. But these details tended to be lost in the misleading discourse of First Amendment martyrdom surrounding WMCA's eviction of Coughlin from its programming roster. Allen Zoll, the Presbyterian anti-Communist and anti-Semite, roused 2,000 Coughlinites to march on WMCA studios in support of the priest's freedom of speech. Zoll also organized daily picketing and nightly "vigils" for Father Coughlin.[39] The Zoll blueprint was so effective that he soon took his picketing playbook to Boston. There, he linked up with Moran.

In January 1939 Zoll gave a CDACR-sponsored lecture to an audience of 800 at Boston's prestigious Mechanics Building. While defending Father Coughlin against the supposed censorship he was suffering, Zoll announced that "Communism was the greatest national danger" facing the United States. "I know of no Fascist or Nazi who is a member of the government, but I can give you the names of hundreds of Communists who are members of the government and even members of the cabinet," Zoll declared. Although Zoll and Coughlin each denied any association with the other, they were strongly aligned politically, and Moran's group was making a name for itself by profiting from Zoll's and Coughlin's intersection.[40]

It is no surprise that, in New York, Cassidy's organizing and recruitment efforts were also taking off at this exact moment. But, in what may be another reflection of cultural differences between Boston and New York, only Cassidy was a press darling. Thus in March, when Moran allied with Sybil Holmes to support creating a Division of Citizenship within the state Department of Education, Moran and the CDACR were not quoted in any news stories. The proposed agency would conduct background checks on teachers and staff, to "meet the threats of both Communism and Nazism in the education department," Holmes said. The press did not quote Moran directly, although one newspaper pointed out that the division was "advocated principally by the special commission" on which Moran had served.[41]

Sometime between April and October 1939, the CDACR morphed into the Boston wing of the Christian Front. It is impossible to pinpoint an exact date. Whereas we know precisely when Father Coughlin commissioned Cassidy to lead the New York Christian Front, there is no similar documentation with respect to Moran. Coughlin's blessing for Moran—if there was one—may have been contained in a letter stolen by the Boston Police when they illegally swept Moran's office at the Copley Square Hotel. In January 1940 officers

William J. Goldston and Benjamin Goodman of the Radical Squad broke into the office and, according to an FBI report, "managed to secure a copy of a letter addressed to Mr. Frank Moran, Copley Square Hotel, Boston from the Rev. Chas. E. Coughlin, Royal Oak, Michigan." It seems that in fact the police took the original, not a copy; the Radical Squad was adamant that "no other copies were in existence." Whatever the case may be, the letter is nowhere to be found.

We might nonetheless suspect that Moran was officially installed as chief of Boston's Christian Front because in March 1939, the very month that Cassidy was elevated in New York, the CDACR's outreach began to wane. Although the CDACR continued to publicize events, Moran stopped writing letters to the editor on the CDACR's behalf and no longer sought press for the organization. One way or the other, the transition was clear to Phillip Young, the manager of the Copley Square Hotel. He must have had his suspicions: the day after the New York arrests, he ventured to Moran's office suite on the second floor unbeckoned. "Entering with a pass key," he found nothing out of place, with one exception. About a year earlier, he had rented the office to Moran, "who represented himself as the head of a 'Committee for the Defense of American Constitutional Rights.'" Now there was no sign in the office of any organization operating under that name. Instead "near the wall there was a large placard reading: 'CHRISTIAN FRONT,'" the name of the organization the US government had just accused of revolutionary activity. Moran had changed colors in plain sight. His skills in evasion would keep the Christian Front operating in Boston, both above and below ground, for another five years.[42]

CHAPTER 5

A Rather Bold Agitator

THE CHRISTIAN FRONT PLACARD IN FRANCIS MORAN'S OFFICE REP-
resented more than a name change. It was also evidence of determined organizing. In some respects, Moran followed a playbook similar to Cassidy's. Both recruited largely from Catholic communities, where they found audiences steeped in Mystical Body theology. And the dubious claim of government censorship that stoked fevers in New York also moved the crowd in Boston.

But alongside the similarities, there were differences that contoured the paths the two Christian Front groups would walk. Most importantly, while Cassidy rapidly built up paramilitary capabilities and planned terrorist activities, Moran's approach was nonviolent. The process in Boston was also slower. Moran struggled for much of 1939 to make headway, then had enormous success in the fall. Cassidy also had the advantage of a New York press corps excited to drum up the story of right-wing activism. For Moran, news coverage was harder to come by. While New York journalists came to Cassidy for quotes, in Boston, even a grand spectacle attracted little coverage. The two men also had different strategies for motivating their flocks. Cassidy's events featured films and guest speakers, including numerous men of the cloth. Boston was the Moran show. Bostonians gathered by the hundreds to hear the lecturer of the Christian Front. The dais was Moran's native habitat, and so much the better because priestly support was often difficult to come by—except at a key September 1939 rally, where Moran still stole the show. And while the substance of Christian Front ideas was consistent between New York and Boston—Mystical Body theology, Catholic Action, the phantom of Judeo-Bolshevism, and grievances against Spain's Popular Front were always the coins of the realm—in Boston, anti-Semitism was justified by lived experience rather than theory alone. The problem with Jews was not just that they supplied the Communist vanguard, but also that they were undermining livelihoods in the here and now. Apparently when Jews were not trying to undermine capitalism, they were cheating their way into its winners' column, or so Moran's supporters felt. Like their leader, fronters in the Boston area were upset by the perceived role of Jews in putting them out of work during the Depression.

For the Boston Christian Front, the crash came in the spring of 1940. The arrests of the New York fronters had little impact in Boston, but the trial itself resonated and inspired more focus from the FBI and opposing community organizations, particularly Jewish groups. Moran was forced to duck the limelight for a time. After the trial concluded with no convictions, Moran returned to public life, but his organization was on shaky footing. By summer, there was no telling what would come of the front in Boston. But what never wavered was Moran himself. He kept his passion and his wits. Above all, he kept his faith—in Coughlin, in the front, in his own ability, and in Christ.

Into the Arena

For most of 1939, the Committee for the Defense of American Constitutional Rights made scant progress. Moran needed to make a splash, both for his group and for himself. He had just found a place in public life via the Holmes commission, and the descent back into obscurity could have been no less rapid. For Moran, it was not enough to scribble strongly worded letters to politicians and newspaper editors. He wanted a profile, and he wanted to see the world remade according to his vision of the good. For help, he turned to the voice from Royal Oak.

The result was a massive success, as Moran and Father Coughlin organized events on a scale that quintupled any Christian Front meeting ever held in New York City. A September 8, 1939, Christian Front rally in Boston at Boston Arena reportedly attracted a crowd of between 8,000 and 12,000. Moran was joined on stage that night by Father Cyril Keating, Coughlin's adjutant and rectory-mate and a writer for *Social Justice*. Coughlin himself was piped in via telephone. Another Boston Arena event, on October 24, reportedly brought in at least 4,000 people to hear speeches by syndicated columnist and radio host Boake Carter, Cassidy, and Moran. Moran advertised the mass meetings under the sponsorship of the Committee for the Defense of American Constitutional Rights, but when the night came, he was emphatic that it was the Christian Front that had brought out such celebrities.[1]

For celebrities these were. Cassidy was now a nationally known figure, thanks to Coughlin's support and the attention of the New York media. As for Boake Carter, although forgotten today, he was one of the three most popular newscasters of the 1930s and was "familiar in almost every American household." In 1938 Carter was voted the nation's "most popular commentator" by readers of *Radio Guide*. He was also one of the first newscasters in America to have his own sponsor, Philco Electronics. Carter's style, novel at the time, was to read newswire releases dispassionately over the air, peremptorily introducing his own sardonic commentary into the staid stories. But his editorials could be cutting, and he picked fights with powerful enemies. Among these were John L. Lewis and the union body he helmed, the Congress of Industrial Organizations. In late 1937 "the CIO-led union that organized the Philco manufacturing plants grew weary of Carter's constant attacks on Lewis and the CIO." In one of the most bizarre moves in American labor history, the CIO helped to organize a boycott against Carter and Philco radios—the very product that CIO workers were manufacturing to earn their livelihoods. The boycott hurt Philco sales so badly that the company soon parted ways with Carter. Carter's isolationism and anti–New Deal rhetoric also alienated listeners; with his sponsorship dried up and ratings down, stations began taking him off the air. Yet, like Father Coughlin, Carter believed he was actually the victim off a conspiracy, forced from the dial by liberals within the Roosevelt administration. Thus Carter, too, became a free speech enthusiast, even though the government was not involved in the private decisions of the broadcasters that deserted him. As early as May 1938 he was headlining a Christian Front–sponsored Great Pro-American Mass Meeting at Carnegie Hall, where spoke on the topic "free speech and the news."[2]

In October 1939 Moran, the master of ceremonies, had no compunctions about compelling expression. He opened the evening by instructing the crowd stand and salute the flag as the Star-Spangled Banner played. "I trust that none of you will refuse to salute the flag," Moran stated. "I recognize your rights as citizens, but I demand that those who do not intend to salute the flag leave the hall." Then, issuing a veiled threat of violence, he told the audience, "Look around you and if they refuse to leave ask officers to give a little help."

Carter used his time to bellow about the National Association of Broadcasters' (NAB) new broadcasting code. Carter called out the NAB for infringing free speech, since its code banned editorializing while reading a news report. There was more heft to this complaint than Carter's earlier ones, as the NAB, though a private organization, was creating federally enforceable standards. The Communications Act of 1934 had established the radio airwaves as a kind of public utility, which the federal government was empowered to regulate, and the NAB was drawing up the rules on behalf of the new Federal Communications Commission. "The party in power in Washington has thoroughly abused the freedom of radio in the United States," Carter insisted, arguing that Democrats were clipping the wings of any newscaster who was against America entering the war in Europe.

After Carter, Cassidy took the stage to rail against Communism. "Jail is too good for Earl Browder," Cassidy declared, referring to the leader of the Communist Party of the United States. Cassidy's speech foreshadowed his cockamamie paramilitary doctrine of false-flag operations and defensive counterattack. "Communists plan to use the next general strike to start a revolution," he thundered to the Boston crowd, adding that he would like "every one of them kicked out of the land."[3]

Moran spoke next. While Cassidy spent his time on stage issuing political dicta and castigating Communists, Moran led what was apparently a raucous religious celebration, but because coverage of the October event was so minimal, little is known of what was said. We do know that Moran also took up the theme of censorship, announcing from the stage that, once again, Coughlin had been taken off the airwaves in Boston. This was false: Coughlin had never been forced from any Boston stations, although after the controversy surrounding his 1938 Kristallnacht speech, he had agreed to stay off the radio for a few weeks. He then returned to record-setting audiences, with plenty of complaints about his supposed removal. As for the situation in fall 1939, just two weeks before the October rally, Coughlin had renewed his contract with WAAB in Boston. Moran had arranged for 500 picketers to "protest against the ruling curtailing Father Coughlin's radio broadcasts," yet there was no such ruling. No matter, Moran lied to the Boston Arena crowd, claiming that he personally had arranged for Father Coughlin to resume his Sunday afternoon radio talks in Boston. The announcement met with stormy applause.[4]

We know more details about the September rally, thanks to a nuanced account written by one Eugene Smith, a part-time Congregational minister in attendance. Smith found the Christian Front's anti-Semitism concerning, so he made a point of bearing witness and recording his thoughts. What Smith saw and heard disturbed him deeply, and after the New York arrests, he shared his rally notes with the FBI, which preserved them.

From the start, Smith wrote, "anticipation and subdued excitement pervaded the air," and "the floor and both galleries were filled." Massive speakers stretched from floor to ceiling. The program began with a large assembly of musicians, "boys and girls from twelve to sixteen" years old, marching onto the floor by the colors—an American flag and a large blue Christian Front flag. The band played "God Bless America" while children carried placards high above their heads. "CHOKE THE VULTURE COMMUNISM," "TEAR DOWN THE WEB OF LIES," "DRIVE OUT THE POISONOUS REPTILE," and "KEEP US OUT OF WAR," the placards read.

Smith was taken with Moran, who moved effortlessly on stage, passionately orating in front of thousands. Moran opened the event declaring that "Father Coughlin is the greatest American in the United States today." When the cheers died down he pledged, "My organization is at his entire service." As for Father Cyril Keating, who took the stage after Moran, Smith thought he was "eloquent and handled the audience with power." Keating spoke for forty-five minutes. "I have lived and eaten with Father Coughlin," Keating shouted, "there is not a lazy bone in his body." "He gets no money from neither big business nor Russia nor Nazi Germany. Father Coughlin wants to apply Christian economics to this country. Are you ready for it? Father Coughlin is *always* right! HE IS THE TRUTH! ARE YOU WITH HIM?" Although, according to every Christian denomination, only Jesus Christ is to be referred to as "the truth," the crowd "cheered Keating with shouts of YES!"

"We need more workers for Father Coughlin and the Army of the Kingdom of God," Keating declared, doubling down on Coughlin's personal divinity. Then Keating led the crowd in hypnotic repetitive cheers:

> ARE YOU READY? ARE YOU READY TO FIGHT FOR
> SOCIAL JUSTICE?
>
> ARE YOU READY TO GET NEW SUBSCRIBERS FOR
> *SOCIAL JUSTICE?*
>
> WHAT DO YOU SAY? SAY IT AGAIN! ARE YOU READY
> TO FIGHT?

Excited cries of affirmation filled the arena as Father Keating took his place in the growing pantheon of priests advocating for the Christian Front.

Before leaving the stage, Keating flattered the audience. Father Coughlin "often spoke of the courageous works of the priests and laity of Boston" and "read every letter" sent to him from New England. Then Keating concluded with an invocation of Mystical Body theology, albeit in twisted fashion: "We belong to the same Church of which he is part of the Head; we are all the members and all bound to one another!" Keating cried. But Keating was referring to Coughlin, not Christ. In Keating's mind, and perhaps in the arena that night, Christ was secondary to Coughlin.[5]

We do not know what Coughlin himself told the audience, because Reverend Smith left Boston Arena just as Moran was preparing the closed-circuit connection. Smith could not stand listening to the voice from Royal Oak. All he heard of the speech was "a metallic cracking, low at first, and raucous continuance." Smith quickly walked home and wrote down his thoughts. "The Christian Front movement in this nation is very dangerous," he believed. "Father Coughlin has started a fire." Smith was blown away by "the loyalty of the audience; their emotional intensity," and "the power of Father [Keating] to arouse people, to sweep them onward without questions or critical thinking." Smith was still "more impressed with the words of Mr. Moran, chairman of the evening."

In closing, Smith described the rally as "Father Coughlin's coup in Boston." The minister seemed to understand that virtually nothing would be done to contest the forces Coughlin and Moran were unleashing. "The city has literally no knowledge of what occurred here."[6]

* * *

As ominous as the rallies were, there was an even more sinister coda. While Cassidy was speaking in Boston, his group was very likely training with two Browning machine guns stolen from a nearby armory. The released Christian Front FBI file reveals information that never arose at the New York trial, even though this information was in the bureau's possession months before the proceedings began: on October 27, 1939, less than a week after the Boston rally where Cassidy effectively laid out his paramilitary doctrine, New York fronter William Bishop told FBI informant Denis Healy that "two Browning Light Machine Guns had been stolen from armories in Boston." The guns,

Bishop said, were "at present time in cold storage" and would be used "for firearms training" in the future. During their raids, FBI agents found 750 rounds of Browning ammunition but no machine guns. Yet here was one of the defendants boasting to the FBI that the front had stolen the guns from the National Guard, just as prosecutors initially alleged before setting aside a charge they claimed they could not hope to prove.[7]

Word of the guns got out on the street, if not in the courtroom. By late January 1940, after the arrests but before the trial began, rumors were circulating in New York about machine guns gone missing in Boston. Newshounds linked the lost machine guns to the Irish Republican Army. To quell these rumors, the FBI deceived the media, telling the Associated Press that "no National Guard Arms had been reported missing" in Boston. That was technically true—the National Guard had not reported any lost guns—but also misleading.[8]

Healy's finding was recorded in Agent Peter Wacks's December 1 report, which was forwarded to Boston on December 7. Yet it would take nearly two additional months before Boston agent J. D. Noble notified his boss, Special Agent Virgil Peterson, that "two Browning automatic rifles . . . serial nos. 105707 and 29188" were "reported missing from the National Guard Armory in Waltham, Massachusetts," a Boston suburb. Neither Peterson nor E. J. Connelley—the New York special agent in charge, who learned from Wacks about the missing guns—mentioned the matter to Hoover or his deputy, Edward Tamm. Nor did anyone ever inform the Boston Police that two high-powered machine guns were lost in the area.

The Boston FBI office ignored the forwarded Wacks report, probably because its contents were described as "information" rather than actionable intelligence. Only after an unnamed Boston FBI agent heard separately about missing guns did the office follow up. The unnamed agent's source was a guardsman at Battery G, in Falmouth, Massachusetts. On January 19, 1940, the guardsman casually told the agent that "a few months ago he was at the Armory in Natick"—another Boston suburb—"and heard rumors that while returning from maneuvers the National Guard lost two machine guns from a truck." Upon further investigation, the agent learned that the guns had indeed gone missing but had already been returned.

It turned out that the guns were known to be missing since at least mid-September. The guns had first left the armory in Waltham on July 12, when Captain Archie McFayden turned them over to Federal Caretaker William

Marshall at the Charlestown National Guard facility. The guns were to be stored in Charlestown while Waltham's National Guard company was out on maneuvers. Around September 15, Captain McFayden asked Marshall to return the guns, but Marshall replied that he had already done so. Presuming that the guns had incorrectly wound up in Natick, McFayden inventoried the armory there but could not find them. Finally, on December 3, Marshall delivered gun 1057072 to McFayden. "Bipod missing, bolt missing, barrel very dirty," McFayden noted. The next day, Marshall appeared again, this time with gun 29188 "in good condition." Noble wrote, "Captain McFayden could not state where the rifles were located from the middle of September to December 4, 1939." Those dates synched with Christian Front target practices. Neither McFayden nor Marshall ever informed their superiors or notified law enforcement.

How exactly Marshall came to possess the stolen guns is unknown. He refused to talk when approached by the FBI investigator, and McFayden had little to add. McFayden told the agent that "he did not consider Marshall to be the type of man who should be a caretaker," but at the same time said that the incident "should be kept confidential." McFayden "did not want to go on record," since the incident would "not sit well with [his] Colonel." Pressed by the FBI investigator, McFayden refused "to quote any acts of Caretaker Marshall." The guardsmen were clamming up and covering up to protect themselves from military discipline, at the very least. Whether they had any other interests—whether, for instance, either was in league with or at least sympathetic to the Christian Front—is a matter entirely for speculation.

The Boston FBI field office concluded that "inasmuch as rifles Nos. 105707 and 29188 were missing from the place they were supposed to be, it is possible that they were stolen and returned."[9] What this meant was that, more than likely, William Bishop's enthusiastic note to Cassidy was true: the Browning light machine guns *were* rattling and echoing along the sides of the Allegheny Mountains in West Virginia in fall 1939. The upshot of the machine gun caper was that as John Cassidy stood in Boston Arena in late October 1939 spewing his harebrained rhetoric about a Communist revolution in the United States, at least two military-grade, combat-ready machine guns were missing from an armory in a neighboring town, and these guns almost certainly were in the Christian Front's possession—with Cassidy's knowledge. The police and the public had no idea, of course, and neither did the rally's organizer. Moran did not know he was taking the microphone from a revolutionary planning a religiously motivated terrorist attack.

At that moment, Moran was flying high. He would spend a few more months soaring, before the New York trial changed his fortunes again.

Building a Base

From September 1939 until January 1940, the Christian Front was booming in New England. During this period, Moran organized Christian Front groups in Pawtucket, Rhode Island, and Hartford, Connecticut.[10] In Lowell, Massachusetts, a so-called Social Justice Platoon convinced the city council to "go on record . . . protesting the action of the National Association of Broadcasters," which was seen as prohibiting the discussion of controversial subjects on the air. "Several hundred persons crowded the city council chamber at City Hall." Moran took the floor to argue that "if such subjects were to be banned, it was the public's duty and not that of the radio operators," a contention that goes some distance in clarifying his eccentric understanding of free speech. His frequent complaint of censorship by private corporations appears nonsensical, but perhaps Moran believed that in fact the state had every right to suppress speech. It was *only* private entities, maybe specifically press entities, whose actions could be said to violate constitutional rights of free expression. As discussed below, Moran defended this position even when challenged to consider its authoritarian character. Of course, it may also be that Moran had no coherent views on free speech and simply argued for whatever was politically expedient. In any case, the Lowell resolution passed unanimously, irking the highest levels of the NAB.[11]

Two weeks after the Boston Arena rally, Moran traveled to Pawtucket, where he shared the stage with Father Curran. At that event, Moran referred to the president as Mr. "Rosenfelt," described his administration as "anti-Christian," and insinuated that "first lady Eleanor Roosevelt frequently visited CPUSA headquarters." Moran also "charged the President with treason in connection with the alleged sale of United States military secrets to foreign governments." "The audience was in accord with the speaker," one spectator noted of the thousand-strong Pawtucket crowd.[12]

An observer from Boston's Jewish Community Relations Council who infiltrated a Christian Front meeting the day before the Pawtucket rally offered a possible reason for the crowd's allegiance to Moran. "Most of them are in very poor circumstances," the writer noted. "They are against the present economic order because they can't get what they want and seem to find within this group a chance to 'strike' at the person or persons whom they believed responsible for their plight."[13]

Economic grievance was indeed essential to Moran's success, in particular that of his anti-Semitic message. This is evident in an early 1940 FBI encounter with Christian Front supporters in Lynn, Massachusetts, a city north of Boston. The Lynn fronters described themselves less as members of an organization than as a "roundtable" of Coughlinites who "also attended the meetings in Boston of the Christian Front held by Francis Moran," where "the principles of social justice ... and the doctrines of Father Coughlin" were discussed. FBI Special Agent Edward Boyle met with several of the Lynn fronters after one of them, an insurance agent and "ardent Catholic" named Thomas Feeney, reached out to law enforcement in the wake of the New York arrests.[14]

Feeney explained to Boyle that Moran's speeches "were instructions on the economic encyclicals of popes Pius XI and Leo XIII." Moran talked about "Communism and its evils and encouraged the audience to watch out for it and fight against it." What Boyle gathered was that "Communism is discussed as a spreading evil," and there was "no specific anti-Semitism except insofar as it [was] connected with Communism." Boyle noted that Feeney and the other Lynn fronters he met seemed "anti-Jewish," but the FBI agent decided that this sentiment was grounded in the economic realities of Lynn: "Jews had driven all the good Christians out of business in Lynn." Feeney and two Lynn compatriots who met with Boyle, Frank Harney and Dr. Charles Flood, all "cited hearsay cases" about Jews. "Harney had been a former shoe manufacturer in Lynn, producing 2000 to 2500 shoes a day before the World War," but "when the war came he was drafted, was forced to close down his factory, and as a consequence he suffered the loss of several thousand dollars. After the war, he came home and the Jews had his business." Harney "had not been able to break into the business again because of the Jews." As far as Harney was concerned, he, like Moran, had been economically displaced by Jews—and for doing his patriotic duty.

Agent Boyle seems to have been quite taken. His report downplayed the potential danger of the front and its sympathizers, asserting that these were just "the opinions of a few men" who belonged to "no real organization." Feeney, Harney, and Flood "were happy to see that at least one man, Francis Moran, had the courage to get up and talk social justice along Christian lines."

Boyle added that "the men had a high opinion of Moran," claiming "he is a very intellectual man with high principles and an earnest purpose to instruct the people in the subversive doctrines being disseminated around them, and to warn them of the same."[15]

Moran was winning support by proposing that the struggle against poverty was not a political one, as the Communists would have it, but rather a religious one. Driven by Coughlin's interpretation of Catholic social justice as a mission on behalf of Christians exclusively, Moran sought to counter Judeo-Bolshevism with what Keating called "Christian economics." That did not mean promoting economic systems inspired by Christian teaching but instead protecting the financial interests of Christians. The good life was for the faithful.

As a "kitchen-table" activist, concerned with the welfare of Christians in the here and now, Moran had a message that appealed beyond the ranks of leading citizens and the exceptionally pious. It should therefore come as no surprise that his big tent welcomed a great many women, who of course were no less attuned to economic hardship than men were. Indeed, many far-right Catholic movements of the 1930s and 1940s counted large numbers of women supporters. Historian Glen Jeansonne pointed out that Father Coughlin "attracted thousands of female supporters, and women joined the Coughlin-influenced Christian Front." Elizabeth Dilling, the anti-Communist speaker and author who shared the podium with Father Curran at the 1938 Pro-American Rally, was a leader in the National Legion of Mothers of America, which billed itself as a patriotic organization and counted a membership between 5 and 6 million by 1941.[16]

Moran seems to have exhibited the same level of magnetism for Catholic women as Father Coughlin, perhaps more. "These women work their heads off for Moran," one confidential source reported to the FBI, who suggested that the women had "come under his spell." Marie Ballem of Winthrop, Massachusetts, wrote to *America* magazine, "I spent every spare moment of my time after work selling *[Social Justice]* and opening up new districts." Ballem was interested in helping financially one "boy with a wife and child who had been discharged from Jordan Marsh Co. department store because he was seen selling *Social Justice* on Washington Street beside rabid Communists and socialists sent out by the General Jewish Council." Here was a Catholic woman who understood full well the Judeo-Bolshevist menace to working-class America.[17]

An FBI confidential source seemed to think that Moran's celibacy played into his mystique and provided a modicum of sex appeal. One "woman said that she always thought M. was giving his life up to do this big work." The source predicted that if Moran ever got married the other Christian Front women would become "angry."[18] There is, however, every reason to believe that Moran's women supporters were primarily interested in his views and arguments, not his hand in marriage. It is not as though women were on the sidelines of far right generally, participating only to find suitable husbands or facilitate enterprises cherished mainly by the men in their lives. Recall Sybil Holmes, the champion red-baiter of the Massachusetts State House, who justified anti-Communism on the basis of Christian devotion and allied with Moran more than once. And there was Dilling, very much out front, who could likewise count on Moran's support. In early 1941 Moran spoke out on behalf of Dilling and her women colleagues who were then protesting the passage of the Lend-Lease Act, which built on President Roosevelt's cash-and-carry scheme and enabled further US support of belligerents in the wars in Europe and Asia. Moran thundered to an audience of reportedly 60 percent women that "hundreds of other women, mothers, who had made great sacrifices to come to Washington and protest the atrocities of the Lend-Lease Bill were not permitted to speak even to their representatives."[19]

Dilling and Moran both argued for isolationism not only because they opposed alliance with Britain and later the Soviet Union against the Nazis, but also in support of Christian pacifism, inspired by the fabulously high casualty rates of World War I. For the mothers, Christianity could save the nation from Communism, and Christian pacifism could save their sons from what they considered a pointless—even counterproductive—sacrifice.

Exercising Influence

During fall 1939 Moran was generating high-profile protests, gaining publicity, gathering a core of supporters, and encouraging public debate. Contrariwise, Cassidy's New York outfit was street-fighting and becoming more truculent in its anti-Semitism. Cassidy was pursuing militarism, while Moran was focused on an intellectual exhortation of the faithful. And while the likes of Carridi in New York were openly anti-Semitic, Moran and other organized right-wing New England Christians kept their anti-Semitism behind closed doors, or else they filtered it through economic griping. The result was a more genteel anti-Semitism in New England—less publicly antagonistic but more insidious behind the veil of supposedly legitimate grievance.[20]

Moran worked hard to build on the momentum of the huge September and October rallies. The moment was opportune, as the public's interest in isolationism and pacifism was increasing in response to the war in Europe, which had recently begun with Germany's invasion of Poland on September 1. At a meeting with 800 Christian Front members in Roxbury's Hibernian Hall on November 8, Moran bragged that "we are doing very well in Lawrence, Lowell, Providence, and Lynn," but he was not content to rest on his laurels. "It is essential that chapters be formed in Roxbury, Roslindale, Dorchester, and other sections of Boston," he explained. Priests in New Hampshire were cooperating but "in a very quiet way." Boston clergy were more trepidatious, but Moran thought they would "come forth when the proper time arises." Calling upon the supranational character of the Mystical Body, Moran concluded, "We are not going to get caught napping as we were in Spain."[21]

From Madrid to the mills of Lowell and Lynn, from Barcelona to Boston, Moran was continuing the fight for Christ. He took the fight to Washington, too, putting pressure on one of the giants of twentieth-century Massachusetts politics: John W. McCormack, who represented a Boston district in the US House and would go on to become speaker of the House in the 1960s. By 1939 McCormack was a major player in federal politics, on the brink of becoming the House majority leader. He was also vacillating on renewal of the Neutrality Act. If passed, the bill would end the US munitions embargo against belligerents in Europe and replace it with cash-and-carry, marking a giant step away from isolationism. On September 18 Coughlin called on his followers to inundate Washington with telegrams and letters of protest. The response was immense. A whopping 256,000 extra pieces of mail flowed into the US Senate in the week after Coughlin's appeal, and 400,000 extra pieces slammed the House. It is a testament to Moran, who mobilized the Coughlinites in Boston, that McCormack alone received 20,000 of these letters. Largely in opposition to renewal, the letters had a strong Catholic imprint and came from parishioners and priests alike.[22]

Moran also threw his weight around in the broadcast war. "A local radio program is of prime necessity," he wrote to all New England Christian Front members on October 6, 1939. "We must go to those people who will not come to us." Behind the scenes, Moran was trying to do just that, working with another giant of twentieth-century Massachusetts politics: the "Rascal King"

James Michael Curley, recently departed from the governor's office but soon to be restored as Boston's mayor, for the fourth time. In the critical weeks after the outbreak of war in Europe, Moran teamed up with Curley to try to purchase Boston's WAAB.[23] WAAB was a key radio station, its signal blanketing metropolitan Boston. The venture may have marked a first attempt at creating an all-right-wing station, a concept that would not be realized until the late twentieth and early twenty-first centuries. Moran believed strongly in the need to counter what he considered Jewish control of local media; Curley's interest is less clear, though surely he would have appreciated access to a friendly outlet. As fate had it, WAAB had just spent $25,000 (the equivalent of $440,000 in 2020 dollars) refurbishing its studio in Central Square, Cambridge, putting the sale price out of reach for Moran and Curley.

With his radio venture off the table, Moran found his next target in Alfred Duff Cooper, a Tory politician and former first lord of the British Admiralty who spent fall 1939 touring the United States, delivering lectures in which he urged Americans to stand up to the Nazis. Cooper was internationally known as a hawk and a man of unusual political courage, who had resigned his cabinet post in opposition to the Munich Agreement appeasing Hitler. Cooper "was featured prominently in Nazi propaganda as one of the three most dangerous Tory warmongers," according to historian Michael Stenton. All this made Cooper a conspicuous adversary for the Christian Front and other anti-Semitic isolationists, who claimed his intervention in the US scene was a ploy by Jewish bankers to push the country into Europe's war. As Cooper's Boston visit neared, Moran stoked such sentiments, while playing up anti-British views within the heavily Irish-American Christian Front.[24]

"This is Great Britain's war, and we are not going to grab the hot chestnuts out of the fire for them," Moran declared at the November 8 Hibernian Hall gathering, which served as a planning meeting for Cooper's arrival in Boston later that month. Cooper's tour had begun in September, giving Bostonians plenty of time to prepare. One idea Moran threw out to the crowd was to "have three men dressed in costumes representing the Spirit of '76 walking back and forth—with fifes—and a drum. Also, a wounded soldier with [a World War I American Expeditionary Force] band on his arm." Moran, always shrewd, wanted to take advantage of Irish bitterness without appearing provincial, which would limit the appeal of his message. So he primed the front with universalist arguments. "We have great sympathy for the people of England, France, Germany, and India—for their governments are not true democracies," Moran intoned. "But this is their battle." Moments like these demonstrated a kind of rhetorical genius, as Moran managed to strike a pose of principle while disclaiming any US interest in the war, reminding listeners of odious British imperialism, and suggesting that nothing separated Britain and Germany politically.[25]

Cooper spoke at Boston's Symphony Hall on November 28. Moran mustered only fifty picketers outside, but what happened inside the hall was more significant. "Before Duff Cooper finished, the entire Hall was in an uproar," an FBI source from the Anti-Defamation League recalled. Cooper, joined by his elegant wife Lady Diana Manners, faced what the *Boston Herald* described as a "barrage of hostile questions." "How about Palestine? What about India? What is England doing with the Arabs?" rang from the balcony, while the hecklers meticulously kept clear of the Irish question. The final jab of "we'll just settle for the war debt" raised some chuckles among the otherwise tense crowd. In his autobiography Cooper lamented the "organized opposition" he encountered on his tour, mentioning Boston specifically. Demonstrating his own prejudice, he blamed "the embers of the ancient Irish feud," a comment that absolved the British of responsibility for ongoing oppression of the Irish while reimagining a long-standing and one-sided policy of dispossession as a sort of family tiff in which all parties were equally at fault. For its part, Boston's upper crust was embarrassed by the outbursts in the gilded confines of Symphony Hall. The *Boston Globe* reported that "the leaders of Boston Society" were "generally sympathetic" to Cooper's speech, and in his autobiography Cooper thanked Bostonians who "came to apologize for the tone of some of the questions that had been asked."[26]

Moran was only too happy to annoy Cooper and "the leaders of Boston Society," but he did not want merely to rouse the rabble. That was the New York model, full of street picketing and fisticuffs. Moran hoped to be a little more sophisticated. So it was that in the early afternoon of January 14, 1940, Moran found himself sitting at the Boston Community Church on Byron Street, on a panel with Doctor A. G. Dieffenbach, religion editor of the *Boston Evening Transcript*, and Reverend W. Ellis Davies of the Unitarian church in Wollaston, Massachusetts. It was Moran's first visit to the progressive Boston Community Church, a Unitarian-Universalist congregation under the direction of the minister Donald G. Lothrop. Lothrop had a reputation for inviting controversial speakers into his church. These included speakers on all sides, whether Moran or the Communists Lothrop "warmly welcomed all . . . to his congregation," leading to widespread speculation that he was himself a Communist.[27]

Before an audience of more than a hundred, the panelists debated the following question: "Should Communists and Nazis Have the Constitutional Rights of Freedom of Speech, Press and Assembly?" Moran "spoke with absolute directness and frankness of his personal attitude toward the Constitution." Agitating Lothrop, who served as moderator, Moran indicated that progressives and progressive organizations "are a part of Communism without knowing it." Moran argued that Nazis, Fascists, and Communists all should be denied constitutional protections because they were revolutionary agitators. How could those who wished to eliminate the United States be protected by its Constitution, Moran wondered. Moran wanted to see "a bureau within the central government" decide which citizens had constitutional rights: "What [the federal government] said was wrong would be wrong, what they said was all right I would permit." Lothrop challenged Moran, asking, "Is not this about what Hitler has now in Germany?" According to one of the attendees, "Moran smiled pleasantly and shrugged his shoulders."[28]

Within twenty-four hours, the New York Christian Front raids were making headlines, and the time for pleasant smiles was over.

Persistence

"Francis P. Moran, 31, organizer of an autonomous Christian Front in New England claiming a membership of 20,000, was 'astounded' last night when informed" of the arrests. "Good heavens," Moran gasped as the *Boston Globe* reporter explained that Cassidy and his group were accused of sedition. As far as Moran was concerned, the very notion was impossible. The purpose of the Christian Front, he told the paper, was "to uphold the Constitution," since "the Constitution is based on the principles and moralities of Christian civilization." Moran made every effort to distance himself from whatever was happening in New York. "I can assure you, there has never been and never will be any talk about bombings in New England," he protested, adding that he was no bosom buddy of the New York leader—he "knew Cassidy very slightly." Moran also defended the Christian Front against the "false allegation" of anti-Semitism. "We have denounced the leadership of Jewish radicals," Moran clarified, promising that there was no anti-Semitism in the good fight against Judeo-Bolshevism.[29]

What to do now? Moran had three choices. He could close shop, go underground, or continue organizing publicly—a dicey proposition given that law enforcement might be coming for him. The day after news of the arrests broke, the *New York Times* was predicting "Saboteur Arrests in Boston." Yet Moran persisted, and in full view. It is in some ways an astonishing decision but also in keeping with Moran's history and commitments. He tangled with politicians, but he understood his work as religious, and there was no end to faith, or else it was no faith at all. What is more, to forswear the Christian Front would be a second black mark, a second failure to follow his vocation after his departure from the seminary. He would be a failure in the eyes of his community, which saw him as a spiritual leader. And he would be a failure in the eyes of God. This was another teaching of Mystical Body theology, which enjoined Catholics to endure any hardship. As the Dominican Order's Thomas A. K. Reilly wrote in *America* during World War I, "The mystery of the Cross"—a symbol emphasized by Mystical Body theology in particular—"lures stalwart souls through faith to the top of the narrow way." Reilly was demanding of the body of the Church "an extreme or consummation of perseverance" on behalf of the divine.[30] For Moran, maintaining the Christian Front was undoubtedly a choice for Christ.

Moran would follow his religious discernment into the teeth of the national security apparatus. Fortunately for him, that apparatus still was not focused on his group. As we have seen, Peterson, the special agent in charge of the FBI's Boston office, had not even heard of the Christian Front before Moran visited him in the wake of the New York arrests. And even after the arrests, the FBI thought Moran's followers were simply opinionated people with "no real organization." The press also continued to give Moran a pass. The initial bad publicity subsided quickly, and the papers did little to link Moran with the seditionists a few hours away. Henry Levy, New England regional secretary of the American Jewish Committee, wrote to his New York counterparts, "The tie-up between the Boston and New York [Christian Front] office should have been made clearer by the papers." Evidently there were some papers that actively refused to draw the connection: a Levy associate inside the Hearst newspaper chain insisted that the company would not poke Coughlin by suggesting that he was the spiritual leader of a nationwide terrorist organization. "Pressing the tie-up between Detroit, Boston, and New York," was impossible "from the standpoint of religion and good business," Levy lamented.[31]

Moran's plan at this point was to keep on doing what he had been doing. Thus on January 18, 1940, just three days after the arrests and on the day he spoke with Peterson, Moran kept a scheduled speaking engagement at the Knights of Columbus Hall in Somerville. The evening, which was sponsored by 200 male Coughlin supporters who billed themselves as the United Minute Men, was an opportunity for Moran to present the aims of the Christian Front to an audience of sympathetic nonmembers. He also used the occasion to distance his loyal New Englanders from the New York seditionists. Moran "made a long speech explaining the motives and purposes of his organization . . . warning of the dangers of Communism."

Suddenly, one of the attendees spoke up. "I should like to say a word," he interjected. It was Lothrop, ready to refute Moran at one of his own assemblies. "You, Francis P. Moran, spoke at my church last week, tonight I would like to speak at your meeting." Taking the floor, Lothrop despaired "the use of the term Christian Front by so un-Christian a group." He accused the Christian Front of being anti-Semitic, tied to the New York seditionists, and beholden to Father Coughlin. Moran denied every allegation. Lothrop then read what looked to be a prepared statement citing historical evidence. But Moran refused to engage. "I defy you to show any proof of Father Coughlin's connection," Moran said, splitting hairs. He acknowledged that he was personally in contact with Coughlin but protested the claim that Coughlin had any relationship to the Boston Christian Front, specifically. An operative of Boston's Anti-Defamation League, in attendance at the meeting, described a "heated discussion" between Lothrop and Moran. When Lothrop accused Moran of being anti-Semitic, "Mister Moran accused Mister Lothrop of being a Communist, and stated that the Community Church was Communistic."[32]

Almost as if he had anticipated Lothrop's arguments, Moran produced, with great fanfare, a stack of "photostatic copies" of a letter from Father Coughlin. The letter, addressed to "My Dear Frank," outlined a benign project. Coughlin encouraged Moran to provide "local intellectual leadership" to "Social Justice Groups" in an effort "to teach and inform, rather than to organize a motley mass." Coughlin further urged Moran to "keep clear of all politics" and "advise" his followers that they "be temperate in their language and actions." Of course group members must refrain from "committing any act which might embarrass our cause or making any statements which might be misconstrued." The letter was dated simply December 1939. Most likely it was concocted by Moran and Coughlin in the wake of the New York arrests and backdated to provide cover in case the Boston front was accused of harboring violent intentions.[33]

Lothrop was caught off-guard by Moran's return salvo. Instead of being cowed, "Moran stated that the Christian Front from now on will fight harder than ever before." He invited all of those in attendance in Somerville to the next Christian Front meeting the following Monday at Hibernian Hall in Roxbury. Amid cheers, Moran flippantly "requested that the audience not be afraid to come as there would be no knives or bombs thrown."[34]

Levy stayed on Moran's case. In February Levy contracted with Maurice Goldsmith, an agent for New York City's Jewish Peoples Council against Fascism and Anti-Semitism, to infiltrate Moran's meetings. Since 1936 Goldsmith had been attending Nazi and Fascist gatherings in New York, sometimes heckling and sometimes silently taking notes. In Boston, Goldsmith casually entered the February 12, 1940, Christian Front meeting at Hibernian Hall. He sat in the last row, where he noticed a young man "eyeing him suspiciously." After Moran finished his introductory remarks, the same young man "walked down the aisle with [a] slip of paper in his hand, which he gave to Moran."[35]

"We have a pleasant announcement to make," Moran shouted. "We are being graced this evening by Mr. Maurice Goldsmith, a representative of the American Jewish Committee." Moran continued, "If you behave yourself, Mr. Goldsmith, you will be able to stay." One can imagine Moran's glee as he held forth. "I know why you are here anyway," he said, "as an undercover man for the AJC, the B'nai B'rith, and a whole lot of other Communist front organizations." Moran then spoke for roughly half an hour about Communists in government and about his trip to New York to visit Cassidy and the other Christian Front defendants. It was on this same trip that Moran met with the defense lawyer, Leo Healy, and with Father Curran, although there is no evidence that he brought this up at the meeting. Suddenly Moran "challenged Goldsmith or any Rabbi . . . to refute anything he had to say." Moran also insulted Goldsmith, saying he was "yellow" and "didn't have the guts" to work out in the open like the Christian Front.

Moran then asked if there were any undercover FBI agents in the audience and spent the next ten minutes berating the bureau. The tirade was eventually interrupted by a commotion in the back of the room. Abruptly "one woman stood up and shouted, 'Why don't we throw Goldsmith out?'" "No, no, no," Moran insisted, "we are not going to gang up on him or his kind. We can take care of them single-handed if we have to." At that point, a Christian Front member notified Moran that the crowd was now overflowing into the street and would need to "move to the larger hall on the next floor." In his report, Goldsmith noted that "the attendance seemed to be about 700—many young people."[36]

Under Pressure

In the weeks after the New York arrests, nothing could stop Moran. He continued to attract large crowds, and no doubt the Lothrop and Goldsmith episodes only added to his mystique. It seemed that his faith was being rewarded, as the Boston front went from strength to strength. Certainly Moran's ego was in no need of salvage. Here he was hatching plans with the former governor and besting Communists in public debate, if underhandedly. He even had what was supposedly a letter from Father Coughlin praising his "intellectual leadership."

But by March, pressure was ratcheting up. For one thing, the FBI was finally taking a closer look at the Christian Front in Boston. On March 8, while federal prosecutors were putting together their jury in Brooklyn, Hoover wrote to Special Agent Peterson requesting "full information concerning Moran be obtained at once." Of course, Moran could not have known this, and, as usual, Peterson was dilatory. When surveillance of the front restarted at its March 11 meeting, it was an operative of the American Jewish Committee in the room, not of the FBI. Moran did not know this, either. What he did know was that only 250 people attended the gathering, a reflection of how hard it was to recruit and organize in the midst of the sedition trial. The meeting was a pathetic exercise in self-defense. First, a Boston fronter denied that the Christian Front was an anti-Semitic organization. "We are not anti-Semitic but we are against atheist Jews and atheist Gentiles," he protested. Then Moran took the stage and explained that "it was difficult for him to get good speakers to come to the meetings" and that many who had been previously booked had stayed away "for fear of spoiling their reputations."

The press may not have been connecting the Boston front to the New York seditionists, but it was nonetheless getting harder to keep afloat an organization that shared its name with a clutch of alleged revolutionaries. Moran realized that he would have to step back for a time. To the astonishment of the relatively few assembled, he announced that he would be taking a break.

"I will be comparatively quiet until after the trial is over," he said. "Then you will hear plenty from me." [37]

Moran did not need to witness the small turnout to decide that it was time for a hiatus: he had come to the meeting prepared to exit the public eye. That evening he distributed the first of his newsletters, which would be a major project while the front lay low. Single-spaced and typewritten on legal-sized paper, the pages contained all of Moran's latest relevant thoughts, suggestions, and announcements. This was a new way of reaching the streets, in plain-talking style. The first issue wondered "why for years we have been told that the Communists could not be prosecuted, despite their open advocacy of sedition, unless they perpetrated an overt act . . . but in the Christian Front affair . . . the FBI says it is not necessary to commit an overt act and that seditious utterances are sufficient for conviction?" The newsletter ended benignly with the announcement of a "Christian Front Dance and Penny Sale" in two weeks.[38]

According to the extant newsletters, only four meetings were held between March 25 and June 17, as compared to the twice-a-week meetings of 1939.[39] As Moran explained it, he was biding his time, but this was a feint. Like the rest of the public, he had no idea what would come next in the trial. In hindsight the verdict appears foreordained, but as far as Moran could tell in spring 1940, the New Yorkers faced the real possibility of decades in prison, and the name of the Christian Front would forever be sullied. Already Moran was losing members—and their cash. Like many Christian organizations, the front took collections at the end of meetings. Fewer meetings and reduced attendance meant financial strain; Moran was threatened with eviction from the Copley Square Hotel. And in late March the House Un-American Activities Committee announced that it would look into the Boston front. In fact, there was no investigation: the committee was being pushed to take the front seriously and mollified critics by promising an investigation that it never pursued. In real time, however, it must have seemed as though the Boston Christian Front was hurtling toward dissolution.[40]

The conclusion of the trial on June 24 had the potential to change the course of things. Although the defendants were not technically acquitted, in the eyes of their supporters, the vindication was total and worthy of grand celebration. On July 1 Hibernian Hall was "packed to capacity . . . standing room only" for a meeting of the Christian Front. This time, "a large percentage seemed to be family groups," with one source reporting that "the audience was one of the most demonstrative ever witnessed—there was stamping of feet, applause, and side remarks approving of the speaker." Moran blamed the arrests of the New York fronters on the B'nai B'rith, crowing, "I guess we showed them down in New York." He announced that new Christian Front groups would be started in Lowell and in Keene, New Hampshire. After months pent up, Moran was on offense, praising Hitler and castigating Jews.

"Hitler was the man," Moran shouted. He rationalized Hitler's actions on the grounds that someone in Germany had to "right the wrong" that was the Versailles Treaty. "All the stories about murders and attacks on Jews are lies and mere propaganda," he asserted. Hitler's "aggressiveness" was an understandable response to the depredations "of the international bankers and Communists in high places." His confiscation of Jewish property was "justifiable," due to the Jewish "minority control" of "sixty per cent of the entire wealth of the country." "There had to be a reckoning—a restoration of balance." Any refugees from Germany were said to be leaving "voluntarily."

Moran was deluded, but he was not stupid. Demonstrating a supple political mind, he managed to commend Hitler while criticizing Nazism. "We disapprove of the moral platform of Hitler's government," Moran explained. "Our religion is based around the home while the Nazi platform is based around the state." Moran was offended by the Nazi view of "amassing good blood through any means," particularly that of promoting births outside of wedlock. "The fostering of illegitimacy is against our religion," he noted.[41]

One strong meeting was not enough to restore the Boston Christian Front. Moran, however, seems to have had a talent for obtaining well-placed support just when he needed it: so many times when he was about to fade off into obscurity, an outstretched arm would save him at the last minute. First there was Father Coughlin, then Sybil Holmes, and now came Father Michael Ahern. Ahern was the last person one would expect to back the front. A polymath and "fundamentally a scientist," Ahern chaired the department of chemistry and geology at Weston College, a Jesuit seminary on the outskirts of Boston. He dabbled in everything from fire-suppression systems to floriculture to seismology. But what made Ahern such a strange fit as a front supporter was his career promoting tolerance and interfaith dialogue. In 1931 "his friends of all faiths" gave him $12,000 to install a world-class seismograph in Weston. The benefactors wanted to make sure Ahern received the money as a tribute to his "life combating religious prejudice in the United States." Indeed, Father Ahern was a charter member of the National Conference of

Christians and Jews, the foremost pre–World War II Jewish-Christian dialogue group in the United States. And as a young priest, he joined the Harvard Seminar on Religious Intolerance, a group of rabbis and Protestant ministers who discussed the problem of prejudice. "Better understanding must eventually bring results among fair-minded people," Ahern wrote in 1930.[42]

Ahern was not only an ivory tower liberal. He took his message to the airwaves, becoming in 1929 New England's own radio priest. His *Catholic Truth Radio Hour* aired on WNAC, which "dominated the dial" of Boston radio in the 1930s. By 1940 Ahern's Sunday show was on the Yankee Network, a twenty-four-station powerhouse broadcasting him from Bangor, Maine, to Bridgeport, Connecticut. "Catholic Question Box," a weekly column in the archdiocesan newspaper the *Boston Pilot*, gave Ahern even more exposure. Ahern's commitment to tolerance was diametrically opposed to the views of Coughlin and Moran. Moran at one point "denounced Father Ahern for his activities in such movements as the National Conference of Christians and Jews."[43]

Despite all this, Father Ahern proved again Tillich's foresight, becoming the next priest to give cover to the Christian Front. Ahern's support came in a memorable radio broadcast on July 14, while the New York trial was still fresh on listeners' minds. The thesis of the address, entitled "What is the Christian Front?" and lasting nearly an hour, was that the front was a mainstream organization doing good work for the faithful. Here was Catholic Action in practice: "Catholics applying their faith" with "confirmation, or approval" by the clergy. That confirmation was in fact coming from Ahern himself. Until this point, no priest or bishop had publicly lent his approval to the Boston Christian Front. There was every need for a Christian Front, Ahern argued, to face off against Spain's Popular Front, which "purported to defend . . . the proletariat . . . against . . . 'the forces of reaction.'" Sounding strangely like Father Curran and Leo Healy, Ahern classed the Christian Front alongside so many similarly situated groups: "the Protestant Front, the Atheistic Front, the Labor Front, the Jewish Front, and so forth." To the extent that some of these fronts advocated against Christianity, a Christian Front was a necessary rejoinder. "The term Christian Front began to be used to designate those forces . . . which aimed to offset the anti-Christian ideologies," Ahern explained.[44]

Although Ahern had spent his life seeking a more tolerant world, his feelings about the plight of Spanish Catholics led him to promote a message hardly different from Coughlin's, putting him at odds with his fellow liberals. For instance, Ahern received a serious lashing after speaking in favor of Franco during a 1938 event at Boston's Old South Meeting House, the venerable Congregational Church building famed in history as the gathering spot for the Boston Tea Party. For a Catholic priest to speak in such an environment was extraordinary, but when he began praising the Spanish Nationalists, he was met with "boos, hisses, and several near fistfights" before being "heckled from the floor." The experience jolted Ahern. He had been invited by activists sympathetic to the Popular Front, and when he asked them to recognize the real evils the Popular Front had committed, those activists proved combative and unruly. Was the Christian Front so much worse? By the time Ahern gave his radio speech, the Christian Front's supposedly violent seditionists had been spared earthly judgment, while the priest had seen with own eyes what Popular Front supporters were capable of.[45]

So it was that in July 1940 Ahern could be at peace recommending the Christian Front to Catholics across New England. "Whatever activities certain units of the Christian Front may have undertaken were purely their responsibility, and not the responsibility of either the Catholic clergy, or the Catholic laity as a whole," he asserted. Then Ahern made a mystifying statement that seemed to jettison all of his previous work in Christian-Jewish relations. "Anti-Semitism, by the way, is no more a federal offense than is anti-Catholicism or anti-Protestantism," he said. Ahern's statement cannot be set aside as a bit of freelance legal hair-splitting; anti-Semitism was never mentioned in Cassidy's indictment, "nor did these attitudes come up in the trial," as Ahern himself admitted. His defense of the front need not have touched on the subject—why bring it up at all, except to sanction Catholic bigotry?[46]

Ahern went on to defend the Christian Front on the grounds that, at trial, the group had not been considered a religious organization. With Catholic anti-Semitism discarded as a motive, anti-Communism came to the fore. "Their initial intention was perfectly good," Ahern wrote in a later reflection, "and within the law." During the radio address, he explained that "the issues of the Christian Front and anti-Semitism so prominent in the scare-headlines in January were already quashed weeks before the end of the trial in June. As a matter of fact, they were never issues in the case at all." Criticism of the speech left Ahern nonplussed. "In referring to the trial of the 14 men in Brooklyn for conspiracy against the United States, I pointed out that their membership in the Christian Front unit was not mentioned in their trial,"

Ahern said, joining Curran, Leo Healy, and the prosecution in demanding that the Christian Front itself was not on trial. The power of Curran's and Healy's arguments was such that even Ahern was moved. So convinced was he that he could not understand why anyone would disagree. "The bald assertion that I had, in that broadcast, defended a group that was un-Christian and un-American was, to say the least, a considerable shock," he wrote.[47]

Moran took immediate advantage of Ahern's unexpected support. The day after the broadcast, July 15, 1940, Moran held a Christian Front meeting, where he told the audience "that a real champion had stepped forward." Previously, Moran said, "the Front has been unable to secure the approval of members of the clergy 'openly,' although many of them privately approved." Now "Father Ahern has rendered his approbation over the air." Of course, many priests had openly supported the front or the idea of a front, but they were not New Englanders. Ahern was the first local priest to throw his weight behind an active organization calling itself the Christian Front. His speech was also published in full on the front page of the July 20 *Boston Pilot*, lending the Boston Archdiocese's imprimatur to the broadcast.[48]

Henry Levy was deeply worried. His contacts had penetrated the July 15 meeting and reported back on Moran's joyous embrace of Ahern. Levy wrote to Louis E. Kirstein, the chairman of the General Committee of the American Jewish Committee, that Moran "has already used the Ahern address as a blanket endorsement for his organization." Most concerning was that "Moran said Father Ahern's statement may be considered the attitude of the clergy with regard to the organization." While this was in some ways an exaggeration on Moran's part, it was also in keeping with the theory of Catholic Action: the approval of one priest in good standing with his bishop counted for the sanction of the whole Body of Christ. More concretely, the approval of the *Pilot* was a statement on behalf of the Boston Archdiocese. The secular press, meanwhile, was almost entirely silent. The *Boston Evening Transcript* was the only local newspaper to chastise "the Boston archdiocese" for its "hands-off policy regarding the local branch of the Christian Front."[49]

Ahern's speech was a victory, but it was not the whole ballgame. Moran built on the endorsement by pursuing the archdiocese's formal recognition of the Christian Front. He knew that direct and public approval by a bishop was worth more than Ahern's words; a bishop's support would guarantee the Christian Front's standing as a religious organization extending the work of the church. On July 17, three days after Father Ahern's speech, Moran reached out to William Cardinal O'Connell, the archbishop of Boston. "Your Eminence," Moran's letter began, "my sincere thanks for any effort you may have made in behalf of . . . those laymen, who, like myself, are fighting with outside organizations for the principles of Christianity." Moran went on to praise Ahern. Moran then asked the cardinal for "the honor of another interview," a puzzling request because the archdiocesan archives contain no record of Moran meeting with O'Connell previously. "Wisdom is necessary in the conduct of movements such as this," Moran closed, before signing off, "cordially and obediently yours."[50]

Cordial obedience was not the characterization of Moran that O'Connell was receiving from his staff. "This Francis P. Moran, the Director of the Christian Front, is making a lot of threatening statements" diocesan chancellor Father Francis L. Phelan wrote to the cardinal's secretary in an undated note. Moran, in Phelan's opinion, was "a rather bold agitator." The chancellor "felt His Eminence would wish to know it," a signal for the secretary to forward the information directly to O'Connell. "N.A."—no answer—O'Connell scribbled at the top of Moran's letter, "file and save letter."[51]

Who knows if Moran paced the days away, awaiting a response that never came. The rejection must have been crushing, the latest dip in a year that had already featured its share of highs and lows for Moran and Boston's Christian Front. Nineteen-forty had begun with enormous promise, thanks to the successes of the previous fall. And even the initial bad press of the New York arrests wore off quickly. Soon enough, infiltrated and unsure about the trial, the Boston front entered its leanest period, only to experience the jubilation of the June verdict and Father Ahern's commendation. But Cardinal O'Connell's brush-off left the Christian Front at another impasse. The Boston unit had not yet recovered from the losses of the spring and remained spurned in polite society and the secular press. Ahern could not be counted on; he had received nothing but opprobrium for backing the front and, in any case, was a strange ideological bedfellow. The future was uncertain. Would another outstretched hand emerge from Boston's foggy clime?

CHAPTER 6

A Nazi in Boston

MARY BRYANT PRATT BRANDEGEE INHERITED $20 MILLION IN 1891, an amount that today would equate to well over half a billion dollars. By the time she met Herbert Wilhelm Scholz, she may have been Boston's wealthiest citizen. Scholz arrived in November 1938, to take up duties as Germany's consul in the city. An educated, good-looking man with perfect English, a cosmopolitan manner, and a charming wife, Scholz immediately won over Boston's elite. But Brandegee had her doubts.[1]

In June 1940 Brandegee marched down from Faulkner Farm—her Brookline estate, which is now a National Historic Landmark—to the FBI field office in Post Office Square. "The present German Consul and his wife," Brandegee explained, are "being lavishly entertained by the Back Bay Social Set." Perhaps wondering if it was a crime to eat caviar and spill Margaux, Special Agent Virgil Peterson nonetheless listened graciously to Brandegee. Eventually she came to the point: this Scholz was a suspicious character. Outside the confines of official diplomacy, the consul was using his position to gain access to President Franklin Roosevelt's circle. For instance T. Jefferson Coolidge, Roosevelt's recently retired undersecretary of the treasury, consistently entertained Scholz in his Brookline home.[2]

Brandegee had been spooked for months by Scholz's quick entrée into Boston society and his closeness with influential figures in the political and business worlds, but what finally inspired her to report her worries was something Scholz said at a dinner party. The occasion came shortly after Hitler had ordered unrestricted submarine warfare, a move that threatened US interests in the Atlantic and significantly ratcheted up tensions with Washington. The order also put the Germans and Soviets on a collision course in the Baltic at a time when the Molotov-Ribbentrop pact supposedly guaranteed peace between Berlin and Moscow. Brandegee was sitting across the table from Scholz when he "started to discuss the war with a friend of hers." This friend told Scholz to his face that she was "decidedly pro-ally." In response, Scholz stared across the table into the woman's eyes and pronounced coolly, "Then we are enemies." Shocked, the Back Bay socialites sat nervously fidgeting at the table until someone suggested, "We had better talk about the weather." Brandegee's message for Peterson was a harrowing one: Scholz was not a diplomat from a neutral power but rather an agent of a foreign adversary.[3]

Peterson did not bother to follow up. He had little concrete information about untoward activities involving Scholz and no basis for an investigation. In any case, the State Department preferred that the FBI stay out of Scholz's business, and so did the president. During 1939 and 1940, the US government did not know it was on the brink of war with Hitler. Roosevelt was doubtful that the Nazis would cause much damage and was, in any case, ambivalent about whether Nazi successes were a serious problem for the United States. His strategy was to not "further enrage Hitler," which meant treating German diplomats with kid gloves. James Clement Dunn, a political adviser at the State Department, told British diplomats that the United States had a policy of not paying attention to men like Scholz. The "federal government," he explained, was "being careful to leave the task of watching it (Nazi activity) to local, state, or municipal authorities."[4]

Few journalists were inclined to pick up the slack. One Bostonian who shared Brandegee's concerns got nowhere prodding Arthur Conant, Jr., editor of the *Boston Evening Transcript*, to look into Scholz. "His case was the first where a Nazi Party member who had no training whatsoever in diplomatic service, had been appointed to an embassy of the Third Reich," the correspondent wrote. "Dr. Scholz has never taken an attaché course, nor has he ever submitted to any of the diplomatic examinations every member of the diplomatic service customarily takes." He had been appointed "solely on the basis of his membership in the National Socialist Party." Conant ignored the letter, placing it in a file labeled "Nazis in the US," where it languished for the next three years.[5]

It turns out that Scholz was exactly what Brandegee feared—he was a spy operating under diplomatic cover. In fact Scholz was on assignment from the Schutzstaffel (SS), where he was an officer in the espionage division known as the Liaison Staff. During his time in Boston, Scholz found a willing intelligence asset in Francis Moran. Desperate and rejected by the institutional Roman Catholic Church, Moran fell into the arms of Nazi Germany. Moran did not have classified information to pass along to Scholz, but he did do the consul's bidding, dedicating countless hours to causes Scholz directed: the defeat of Roosevelt in 1940, stirring up anti-Semitism in Boston, promoting the Nazi line, and even pushing the US military to take up operations that would benefit the German war effort. As discussed later in this book, the union between Moran and Scholz was a criminal one. Moran never registered as a foreign agent, as required by the Foreign Agents Registration Act of 1938. And his work for Scholz arguably violated the Smith Act of 1940. Their partnership would become one of the most effective espionage and secret propaganda relationships of World War II.

For quite a while, Moran got away with being an underground collaborator, despite Dunn's assertion that "local authorities manage[d] perfectly well" in unearthing Nazi activity on the home front.[6] Dunn was apparently unaware of charges of police favoritism toward the Christian Front in both New York and Boston. Privately, Moran bragged to Derounian, reporting undercover, that "sixty per cent of the Catholic priests in Boston were with him, and that practically all of the cops were also with him." Derounian followed up on Moran's assertion and found that "later checking up seemed to confirm his declaration on the cops."[7]

Moran's reconciliation of Catholicism with Nazism was a complex act of moral flexibility, driven above all by his conviction that his faith enjoined anti-Semitism. John Franklin Carter wrote that Moran was drawn to "the Mystical Body of Hitler," but this overstates the case. As detailed in the next chapter, Moran did not embrace Nazism, much less substitute Hitler for Christ. He compromised with Nazism because he thought it was the right thing for a Christian to do in light of the Judeo-Bolshevist threat. And it was Scholz who gave Moran a reason to compromise. A detour through Scholz's story provides fascinating insights into a key figure in the tale of American Nazism, albeit one as dim in historical memory as Moran, Cassidy, and the Christian Front. It was not just any Nazi who could have won Moran over.

Scholz was a powerful believer in the rightness of the Nazi cause, who articulated his views in the kind of philosophical terms that Moran appreciated. Moran, after all, was a "lecturer," an "expert," and a "student." Scholz spoke the activist-intellectual language.[8]

And perhaps Scholz noted a kindred quality in Moran. Their backgrounds were quite different—Moran the son of working-class immigrants, Scholz the scion of the cultured upper-middle classes. But both men spent their early years looking for a way to believe in themselves, and both found the answer in varieties of nationalism and anti-Semitism. Both also knew what it meant to be lucky. When Moran met Scholz, the Bostonian had repeatedly been saved from irrelevance by the intercession of a patron and was on the lookout for a new one. Scholz had had many patrons, too, politically connected men who gave him opportunities he had not earned and who may even have saved him from death during the infamous Night of the Long Knives in 1934. Scholz had a knack for knowing the right people and being in the right place at the right time. This good fortune, combined with a real intelligence, helped Scholz navigate the competitive world of the Nazi bureaucracy, in which power plays were as constant as they were violent. It can seem as though the Nazi upper echelon trained for the Holocaust by first murdering each other. For Scholz, Boston would be a refuge from the infighting of Munich and Berlin and an opportunity to bring new supporters into Hitler's fold.

A Spy Is Born

Herbert W. Scholz was astute and circumspect, manipulative and inspiring. He was a survivor. Journalists were cautious about probing into his story, for he always fought back. But if there was not much written about Scholz in his own time—and a good deal of what was written is suspect or contradicted by other sources—his biography can be pieced together from assorted writings in German and English.

Scholz was born on January 29, 1906, in the southwest German city of Karlsruhe. His family was one of wealth and standing. His father, Wilhelm Gustav Scholz, was technical director and part owner of Waggonfabrik Jos. Rathgeber, a Munich-based producer of railway and street cars. Companies like Rathgeber led Munich's industrialization in the years prior to World War I, and the executives of such firms were highly esteemed. As the son of a prominent German businessman, Herbert Scholz was expected to be well educated and was sent to the Realgymnasium München, a school established by King Ludwig II of Bavaria in 1864 as an advanced and experimental "new language high school." Accordingly, Scholz mastered multiple foreign languages from an early age—French, Italian, Hungarian, and English. But Scholz was rebellious. He seems to have been unsure of what direction to take next. After finishing his course at the Realgymnasium at age eighteen, he spurned the liberal arts and instead chose legal studies. A year later he quit and became a volunteer at a bank in Munich. Whether in law or banking, Scholz seemed reluctant to tie himself to either track.[9]

In 1925 the nineteen-year-old Scholz became politicized and joined the Freikorps Oberland, a "free" regiment of paramilitary militia fighters who famously battled against the short-lived Munich Soviet Republic in April 1919. The Freikorps' "citizens' guard" joined hands with the Reichswehr—the regular German army—in fierce fighting that cost hundreds of civilian lives, alongside a similar number of combatants. The suppression of the Munich Soviet was politically significant; Hitler viewed the destruction of the short-lived republic as the first inkling of "the resurrection of the German people." Communists were tried and executed on the judgment of Freikorps leaders. In 1921 the Weimar government banned the Freikorps, but it lived on unofficially as the Bund Oberland Club. In 1925 the militia was reorganized and allowed to return to operation under its original name.[10]

The Freikorps was a formative institution for a number of high-ranking Nazis. The Freikorps' logistical mastermind during the Battle of Munich was Rudolf Hess, who would go on to become the Nazi Party's deputy führer. Heinrich Himmler was an agricultural student at Munich's Technical University and Freikorps member in 1919. Later he served for sixteen years as the chief of the SS and was a key planner of the Holocaust. As Hitler biographer Allan Bullock put it, "The Freikorps were the training schools for the political murder and terrorism which disfigured German life up to 1924, and again after 1929." Scholz's induction into the Freikorps was thus a critical career decision. Too young to have gained heroic status serving in World War I, he made his way upward by joining a paramilitary group whose political ideals were well aligned with those of the Nazis. Service in the Freikorps also showed a willingness to fight and possibly die for those ideals, enhancing Scholz's credibility as a far-rightist.[11]

In 1927, after two years in the Freikorps, Scholz relocated to Leipzig to attend university. On the face of it, this move looks like a sign of obedience to his father, a way to placate the family, and possibly even a rejection of Nazism. Instead of nationalism and bullying, the twenty-one-year-old Scholz was turning to the life of the mind—a peaceable dedication to thought and learning rather than a zealous commitment to the fatherland. But Scholz had other ideas. He did wish to become a student again, but what he wanted to study was the philosophy underlying Nazism. Still, Scholz took an intellectually flexible approach, taking in lectures on a range of topics and from professors with widely varying views. For instance, he took classes with Hans Driesch, a renowned biologist who undertook philosophical studies of embryology. A pacifist and Nazi critic, Driesch was eventually removed from the classroom by Hitler's censors. Scholz also took courses with Hans Freyer, who combined philosophy with sociology and was at times an overt Nazi. Freyer was known for supporting purges of anti-Nazi colleagues and, even when he was not directly involved in politics, for writings propounding racism, anti-Semitism, and authoritarianism.[12]

Sometime in the late 1920s, presumably during his years in Leipzig, Scholz joined the Sturmabteilung (SA), the brown-shirted "storm troops" of the Nazi Party. The SA was a kind of successor to the Freikorps and the Bund Oberland Club, members of which "constituted the core of the Sturmabteilung in Bavaria" by 1925. Like the Freikorps, the SA was a right-wing militia. The difference was that the SA was officially aligned with the Nazi Party, whereas the Freikorps had been an unofficial supporter of the German army. Historian Daniel Siemens describes the SA as "a highly centralized, nationwide organization that ultimately challenged the state's monopoly on violence." Commanded by Ernst Röhm, "a barrel-chested, scar-faced desperado" and former mercenary, the SA allowed Hitler to "cut out any dissent in the streets and portray himself" as "the strong arm needed to control the nation." Röhm saw the SA as "the most effective protection against the Bolshevizing of Germany and the rest of Europe" and deployed his forces to prevent Communists from disrupting Nazi Party speakers.[13]

Scholz's SA membership put a definitive end to the possibility that he would follow his family's expectations. The Scholz family were members of the *Bildungsbürgertum*, who emerged in the eighteenth and nineteenth centuries by accumulating material wealth through industry and thereby gaining social position. These privileged Germans were anchored in cities and emphasized education and the appropriation of elite culture and manners. They were, in other words, Germany's successful strivers: they had the wealth to compete with the upper class but not the breeding. The Bildungsbürgertum had to work for their place in society.[14]

The wearing of the brown shirt represented the ultimate rejection of Wilhelm Gustav Scholz's project, and of the Bildungsbürgertum. Wilhelm wanted his son to become a captain of industry; Herbert wanted to be a captain in the SA. Perhaps Herbert's political activity was a psychological rebellion aimed at his family and its values. And certainly the SA offered something precious to a searching youth like Scholz: a supportive community and a sense of identity— a connection to a project that mattered. "Today I attended the general mustering of the SA," Nazi propagandist Joseph Goebbels wrote in his diary in early 1931. "We can set ourselves to the great work now. Assault is followed by assault. Blood pours. Binder for the new community!" That blood, the binding agent of the SA, was the blood of Communists.[15]

It is difficult to recreate a profile of Scholz's work in the SA. His Nazi Party file at the Berlin Document Center contains no reference to his party status prior to June 1933. A US State Department interrogation of an unnamed source from July 1945 indicated that much of Scholz's efforts in the SA prior to 1933 consisted of "work for Hitler . . . outside of Germany," suggesting that the SA was putting his language skills to work. Such activities would have been in keeping with Röhm's view of his organization as an agent for the "Germanization" of Eastern Europe. Young Scholz's fluency in Hungarian would have been useful in this respect. While Scholz never had official diplomatic training, he may have had his introduction to the craft in the SA.[16]

But before Scholz was a diplomat—or, rather, a spy posing as a diplomat— he was a philosopher. He began writing his dissertation in 1930, under the direction of Werner Schingnitz, a student of Dreisch's who never reached the professional level of his mentor. In fact, of all the scholars on Scholz's dissertation committee, Schingnitz ranks last in order of distinction. But working with Schingnitz would prove a shrewd decision, although Scholz could not have foreseen this. What Scholz did know was that Schingnitz shared his own zeal for National Socialism. Schingnitz was arguably the top Nazi at the University of Leipzig and in November 1933 was appointed Nazi Party official responsible for *Philosophie und Weltanschauung* at the university. Shortly thereafter, he became head of the National Socialist Teachers League for Saxony. By the time he finished directing Scholz's thesis, Schingnitz had fully subordinated his intellectual life to Nazism. As a disciple of Schingnitz, Scholz was abandoning scholarly inquiry in favor of propagandizing on behalf of Nazi power.[17]

Scholz was to take part in Schingnitz's great project: the crafting of *Philosophisches Wörterbuch (The Philosophical Dictionary)*, a survey history of German philosophy driven by the conviction that subordination to Nazism was the people's natural state. The work would outline advancements in "pure" German thinking and rescue it from Jewish influence. For instance, Schingnitz wrote an entry on Henri Bergson, arguing that the French-Jewish philosopher plagiarized his views from Arthur Schopenhauer and made this theft and bastardization palatable to unwitting Germans by employing "positivistic, Jewish mysticism." Schingnitz also attacked Edmund Husserl, the architect of what would become known as phenomenology, for engaging in "typical Jewish rationalism." Husserl had to be struck from the pantheon of German thinkers and in fact was ejected from his emeritus chair at the University of Freiburg in early 1933 "for being a Jew."[18]

Scholz's contribution would be to study the obscure nineteenth-century psychologist Oswald Külpe and write a dissertation that would serve as the basis for an entry in the dictionary. Külpe receives little attention today, but he was a significant early theorist of cognition and reflection—specifically, the role of thought processes in carrying out action. Formally speaking, Scholz's topic was Külpe's concept of "imageless thought": the effect of linking introspection and awareness to sensory content. But evidence suggests that Külpe was a Jew, so Scholz's real task was to prove Külpe's unworthiness as a German philosopher. Scholz's thesis was a brilliant piece of falsehood—impressive in its methods, with each claim leading inexorably to the next, but premised on an extremely unsound foundation. He accused Külpe of "duplicity" and deemed the man's entire corpus "problematic" and "illogical." Later, in his dictionary entry, Schingnitz charged that Külpe tried to "justify" an essentially Jewish philosophical system and impose it on Germans. Scholz submitted his thesis in April 1932 and was granted his doctorate.[19]

With his credential in hand, Scholz prepared to move into the public realm. "Herbert had some political aspirations," Ruth Dwight McVitty, heir to the Arm & Hammer baking soda fortune and a one-time girlfriend of Scholz, wrote after their break-up around 1930. His goal had never been to work as an academic but rather to gain firm grounding in Nazi political philosophy and put a Nazi seal on his education, thereby positioning himself for upward mobility in Hitler's regime.[20]

Scholz's first job after receiving his doctorate may seem quite menial, but, in a stroke of good fortune, he wound up in the perfect position for a young Nazi on the make. Scholz became a secretary to the Deutsch-Japanische Gesellschaft—the German-Japanese Society in Berlin, which managed Japanese and German scholarly exchanges and sought to tighten cultural relations between the two countries. Scholz had no expertise concerning Japan, and the job placed him outside the loop of Nazi bureaucracy. But the German-Japanese Society happened to be run by Hitler's private secretary, Rudolf Hess. Unlike Scholz, Hess had a genuine interest in Japan and was a kind of Nazi resident expert on the country and its place in global affairs. But if Scholz was ignorant of Japan, he was carefully attuned to power. Reporting directly to Hess, Scholz was routinely face-to-face with the man who was always by the führer's side.

Indeed, soon after Scholz arrived at the German-Japanese Society in 1932, Hess became an even more important figure. That summer Hitler broke with the powerful socialist-leaning Nazi politician Gregor Strasser, forced Strasser out, and consolidated his own grip on the party. One of his first moves was to name Hess chair of the party's Central Political Commission. Then, shortly after Hitler gained the chancellorship in 1933, Hess was appointed deputy führer. Scholz's entry-level job was now a direct conduit to the second most powerful person in Germany.

But Scholz was also stuck between two camps engaged in an epic power struggle. On one side was Röhm, who sought a socialist restructuring of the German economy and wanted to amalgamate the SA into the Reichswehr, Germany's regular army. On the other side were Hess and Himmler. Both opposed socialism as an existential threat to the regime. They also had different plans for the military and the future of German rearmament, as the country's forces were still limited by the terms of the Versailles Treaty. As SS commander, Himmler wanted his own troops to reconstitute the military, and Hess was in his corner. Scholz was torn between allegiance to Röhm and the SA, on one hand, and Hess on the other. But Scholz ultimately put his lot in with Hess and Himmler. When Scholz began at the German-Japanese Society, he was also "foreign policy officer in the ministerial office of the supreme SA leadership." By the time he ended his association with the society in 1933, he was an officer in the SS.[21]

This transition was a complex one, and it is not entirely clear how Scholz became deregistered with the SA and signed up with the SS. The move certainly came at the right time, though. In 1932, just as Scholz was finishing his dissertation, it was revealed that Röhm was gay. Hitler, a long-time Röhm ally, downplayed his sexual activity in private, but Hess, Himmler, Goebbels, and other Nazi potentates lined up against Röhm and pressed Hitler to be rid of the SA chief. Germany was a democracy at the time, and the revelation of Röhm's homosexual acts was weighing the party down, not least because gay sex was a crime according to Germany's Basic Law. The Nazis were not Germany's only nationalistic or conservative party, which meant that a scandal had real potential drive voters into the ranks of the competition.[22]

It may have been Schingnitz, Scholz's academic advisor, who engineered Scholz's move from Röhm's SA to Himmler's SS. The source of the outcry surrounding Röhm was his leaked correspondence with Karl-Günther Heimsoth, a physician and astrologer based in Leipzig. As the Nazi cultural-political officer in that city, Schingnitz was involved in the official response. When it became clear that Röhm had asked Heimsoth to decipher whether the time and date of his birth caused his homosexuality, Schingnitz was ordered to purge the Leipzig-based Astrological Society. This is how Schingnitz became privy to the inner circle's opinions of Röhm. Naturally, Schingnitz would have wanted his recent star graduate to get out from under Röhm's aegis. It is possible, then, that Schingnitz pulled strings on Scholz's behalf, resulting in the appearance of a peculiar May 26, 1933, letter in Scholz's personnel file. There is no letterhead or return address on the document, and the signature below the closing "Heil Hitler" is indecipherable. The letter, addressed to no one in particular, states that Scholz had been moved into the "Brown House Group" and would "therefore leave . . . his previous *Ortsgruppe*"—that is, his local branch of the SA.[23]

Wherever the opportunity came from, the chance to move into the Brown House was not to be missed. A freshly renovated palace just off the Königs-platz in Munich, the Brown House was the headquarters of Nazi leadership. Hitler, Himmler, Hess, Goebbels, and top Nazi politician Hermann Göring all maintained offices in the Brown House. On special occasions, a quasi-shrine on the first floor displayed the *Blutfahne*, the blood-stained Swastika flag carried during the Beer Hall Putsch of November 1923—the failed Nazi coup attempt against the Weimar regime, which introduced many Germans to Hitler and became a galvanizing moment for the young party. Scholz had arrived at the nerve center of Nazism. On a daily basis, he was face-to-face with the "true believers," as historian Arnold Krammer called them. People "whose blind faith, considerable administrative skills, and public appeal helped make Hitler successful." As for Röhm, his presence at the headquarters was "as good as never," according to Ernst "Putzi" Hanfstaengel, a Hitler confidante and Nazi press secretary who also had an office in the Brown House.[24]

On June 26, 1933, exactly one month after his removal from the SA, Scholz accepted an appointment as *Sturmbannführer* in the SS, a rank similar to that of an army major. Himmler was seeking educated men for leadership positions in the SS, and Scholz took the opportunity. Here was a signal of Scholz's political acumen. At this point it was not yet clear whether the SA or SS, Röhm or Himmler and Hess, would win the day. Hitler and Röhm were devoted friends, and Röhm was doing all he could to maintain his influence. His SA was also popular with the public and vastly larger than the SS; whereas the SA had more than 3 million members in 1934, just two years earlier the SS numbered only 50,000. The SS also had not yet achieved its vaunted place within the wider Nazi organizational structure and was still proving itself as the locus of unconditional loyalty to Hitler. For Scholz, sticking with Röhm would have been a big risk, but casting his lot with Himmler and Hess was no sure thing, either. Scholz's gamble would pay off.[25]

It was in his role at the SS that Scholz became involved in espionage. Himmler assigned him to the Berlin-based *Verbindungsstab*, the Liaison Staff of the deputy führer, which was Hess's personal office. "Among other duties," the office "oversaw the activities of German agents abroad." Scholz also was the SS reporter on the ideological devotion of German Foreign Office representatives, many of whom were career civil servants without Nazi connections and so were politically suspect. It was Scholz's job to gauge the zeal of each German diplomat and suggest remedies if their dedication to Nazism was insufficient. Scholz thrived in the role, and less than six months after joining the Verbindungsstab was promoted to the rank of *Obersturmbannführer*, equivalent to a lieutenant colonel in the German army.[26]

The work of the Verbindungsstab included domestic matters, such as pressing for the union of industry and the state. But many historians see the agency primarily as a spy hub. This function was created by Hess, who considered himself an espionage specialist. Whereas other offices, such as Reinhard Heydrich's *Sicherheitsdienst*, handled domestic intelligence, foreign intelligence and surveillance of party members abroad were the Verbindungsstab's brief. British Intelligence described the Verbindungsstab simply as "the intelligence agency set up by Hess." Curt Riess, one of the few German anti-Nazi journalists fluent in English, had a more revealing take. In 1941 he wrote, "The Liaison Staff had three basic principles: Everyone can spy; Everyone must spy; Everything can be found out."[27]

Herbert Scholz had not set out to be a spy, but life took him in unexpected directions.

A Family Affair

"She is a lovely looking creature," William Castle, a former US ambassador to Japan, wrote of Liselotte von Schnitzler after meeting her at a resort hotel in Hot Springs, Virginia. Her uncle, Herbert von Dirksen, had been the German ambassador to Japan, and from 1938 to 1939 served Hitler as ambassador to Great Britain. Lilo, as she was known, possessed a keen mind, impressive language skills, and was "tall and blonde, with beautiful blue eyes." In the late 1920s she spent two years in London studying English, and in the early 1930s she moved to Paris and spent two more years at the Sorbonne, receiving a diploma in "the study of French Civilization." At Hot Springs in 1938, she conversed with Ambassador Castle about Hitler's recent meeting with Mussolini. "She wanted me to know there was perfect harmony in every way," Castle wrote of his chat with the beguiling Lilo. "She's a pretty good politician."[28]

In addition to her intellect, beauty, and political skills, Lilo possessed stature in Berlin society. Her grandfather, Paul Wilhelm Schnitzler, was a member of the hereditary Prussian aristocracy and sat on the supervisory board of IG Farben, the multinational chemical concern that would become a key industrial ally of the Nazi war effort, manufacturing fuel, explosives, rubber, plastics, medicine, and the Zyklon B gas used to murder Jews and others during the Holocaust. In 1945 General Lucius Clay, the American deputy military governor of Germany, called Farben "the largest and most influential chemical company in the world." Lilo's father Georg followed in his father's footsteps at Farben and by 1934 was a board member and its chief sales director, making him a man of consequence in prewar Germany.[29]

Lilo was an early adopter of Nazism. By the early 1930s she was "almost a steady guest at the [Reich] Chancellery." Hitler was not yet in power, or fully accepted by Berlin society, but, according to Curt Riess, Lilo "was philosophical about it." For her, "it was perhaps just as well to be on the inside" in case the Nazis did take over. Journalist Bella Fromm claimed that both Lilo and her mother Lilly, a Berlin socialite, "asserted themselves as ardent Nazis." The Nazis, of course, kept rising, and by 1933 Lilo had had her pick of the Berlin bachelor scene. *Washington Post* society reporter Evelyn Peyton Gordon even hinted at a brief flirtation with Hitler. While at the Frankfurt train station in 1933, Lilo suddenly looked up to see Hitler sitting in a car across the platform. The führer was staring at her intently with a "penetrating gaze," which "made her heart nearly stop beating." She wished to greet him, but "emotion choked me," she recalled. Later, when they met again in Berlin, Hitler referred to Lilo as "lovely," and she called him "wonderful—just too wonderful." Riess suggested that Lilo was "a presence in Hitler's house" and that this is where she met Herbert Scholz. They quickly fell in love and decided to marry.[30]

As an SS officer, Scholz could not marry just anyone. In late 1931 Himmler had issued an "engagement and marriage order," which sought to ensure that members of the SS created "hereditarily healthy" and "Nordic" families. The SS considered German women to be "the protectors of the most holy source of blood and life," historian Lisa Pine has written. In practice this meant that Scholz and other SS men were obliged to have their fiancés vetted by Himmler's office for racial suitability.[31] The process was not a smooth one, as Himmler's aides became obsessed by a potentially non-Aryan ancestor of Lilo's, one Jean David of Boezinge, Belgium, who sounded like he could be a Jew. Much sleuthing only left more questions, but eventually a Belgian curate sent a notarized copy of the Roman Catholic baptismal certificate of Matheus Benedictus David, Jean David's son. It was not definitive proof of Lilo's Aryan bloodline, but it was enough to satisfy the administrative requirement, and on March 26, 1934, Himmler granted his permission. Scholz and his intended had no idea what was going on behind the scenes; all they knew was that their request to marry was approved. It was another moment of good fortune for Herbert Scholz, not least because the relationship with Lilo and her family would be integral to his future and may even have saved his life.[32]

Scholz's peril was a product of his SA background, and Röhm was trying to make a case of it. It took Röhm some time to discover that Himmler had poached Scholz, but when Röhm found out in June 1934, he exploded with rage. In a scathing letter to Himmler, Röhm complained bitterly that Scholz had been commandeered. Scholz, Röhm argued, had been "lifted" by the SS in a manner both "illegal and illegitimate" because the SA had not approved the decision. Ever the devious administrator, Himmler replied that the move "was not . . . against the norms of the SA because Scholz was not officially listed as a member of the SA on the day of his promotion."[33] This of course was a consequence of Scholz's mysterious deregistration the previous year. Himmler had covered all his bases. On its face, the exchange is hardly extraordinary, but it does reveal something important: Röhm's utter naïveté about what was coming next for him. At this very moment, Himmler and Göring were assembling a hit list of Nazis who had to be gotten rid of in order to firmly and finally establish the supremacy of the SS and its leadership within the party. High on the list was Röhm, who, oblivious to the threats against him, was busy warring with Himmler over the departmental status of Herbert Scholz. The question for Scholz was whether his new status would save him, or whether Himmler would turn on him as well.[34]

In short order Himmler convinced Hitler that Röhm was plotting to over-throw him and take over the party. Historians doubt that there was any sub-stance to the allegation; nevertheless, from June 30 to July 2, at Himmler's direction, "the Schutzstaffel executed without trial an unknown number of Sturm Abteilung members."[35] The SS also targeted three of the most recent chancellors of the Weimar Republic, resulting, respectively, in their arrest, exile, and murder. In total, thousands were arrested and hundreds executed. Concentration camps began to open to take in the detainees. Röhm was ex-ecuted in dramatic fashion at Munich's Stadelheim Prison on July 1. The purge became known as the Night of the Long Knives.

As for Scholz, Columnist Helen Lombard contended that he "barely es-caped assassination." According to Fromm, this was thanks to Himmler, who "seems to have saved Scholz's skin from the general purge." Riess, however, put the credit elsewhere, arguing that Scholz's survival was only "due to Schnitzler's influence"—Georg von Schnitzler, that is, Lilo's father. All we know for certain is that Scholz and other SS men with former SA connec-tions were sidelined for nearly a month. Scholz's personnel file states that he "left Berlin in a hurry, hiding out in Bavaria, in the vicinity of [Lake] Chiemsee" from June 30 to July 27.[36]

There is some reason to believe that it was the Schnitzler connection that saved Scholz. Most importantly, Schnitzler was a major donor to the Nazi cause. In February 1933, with Nazi coffers running dry just ahead of a cru-cial round of elections, Hitler asked a group of leading industrialists for do-nations. At the time, big business was flocking to the Nazis as a bulwark against the Communists, who had made gains in the 1932 election. Schnitzler was one of the businessmen who stepped up. "While others hesitated, von Schnitzler made the first substantial contribution . . . without even bothering to consult his board," columnist Sylvia Porter wrote, alleging that Schnitzler promised a million Reichsmarks on the spot. More recently Adam LeBor and Roger Boyes put the figure at 400,000 Reichsmarks. Whatever the exact sum, it was "the largest single contribution from German industry to the Nazi coffers." Hitler owed debts to Schnitzler, which would tend to improve the standing of his future son-in-law. On July 27 Himmler ordered Röhm's successor, Viktor Lutze, "to return [Scholz] to the Reichsführer-SS for further use."[37]

Another reason to believe that Scholz received special treatment is that Rolf Reiner, a friend and former SA member who defected to the SS with Scholz, seems to have met with a very different fate. Unlike Scholz, Reiner was arrested and imprisoned. Journalist Martha Dodd insisted that Reiner was eventually released from prison and "came out pale, with his hair shorn, having missed execution by the skin of his teeth." Stephen H. Roberts disagreed, claiming that Reiner was executed after an extrajudicial hearing. What we do know is that Reiner's name is conspicuously absent from an August 22 memo confirming the final transfer of Scholz and two other former SA members back to SS ranks.[38] Scholz certainly was the luckier. This latest round of good fortune behind him, he married Lilo on September 22, 1934.

The day of the wedding coincided two events that testify to the Nazi effort to subordinate Christianity to the state. In the Berlin Sportspalast, Dr. Ludwig Mueller, of the Nazi Protestant German Christians, was consecrated *Reichsbishop* in a ceremony laden with "hundreds of swastika flags." The *New York Times* reported, "There was literally nothing in the hall to remind an observer that they were in a Christian assembly." Christians in brown Storm Troop uniforms shouted, "'Heil!' and again 'Heil!' and on all sides arms were raised in the Hitler salute."[39]

If some Protestants were moving closer to Hitler, Roman Catholics were finding only distance. Across town, at the Reich's Chancellery, diplomatic negotiations between Hitler's government and the Holy See collapsed. Vatican Secretary of State Eugenio Pacelli was infuriated by Hitler's refusal to abide by the 1933 German-Vatican Concordat, which guaranteed the rights of the Catholic Church in Germany, in exchange for political quiescence to the Nazi state. But the Germans violated the agreement routinely, and Cardinal Pacelli threatened a papal denunciation of Hitler's tactics. By 1934 Pacelli considered Nazi persecution of Catholics to be "of greater harshness and arbitrariness" than Bismarck's Kulturkampf.[40]

Yet the Christian Front never seemed concerned that the Nazis were bridling Christianity and undermining Catholic institutions, thus Moran could embrace the likes of Scholz when the chance came. Within a few months of his wedding, Scholz was posted to the United States, a respite from the backstabbing of Berlin and Munich and a means to escape scrutiny after the Night of the Long Knives, which quickly was becoming known as the Röhm Putsch. For Moran, inculcated as he was in German nationalism and the German language, Scholz was a gift from the heavens—no matter that the Nazis were, in their own way, cleansing Christianity from their realm as effectively as the Soviets or the Popular Front.

Father Coughlin, speaking in Boston at the former Braves Field in 1936.
Boston Herald-Traveler Photo Morgue, Boston Public Library

Five members of the Christian Front pose with their rifles during target-shooting practice in Narrowsburg, New York, fall 1939. Macklin Boettger (second from left) and John Viebrock (second from right) were two of the group's top organizers and leaders of its paramilitary wing. Bettmann/Getty Images

A cache of weapons, ammunition, and homemade bombs found by the FBI in the Brooklyn home of Christian Front member John Viebrock. Bettmann/Getty Images

John Cassidy (left) and William Bishop, two key members of the alleged Christian Front plot to overthrow the US government, on January 15, 1940, after their arrests. *New York Post* Archives/Getty Images

Members of the Christian Front on trial in New York, April 3, 1940. Lawyer Leo Healy, holding a sheet of paper, poses with defendants. Shutterstock

Francis Moran, New England director of the Christian Front, on January 16, 1940, the day after the New York Christian Front arrests were reported in the press. *Boston Herald-Traveler* Photo Morgue, Boston Public Library

Father Charles Coughlin shakes hands with Massachusetts Governor James Michael Curley at the State House, Boston, on August 13, 1935. *Boston Herald-Traveler* Photo Morgue, Boston Public Library

Father Coughlin (right) receives a headdress, making him chief of the Tea Party group of Massachusetts, August 17, 1936. *Boston Herald-Traveler* Photo Morgue, Boston Public Library

The German Consulate in Boston at 39 Chestnut Street, where Christian Front leader Francis Moran secretly met with Consul Herbert W. Scholz, an SS officer and Nazi spy, in July 1940. Courtesy of Revolutionary Spaces

Ernst Röhm, cofounder with Adolf Hitler of the militia Sturmabteilung (Storm Battalion), was a mentor to Herbert Scholz, the German consul who provided direction to the Christian Front in Boston. ullstein bild Dtl./Getty Images

Herbert Scholz with his American girlfriend Ruth Dwight McVitty at Zugspitze, Germany's highest peak, in 1930. McVitty was heir to the Arm & Hammer baking soda fortune. Courtesy of Antony Taquey

Herbert Scholz, reading the news of President Roosevelt's order closing all German consulates on June 16, 1941. *Times Wide World/Redux*

Boston Christian Front leader Francis Moran shows off the group's pamphlets. In January 1942 police seized these and other materials from Hibernian Hall in Roxbury. *Boston Herald-Traveler* Photo Morgue, Boston Public Library

Boston Police Commissioner Joseph Timilty displays two books
distributed by the Christian Front, which were declared Nazi
propaganda and banned from sale in the city on January 5, 1942.
Boston Herald-Traveler Photo Morgue, Boston Public Library

Father Edward Lodge Curran,
president of the International
Catholic Truth Society of Brooklyn
and principal theologian of the
Christian Front. Curran, who was
also a lawyer, developed the
defense strategy used by the New
York fronters at their 1940 trial and
worked frequently with the front's
Boston unit during the group's
public, underground, and postwar
phases. Irving Haberman / IH Images /
Getty Images

CHAPTER 7

Hitler's Spymaster on Beacon Hill

FOR THOSE WHO WERE WILLING TO TAKE SERIOUSLY THE "PARA-noid fringe," there were plenty of warning signs concerning the German consul. In the summer of 1940, around the same time Mary Brandegee shared her suspicions with Virgil Peterson at the Boston FBI Office, no fewer than three government officials involved in national security and foreign policy raised the prospect that Herbert Scholz was up to no good.

The first was FBI Special Agent L. K. Cook. On June 4, 1940, he sent a memorandum to FBI Assistant Director Hugh Clegg explaining that he, Cook, was developing a possible informant who had a close relationship with Scholz. What exactly Cook suspected is unclear. In Scholz's FBI file, which was released in 2017 under the Freedom of Information Act, the Cook-Clegg memorandum is highly redacted: it is not known whether the memo spells out evidence that Scholz was using his position to spy on the United States or engage in propaganda activities. We do know from the memo that Scholz was pressing the potential informant to join a small circle of German Americans who had regular, secret meetings with the consul. Through an intermediary, the potential informant told the FBI he was "anxious to coop-erate with American authorities" but at the same time was hesitant to "con-tact the Bureau himself because he felt it would endanger his life." US au-thorities may have thought Scholz benign, but this informant believed otherwise, figuring he could not rely even on the FBI to protect him from the SS man.[1]

Given the sensitivity of snooping around a foreign diplomat, Cook needed permission to pursue his lead. Clegg passed the request along to Hoover, and on June 12 the FBI director wrote to Peterson, encouraging him to interview the middleman who was talking to Cook on behalf of the potential informant. But in closing Hoover warned that Peterson "should not, of course, conduct any investigation in this matter relative to Herbert Scholz, the German consul, without specific authority from the Bureau." That authorization never came. An unsigned June 26 State Department memo claimed the FBI had opened an investigation into Scholz, but this was a false alarm. The FBI neither took up Cook's lead nor opened an investigation of Scholz in June 1940.[2]

On the same day the State Department put out its erroneous memo, Lieutenant D. J. Harkins of the Office of Naval Intelligence wrote to his superiors in Washington, urging them to pay attention to "the situation in Boston." Harkins, who was posted to the Boston headquarters of the First Naval District, deemed "it best to review entirely the facts concerning the Boston situation because present-day happenings indicate that nothing can be considered too far-fetched and fantastic." The happenings in question were the New York Christian Front's alleged seditionist activities. Only two days earlier, the fronters had been let off at trial. Harkins did not join the public and the Catholic hierarchy in discarding the New Yorkers as mere crackpots; he considered the New York fronters genuinely dangerous and feared that others like them were operating in Boston, potentially at Scholz's direction. Writing to Captain Elliott Bodley Nixon, the Office of Naval Intelligence's counterespionage chief, Harkins described Scholz as "an Obersturmengruppenführer in the Schutz Staffel (Colonel of the elite Himmler Black Shirt Guards) . . . who is very clever and thorough" and who "might have approached or been approached by extremist elements" in Boston. In particular, Harkins worried that Scholz was targeting "meetings of persons who are interested in combating Communism."[3]

Harkins dared to take the paranoid fringe at face value, and his instincts were correct. But Nixon never responded or set any investigations in motion. Instead he shelved the memo for a year. The fact was that Nixon was more concerned about Harkins than Scholz. Under Nixon, Navy intelligence was "plunged . . . into the dark world of spies, surveillance, and secret operations" at home. Mole hunts are common side effects of counterintelligence, and Nixon thought Harkins himself might be a Nazi spy. Only on June 27, 1941, did the Harkins memorandum finally make its way to the FBI.[4]

A third official who was wise to Scholz was Roosevelt's deputy undersecretary of state, Sumner Welles. "Are you sure that the FBI is doing all that it should be doing in this very important matter?" Welles asked Assistant Secretary of State Adolf Berle, the State Department's point person on security. "I have every reason to believe that Dr. Scholz is doing far more than merely giving Sunday night suppers at his house." But Welles, writing on July 5, 1940, was too quick on the draw. America's fledgling intelligence apparatus was not yet ready to focus on the likes of Scholz. Even after the United States entered the war, "Nazi secret service covert penetration . . . was considered a distant priority," according to historian Christopher Vasey. It was the Japanese who attacked the United States and forced Washington to join the conflict, and it was the Japanese who got most of the attention. Nazi espionage in the United States was in fact robust, including successful efforts to recruit conservative Protestants and former KKK members to form an organization similar to the Christian Front. But no one was listening to Welles in 1940, just as no one was listening to Harkins, Cook, and Brandegee.[5]

Moran, however, was listening to Scholz, and the leader of the Boston Christian Front liked what he was hearing. The first known meeting between the two men came in late July 1940, although it is probable that their relationship began earlier. Joining the July meeting was Dr. Heribert von Strempel, a German aristocrat and the first secretary of the German Embassy in Washington. But Strempel, like Scholz, was not just a diplomat. While under interrogation after the war, Strempel admitted that he was also the chief administrator of "the fund called the *Schmiergeld*," which the Nazis used to make payments to their US agents.[6] This made Strempel—again, by his own admission—"one of the major pay-off men for German propaganda activities in the United States." During the July 1940 meeting, Strempel "explained to Moran that he represented a German-American group in New York which was interested in his work." Thus did Moran find his next outstretched hand, emanating from the German Consulate.

Working with diplomats was no doubt intoxicating for Moran. Even better, one of them was a baron. Moran's fluent German, and the firm respect for German culture and nationalism he had learned at the seminary, stood him well. And payments from Strempel's fund would stabilize the Christian Front's finances. In return, Scholz would gain a useful agent in Boston. In his postwar interview, Scholz explained that, before he took up with Moran, he had found it difficult to do serious propaganda work in the city and the wider region.

"I had no German-American Bund or other German societies to help me," he said. Boston was not a heavily German area, and, in any case, German nationals and societies were the focus of intense surveillance by US intelligence and law enforcement agencies. US officials presumed that only German immigrants and citizens of German extraction would be tempted to spy for the fatherland.[7]

That made Moran an extraordinary asset: a homegrown American who was known for his patriotism. Moran was strongly associated with Catholicism, Americanism, and anti-Communism, but he was not widely recognized as an anti-Semite. It was only Jewish activists, undercover journalists like Derounian, and SS officers like Scholz who seemed to recognize Moran's latent Nazi potential. And as a US citizen, he benefited from the full range of constitutional protections, making him difficult to investigate. Indeed, because his organization was religious in nature, Moran was powerfully insulated from government scrutiny. Religious freedom may not have inoculated Moran against suspicion, but it did mean that law enforcers and intelligence agents would have a hard time penetrating the Christian Front. This was especially so after the trial had ended without guilty verdicts. To go after the Christian Front again might be perceived by the public as an unconscionable exercise in double jeopardy, which would leave the FBI and others extra cautious.

There was a potential snag, however. Although Moran was a convinced, if semi-covert, anti-Semite, he was not an obvious friend of Nazis. He had publicly denounced aspects of Nazism, even as he justified Hitler's oppression of Jews. And by 1940 Moran was not looking for anyone or anything to believe in. He knew where he stood: he was as ardent a Catholic as one could hope to find, in lockstep with Church doctrine. Moran was as true a believer in the Mystical Body as Hess and Himmler were in the wisdom of National Socialism. The Swastika could never have replaced the sign of the Cross, Hitler could never have replaced Coughlin, and the German volk mattered to Moran only insofar as he understood them to be Christians under assault from Judeo-Bolshevism.

Moran was willing to do Scholz's bidding because he recognized that what was good for the Nazis was also good for the front and because he was able, ultimately, to reconcile Nazism with his faith in Christ. This is a critical point to remember, as we dive into Moran's career as a Nazi propagandist: he was never a double agent. Although he took orders from an SS officer, his allegiance remained firmly with Christ and with a Christian-nationalist view of

America. He was able to square the circle thanks to certain developments in Catholic thought. Perhaps counterintuitively, the most important of these developments was the Catholic embrace of the nascent doctrine of human rights. Indeed, Father Coughlin was one of the most forceful exponents of human rights in the United States at a time when the overwhelming majority of the public had never heard of the concept. Catholic human rights taught Coughlin, and Coughlin taught Moran, that all people could be saved by joining Christ's body. No one was so intrinsically tainted as to be beyond communion with the divine. Thus Moran could not align with Hitler in seeking to eliminate Jews as a race, for doing so denied the innate capacity of every Jew to become a Christian and therefore to be saved. But nor could humanity be saved in the absence of Christ's body, which Communists wished to destroy. Moran understood that Nazi racism was antithetical to his religion, but he also understood that, without his religion, there was no future for humanity. The Nazis were the enemy of Moran's enemy, and so became his friend.

A Catholic Makes Peace with Nazism

As we have seen, Moran strongly opposed certain elements of Nazi policy. In particular, he scorned Nazi efforts to tailor the human population with an eye toward "racial hygiene." Moran was pro-natalist, favoring policies that encouraged childbearing. But his interest here was spiritual rather than political. Raising a family was a religious good, not a matter of concern to the state—although Moran had no complaints about the state using its power to promote his preferred spiritual ends. In any case, the goal of his pro-natalism was to build Christian societies, whereas the goal of Nazi pro-natalism was to build Aryan societies, an objective that was meaningless to Moran. And as a doctrinaire Catholic, he could never have supported Nazi eugenic policies that allowed abortions on racial grounds. Most broadly, while the Nazis were driven by a particularistic interest in the fortunes of the German volk, Moran thought of himself as something very different: a humanist, concerned for the spiritual lives of all people rather than the political ambitions of any one nation.

Moran's humanism was not without complications, of course. His Judeo-Bolshevist anxieties made him profoundly anti-Semitic. But his anti-Semitism was religious and cultural in nature, not racial. Moran's anti-Semitism occupied a separate space; it was neither Nazi racism nor the old Catholic anti-Judaism. Catholic anti-Judaism reflected suspicion and condemnation of Christ killers, while Nazi anti-Semitism considered Jews racially impure. Moran's anti-Semitism, in contrast to both of these, was grounded in what historian Kenneth Stow calls "the centuries-old fear of Jewish pollution." On this view, the Jews were an ongoing challenge, not merely the unapologetic heirs to deicide. But the pollution Moran had in mind was not the genetic pollution the Nazis stamped out by means of the Final Solution. The problem from Moran's perspective was the Jewish propensity toward Communism, which he saw as an ontological deficiency within Judaism, not a biological deficiency within individual Jews. Recall Father Coughlin's distinction between good Jews, who upheld the covenant with God, and bad Jews—atheists who tried to destroy that covenant, and all religion, using the weapon of Communism. As always, Moran was in Coughlin's camp. Unlike Nazis, Moran thought Jews were redeemable, even if, in practice, many did not want to be redeemed and sought to prevent the redemption of others.[8]

Moran's refusal to countenance racial anti-Semitism was in keeping with "modern" Church positions that emerged from the revolutionary development of personalism in the nineteenth century. Within Catholicism, personalism was a response to scientific rationalism, evolutionary thought, and enlightenment political movements toward liberalism, on the one hand, and collectivism, on the other. Personalism encompasses a complex of views, full of nuance and driving toward diverse conclusions. Rather than explore personalism deeply here, it is enough to establish that the Catholic embrace of human rights and attendant anti-racialism followed from a theological focus on the person.

Moran imbibed his humanist ethic from Father Coughlin. What has gone unexamined by Coughlin's numerous biographers and in the 350-plus books written about him is that Coughlin was the first prominent priest in the United States to champion human rights. His human rights discourse started as early as 1934, with his "Sixteen Points of the National Union for Social Justice." In the last of these points, Coughlin announced, "I believe in preferring the sanctity of human rights to the sanctity of property rights." The "chief concern" of government should be the poor, whereas "the rich have ample means of their own to care for themselves." Or, as Coughlin put it in another context, "human rights must prevail over commercial rights greedily guarded by a few."[9]

These words are startling both because few today would associate a strident anti-Semite and Christian chauvinist like Coughlin with human rights discourse and because that discourse was virtually nonexistent in the 1930s. But Coughlin was consistent in his views. For instance, he fought a long rhetorical battle with the American Liberty League, a group of conservative businessmen, on the basis of human rights. "They minimize the sanctity of human rights," Coughlin said of the league bankers, who cared about only their "bonds and their assets." Under the Liberty League's philosophy, Coughlin argued, ordinary people "own no property, possess no human rights, [and] are economic slaves." So resolute was Coughlin in his human rights thinking that he even turned against his betters in the Catholic hierarchy, when he insinuated that William Cardinal O'Connell of Boston deserved criticism for allegedly supporting the league.[10]

Moran and the Christian Front repeatedly demonstrated their humanistic worldview and the anti-racialism this worldview inspired. One straightforward example is Moran's response to Max Bradley, a Boston-area pro-Nazi speaker who wanted to debate Moran on the question, "What, if anything, besides religion, do you hold against Hitler?" At the Christian Front meeting of July 1, 1940, Moran declared that he would never let Bradley take the stage. Moran "wanted to show his disapproval of Hitler's intolerance." As far as Moran was concerned, Roman Catholicism was a vehicle of salvation for all humanity and all humanity had the opportunity to accept Christ; as a Christian religious organization, the Christian Front was bound to promote this worldview. Nazi racists like Bradley would not be welcome because they eschewed the common humanity that true religion incorporated.[11]

Two weeks later, on July 15, an aggrieved Bradley showed up for the Christian Front meeting at Hibernian Hall and demanded to speak. He had come with what he called "definite proof that Teuton blood is whiter than any other kind of blood." But Moran refused even to discuss the issue. "The beliefs of the Front are diametrically opposed to those of Mr. Bradley," he thundered. An African American woman seated in the back of Hibernian Hall "stood up to state that she was living proof that Mister Bradley's theories were false." "Colored blood flows in my veins," she announced proudly. Bradley was hustled out of the hall without finishing his diatribe.[12]

It is worth lingering a moment on episodes like these, for they reveal much about the intellectual currents in which Moran and the Christian Front swam. Some historians have taken for granted that the Christian Front was grounded in white supremacy, but such assumptions betray a presentist mindset that fails to account for the kinds of nonracial bigotry exercised in 1930s and 1940s

America.[13] Certainly the front expressed views that overlapped with those of white supremacist organizations like the Klan. The front and the Klan were united against Communism, for instance. But the front did not join the Klan in mourning the Confederacy and promoting white supremacy. The front's anti-Semitism was a product of Catholic doctrine rather than racist beliefs; the front was anti-Semitic because it equated Jews with Communists and Communists with enemies of Christ, not because it saw Jews as insufficiently white or as race traitors. In fact, while American racists were lynching and sterilizing African Americans, agitating against "race mixing," and seeking to return African Americans to plantations—whether via forced prison labor or the renewal of slavery—the front allowed African Americans in their ranks. Joseph McWilliams, who was sometimes called "Joe McNazi," even recruited in Harlem. On one occasion he stormed into the neighborhood and inveighed against "the slave market of the North Bronx, where the Negro women stand around as if on a slave block and fat, lazy, kikes come around and offer them 15 cents an hour to clean their apartments." McWilliams claimed that the Christian Front would "mobilize all the Negroes" in Harlem and that, "on the day of reckoning, the Negroes will join with the Christians in annihilating the common enemy." Chillingly, McWilliams promised African Americans who responded to his call that they "would get first choice on his extermination squads."[14]

McWilliams's story is especially complicated because he had previously been associated with the Klan. But he must have bought into Coughlin's and the Catholic Church's turn toward human rights. By the time he was in New York, McWilliams was suffering the Judeo-Bolshevist fever, and he was prepared to spread the virus even among the Klan's racial enemies. African Americans were little interested in heeding the call, though. McWilliams's attempt to recruit Harlemites into the Christian Front came to nothing, according to a report for the NAACP by the Baptist minister and future US congressman Adam Clayton Powell, Jr. Powell also found no evidence of Christian Front organizing in Harlem beyond McWilliams's exhortations.[15]

Like McWilliams, Moran was happy to work with African Americans who shared his anti-Semitism, a position blessed implicitly by the modernizing, human rights–oriented Church. One of these African Americans was Lawrence Dennis, the Harvard-educated author of *The Coming American Fascism* (1936). Dennis has been called "a black voice in the right-wing wilderness," and Moran was proud of his autographed collection of Dennis's books. Moran told one FBI informant that he thought Dennis had "class."[16]

It is not my aim here to suggest that Moran held liberal positions on civil rights or that he was even representative of his community. Interactions like Moran and Dennis's were extraordinary in 1930s Boston, where white Catholics were noted for their "unhappy social prejudices." As historian William Leonard put it, "Very little truly interracial activity existed between white and black Catholic Bostonians during the first half of the twentieth century." My point, rather, is that we will misunderstand the Christian front's motivations if we insist that currently popular logics of racism and anti-Semitism held universally during the Christian Front's heyday. For Moran, Coughlin, and others in their camp, Catholic human rights simultaneously rejected racism and required anti-Semitism.[17]

It is via anti-Semitism that Moran and some other Catholics reconciled with Nazism. The humanism that rejected racial thought could also inspire an anti-Communist frenzy, which the Judeo-Bolshevist myth refracted into anti-Semitism. This much was clear in the work of German theologians such as Robert Linhardt, a Jesuit priest and author of the 1933 treatise *Constitutional Reform and Catholic Conscience*. Linhardt argued that Catholic political theory should welcome "the inalienable human rights of the person," as historian James Chappel recently put it. Linhardt also stressed "human dignity" as the backbone of Catholic political thought. Such statements led some to presume that Linhardt was a democrat, if not a socialist. But historian Kevin Spicer has confirmed that Linhardt "suppor[tted] the NSDAP in his preaching and teaching."[18]

This reckoning was possible, for Linhardt and others, because both Nazism and Catholic humanism were deeply opposed to Communism and because the Nazis, despite a fractious relationship with established churches, were not overtly hostile to Christianity itself. As Alfred Rosenberg, Hitler's most influential religious theorist, argued in *The Myth of the Twentieth Century*, Christianity needed to be "reformed and saved from the 'Judeo-Roman' infections of its clerical representatives." Reformed, not scrapped. Rosenberg was careful never to attack Jesus Christ.[19] Given the options— Fascism or Communism—the choice for Catholic humanists was clear. A theology of personalism and human rights could flourish only if Christ were present; under Communism there would be no such presence, whereas under

Fascism at least some form of the Mystical Body of Christ would survive. As a result, "anti-Communism was paramount."[20]

Nothing could be more important for the new, human-focused Catholicism than stemming the Communist advance, and so nothing could be more important than a war on Jews—even if the most able allies in that war were Nazi racists. Moran discovered this just as Lindhardt had.

The Propagandist

In October 1940 Moran described to Arthur Derounian the anatomy of the Christian Front's anti-Semitic message. "I never come out with the Jews," Moran explained, meaning that in his public speeches, he was careful not to explicitly attack Jews as such. "I always put it this way: Of course, it is too bad that Jewish leaders are leading astray the Jews of America . . . I consider most of them good people, but the leaders, tsk, tsk." Moran characterized this method as "slyly hitting at the Jews," and his experience suggested that "it works amazingly well." Indeed, "it is the ONLY approach in a town like Boston, where the people are conservative, yet resent open persecution of any minority," Moran said, admitting that his goal was indeed persecution. This sort of language was justified, Moran said, because the Christian Front was "sincerely engaged in fighting for Christianity, and against Communism."

Derounian, who at this point had been covertly following Moran for some two years, was alarmed. "The impression one gets is that this man is highly calculating, highly dangerous, a ruthless personality." While most governmental observers viewed Moran as nonthreatening and consistently downplayed the effectiveness of his activism, Derounian's opinion was the exact opposite. "This man strikes in the dark. He strikes like a rattler without warning. And his sting is apt to be deadly. Subversively, undercover, smiling in public, conniving in private, he is capable of shaking your hand and at the same time stabbing you in the back." Derounian's final assessment was perhaps his most astute. "He is far advanced as a propagandist," outdoing even "those in New York." "By every standard," Derounian concluded, "Moran's office, and Moran's position is that of propagandist."[21]

What Derounian did not know at this time was that Moran had taken on his propaganda role at Scholz's request and with the consul's assistance. In an astonishing 1943 interview with Derounian, again reporting undercover,

Moran confessed that he and Scholz had designed the propaganda strategy together:

> Scholz and I worked out this plan: you can't win this fight with terrorism—with storm troopers, or risk just yelling 'Jew.' You've got to lay the groundwork first. You've got to be subtle about it so that they can't pin an anti-Semitic label on you. We're all working for the same end. It's the tactics that are important. You can lose this fight with the wrong tactics.

Incredibly, this interview, which was published in the *New York Post*, prompted neither investigations nor legal action. Moran was admitting to being a foreign agent, even though he had not registered with the federal government under the Foreign Agents Registration Act. Somehow this too escaped the FBI.[22]

In aligning his religious anti-Semitism with Scholz's propaganda goals, Moran was agreeing to work for the fulfillment of one of Hitler's major wartime objectives, which was laid out in the Führer's Order of September 8, 1939, one week after Germany's invasion of Poland. The idea behind the Führer's Order was to prioritize a propaganda campaign "to persuade neutral states to take Germany's line." This approach was a good fit for Moran's style. He had never gone in for terrorism, thuggery, and intimidation. He was not a fistfighter like Carridi, a paramilitarist like Cassidy, or an aspiring executioner like McWilliams. Scholz was urging Moran to do what he was naturally good at. The consul saw Moran's gifts as clearly as Derounian had in the course of their 1940 interview.[23]

These gifts were on full display in June 1940, when Moran made his first propaganda ploy on Scholz's behalf. Whether Moran was at this point an agent working in Scholz's employ is unclear. The first documented meeting between the two men would not arrive for several weeks, when Moran visited Scholz and Strempel at the consulate on Beacon Hill. It is entirely possible that Scholz and Moran had communicated prior to this meeting, but if Moran was instead freelancing in June 1940, he was putting on quite a display. Either his propaganda effort was coming at Scholz's direction or it was an impressive audition, leading in short order to Moran's recruitment.

The precipitating event was the publication by the *Boston Herald-Traveler* of a scathing editorial about the führer. This was an unusual move by the newspaper. The staid and steady afternoon edition of the *Boston Herald*, the

Herald-Traveler had a reputation for taking positions on the nitty-gritty of local affairs, not geopolitics. But on May 28, 1940, two weeks after the Nazi blitzkrieg had overwhelmed Belgium and the Netherlands, the paper came out swinging. The editorial referred to Hitler as "a wild beast" possessing "satanic" methods. "Hitler is merely an ex-guttersnipe, a mediocre little man with a mediocre mind." Not mincing words, the editorial argued, "This creature Hitler will never be beaten by the rules of civilized warfare. Somebody needs to get right down in the gutter with him and fight the way he fights, only more cruelly." In conclusion, the newspaper waxed religious: "If a beneficent God cast an archangel into eternal fire, why should we be choosy about what we have to do to Hitler the Horrible and his horde?"[24]

In response Scholz made a formal démarche. The consulate's official word, issued in a letter to the editor by Consular Secretary Kurt Bohme, was that the *Herald-Traveler* had impugned "the head of a nation, with whom the United States of America entertains diplomatic relations." Hitler had been "insulted in such uncivilized expressions, that this Consulate in the future must refuse to give [the] paper any information in whatever matter it may be." The rejoinder backfired, earning condemnation all over Boston, as elites accused the consulate of trying to punish the newspaper for exercising rights protected by the constitution. Boston City Councilor Maurice Sullivan petitioned US Secretary of State Cordell Hull for the "immediate recall" of Scholz. The German consul "manifested an absolute disregard for the rights conferred upon the press through the American Constitution," Sullivan roared. He also urged the Boston City Council to classify "Scholz as a persona non grata in our city and in a nation where Americans still cherish their constitutional freedom." *Time* got hold of the story and reported that "some half-dozen New England Congressmen" and "three Senators rose to defend the freedom of the press."[25]

Moran immediately came to Scholz's defense. On June 5 he wrote a long letter to the *Herald-Traveler*, a strange but agile apologia. "For Hitler we have no sympathy nor condemnation," he wrote ambiguously, but the paper was in the wrong employing language "meant to stir up hatred." Turning around the editors' religious rhetoric, Moran wrote, "No Christian is justified in fighting for hatred." The author of the editorial must have been "controlled" by an outside force, Moran asserted—the Jews, presumably. Are American newspapermen, he asked, "being forced to write against their will?" Returning to the theme of Christianity, Moran closed by excoriating the editorial writer for "placing yourself on par with Almighty God; comparing your ability to judge with His, and thus justifying yourself: Unspeakable!"[26]

The *Herald-Traveler* made no reply and did not print the letter. So Moran repackaged his missive as a handsomely styled handbill titled, "An Open Letter for Every American with a Sense of Fairness." He printed hundreds of copies and on June 8 dispatched Christian Front members to distribute them during the annual parade commemorating the Yankee Division homecoming of 1919—the return of the Boston-based 26th Infantry Division at the close of World War I. A major affair, the 1940 parade featured 25,000 World War I veterans and 5,000 National Guard troops with slung rifles, marching through the city to Boston Common. More than a hundred thousand Bostonians braved downpours to celebrate their veterans and guardsmen. And some of these attendees went home with Moran's flyer defending Hitler and his Boston consul.[27]

It is difficult to gauge whether the handbill effort was effective, but what is clear is that in the spring and summer of 1940, as the New Yorkers were on trial and the future of the front appeared uncertain, Moran was developing a pro-Nazi mindset. He was not persuaded of Nazi ideology, but he was all in for the defense of Christ and Catholicism against the Judeo-Bolshevist menace and the Nazis were natural partners in this cause. This position might have been hard to square with the reality that, at the time, the Nazis were still treaty allies with the Soviets, the ultimate Judeo-Bolshevists and chief enemy of Christianity globally. But the anti-Semitism Moran shared with the Nazis was enough to dissolve any doubts that might have crept into his mind. And by July Moran was empowered to take essentially any political action he wished, as long as he could find support—which Scholz and Strempel provided. Working under the auspices of a religious organization, Moran could shield himself and his patrons from scrutiny. He was not Scholz's only man in Boston—several others, involved in more traditional espionage, rounded out Scholz's stable of agents. But Moran became the most successful. The second half of 1940 and first half of 1941 would be heady days for the Boston Christian Front, thanks to the partnership with Scholz, Hitler's spymaster and Boston's highest-ranking Nazi.

CHAPTER 8

Rifles and Rhetoric

IN MAY 1934 DR. HEINRICH BRÜNING BURNED HIS PERSONAL PAPERS and fled Germany. Brüning had been chancellor of the Weimar Republic from 1930 until 1932, navigating the ship of state through the thick of the Depression. Now he was just steps ahead of the Gestapo, the secret police controlled by Himmler. Brüning probably would have been caught but for the aid of an unlikely guardian. "Goebbels saved my life," Brüning later recalled. Joseph Goebbels, the Nazi propaganda chief, had gotten word to Brüning's secretary, urging that the former chancellor "not go by the usual streets." Brüning needed to get far away. He took a position in the political science department at Harvard and headed to Boston.[1]

Brüning spent his first few years at Harvard in isolation, concentrating on teaching and academic affairs. He "resided like a monk" and rarely spoke out on events in Germany. But then came November 1938 and Kristallnacht. Brüning broke his silence with a flurry of highly charged articles characterizing Hitler and his men as "torturers" of Jews and predicting that Nazism would soon die out. Herbert Scholz did not like the sound of that. Himmler's henchman arrived in Boston just as Brüning's press campaign was gaining momentum. There is every reason to suspect that Scholz was sent to Boston specifically to seal Brüning's lips again, but no one connected these events at the time. The American press speculated that Scholz's assignment was a demotion following an unspecified diplomatic faux-pas in Washington.[2]

Scholz spent part of his first year in Boston investigating Brüning and devising a scheme to undermine him. Then, in October 1939, Brüning received a stunning letter from the consulate. The German Foreign Office, Scholz explained, had "received certain information" to the effect that the former chancellor would spend the upcoming semester lecturing at the University of Oxford. Scholz reminded Brüning that Germany and Britain were at war and asked that Brüning contact him to "discuss the matter . . . now." Brüning made no reply. His plans were not public knowledge, which meant that Scholz was spying on him.[3]

Brüning had every reason to feel threatened. He knew Scholz's father in law, Georg von Schnitzler, and the implications of that relationship: Scholz was close to the heights of Nazi power. Indeed, via Schnitzler, Brüning likely was aware that Scholz had spent time at the Brown House and was now an SS officer, which meant he took orders from Himmler, the man whose death squads Brüning had narrowly escaped. Describing the "purge list" compiled for the Night of the Long Knives, Brüning told an interviewer, "I was at the head. Then came Schleicher. They got Schleicher." Former Chancellor Kurt von Schleicher and his wife were murdered in a hail of bullets on June 30, 1934, as they answered a knock on the door. Brüning harbored no illusions about Scholz and worried both for himself and for loved ones back in Germany. Refusing to respond to Scholz was a tactical mistake, though. Soon more letters arrived, each one adding to Brüning's fears.[4]

Scholz's interventions had their intended effect, scaring Brüning into quiescence just as his anti-Hitler activities were beginning to take off. These included not only outspoken protests but also clandestine efforts to directly undermine the Nazi regime, such as Brüning's behind-the-scenes backing of Adam von Trott, a German diplomat and early Nazi resister. In November 1939 Trott wrote a sensitive memorandum to the State Department "soliciting the assistance of . . . individuals in the United States in supporting a movement involving the overthrow of the present regime in Germany." Brüning arranged for Trott to meet with Assistant Secretary of State George S. Messersmith, perhaps the foremost anti-Nazi in the State Department at that time. But in the wake of Scholz's harassment, Brüning cut off contact with Trott. The dissident found no further support in the United States, and his influence campaign went nowhere, as the country remained stubbornly on the sidelines of the war in Europe until 1942. Trott returned to Germany and continued his work, eventually getting the noose in 1944 after joining Colonel Claus von Stauffenberg's plot to assassinate Hitler.[5]

The intimidation campaign against Brüning was hardly the only intelligence work Scholz did for the SS while stationed in Boston. Scholz was not in Boston long—by summer 1941, he was expelled from the United States along with the rest of Germany's diplomatic corps. But his sojourn was an energetic one and often fruitful. He owed his effectiveness to a number of factors. One was his own creativity. Scholz pursued a range of activities, from coercion of dissenters to secret and overt information warfare. One day he developed intelligence, and the next he engaged in sabotage. His stable of agents included Fascist- and Communist-sympathizers alike. A true master of spy craft, Scholz knew every trick in the book and many besides.

A second source of Scholz's accomplishments was the ineptitude of US security officials. Virgil Peterson, a Chicagoan whose true interest lay in busting that city's organized crime syndicates, never got the hang of counterintelligence or counterterrorism. From the vantage point of history, it seems that, as far as Peterson was concerned, bad guys were motivated by money, not God or politics. He spent his years in Boston a passive observer of both the Christian Front and its Nazi handlers. Meanwhile officials in Washington were stuck in neutral. The American public was well and truly at odds with itself over the war in Europe, making a concerted counterespionage effort politically contentious. For every member of Congress who wanted the national security apparatus to do more to root out German agents, there was another who insisted that there were no such agents. These politicians did not consider Hitler a friend, but did he really need to be an enemy? It is also worth keeping in mind that US intelligence was in its infancy, growing to behemoth proportions only during the Cold War.[6]

Finally, Scholz could credit a good deal of his work to Moran. Among all of Scholz's espionage efforts, his most ambitious may have been a project to undermine the US military—a project of which Moran was the public face. It was a remarkable transformation for Moran and another demonstration of his quick wits and rhetorical talents. Unlike the many Army and National Guard veterans of the New York front, Moran the lecturer had never focused on weapons of war. Yet he learned fast and became a foremost activist on behalf of the M1941 Johnson semiautomatic rifle, which he hoped first the US Army and then the Marines would adopt. It is safe to say that Moran would not have uttered a word about the Johnson rifle had Scholz not seen a US commitment to the new firearm as advantageous to Germany in a possible war with the United States. The effort to install the Johnson as America's standard-issue rifle ultimately came to naught, but it was the beginning of Moran's interest in military affairs. He would soon be found discouraging recruitment by convincing listeners that the army was encouraging enlistees to engage in sinful sexual behavior. Later he would assert that recruits were going mad in their army camps and that Germany was so powerful it was not worth fighting.

With Scholz's guidance, Moran's attitude and style changed markedly. He spent the second half of 1940 blazing from his pulpit on behalf of Hitler. On some occasions, he discarded his cautious approach to anti-Semitism. He continued to protest that he was not anti-Semitic, merely pro-American and pro-Christian. But his language grew more forceful as he came under the sway of Nazi ideas. His oratory also became more political and less religious. This is not to say that Moran foreswore Christianity—not by any means. But he allowed priests like Brophy to handle the theological talk while he, Moran, appealed more to secular principles. Moran's work with Scholz coincided with a period when US politics was moving, however slowly, in the direction of the Allies. As the challenge of securing US neutrality became more pressing, so Moran's Nazi activism became more vehement and more dangerous.

Spy Craft

On July 9, 1941, George Johnson Armstrong gained an ignominious distinction. He was the first British subject to be executed under the 1940 Treachery Act. Armstrong never achieved much as a spy. His crime lay primarily in trying to become one, and the man who recruited him was Herbert Scholz.

Armstrong fit the profile of a Scholz agent. As a British national, Armstrong did not raise suspicions in the way German nationals did. As an engineer, Armstrong was in a position to secure technical information. And as a sailor in the British Navy, Armstrong was well placed for foreign work. Moran was the rare Scholz agent who remained stateside; otherwise, the consul consistently had his agents either join the US or Allied militaries or stay in their military jobs and request overseas assignments. From abroad, they could report to German handlers and make dead drops of time-sensitive information. Armstrong was much more valuable to Scholz as a merchant mariner on the other side of the Atlantic.

Lastly, Armstrong's idealism made him a fine recruit. Armstrong was a Communist, a view that would not have left him happily disposed toward his own government. But, as far as he knew, the Germans were different. When Armstrong passed through Boston in 1940, the Molotov-Ribbentrop Pact was in effect, sealing neutrality between Stalin and Hitler and raising the Nazis' standing among those sympathetic to the Soviet experiment. At the same time that Scholz was meeting secretly with Moran, the SS man was also furtively enlisting Moran's opposite. It is unclear what would have made Moran angrier—Armstrong's Communist views or his British passport.[7]

It was Armstrong who approached Scholz, in the form of a letter offering to spy for the Germans. But British intelligence intercepted Armstrong's communications, leading to his arrest, extradition from the United States, and trial. He was accused of "conduct to the prejudice of public safety, the defense of the realm, and intent to assist the naval, military, and air operations of the enemy." Armstrong defended himself, claiming he had hoped to use his access to Scholz to learn about Nazi spies carrying out espionage in the United States and Britain. But Armstrong's story was not convincing enough to rescue him from the gallows.[8]

A more substantial Scholz contact was Fritz Fenthol. In spring 1940 Fenthol traveled from Germany to Russia, China, Japan, and then the United States. In late July he spent four days with Scholz and Lilo at their fashionable residence on Reservoir Road in the affluent Boston suburb of Chestnut Hill. A "confidential informant believed to be reliable" told the FBI that Fenthol came to America "under the personal orders of Adolf Hitler and the German General Staff." It is unclear what Scholz and Fenthol spoke about in private, but J. Edgar Hoover was convinced that "Scholz was obtaining national defense information." The FBI director was horrified to learn that this Scholz spy had apparently penetrated the New England Defense Conference, a liaison group overseeing US military research conducted at universities in New England. Rather than risk embarrassment, Hoover kept the information on Scholz's military spying from the State Department, which was informed of the breach only after the war was over.[9]

Another Scholz spy, whom the FBI would eventually catch, was William Curtis Colepaugh. An engineering student at the Massachusetts Institute of Technology and a US Naval reservist, Colepaugh came under the influence of both Communist and Nazi propaganda and in spring 1940 decided to join the German army. He immediately contacted Scholz. The German consul was receptive but encouraged Colepaugh to set aside his desire to enlist in the Wehrmacht. Instead Scholz wanted Colepaugh to stick with the Naval Reserve and, as an ordinary deckhand, "ship aboard a British vessel . . . and bring back information on the operation of British convoys." Colepaugh did as instructed, landing a job on the freighter *Reynolds*, bound for Scotland. He "assiduously noted what patrols accompanied the convoys and how they guarded them." After his return voyage, he remained in the US Naval reserve until he was discharged in 1943.

In January 1944 Colepaugh sailed as a mess boy on the liner *Gripsholm*, jumped ship in Lisbon, and presented himself to the German Consulate as a friend of Herbert Scholz. Colepaugh was then sent to the Nazi spy school at The Hague in the Netherlands, where he was trained by Otto Skorzeny, the legendary SS officer who commanded the daring glider raid in the Apennines to liberate Mussolini in 1943. On November 29, 1944, Colepaugh and fellow spy Erich Gimpel were offloaded from a German submarine near Hancock Point, Maine. Ordered to gather technical information on the Allied war effort and transmit it back to Germany, Colepaugh instead spent a month on the lam and then turned himself in to the FBI.[10]

Spies like Colepaugh and Armstrong were expendable. Scholz hoped they would be useful, as Colepaugh was. But if they failed, as Armstrong did, so be it. Scholz's job was to recruit them and get them into the espionage pipeline. In this respect, he was successful. He was also good at sabotage. For instance he implemented a small but effective plot to starve the US Army of manpower. In October 1940 the Army's Military Intelligence Division learned from a "reliable" source that Scholz was secretly providing "German males" living in the United States "with birth certificates, either putting them under or over the draft age." Scholz could not have singlehandedly prevented the expansion of the US armed forces, but he did what he could, and cleverly. Nothing came of the Army's intelligence discovery. Even when Scholz was caught in the act, US officials turned a blind eye rather than hold one of Hitler's men accountable.[11]

The Johnson Rifle

Scholz's interest in Colepaugh and Armstrong reflected wider Nazi intelligence priorities in the United States prior to Pearl Harbor and the US declaration of war. Technical information was a key area of interest for Nazi spies and was arguably the area in which Nazi spies proved most effective. Engineers like Colepaugh and Armstrong were thus valued targets for recruitment. But one did not have to be an engineer to be useful: Scholz was equally eager to put Moran to work in the area of technical espionage. What emerged in Boston in summer 1940 was a strange mix of politics, religion, and rhetoric aimed at swaying members of the Christian Front to become theologically invested in, of all things, Congressional debates surrounding a rifle.[12]

The question was whether the army should adopt the M1 Garand as its standard-issue service rifle, or else take up the Johnson semiautomatic rifle. At the August 19 and August 26 meetings of the Christian Front, Moran made impassioned pleas for attendees to write their members of Congress, pushing for adoption of the Johnson. This was a confounding departure for Moran, who had been lurching pacifist. In 1940 alone, he had delivered at least four speeches on just war theory, arguing that the United States was not justified in resorting to war.[13]

Melvin Maynard Johnson, a 1934 graduate of Harvard Law school, amateur inventor, and member of the US Marine Corps reserve, had designed his weapon to compete with the Garand. Both were semiautomatic rifles, but the Johnson had advantages, such as a larger magazine capacity. As one firearms enthusiast put it, some thirty-five years after the debate over the two guns, the Johnson "was reliable, accurate, and easier and cheaper to make than the M1 Garand." The Johnson also had its backers in government. On May 10, 1940, the Senate Military Appropriations subcommittee traveled to Fort Belvoir, Virginia, to test both rifles, and Senator Ernest Lundeen of Minnesota, a veteran of the Spanish-American War, "scored 28 bull's-eyes without a miss, using both weapons." Yet Lundeen was swayed by the Johnson's ease of use and concluded that the design was "way ahead of the US military mind." But since the US Army had already committed to production of the M1 before the Johnson came to market, ordnance officials and many politicians were reluctant to change course.[14]

It is entirely possible, even likely, that Lundeen conveyed his experience to the Germans. Lundeen was an isolationist and profoundly antiwar. Perhaps he was a pacifist because he had experienced war himself, but he was also thoroughly pro-German. In 1967 historian Alton Frye uncovered that Lundeen had secret talks with the German Embassy in Washington prior to the outbreak of war in the United States.[15]

By coincidence, Lundeen's interest in the Johnson was piqued on the same day as the Germans'. While Lundeen was racking up bullseyes, the Germans were invading Holland. The campaign began May 10 and ended just four days later, as the Dutch came to realize that the German Air Force would easily decimate their cities. The Dutch defeat brought an intelligence coup for the Germans. Earlier in 1940, the Dutch government became Johnson's lone volume buyer, purchasing a large shipment of his gun for use in the Dutch East Indies. Consequently, when the Nazis took over the Netherlands, they came into possession of as many as 30,000 Johnson rifles.[16] In short order, the Nazis knew everything there was to know about this quite esteemed US-made firearm, which was a great help because the Germans were struggling to develop their own semiautomatic. They could reverse-engineer the Johnson, learn its secrets, build a superior weapon, and outgun the Americans on the battlefield.

If, however, the Americans adopted the Garand, the Germans would be out of luck, or so they believed. As it happened, the Garand was arguably the lesser firearm, but the Germans did not know this. In fact, they did not know how the Garand worked—and this was precisely why they had reason to hope the Americans would instead choose the Johnson. The plans for the Garand constituted one of the few US technical secrets the Germans were unable to steal, though they came close. In 1939 the FBI discovered that a German spy ring headed by a South African agent named Fritz Joubert Duquesne had pilfered the Garand's technical specifications. Specifically, Duquesne was able to get hold of the plans for the gas-operated breech mechanism, the heart of the semiautomatic loading action. Duquesne was just about to ship this vital battlefield intelligence to Germany when the FBI raided his office, stymying the information transfer. It was after this failed effort to compromise the Garand that the Nazis began covertly persuading the Americans to adopt the Johnson, the rifle they could study in depth.[17]

In the wake of the Dutch conquest and Lundeen's show of marksmanship, Moran began to lobby vigorously for adoption of the Johnson. He pushed his followers to support a bill sponsored by Senators Morris Sheppard and David Walsh, which aimed to make the Johnson the US Army standard. This pressure campaign preceded Moran's first documented meeting with Scholz, another reason to believe the two men were working together before that secret liaison joined by Strempel. Moran had never previously shown interest in military ordnance: Why else would he care, except to help his German handlers gain the upper hand in a seemingly imminent war with the United States?

In early July, the Sheppard-Walsh bill was defeated, but that did not stop Moran. He shifted his attention to the US Marine Corps, launching an even more strident initiative than the Sheppard-Walsh push. On August 26 Moran invited a "past commander of the Massachusetts Marine Corps veterans" to address the Christian Front. The unidentified Marine's speech focused on the topic of how "the Garand rifle recently accepted by the US Army is vastly inferior to the Johnson rifle." There were about 750 listeners in the audience that night.[18]

A few months earlier, Moran barely mustered a third of that number; suddenly, with the cloud of sedition lifted and Scholz providing the front new purpose, New Englanders were flocking to Moran's gatherings. These were mostly supporters, but members of local Jewish organizations were there, too, listening to Moran hold forth on munitions. The Boston Police Department's Radical Squad, though primarily attuned to Communist organizing, also attended. No doubt these outsiders were spooked by the possibility that the Boston Christian Front was going the way of the New Yorkers. Just a few weeks earlier, they had been let off at a trial where their own rifles and bombs—purchased legally or assembled from readily available parts—were on display. Was Moran promoting the next weapon of far-right revolution? If so, he was doing it obliquely. Observers seemed confused by Moran's gun talk. Either they did not understand what was being discussed, or Moran's shift to this new martial position escaped their analysis. Moran seemed genuinely concerned that the US military equip itself with the Johnson rifle, even as everyone who followed his work knew that the Christian Front was committed to keeping the United States out of the war.[19]

In the end, the Marines also declined the Johnson as a standard-issue rifle, although the gun saw some action with Marine paratroopers in the Pacific theater. The chilling fact remains, though, that Scholz was able to subvert the conversation on the matter. He fostered what looked like an ordinary democratic debate, which in fact could have produced a direct effect on the battlefield conditions of World War II. As the Christian Front morphed from a religious organization into a Nazi-controlled political one, it was becoming something more than a propaganda enterprise. Ordinary Roman Catholics in Boston were unconsciously aiding a state with which their own would soon be at war.

Momentum

Under Scholz's influence, the Boston Christian Front experienced a large up-tick in membership and won more publicity than it was previously accustomed to. One factor was Moran himself. Even when the front was at a low ebb during spring 1940, he was coming into his own, operating like a neighborhood political boss crossed with a local parish priest. He inspired confidence and loyalty. At a Christian Front meeting on May 24, 1940, one observer was impressed by "Moran and his assistants [who] seemed to know most of the people in the audience." Moran "addressed many of them by their first names and was apparently on friendly terms with them."[20]

But the front's newfound success bears clear imprints of Scholz as well. After July, Moran and the Christian Front changed. Moran's secret meeting with Scholz heralded a new style of Christian Front leadership, focused on pro-German sentiment and blunt anti-Semitism. Moran jettisoned his earlier approach of providing an escape clause for his anti-Semitism, and he stopped leavening his praise of Hitler with criticisms. He also started spewing invective at the US military. To make room for all this political chatter, Moran largely set aside religious oratory. He was not abandoning Christ in favor of Hitler; Moran simply relied on friendly priests such as Father Brophy to serve as the front's religious pillars while Moran himself concentrated on distributing Scholz's Nazi-friendly message. An observer from the American Jewish Committee in New York City noticed the new priestly trend when he infiltrated a series of Boston meetings. "Almost at every meeting there is always one or more clergyman present," he noted. Echoing Tillich, the infiltrator worried that, with so much clerical backing, "this movement will spread and become more powerful and more dangerous than the late Christian Front."[21]

These shifts showed themselves early. At the Christian Front meeting on August 12, about two weeks after his first confirmed meeting with Scholz, Moran warned his followers that some Boston Jews were concerned about "correcting any misinformation which might be distributed at Christian Sunday schools." Moran was incensed. "The gall of these——Jews, who try to interfere with the observance of our religion," he fumed. There is no indication of the exact expletive uttered, but it is the first documented example of Moran resorting to coarse language.[22]

It was also during the Scholz period that Moran started generating circular letters. Unlike his earlier newsletters, these documents were not intended to substitute for public meetings while the front was underground. Rather, Moran gave out the circulars only at meetings, so that fronters would have literature to distribute in their communities. It may be that Scholz encouraged Moran down this road. In any case, the letters reflected Moran's newfound focus on military matters of special interest to the Germans. For instance, Moran's September 9 circular was counter-recruitment activism sung in the key of Catholic sexual morality. Moran decried the distribution of condoms at Army training camps, where enlistees were "supplied with contraceptives upon arrival." Training in the US Army was "the safest way to become immoral," Moran asserted, lamenting that soldiers were being encouraged to engage in the sin of extramarital sex. The army's birth-control policy was a sure sign that "the family was no longer sacred." The right thing to do was to stymie enlistment. "We presume that those of you who practice Christianity . . . will object to such temptations being placed in the way of your sons."[23] Sexual morality and the politics of reproduction were, in general, strategically important for Moran. At a 1941 meeting, he asked his listeners to vote against Roosevelt in the coming election because of his position on birth control and because the president supposedly preferred "that masturbation be sanctioned for youth."[24]

Sometimes Moran's focus on political controversies crowded out his religious message entirely. The October 7, 1940, meeting at Hibernian Hall was devoid of religious content. Moran railed against Roosevelt, saying the president wanted "to acquire more power through a stronger and more centralized government." This accusation was also a defense of Hitler. "President Roosevelt, who talks against Hitler, is actually a greater advocate of centralized power than Hitler." And as for Hitler, his "actions are actually not as bad as his talk," Moran thought. "I promise to be far more radical in the future," he announced. With war looming, there was no place for moderation when it came to Roosevelt or "those atheistic—Jewish Communists." Comments like these won the audience's enthusiastic approval. The free-will offering taken up at the end of the meeting netted $62 ($1,166 in 2020 dollars), an increase from $35 the previous week.[25]

The surge in heated rhetoric testifies to the increasing difficulty of the challenge facing Moran, Scholz, and others carrying out the Führer's Order. Hitler wanted to persuade foreign powers to remain neutral, but neutrality was looking like a more and more untenable position. By fall 1940 the Germans had toppled nonaligned states like Belgium, Luxembourg, and the

Netherlands, demonstrating how little respect the Nazis had for neutrality. Yet Moran had to convince his fellow Americans that neutrality was the best choice for the United States. In his October 7 circular, Moran wondered aloud what patriotic Americans should do "if a declaration of war is made by a power-mad administration against the will of the people." The British, Moran wrote, did not deserve America's help, because they were not fighting "for principles which are the basis of American life." Indeed, Moran thought the British were duped into the war by Jews. "We ask you, do you believe the English people are fighting even for themselves?" he asked rhetorically, while rambling about Jewish infiltration of the royal family and the Bank of England—"there is not one Gentile on the Governing Board of the Bank of England." No, Britain was fighting "to satisfy the hatred of the Jews for Hitler." The choice for Americans was obvious. "We of the Christian Front of America, as Christians and as citizens, therefore would refuse unequivocally to participate in a war at the demand of a corrupt administration except in the case of invasion."[26]

Moran was no stranger to isolationism, but this felt different. Despite his closing lip-service to readers' status as Christians, his argument had virtually nothing to do with Christianity. Nor did Moran make his usual claim that, whatever Americans thought of Hitler, the real enemy was Communism. The circulars were supposed to introduce the wider world to the vision of the Christian Front, yet the foundational myth of Judeo-Bolshevism was nowhere to be found in the October 7 letter. Instead of explaining why Judeo-Bolshevists threatened Christianity, Moran argued that America simply had no place in a war to protect another people, Jews, who had in any case courted their own disaster. And instead of appealing to the Mystical Body, he appealed to civic values of democracy and limited government. It is impossible to say whether Scholz had a hand in the new messaging, but one can readily imagine that Moran saw the need to make secular appeals if he was going to convince the wider public to stay neutral. It was one thing to exhort conservative Christians to keep reds out of school classrooms. It was another to move the weight of public opinion in hopes of influencing national security policy coming out of Washington.

Scholz's impact is clear in Moran's sudden fascination with the liberal arts. Moran had always been well spoken, and he had clearly done readings in biblical interpretation. But he was no longer content to quote scripture and theologians. Now he began to cite the sorts of secular thinkers one might study in the philosophy department at, say, Leipzig. An FBI informant who attended the October 4 meeting noted that "he talks about Voltaire, Spinoza, and other philosophers." Presumably the Jewish Spinoza provided a negative example. "Moran must have his speeches prepared for him by other people," the informant thought. Audiences were awestruck. "Talking in his usual calm and persuasive manner, his voice never rising above nor falling below an even level, he kept his audience of 700 spellbound," one observer from the Anti-Defamation League (ADL) wrote after the October 21 meeting.[27]

Although Moran's rhetorical style had changed, the thrust of his oratory had not. In February 1941, another ADL report marveled that "Moran has the ability without exhorting or gesturing to keep his listeners glued to their seats—while he spouts a steady flow of words that are bristling with hate." This observer also noticed that the police seemed to be treating Moran as though he were no longer a threat. "Perhaps the most significant thing impressing a listener who has made it a habit of attending these lectures in the past, is the conspicuous absence of police," the ADL plant wrote. Previously he had witnessed both uniformed and plainclothes policemen dotting the hall while Moran held his meetings. But during the fall of 1940, the Boston Police went on hiatus. "Can it be that they had lost interest in a man who through his naïve mannerisms can throw them off track by his casual manner of talking?" the ADL observer wondered. It is not clear whether Scholz had anything to do with the decreased police presence. Perhaps the outcome of the New York trial had mollified the police. And one cannot discount the extent to which the police were on Moran's side. As Derounian discovered, Moran was not idly boasting when he claimed to have coopted the balance of the local police.[28]

"Words that are bristling with hate" would also be an apt description for the pronouncements of Moran's priestly spokesmen. On October 24, Father Brophy arrived in Boston to address a group of Christian Front dignitaries at the stately Westminster Hotel in Copley Square. The occasion was a dinner party to celebrate the forty-ninth birthday of Father Coughlin, and Brophy was prepared with a suitably lighthearted opening. "I come from New York City. I don't know Yiddish yet, but suppose I'll have to learn it," he joked, as the audience laughed in appreciation. Brophy, though, had not come to Boston to deliver a standup comedy routine. In his encomium for Father Coughlin, he described the radio priest as one who "has striven at all times to link up the scattered forces of the Mystical Body of Christ into a single battle line so that with united force, we might remain unwavering against the common enemy." Brophy did not have to specify who that enemy was, but, going off-script, he explained the obvious. "How can any of us today trust the Jews?" he shouted, "when Jesus couldn't!" According to an FBI report based on later conversations with Moran, "The room rocked with applause, with clapping and stamping."[29]

Composing himself, Brophy returned to the theme of the Mystical Body, lamenting that "non-Christians"—his preferred euphemism for Jews—were more cohesive than his own Christian brothers. "These non-Christians have wonderful organization because they are all united," Brophy asserted. "If a non-Christian in Yugoslavia has a toothache, all of the non-Christians in New York get a headache." This was street-level theology. Brophy was making Pauline biblical principles accessible to ordinary Catholics, but he was adding his own grotesque twist. It was imperative that Christians "likewise unite," and the vehicle for that unification was the organization Coughlin had inspired. "A nucleus has been started—the nucleus is the Christian Front." For Brophy, the Christian Front was the material realization of the Mystical Body of Christ. In effect, he was telling his audience that the Body of Christ would shrivel and die unless it was nourished by Jew hatred.

"We must be good Christians," Brophy announced, "but that does not mean being weak-kneed, and letting all the non-Christians get the power." To murmurs of disgust, Brophy declared that the National Conference of Christians and Jews had recently condemned anti-Semitism. "Anti-Semitism equals fortitude for Christians, Christian fortitude," he bellowed. Here again Brophy was sacralizing anti-Semitism. As one of the seven gifts of the Holy Spirit, fortitude occupies an important place in Catholic theology. For Catholics today, fortitude is the willingness to stand up for God and God's truths, even when doing so means facing down fear. For Catholics in 1940, fortitude meant "being able, in the spiritual contest, to fight manfully and to resist our most wicked foes." If anti-Semitism was fortitude, then Jews were the "wicked foes" whom Catholics were divinely enjoined to resist.[30]

Brophy repeated his Mystical Body speech on October 28 at the Christian Front meeting at Hibernian Hall. An observer counted "about 350 to 400 people in the audience . . . jammed to standing room only capacity. The group consisted of youngsters in their teens . . . and a lot of young men in their 20's." Moran's strength had been among men and women with families. Now his message was attracting younger Bostonians. Indeed, his movement seemed to be growing geographically as well. The US Army's Military Intelligence Division reported that Moran's Christian Front handbills had been found as far west as Cincinnati, plastering the lockers of a local bus station.[31]

Like Brophy, Moran took for granted the idea that Jews comprised their own closely held body and that their insidious power lay in unity. In an effort to encourage similar unity among Christians, Moran organized a "buy Christian" campaign for the 1940 Christmas season. "Christians would do well," Moran wrote in his weekly circular of December 9, "to learn from the Jew that quality in which he most excels—LOYALTY TO HIS OWN PEOPLE!" To this end, Moran urged his followers to "buy their Christmas cards, presents, and decorations . . . from those who join us in our love of Christ." He provided a list of fifteen stores owned by "fellow Christians," which should be patronized during the Christmas season. Displaying his meticulous research, Moran indicated that Kennedy's, then Boston's premier clothing store, should be patronized except for the womenswear and boys' shoes departments, which were "leased out," presumably to Jews. "We are not advocating a boycott," Moran offered. "We have simply suggested where any Christian with a brain in his head should trade.[32]

The whirlwind year of 1940 closed with Moran in an aggressive posture. The ups and downs of the first half of the year gave way to momentum in the second half, as Moran peddled Scholz's line behind the protective walls of religious freedom and isolationist politics. With the police backing him, and federal counterintelligence indifferent, it seemed there was nothing standing in Moran's way, at least from a legal standpoint. His views were by no means universally accepted, but he had the liberty and the resources to press them with ever greater force on the body politic. In the coming year, as the United States inched closer to war, Moran's work on behalf of the Nazis would become that much bolder and more urgent.

CHAPTER 9

Kissing Hitler

THE *PAULINE FRIEDERICH* HAD BEEN TIED UP SINCE SEPTEMBER 2, 1939. The tanker, carrying a million dollars of lubricating oil, was stranded in Boston Harbor just as the war in Europe commenced. Rather than expose his ship to the perils of a naval battle in the Atlantic, Captain Ernst Heitzman decided to stay put. But the crew was restive, wishing to return home, and a mutiny broke out while the vessel sat in maritime limbo. To keep his sailors in line, Heitzman held their wages hostage: anyone who disagreed with his decision would be refused their pay. In January 1940 the leader of the insubordinate wing, Second Officer Wilhelm Harren, filed a claim in US court for $98.60 in unpaid wages. With federal action pending, US Marshals and Navy servicemen took possession of the ship. *Life* magazine called the impounding of the *Pauline Friederich* America's "first win" and a "bloodless victory in the Battle of the Atlantic."[1]

Berlin was not celebrating that victory. Scholz was expected to save the *Pauline Friederich* and save face for Hitler. Scholz and Heitzman were also adamant that neither the United States nor the Allies be able to use the ship and were concerned about the possible forfeiture of its precious cargo. Scholz secretly boarded the tanker seven times while it was docked in Boston Harbor, and it was probably under his direction—and at the very least with his approval—that the loyal Nazis of the crew carried out their next steps.[2]

On March 29, 1941, members of the US Coast Guard boarded the ship for routine inspection. They found holes drilled into the cylinder walls of the engine, pistons destroyed, the thrust bearing smashed, the auxiliary generator wrecked, and the bilge pump and steering engine demolished. These were serious crimes: tampering with the "motive power" of a commercial vessel "with the intent to injure or endanger the safety of the vessel," within the jurisdiction of the United States, carried a potential sentence of twenty-five years in prison. US Marshals arrested Captain Heitzman and nine of his sailors. All pled not guilty; bail was set at the extraordinarily high number of $450,000 (more than $8 million in 2020 dollars). "Outside the courtroom," one Massachusetts newspaper reported, "the crew members greeted Consul Herbert Scholz with hands upraised in the Nazi salute." With Scholz and his compatriots in the midst of a serious legal, diplomatic, and public relations crisis, Moran tried to explain the "injustice" of the case to the people of Boston.[3]

His circular letter for the first week of April took aim at "the seizure of Axis ships by the United States, and the sabotage thereof." There had been no other seizures, but pluralizing "ships" served Moran's propaganda goals. Impoundment was said to exemplify "the corruption and the lack of neutrality in the New Deal administration." Furthermore, the German saboteurs were guilty of nothing; their hands had been forced. "German sailors would never destroy their own ships without good reason," Moran asserted, and the good reason was that the Americans and the British were trying to steal their vessel. The men had to scupper their ship lest it "be seized and sent to England as soon as Roosevelt could discover a legal or quasi-legal excuse." These fine men of duty were victims of "nothing more than a persecution." Moran also suggested that the sailors were being harassed or even tortured in custody, subjected to conditions that "have made it impossible for them to obtain decent sleep." The ordeal of the *Pauline Friederich* threatened to drag America into the war, even though "Germany is more than willing to live at peace with us." If only Americans would "finally wake up to the fact that this is a Jewish and international bankers war."[4]

The *Pauline Friederich* incident was a missed opportunity for federal security agencies both to call out Scholz and to tie him to Moran and the Christian Front. The US Army's Military Intelligence Division knew that Scholz was making routine visits to the ship and meeting with its captain, and MID passed that information to both the FBI and the Office of Naval Intelligence. None of these agencies endeavored to investigate whether Scholz directed the sabotage. In fact, MID made the considered choice to ignore what was going on. Rather than categorize their information on the Scholz-Heitzman secret meetings as "Grade A - immediately dangerous," MID characterized the situation as "Grade B - potentially dangerous," a designation that ensured the case would not be taken seriously. They thereby allowed Scholz, and his relationships with Boston supporters like Moran, to escape scrutiny once again. It was only after the sabotage was discovered that US officials made law-enforcement efforts, and then there was no investigation of Scholz's role. The Roosevelt administration responded to the sabotage by expelling the German naval attaché in Washington, Robert Witthoeft-Emden, but Scholz was free to continue his espionage and propaganda work.[5]

This was in many ways the story of 1941, with respect to Scholz and Moran: they repeatedly slipped through the fingers of intelligence and law-enforcement agents. The men were under frequent suspicion, yet they managed again and again to escape sanction. To an extent, this was a result of their own cleverness—Moran had a talent for violating the spirit of the law while remaining just inside the boundaries of the letter, although eventually it became clear to some in the national security apparatus that he was an unregistered foreign agent. Even then, the attempt to investigate Moran was a lurching affair, mired in official ineptitude.

It is remarkable that Scholz managed to stay out of MID's clutches despite all that the agency knew about him. After MID learned of Scholz's visits to the *Pauline Friederich*, the agency developed a lead from a "reliable informant with a rating of A," who interacted personally with Scholz and informed MID that the consul was up to no good. During a face-to-face conversation, Scholz reportedly told the informant that "information had been received from Germany that the consul who did the most to hinder the national defense of the United States . . . would be awarded a medal" by Hitler. The informant and MID both concluded that this was a ruse—that Scholz made the statement in hopes that it would reach American intelligence agencies "and thereby cause additional effort to be expended by US government agencies [by] keeping the Consuls under surveillance, thus diverting attention from . . . sabotage activities."[6] Thus Scholz either was under orders to undermine US national security directly, or he was playing games with the security bureaucracy in order to achieve that end indirectly. But MID did nothing. Between the informant and the *Pauline Friederich* visits, the agency had intelligence upon intelligence when it came to Scholz, yet still left him room to maneuver and make good use of Moran, his principal asset in Boston.

Camp Crazy

"Two riot squads were called out to maintain a semblance of order," the *Boston Herald* reported of Moran's first initiative of 1941. In the middle of January, Christian Front members showed up in numbers at Boston's Faneuil Hall to support Verne Marshall, an Iowa newspaper editor and founder of the No Foreign Wars Committee. Marshall was set to debate Mayo Shattuck, vice chair of the New England branch of the Committee to Defend America by Aiding the Allies, on a program broadcast from Boston to Philadelphia over the Colonial Network. "Police identified the hecklers of Mayo Shattuck as members of the Christian Front," the American Jewish Committee's Henry Levy noted, with "the heckling growing so loud that Verne Marshall made two or three attempts to stop it on the basis of sportsmanship." But Moran and his crew refused to pipe down. "The heckling grew so loud that the moderator . . . threatened to cut the program off from the air." The riot squads were unable to "restrain hundreds in the audience from booing and shouting at Shattuck, who . . . was still advocating aid to Britain when the nightmare ended."[7]

Moments like these were aberrations for Moran, who was not typically one for public agitation. Only one prior incident, the fall 1939 heckling of Alfred Duff Cooper, resembled the Faneuil Hall episode, and on that earlier occasion there were no riot squads called in. By 1941, however, the tension had grown thicker in Boston and across the United States. A war that once felt far away was now an everyday concern, increasing the sense of urgency among interventionists and isolationists alike. It would be another year before US troops were involved, but the country was very much embroiled in the war economically and diplomatically, and military preparations were intensifying.

These preparations became Moran's major concern. Whether or not he had received specific orders, it was in fact Scholz's job to "hinder the national defense of the United States," and in this effort Moran was an eager collaborator. Their target was the largest military cantonment in the First Corps Area: Camp Edwards on Cape Cod, a 22,000-acre base that would house nearly 40,000 soldiers during World War II. During the first week of March 1941, Moran went to Camp Edwards to address Catholic troops on the subject of Lent. Documents generated around the time of the visit indicate that the retired Captain George A. Moriarty, who was known to the FBI as somehow both "violently anti-Semitic" and "a harmless windbag," may have put in a good word for Moran, helping him secure an invitation to the camp. And army officials were not about to stand in the way of a speaker from a religious organization discussing spiritual matters with the boys. Moran's topic, however, was not so much Lent as anti-Semitism and political grievance. During his lecture, Moran "denounced President Roosevelt and the Jews, stating that they should be treated like traitors." Any citizens who "force us into war should be shot," he raged. When he finally got around to his purported topic, he castigated camp officials for "serving Catholic boys meat on Fridays" in spite of Lenten restrictions and allowing "Jewish boys to have holidays from their duties on Passover." Moran was never asked back to Camp Edwards.[8]

Camp Edwards had become a showcase for Moran's propaganda style. He was seldom a reckless speaker, for he understood that he was involved in a war of words, in which every statement counted. This does not mean that he spoke honestly—far from it. But he was always careful to associate his rumors with a semblance of truth. For example, while there was no indication that Catholic soldiers were in fact served meat on Fridays during Lent, the camp did grant furloughs to Jewish soldiers during Passover. A rumor was more believable when it bore hints of truth.[9]

In his talks at Hibernian Hall, Moran doubled down on the horrors of Camp Edwards. "The Jews have all the soft jobs in the Quartermaster and Medical Corps," he insisted, building on the theme of Jewish cowardice, which had become so prevalent in Catholic circles since the Great War. And as for Jews who weren't pretending to fight for America, "these cheap chiseling rats will profiteer and make a fortune out of the war, even if they have to harm their own country," Moran told a "very enthusiastic crowd." Indeed, the crime of the Jews was much worse than merely profiteering. "They have even sold poisoned food at different camps," Moran alleged without evidence.[10]

The idea that Jews were trying to poison American soldiers was flagrant nonsense, absurd even in the universe of anti-Semitic, isolationist conspiracy theories. Here was Moran arguing that Jews were both trying to rope America into war in their own defense and to ensure that America was too enervated to fight. In reality, it was Moran who was trying to depress American military capacity, by eroding confidence in the armed forces and persuading young men not to join up. The strategy was almost certainly developed in concert with Scholz, who was also doing what he could to undermine US warfighting capacity through his birth-certificate scheme, spy recruitments, and the Johnson rifle ploy. MID knew what Moran was up to—he was speaking in public, after all—although agents failed to connect Moran to Scholz. On April 15, an MID agent secretly attended the Christian Front meeting at Hibernian Hall, where he heard Moran announce that "at US Army camps throughout the United States, men are slowly going insane." These soldiers, he claimed, were becoming "camp crazy." This was "due to the fact that they were not used to the manner of life of being thrown in together by the tens of thousands at one place."[11]

"According to Moran, there have been many suicides in the military camps recently," an Anti-Defamation League plant at the same meeting recorded. Two days later, on April 17, Moran claimed "there was another suicide at Camp Edwards," but, he added, "of course you don't read that sort of news in the papers." And there was "a particularly tragic case" at Camp Lee, Virginia. A young draftee, "losing his mind slowly," walked up to a soldier on guard duty, "wrestled the rifle from his hands, and shot himself in the head." Moran's story "got quite a reception from the audience with many Ohs and Ahs."[12]

Again, Moran's rumors possessed a veneer of believability. For some time, New Englanders had been hearing that soldiers at Camp Edwards were so cramped that they "tripped over each other on the job." Multiple press reports indicated that morale at the camp was high, but there was enough confusion surrounding the state of affairs at Edwards for Moran to gain traction. For instance, in March 1941, as Moran's comments were circulating, camp commanders suddenly and with no explanation dispensed with "fatigue duty," which included menial work such as cutting wood for fuel, road construction, policing camp, constructing buildings, and digging ditches. For those disposed to Moran's point of view, it looked like the army was proving his point. Lieutenant Colonel A. R. Bolling, the chief of MID, rebuked Moran for passing "numerous unfounded stories of conditions at Army camps . . . so as to arouse strong feelings against the military and the government." Bolling played the scold but kept his reports to himself. Moran evaded scrutiny once more.[13]

Moran's most controversial counter-recruitment spectacle came in June, with the Christian Front's screening of *Sieg im Westen* (*Victory in the West*). One of the first films to show the German army in action, *Sieg im Westen* was a masterpiece of German propaganda. It had premiered on January 20, 1941, in the projection room of the Reich Chancellery, with Hitler and director Svend Noldan present. Noldan's specialty was contriving animated maps to represent Nazi conquest, and the use of rats to represent Jews. His animation style influenced Walt Disney, and his politics won him Hitler's admiration. On the evening of the screening, the director and the führer greeted each other with a warm handshake. "Hitler was visibly impressed by the film," historian Rolf Giesen has written, because much of the content "reminded him of his own time as a soldier in the First World War."[14]

The power of *Sieg im Westen* lay in its cinematic treatment of documentary footage. Noldan recut material from newsreels and spliced it with his own animations and artful live-action scenes. Orchestral music and dramatic narration rounded out the "impressionist, emotive, and all-conquering" display, "a blitz of sound and image," as film historian Roger Manvell put it. Hollywood titan Frank Capra was so taken with the craft of *Sieg im Westen* that he later recycled segments of the battle footage for his own propaganda films on behalf of the US war effort, the iconic *Why We Fight* series.[15]

Another American captivated by *Sieg im Westen* was Moran. On June 2, 1941, he screened the movie for more than 600 people gathered at Hibernian Hall. As he prepared to roll the tape, he was sure to mention Father Coughlin, "who more than any other man in the United States . . . has been a leader in the creation of public opinion." Then Moran advised the audience that, while there was no English soundtrack, he would provide instantaneous translation and commentary. As the lights dimmed, he offered the last of his preludes: "What you are about to see tonight [is] the power that America is supposed to fight."

For the next hour and a half, Stuka dive bombers, Panzer tanks, and overwhelming numbers of fast-moving Nazi troops enlivened the screen. "During the showing of the film, Moran made several side comments emphasizing the horror of modern warfare and the hopelessness of fighting a mechanized Nazi army." Faced with such power, Moran warned, America should be like "the little boy who minds his own business and doesn't get into a fight unless someone hits him first." As the lights came back on, Moran "urged the women in the audience having sons in the United States Army to write to their sons and tell them what they had seen in the film and to impress upon them the impossibility of any nation defeating the German army now."[16]

Word of the screening made it as far as Berlin, where Joseph Goebbels and his aides gleefully recounted how, "after the showing of the German propaganda film *Sieg im Westen* (*Victory in the West*) before a Christian Front audience in Boston, Mr. Francis P. Morton [*sic*], characterized the American war against Germany as 'a hopeless conflict . . . and a senseless shedding of blood.'" The US Foreign Broadcast Information Service, which monitored radio transmissions from belligerent countries, picked up on a German radio announcer reveling in Moran's entreaty to "American mothers [to] oppose military service for their sons."[17]

What was cause for celebration in Berlin provoked outrage in Boston. The Veterans of Foreign Wars publicly censured Moran, and members of the Disabled American Veterans wrote an angry letter to Major Patrick Healy, head of the Massachusetts Censorship Board, arguing that Moran should be thrown in jail. "He asked mothers to become traitors to this country," the Disabled Veterans charged. They argued that when, on May 27, 1941, President Roosevelt proclaimed an "unlimited national emergency," Moran became prosecutable under the Espionage Act. Healy, however, believed he had done all he could have. Moran had come to him a week before the screening and was instructed that he could show the film as long as it did not include an English translation. Moran was happy to comply: the film was not heavy on text, and Healy had no idea that Moran could translate as needed. Healy referred legal questions to the FBI, which announced that it could find no federal laws Moran had violated.[18]

Nor had Moran violated state laws. On June 4, two days after the screening, leaders of the Disabled Veterans joined counterparts from the VFW and Massachusetts American Legion to draw up a statement of protest and demand that the state punish Moran for failing to obtain a license to show the film. But a local official told the group that Massachusetts had "no jurisdiction over" the screening, because Moran had acquired a sixteen-millimeter version of the film and had not charged admission. A state license was required only for ticketed screenings of thirty-five-millimeter films, which were associated with entertainment. Sixteen-millimeter films were associated with newsreels and so were classed separately. Massachusetts Governor Leverett Saltonstall also demurred. A member of Boston's Jewish Community Relations Council indicated in a June 4 memo that Saltonstall "felt no action should be taken that could possibly be interpreted as an extralegal suppression of free speech." In deference to the governor, state and local officials decided "to do nothing further on the matter."[19]

Moran rejoiced in the veterans' protest. "I would like to show the film to them first of all," he told a reporter. "Every Legion Post in the country ought to see this film." Indeed, Moran had every intention of showing the film again.

On June 5 he said he aimed to "make it available to the general public at the earliest possible date, probably later in the next week."[20]

Moran's critics were either unaware of a formidable new legal tool at the federal government's disposal or were unwilling to contemplate its use. The Smith Act, passed on February 19, 1940, dropped the wartime parameter of the Espionage Act and criminalized any "intent to interfere with, impair, or influence the loyalty, morale, or discipline of the military or naval forces of the United States." Specifically, it was unlawful to "advise, counsel, or urge in any manner insubordination, disloyalty, mutiny, or refusal of duty by any member of the military or naval forces of the United States."[21] Moran's statements during and after the June 2, 1941, screening—in particular his explicit urging that mothers depress their serving sons with tales of German military might—were construable as violations of the Smith Act.

But if the VFW could be forgiven for omitting a Smith Act analysis, and if state officials were powerless to enforce a federal law, it is harder to look charitably on the federal intelligence and law enforcement agents who turned a blind eye. The Military Intelligence Division had an eyewitness at the June 2 screening, but the agent's report made no mention of Moran's entreaty to mothers of enlisted sons. And while MID was ignoring the evidence of a Smith Act violation, the FBI was seemingly rewriting the law to suit its ideological predilections. Hoover was deeply invested in the Smith Act and understood the fearsome power it represented, but he saw the law, in spite of its language, only as a weapon against Communists.[22]

Attorney General Francis Biddle also opposed the idea of prosecuting Moran for seditious activity, under the Smith Act or any other statute. He informed Hoover that no such charges should be on the table, and Hoover passed the message along to Peterson in Boston, writing, "the Attorney General indicated his unwillingness to authorize prosecutions for sedition." Just a year after the disastrous New York trial, Biddle was not willing to consider another Christian Front sedition trial. Ironically, Biddle would later spearhead Smith Act charges against fronter Joe McWilliams and twenty-nine others, a case that became derisively known as the Great Sedition Trial. The trial lives in infamy as an example of prosecutorial overreach. The government struggled for years to bring forward a coherent argument, and the case ended in a mistrial. In comparison to the McWilliams case, Moran's was cut-and-dried.[23]

But even if Hoover was not able to pursue a sedition prosecution, he was keen to pin some kind of charge on Moran. Hoover had every incentive to at least appear engaged in the Moran case, as many officials in powerful positions were suddenly curious about the Christian Front's activities. For instance, Hoover heard from Arkansas Representative David Terry, who took an immediate interest after learning of the film screening. Terry asked Hoover to investigate Moran and advise about any findings at the "earliest opportunity." Normally a three-term congressman from a Southern state fretting about an incident in Massachusetts would not have Hoover overly concerned. Terry, however, was a member of the powerful House Appropriations Committee, and nothing made Hoover move faster than the prospect of budget cuts.[24]

Hoover got creative. One avenue of possible criminality lay in the origins of the film. Had it been imported illegally? US Customs informed Hoover that they had tracked the film since its arrival at Brownsville, Texas, in March 1941. Because *Sieg im Westen* was neither obscene nor "advocated the overthrow of the United States government," no law prevented its distribution in the United States. Still, it could not have been easy for Moran to obtain the film. The German Foreign Office and the Wehrmacht had restricted foreign distribution to military attachés and diplomats.[25]

Moran was not a military attaché or a diplomat, but finally some well-placed observers were beginning to wonder if he was working for one. One of those observers was Reverend Leon Birkhead, founder of the liberal group Friends of Democracy. On June 5, he telegrammed Secretary of State Cordell Hull with a question: "Has Francis P. Moran, leader of the Christian Front in the Boston area, registered as a propaganda agent of a foreign power?" Under the Foreign Agents Registration Act of 1938, Moran was required to inform the government that he was working for Scholz, which he had never done. The prosecutorial standard for conviction under FARA was high. In Moran's case, officials would have to catch him in the act of taking direction or resources from Scholz. But the idea of a FARA prosecution struck a nerve. Two weeks after the screening, Hull told the press that, since hearing from Birkhead, he "was keeping a careful watch over propaganda material . . . to determine whether the Foreign Agents Registration Act had been complied with."[26]

Moran responded forcefully, and with his usual rhetorical cleverness, in his own statement to reporters. "If I am a Nazi agent because I dared to show that the German army is too strong for us to get mixed up with," he thundered, "then all those people who are sponsoring British relief are working for the British government." Moran also picked up on the involvement of Birkhead who, as a political enemy, was a ready foil. Moran could dispense with the allegation by implying that Birkhead was grinding an ideological axe, and on behalf of Communists, no less. "I shall be the first to volunteer to defend us against the Nazis," Moran said. "May I ask Reverend Birkhead whether he would volunteer to fight against Russia?"[27]

A bit of red-baiting might have been enough to shut down Birkhead, but Moran was now attracting scrutiny from powerful officials who would not be so easily dissuaded. It is particularly important that attention was coming from the likes of Secretary of State Hull, as the State Department had been a major obstacle to investigations of German officials in the United States, thereby preventing revelations about their agents. If the State Department was interested in knowing more about men like Moran, there could be serious trouble ahead for Scholz as well, and for other Americans working for Nazi diplomats. Adolf Berle Jr., assistant secretary of state and a close advisor to FDR, seemed to share Hull's worries. He pushed Hoover to get Peterson "to determine if Francis P. Moran acted as an agent of a foreign principal." Hoover—who had always taken German spies seriously, even if he did not feel the Smith Act was an appropriate response—was enthusiastic. The *Sieg im Westen* affair was turning into a black eye for the FBI, but a FARA prosecution might be just the healing ointment needed.[28]

One obvious investigative direction involved, again, the film itself. But this proved a dead end. As Moran freely admitted to a *Boston Globe* reporter, he acquired his copy of *Sieg im Westen* from Ufa Films, Inc. Moran even gave the reporter the company's street address—1270 6th Avenue, New York City. Ufa, short for *Universum Film Aktiengesellschaft*, was indeed a foreign agency. It was under the majority ownership of the German government and was controlled by Goebbels. But, as Hoover came to understand, Ufa was "registered with the Secretary of State as an agent of a foreign principal." Not only that, but in its FARA application to the State Department, Ufa described its purpose as "the production, distribution, release, and exhibition of motion pictures." In other words, Ufa was operating legally in the United States; it could not be prosecuted for doing precisely what it had received approval to do, nor could its customers be held liable for taking advantage of its approved services.[29]

Berle told Hoover to keep digging. The FBI director ordered Peterson to send agents to interview Christian Front members about Moran's possible association with foreign agents, and for once Peterson seemed inclined to act. He assigned J. W. Coulter and J. H. Foley, agents experienced in national security matters, to investigate. During the late 1930s, the two agents had done a masterful job of creating contacts inside Boston's America First Committee. One of those contacts admitted that her daughter "had attended meetings of the Christian Front, and might possibly have given money to Moran at one time." Coulter and Foley moved quickly to interview her. But the woman had nothing useful to say concerning a secret partnership of which she had no knowledge. She "stated that she knew Mr. Moran personally and considered him a very excellent character who would never stoop so low as to accept money from any foreign government in order to carry out the activities of the Christian Front." In frustration, Coulter became rather ruthless. Unbeknownst to Moran, Coulter scoured his bank account, scrutinized his loans, examined his mortgage, delved into his elderly mother's finances, and initiated a mail cover—at Coulter's request, the Boston Post Office recorded all information on the outside of parcels addressed to Moran. A mail cover is a common investigative technique that does not require the securing of a warrant. In fact, Moran's FBI file does not include a single warrant application. The financial information was voluntarily divulged by bankers.[30]

Coulter's probe came to nothing, and two months after its initial screening, Moran showed the film for a second time at Hibernian Hall. Press coverage "fails to say that the audience cheered Hitler whenever his picture appeared on the screen," a confidential informant reported to Peterson. Moran translated between the cheering. "His German translations were flavored with subtlety," the informant noted. Such subtlety was beginning to annoy Hoover. Foiled at every turn, he acted out, all but threatening to fire Peterson. That Moran could still move freely around Boston reflected "unfavorably on the Bureau," Hoover told Peterson. It would look especially bad "if every effort is not exerted on the part of your office to gather all evidence which is available," the FBI director added menacingly. Hoover sent Peterson at least three letters in fall 1941, pressing the slow-moving special agent to find some crime Moran had committed, but Peterson made no progress. Perhaps he had better things to do. He had agreed to teach a course at Harvard for New England police officials on "the investigation of espionage . . . and subversive activities."[31]

"Heil Hitler!": The Front in Late 1941

On June 16 FDR threw down the hammer and ordered the closure of all German consulates in the United States. A note from Deputy Undersecretary of State Sumner Welles accused German diplomats of "activities of an improper and unwarranted character, inimical to the welfare of the country" and "wholly outside the scope of their legitimate duties." Scholz would have until July 10 to pack his bags and leave.[32]

As soon as the news broke, a gaggle of reporters clamored outside the consulate on Chestnut Street in Beacon Hill. Scholz greeted them at the door, "beaming and rubbing his hands together." He projected an easy air, seeming to treat the whole situation as a farce. "Consulate Closing Huge Joke," the *Boston Herald* reported. "Scholz just laughs and laughs." Perhaps Scholz was beaming and laughing because Moran, of course, would not be coming with him. Scholz knew he could rely on his agent.[33]

That confidence was well placed, as Moran spent the second half of 1941 churning out Nazi propaganda even though Scholz was bound for distant shores. In his July circulars, Moran continued to harp on Roosevelt. FDR's destroyers-for-bases deal, concluded by executive order, was despicable: neither Congress nor ordinary American citizens were consulted about the plan, which saw the United States transferring military technology to Britain in exchange for basing rights in British territories. Here again Moran was delivering a civic argument, not a religious one—a sign that Scholz's lessons had stuck. Moran's position was that the president was "ignoring his duty to consider the welfare of our own country first." Moran also alleged that FDR, if left unchecked, would create a "post-war League of Nations" because "he wants no national boundaries or national loyalties."[34]

As far as Moran, the unregistered foreign agent, was concerned, his own national loyalty was incontestable. His position was not unlike Cassidy's when the New York front leader, from the witness stand, argued that he was not a revolutionary, even though he was trying to take over the government and replace it with a new one. Both men understood themselves to be protectors of the true America, whatever the law required or whomever the people elected. Moran and Cassidy saw no irony in calling out others for treason, foreign allegiances, and anti-Americanism generally, because their intentions were, by their own lights, patriotic. Loyalty did not entail an obligation to follow just laws, support the whole community, or solve problems through the political process. Loyalty was a matter of the heart, and Moran and Cassidy decided that their hearts were pure.

Indeed, just a few days after the consular expulsion order, Moran could feel purer of heart than he had for some time. On June 22, 1941, Operation

Barbarossa commenced. About 3 million Axis and Axis-aligned soldiers, the largest land invasion force in the history of warfare, opened an eastern front against the Soviet Union. The Molotov-Ribbentrop Pact was over. The Germans were at last fighting the red devil himself, and Moran would no longer have to tiptoe awkwardly around the unconscionable Nazi-Communist alliance. The following day, from the stage at Hibernian Hall, Moran shouted, "No matter what Hitler may have done in the past, anywhere, any time, I could kiss him for what he has done." I "could kiss him every hour of the day in spite of his mustache." Manic with joy, Moran grabbed a glass of water and offered a toast. "For what Hitler has done, and for what he is doing, for what he will do—I say 'Heil Hitler.'"[35]

An Anti-Defamation League plant at the meeting recorded Moran's "Heil Hitler" remarks and made sure copies of the report were sent to both Lieutenant Colonel Bolling at MID and to Peterson.[36] Peterson, who must have taken a new interest in Moran, had his own informant on hand for the June 23 meeting. The informant arrived just in time for Moran's kissing-Hitler speech. "If he weren't Irish, he would certainly seem German," this rather spacey new FBI informant concluded.[37]

At a meeting held the evening before Scholz's post was due to close, Moran "spoke angrily of the German Consul being sent home." In fact Scholz was not headed to Germany. Scholz's next assignment was to the German legation in Budapest, where his fluent Hungarian would come in handy. Miklós Horthy, regent of the Kingdom of Hungary, was ambivalent about Hitler and reluctant to accept his status as a Nazi client. He also scuffled with the Nazis over Jewish deportations to the death camps. Himmler must have thought Scholz had done well in the United States, if his next job was to be such a delicate one.

An FBI report from 1942 indicates that Scholz spent his last evening in Boston with Moran. It was a dangerous move. No longer protected by the State Department, Scholz must have expected that he was under intensive surveillance. That he would risk exposing his asset demonstrates how important Moran had become to the Nazi project in the United States: meeting with Moran was a matter of urgency—otherwise it would not have happened. Clearly the men took great pains to maintain secrecy, because the FBI had no idea about the meeting until more than a year later, when an informant dragged the story out of Moran. At this final liaison, Scholz urged Moran to keep up his work, assuring the Christian Front leader that the cause was not lost and he would soon return. Scholz predicted a rout of the Allies. He had put his furniture in storage rather than sell it, confident that he would be back within five years. Scholz also guaranteed that he "never talked in the presence of the consulate secretaries," fearing FBI plants, and that all of his "confidential files" had been burned. Moran was likely gratified when he read that the consulate's tony neighbors on Beacon Hill had called the fire department to complain of smoke emanating from the building. The *Globe* reported that "Lieutenant John Hoar of Engine #10 went to the consulate and found the smoke and sparks were caused by attachés burning papers in the furnace."[38]

Moran kept the sparks flying in Boston. At one summer 1941 Christian Front meeting, he told his audience that FDR needed to be "removed from office by force and violence" after he had treasonously ordered the US occupation of Iceland. Moran spent much of the second half of 1941 on a tour of the East Coast, parts of the Midwest, and Canada, spreading the message that war against Germany was futile. He "travels all over New England," an FBI source reported, where he "talked with everyone from the mayor of a town down to the chambermaid and the local barber." He told Canadians that the fighter planes the United States had sent their way for delivery to Britain "had to be rearmed because the American guns were defective."[39]

On August 29 Moran traveled to Scotch Plains, New Jersey, for a key meeting with the publisher George Sylvester Viereck. Viereck was not shy about his pro-Nazi views. In 1923 he had been one of the first journalists to interview Hitler. Viereck gazed "into Hitler's 'magnetic blue eyes,' and characterized him as a superman."[40] In 1939 Viereck established Flanders Hall Publishers to generate Nazi propaganda pamphlets, of which Moran was a distributor. There is every indication that Strempel and Viereck worked together to get the materials to Moran.[41] But in 1941 it was Moran who came to Viereck, with the intent to effectively take over his operation. Apparently Moran "received a tip" that Flanders Hall was soon to close down. He later divulged that he purchased the pamphlets "to keep them out of the hands of British and the Jews, who wished to destroy them"—such a tip must have come either from Nazi intelligence or from a Nazi sympathizer inside US intelligence or law enforcement. If the tip was from German intelligence, this was a sign that Moran was being promoted, taking over Viereck's role as chief propagandist in the region. However he learned of the coming closure, Moran arrived in Scotch Plains with an ambitious agenda: he bought as many volumes as he could, returning to Boston with 16,000 copies of Viereck's works. Five weeks after striking his deal with Moran, Viereck was in handcuffs, about to stand trial for failing to register as a foreign agent. After a number of prosecutorial stumbles, he was finally convicted under FARA in 1944 and would spend three years in prison.[42]

Moran, demonstrating his always-keen business sense, repackaged the pamphlets into books and used Christian Front members as a salesforce. He took one each of Viereck's seventeen different pamphlets and bound them into a single volume priced at four dollars, a hefty sum but perhaps worth it to fans of Nazi literature. Fronters would buy the books and resell them. A Christian Front member who spoke to the FBI said Moran "urged us all to buy as many as we can, and sell as many as we can." Recognizing that Viereck was under indictment for publishing the very works that he was now distributing, Moran asked Christian Front members to conduct their sales discreetly, "otherwise, you can send me cigarettes in jail!"[43]

Moran spent the rest of 1941 castigating Jews and calling on his clerical supporters to preach the gospel of anti-Semitism. On October 20, at "an unusually large meeting—so crowded that chairs were placed in the aisles," Moran described "the Jews" as "a hindrance and a source of evil to any country that held them." Sounding a novel and disturbing genocidal note, he exclaimed that "there could be no room for two religions at odds with each other." Strangely, he added that "court records would show how evil the Jews really were." Perhaps Moran was suggesting that one day the Jews would be duly tried for their crimes. It is a delusion reminiscent of the New York fronters. They thought they would seed America's next government; likewise, Moran seemed to think that, in a just world to come, his law would reign.[44]

The following week, October 27, the Christian Front met for an evening with Father Brophy, who injected a bit of religion into meetings that were now dominated by antiwar agitation rather than sermonizing. Even the Judeo-Bolshevist threat to Christianity had been receiving short shrift, as Moran focused instead on the Jewish threat to Germany and the conspiracy of Jewish bankers and sympathetic politicians peddling war. Audiences no doubt appreciated this sort of talk, even though it emerged from the Nazi playbook more than that of Catholic anti-Semitism. Those were the wages of Coughlin's style of human rights, after all. But the crowd—to say nothing of Moran himself—still hungered for the holy word. When Father Brophy entered Hibernian Hall, "there was a tremendous ovation, everybody standing up." He received another ovation after he was introduced. "The audience rose cheering and applauded most enthusiastically."

Taking the stage with Bible in hand, Brophy began to read—from all four Gospels—the story of Christ and Barabbas, the murderer whom Pilate released in response to the exhortation of the crowd at the crucifixion. The story was an important one in the annals of Catholic anti-Semitism, for it seemed to show a mob of Jews demanding clemency for a criminal and execution for Christ. After a dramatic pause, Brophy asked, "Is it a sin to hate the Jews?" "Can you love a man who prefers the killer Barabbas?" "Can you love a race which is leading us to war because Barabbas is chosen over Christ?" Brophy did not have to use Moran's increasingly secular rhetoric to reach the same conclusions. "Let them fight their own battles," Brophy resolved. An FBI plant at the meeting noted that the priest "damned the Jews in a perfectly nice religious way."[45]

That said, like Moran, Father Brophy had made his peace with Nazism. An Anti-Defamation League operative in attendance on October 27 wrote of Brophy, "He didn't feel that there was any danger in Nazism, declaring that the real danger was Marxism." Brophy knew what he was getting into. "I will be called a Nazi for that statement—but that doesn't disturb me," he confessed. "I have been called a Nazi before."[46] Here again, the Roman Catholic synergy with Nazism was more a function of shared anti-Communism than theological overlap. Brophy could never have given credence to the pantheistic and mystical elements of Nazism, but Brophy absolutely could have agreed "that the two 'faiths' [Nazism and Roman Catholicism] shared enough common enemies—Communism . . . anarchism, Judaism . . . alleged social and moral decadence—to make collaboration fruitful," as the historian Roger Griffin put it. Moran may have taken a reminder from Brophy. By November, with Nazi Field Marshal Erwin Rommel racing across Egypt, Moran was tempering his June remarks about kissing Hitler and instead presenting Christian collusion with Nazis as a matter of compromise. "It is not that we love the devil in brown," he wrote in a Thanksgiving postcard to Christian Front members, "but we hate the devil in red much more."[47]

That was the last Thanksgiving before the war fully and finally came to the United States. At this point, Moran had seemingly survived just about everything that could be thrown at him. He had gained and lost many patrons and come out in fine form. He had the support of friendly priests and a slew of books to sell. He had found a happy medium between Christ and

Hitler that served his intellectual and political needs and kept him publicly relevant. Usually, his role as a religious figure protected him from legal scrutiny. And when the First Amendment was not enough, he found clever workarounds. Moran could see that government officials were on his case, but he seemed to know the law better than they did and had the confidence to press ahead while they fumbled. Other foes might be more capable, though. Moran would soon find out just how capable, when British spies came for him.

CHAPTER 10

Questions of the Most Delicate Kind

"I DO NOT RECOMMEND VIOLENCE," MORAN BOOMED TO HIS CHRIS-
tian Fronters. Specifically, he was not recommending violence against the
Irish American Defense Association (IADA), a new organization in town.
IADA wanted "to let the world know, and the president in particular, that
Irish-Americans were behind the administration's policy." The front devoted
its meeting of December 1, 1941, to planning for IADA's inaugural gathering,
scheduled for the fateful day of December 7 at Faneuil Hall.

"All good Irish-Americans are definitely opposed to the president's policy,"
Moran told the fronters. Then he "paused very effectively," according to an
observer who shared his thoughts in a letter to Reverend Walton E. Cole, a
Boston minister who was wary of Moran. During that dramatic pause, mum-
bling could be heard throughout the hall. Small groups of fronters seemed
to be discussing creative ways by which they could break up the IADA meeting.
Looking around from the stage, Moran understood what was happening. He
then "as would a very capable actor, threw kisses to the crowd . . . and the
crowd cheered loudly."[1]

Moran had a plan of his own. Fronters would arrive early and occupy most
of the seats. Then a boisterous walkout was to take place. When the day of
the IADA event came, the fronters followed their leader. One eyewitness described "the concerted effort of a group of people walking out." In the middle
of the meeting, "a large number of persons arose from their seats with booing
and raucous laughter" and "moved slowly away." "Several scores of hecklers

stormed from the auditorium," the *Boston Herald* reported. The front's antics were, as one letter to the *Boston Globe* put it, a "dreadful symbol." Just a few hours after the attack on Pearl Harbor, Moran and the Christian Front did not pause to honor the more than 2,400 Americans who had been killed. They went through with their plan and disrupted the meeting.[2]

IADA's emcee that evening was an inconspicuous Bostonian named Frances Sweeney. She wanted to keep a low profile and declined to speak herself. She had been working diligently behind the scenes for weeks to bring the meeting together, only to hear it crash around her, amid jeering about "the Jews who have gotten us into this war" and "President Roosevelt, that tool of the international Jews." Sweeney confessed to a friend that the walkout "left me with my Irish so far up it could never come down."[3]

Sweeney was well connected among Boston's liberal intelligentsia and had solid contacts in the news business. But she was not a public figure, and few knew anything about her murky organization. Among those who were familiar with IADA, however, there was a good deal of suspicion. In New York, *The Irish Advocate* argued that IADA was "fake," suggesting "there is very little Irish about it except the green ink in which it prints some of its literature." The Boston Central Council of Irish County Associations passed a resolution sharply criticizing IADA, which had formed independently of the council and was unknown to it. The Ancient Order of Hibernians, perhaps the most important Irish-American political organization, was skeptical, again because they knew nothing about the group. In the wake of the December 7 meeting, when Bostonians at large found out about IADA, one wrote to the *Globe* expressing his view that the last thing the city needed was another neighborhood political association.[4]

Some skeptics were not sure that IADA actually was a neighborhood political association. Burton Wheeler, a US senator from Montana, thought IADA was nothing more than "an outfit organized . . . to stir up Irish-Americans for war." When Wheeler was asked by a reporter about IADA's announcement that it would not be seeking contributions, the senator scowled, "They don't need any contributions—their expenses will be paid by England . . . or out of the lend-lease money." Like many in official Washington, Wheeler strongly suspected that the British were involved in intelligence activities in the United States, in particular that FDR's newly established Office of the Coordinator of Information was a British "mentoring" project within the US government. But Wheeler was easily dismissed as a partisan with an axe to grind. Formerly an FDR supporter, the senator changed his mind after the court-packing scheme of 1937. Wheeler then became one of the most vociferous isolationists in the Senate. He once described the Lend-Lease Act as "the New Deal's Triple-A foreign policy to plow under every fourth American boy."[5]

Yet Wheeler's instincts concerning IADA were dead on. The organization was in fact a creation of British intelligence, in its effort to sway American opinion toward the war. Sweeney was like Moran in that both were agents of foreign powers, yet genuinely committed to their ideologies and policy goals. Both were also devout Catholics who were moved to their political positions by their interpretations of the Gospel, by the call of Catholic social action, and by their own life experiences. But Sweeney and Moran differed in a key way: Moran knew he was a foreign agent; Sweeney did not know that she was.

As far as Sweeney knew, she was developing her own agenda—influenced by her associates, perhaps, but not by a handler. She executed that agenda through persuasion, skilled organizing, and masterful manipulation of the press. Where Moran stood on stages and held forth, Sweeney wrote letters to news publishers, dunned business leaders behind closed doors, brought together influential people in close quarters, and fed carefully timed stories to the papers. Her schemes were based on superior knowledge of the Boston political and media landscape and on her singular determination to undo the Christian Front and suppress anti-Semitic and Fascist sentiment broadly.

Yet Sweeney was working for an organization both funded and founded by British intelligence. Unwittingly, she was in frequent contact with a person who was, quite wittingly, working for the British. The exact identity of this go-between—referred to, in the parlance of the spy world, as a cutout—has never been established. It must have been a confidante of Sweeney's: someone whom she trusted, with whom she was willing to share plans, and from whom she was prone to take guidance. In other words, the cutout was almost certainly a true friend of Sweeney's, whom the British tasked with recruiting, monitoring, and assisting IADA's leader.

The construction of IADA was a byzantine process involving a heap of UK intelligence agencies nested within each other and interacting via coded messages. Before and during World War II, the British spy apparatus, like the German, was vastly more capable than that of the United States, hence the installation of the Coordinator of Information as a British mentee. Boston, perceived as critical to the development of US public opinion because of the strong anti-British sentiment among the city's politically powerful Irish American community, became a front line in the war, even as no shots were fired there. Even today, Americans are largely unaware of the extent of British and German espionage across the United States as both powers struggled either to prod Americans into the war or keep them on the sidelines.

This black-ops contest was perhaps nowhere more urgent than in Boston, where Sweeney faced off with the Christian Front. The bitter irony of Sweeney's effort is that as soon as she exposed Moran as a Nazi propagandist, the Boston Police swooped in and interrupted. Finally a law-enforcement agency was putting the fight to Moran. Yet it is hard to escape the conclusion that the police, who had long been allies of the front, were still on his side. In January 1942, officers did shut down the Christian Front. But Commissioner Joseph Timilty disrupted more serious investigations at the federal level. And he so clearly violated Moran's civil liberties that he imperiled any chance for prosecution. Ultimately the two would reach a deal to save each other.

A Secret History

IADA was born in New York, at 8 West 40th Street, founded by Christopher Emmet, an American and a longtime British intelligence contact. The idea was to contest John Cassidy and the Christian Front. Emmet's group enjoyed good publicity and was well funded, but once the Christian Front was cut down to size in New York, IADA lost its sense of purpose and began to look like a rather pointless speech-making organization headed by wealthy elites. Historian Thomas Mahl, one of the few who has written about IADA, concluded that, if the group was a British spy asset, it was an ineffectual one, "reduced to whining about 'vicious attacks by the Coughlinite Irish Organizations and Press.'"[6]

In 1998, the same year Mahl's book was released, readers gained access to a landmark compendium of formerly classified British intelligence documents, which showed with certainty that IADA was indeed a UK asset. This compendium, *British Security Coordination: The Secret History of British Intelligence in the Americas, 1940–1945*, presented a selective history of British Security Coordination (BSC), the US umbrella organization of the British

Secret Intelligence Service, also known as MI6. BSC had a robust US presence, with offices located in New York City's Rockefeller Center. The provenance of the material contained in the book is vague. As the story goes, in 1945 the chief of BSC in the United States, Sir William Stephenson, arranged for all of BSC's files to be moved, under armed guard, to Canada. At Camp X, outside of Toronto, three British intelligence officers tasked by Stephenson read the files and distilled them into a single-volume history of BSC, containing accounts of British spying success in North America and Latin America.

But even successful spying is not necessarily suitable for public revelation. Just twenty copies of the history were produced and bound, and the archive itself was destroyed. After the volume was completed to Stephenson's satisfaction, one of its compilers was "instructed to collect the entire BSC archive and burn it . . . thereby ensuring that the twenty printed copies were the only extant historical record of BSC." Eight copies were distributed among President Roosevelt, Prime Minister Churchill, and other principals. Of the remaining twelve copies, Stephenson ordered ten burned. This was done in 1946, at a farm near Montreal.[7] Stephenson retained the last two copies for himself, marked them "Top Secret," and locked them in a bank vault. Editing his own archive via matchstick, Stephenson was not only creating a chronicle of the successes of BSC but potentially expurgating material that might have embarrassed BSC or run afoul of US law.[8]

The 1998 *Secret History* contains eleven paragraphs on IADA, but none of them pertain to its operations in Boston. Rather, the *Secret History's* discussion of IADA focuses on the organization's work pressing the US government to in turn press Ireland itself, which was officially neutral. Both BSC and the United States were never successful in changing that position, although Ireland did at times, without publicity, assist the Allies. Scholars who have written about IADA since 1998 have invariably adopted this theme, viewing IADA as focused on affecting Irish policy. Both the secret history and subsequent authors overlooked IADA's domestic role, including Sweeney's war with the Christian Front.[9]

It is possible that some US writers have, for some time, known more about IADA than they have let on. In September 1989, eight months after Stephenson's death, a 423-page document entitled "British Security Coordination (BSC): An Account of Secret Activities in the Western Hemisphere, 1940–1945," was turned over to CIA historian Thomas F. Troy and *Washington Post* defense reporter David Ignatius. The source of the 423-page document is unknown. Drawing on what he found in the document, Ignatius published the bombshell article "Britain's War in America." There is no way of knowing if the 423-page document reviewed by Ignatius contained the same material as Stephenson's last two locked volumes and whether and how this material differs from what appears in the *Secret History*. Ignatius considered what he found in the 423-page document a "shocking" disclosure of the means by which British intelligence "manipulated" US public opinion prior to Pearl Harbor.[10] Other US journalists, Mike Wallace and George Crile III, have come to similar conclusions concerning British propaganda efforts in the United States. In 1979 Wallace and Crile produced "Target: America," a TV pilot in which former US and British spies talked about BSC. The reporters were stunned by the "dirty tricks and smear campaigns" the British used to discredit antiwar Americans and "get the United States directly involved in World War II." Britain's espionage and covert propaganda operations even seemed to have the approval of President Roosevelt. All the networks balked at the pilot, though. A few years after Watergate, media organizations were not ready to impeach another American president—even in the court of historical memory—and especially not one so admired as Roosevelt.[11]

With journalists either shut down or closely guarding sources they were not authorized to share, it was not until 2016 that a large quantity of reliable information involving BSC's stateside activities was made available. In that year the UK National Archives released a sizable tranche of files from a wartime agency called the Special Operations Executive. SOE was created on the orders of Winston Churchill in July 1940, with the purpose of promoting resistance groups in German-occupied areas. In Churchill's famous phrase, SOE would "set Europe ablaze." But not just Europe. In practice SOE was neither strictly focused on Europe nor solely interested in sabotage and subversion. From the start SOE operated globally and placed officers with BSC in the United States. SOE also incorporated a British intelligence unit called Electra House, which cultivated "black propaganda"—information purported to be from a trusted source on the target's own side. Black propaganda was precisely Moran's specialty while working for Scholz.[12]

This is where IADA comes in. If the Christian Front became a black propaganda outfit for the Nazis, IADA was a black propaganda outfit for the British. This becomes clear in SOE's files—files that Stephenson could not burn. The BSC archive is gone for good, save for the materials chronicled in the *Secret*

History. But the SOE archive contains loads of BSC documents, thanks to the many SOE operatives who were working for Stephenson. As of 2016, those documents are available to us. They reveal a BSC quite different from the one appearing in Stephenson's official *Secret History.* Historian Keith Jeffrey, author of an authorized history of MI6, wrote that "the BSC Official History of 1945 [was] clearly designed to show the organization in the best possible light." The papers released in 2016 reveal something more morally ambiguous. The goals of the real BSC were the same as the one presented in the official history: to induce the United States to join the war. But the methods and attitudes of BSC were not entirely admirable. The agency implemented a robust and entirely undetected clandestine effort in the United States, in which Americans were very much pawns in a game of foreign powers.[13]

The results, as is seemingly inevitable in covert operations, were mixed. From the standpoint of spy craft, BSC's efforts in the United States were often masterful. But many laws were broken, and many lives were ruined. In Boston, Stephenson's campaign of deception generated ripple effects, including violence and civil rights violations. The effort to take down Moran by any means necessary would eventually undermine Jewish-Catholic relations in the city. This was irrelevant, however, from the perspective of British intelligence. BSC understood itself to be at war in the United States, and every war breeds collateral damage.

Battlefield America

As far as BSC was concerned, there was no such thing as American neutrality. The United States was in the conflict long before Pearl Harbor—not as a belligerent but as a theater of action in a propaganda war. Thus one of BSC's tasks was "combatting hostile (American or neutral) influences in the Americas." As the British officer Colonel Sir Geoffrey Vickers wrote in a chilling report for SOE, "The first essential is to regard the U.S.A. as a battlefield and to realize that as it becomes increasingly involved in war it may become more of a battlefield."

Vickers compiled his report after visiting New York in February 1941, at the same time the Democratic-led House of Representatives passed the Lend-Lease Act in a landslide. It might, then, have seemed that the battle for America had been won. Undoubtedly Lend-Lease had its critics, yet the balance of public opinion was in favor, and the largely party-line vote in the

House indicated that the outcome in the Democratic-controlled Senate was not in doubt. Yet Vickers was not convinced that the United States was truly in Britain's camp. "The confused, unstable, yet powerful forces of American opinion are being continually manipulated by pressures, applied by groups of all kinds," he wrote. "Beneath and sometimes under cover of . . . domestic issues, the war is being fought incessantly with weapons varying from humanitarian appeals to knives and poison." Britain would never resort to knives and poison in battlefield America, but pressure and manipulation were very much arrows in BSC's quiver. British intelligence, no less than its German counterpart, aimed to win the contest for American hearts and minds.[14]

To this end, Irish Americans were an early focus of British agents. In spring 1941 Electra House prepared "Notes on Irish-American Opinion," a secret report that argued "Irish America was still a potent influence" on political life in the United States, and that Irish Americans, if left unplacated, could harm the British war effort. Electra House regarded "the Irish dog as sleeping but not dead . . . if it howled loud enough it might arouse a measure of general sympathy." Sympathy for the Irish was not typically in Britain's interest.

If Britain was to secure America's support in the war—if, above all, it was to secure a military alliance—then Westminster would have to take the Irish question seriously on both sides of the Atlantic. Electra House made a number of recommendations. One recommendation was that Britain refrain from occupying Irish ports. The idea of seizing Irish ports was a radical one, but some quarters in London had for years considered it an option in the event of another world war. Electra House argued that such a course of action would have disastrous effects in American politics, swaying Congress and the White House against the UK position. Another recommendation was a carefully tailored black propaganda operation. "Overt propaganda activity," the report warned, "is both risky and superfluous." But "propaganda by qualified Americans . . . might well be effective."[15]

Boston was of particular importance in the battle for Irish American opinion. The Electra House report identified Boston as the "rallying point" for anti-British sentiment in the United States and singled out "Cardinal O'Connell . . . as an ancient monument to implacability." Agents on the ground would soon confirm that Irish Boston was a major obstacle to British interests. When William Agar—a former Columbia University geology professor and World War I pilot, and a BSC operative—delivered a speech at Faneuil Hall in May 1941 aiming to convince US Austrian Catholics to unite against Hitler, he found it was Irish Catholics, not Austrians, who were the problem in New England. Agar left Boston shaken by his experience with the "violent isolationism" of local Irish Catholics, but also convinced that something needed to be done about the situation.[16]

One Irish Catholic Bostonian who spurred British intelligence to action was Father Michael Ahern, who had provided theological cover to Moran in 1940. In July 1941 he went public with more of his ruminations. This time, the Jesuit scientist was the subject of a *Boston Globe* piece in which he "called Communism and Nazism two of a kind." He elaborated on the point while speaking at Harvard University's Littauer Center. "Both ideologies deny the rights of the individual soul, both reject spiritual values, both are vowed to the destruction of the Judeo-Christian outlook on life and on the value of life."[17]

Ahern was not aligning with the Scholz-era Christian Front. He was making a serious theological argument against Nazism, in addition to Communism. But BSC was not a talk shop. Nor did its agents see much advantage in equating Nazism and Communism. The fact was that, at this point in the war, allying with Britain meant allying with the Soviets as well. A month earlier, the Axis had broken off the Molotov-Ribbentrop Pact and invaded the Soviet Union. Stalin was now working with the British and was receiving American Lend-Lease aid. Calling out Hitler and Stalin in the same breath was at best a motion for neutrality, which was as good as useless. The Boston Irish would never swing toward Britain if they were listening to the likes of Ahern.

Five days after the *Globe* published its Ahern story, the wheels started turning at BSC'S New York office. "We are considering formation of [an] Irish-American group to defend democracy," an unsigned telegram to MI6 in London read. "We can probably secure twelve prominent Irish Americans to start this group." The telegram ended with a line that would have horrified every rank-and-file member of the Christian Front: "There is a chance now of obtaining active support here from Irish Communists." The message was addressed to A.C.C.S., the codename for MI6 Deputy Chief Claude Dansey.[18]

Instead of A.C.C.S., the reply, two days later, came from a source identified as U. U recommended caution with respect to "the possible use of . . . the Irish Communists in America" to carry out SOE's black propaganda. "This obviously raises questions of the most delicate kind." But U signaled tacit approval for a Communist-free propaganda campaign directed at Irish Americans by acknowledging that the proposal had been "passed on to 48000," the code name of Stephenson, who was away from New York at the time. It is likely that U was a high-ranking figure, probably Alexander Cadogan, the permanent undersecretary of foreign affairs. Cadogan is known to have "paid serious attention to intelligence," historians Christopher Andrew and David Dilks have written. Cadogan had also read and been "very interested" in the Electra House report. In its own delicate way, the exchange makes clear that the Irish American black propaganda scheme was getting top-level consideration in London.[19]

Within a week of U's reply, Irish Catholics in Boston were being spied on. According to a declassified BSC report, William Agar was dispatched to Boston once more, this time "to soften Cardinal O'Connell and his mouthpiece, Ahern." Apparently Agar gave a speech in Boston "attacking Ahern's stand," but the address was totally ignored in the press. Nevertheless, BSC was encouraged and believed that Ahern was beginning to modify what the agency uncharitably described as "his previous pro-Nazi, anti-English stand." The after-action report on Agar's trip urged British intelligence to continue focusing on Boston. "We should keep up this sort of pounding in that area particularly as Ahern slips back, and Moran of the Christian Mobilizers is more active than ever." This the first mention of Moran in BSC documents. The report mislabeled his organization but rightly placed Moran at the center of anti-British sentiment in Boston.

While in Boston, Agar began the process of organizing a pro-British Irish American group. He found the effort enormously challenging. It was possible to find Irish Americans supportive of the British war effort, but willingness to share those views in public was in short supply. Agar approached two prominent Boston Irish Catholics, "to head up the Committee"—that is, a proposed committee to push for Roosevelt's pro-British policy. But while the two were "in sympathy with the Committee, they say they cannot step out in front." If they did, "the Cardinal or his henchman Ahearn [sic], will attack them from the pulpit and the radio," Agar wrote. He had learned from a local insider that Cardinal O'Connell believed nine in ten Boston Catholics opposed aid to Great Britain. "The worst of it is," Agar concluded, "the Cardinal's assertion is very nearly right."[20]

The British sought Irish American personalities to rival the cardinal. In particular, agents thought the Democratic Party might avail a champion, so agents posed as party activists in order to woo men of consequence. One option was Al Smith, the Irish Catholic former governor of New York and 1928

Democratic presidential nominee, who had endorsed FDR at a key speech in Boston in 1932. But Smith "was reluctant to join any more committees" and worried that IADA, even if well intentioned, would be swallowed in controversy. He declined the invitation. Another candidate was Edward Burke, one of the first Irish Catholics to work at the prestigious Boston law firm of Hale and Dorr (now WilmerHale). Burke was appointed by FDR to the Volunteer Participation Committee of the Office of Civilian Defense and was an important figure in Massachusetts Democratic circles. But when he was invited to lead an organization calling itself the Irish American Defense Association, Burke responded coolly. He believed that "no special committee should be formed" in Boston and argued that public speeches and letters to the press would suffice. By October, a grim pattern had set in. "Several prominent Irish in Boston are working with us," one BSC agent wrote to his superior. "They are not prepared, however, to come out in front in a formal committee."[21]

Fall 1941 was a time of desperation for BSC and the British war effort generally. Britain's military position was faltering, making American entry into the war critical. Barbarossa and its aftermath had been devastating, as the Germans made large gains on the Eastern Front and maintained air superiority. The British mainland was also suffering terribly under the Luftwaffe's barrage. In a July speech reflecting on a recent trip to Britain, *New York Post* publisher George Backer observed, "In London, your eyes get accustomed to the destruction, with the heart of the City all gone." Yet America remained stubbornly on the fence. The same day Backer gave his speech, Viscount Lord Halifax, the British ambassador to the United States, visited the Lockheed plant in Burbank, California, to thank workers there for supplying a hundred Hudson Bombers to Britain. On his way into the plant, the ambassador was met by picketers lofting placards reading "Wake Up America!—The British Are Here!" and "To Halifax with Halifax."[22]

As the days wore on, even Churchill took up directly the challenge of installing a propaganda army in America. That a wartime prime minister staring into the jaws of defeat could devote any energy to such a project demonstrates its critical importance. On November 24 Churchill wrote to Anthony Eden, the former foreign secretary, inviting him to take over the Political Warfare Executive, SOE's new black propaganda branch. "If you feel . . . that not only is the task of building up the 'British Fifth Column' all over the world important, but that S.O.E. is a good machine for constructing it, it would be a very great help if you could arrange for some expression of your views," Churchill implored. That the former foreign secretary was being asked to handle black propaganda speaks further to the conviction within British intelligence that America had to be turned, and that a seemingly homegrown public-opinion campaign was the key. Churchill hoped that, with Eden in charge, "we can really get the S.O.E. machine working as the instrument of policy that it ought to be."[23]

In Boston the British tried to force the issue. A few days after Churchill's letter to Eden, British agents set up IADA offices in the Little Building, at the corner of Boylston and Tremont streets. A Modern Gothic high-rise with a façade of Deer Isle granite and cast stone, the Little Building was perhaps the most fashionable Boston office building of the period. It commanded beautiful views of Boston Common and the Public Garden. But while IADA had a desirable office, there still was no one to fill it.

BSC blamed two forces above all for their difficulties recruiting in Boston. One, as we have seen, was the Catholic Church. Cardinal O'Connell would "crack down immediately" on anyone who stepped forward as "pronouncedly pro-British." BSC realized that the Church was a principal reason that "the Irish in Massachusetts, both 'lace curtain' and 'shanty,' are better organized than anywhere else in the country," and the same Church was not pushing its flock to change its attitude toward Britain's war effort. The second obstacle was "the bigoted American Fascist Christian Mobilizer wing in New England . . . ably led by Francis Moran." BSC was still getting the name of the group wrong, confusing it with that of Joe McWilliams's New York–based Mobilizers. But after a few months of studying the Boston isolationist scene, they knew its leader and understood what he was capable of. "He provides the whole bag of tricks," a BSC report noted, "rabble-rousing, race prejudice, and religious bigotry." Agents also concluded that "he has some behind-the-door support from higher clergy."

It was not just the Church that backed Moran. He seemed to be everywhere, from the heights of the clergy to the union halls. BSC thought "the most amenable Irish-Americans for aid to Britain are in the organized labor groups," but Moran was getting in the way. Union organizers were "entirely willing to help along the program of our Committee," yet rank-and-file members had other opinions. "In the labor unions, Coughlin's *Social Justice* is widely sold around the union Halls," operatives wrote, "this helps generate the following for Moran."[24] There was great concern that, with Moran a thorn in the side locally, national figures en route to Boston later in the year would compound the struggle. "Wheeler—Lindbergh [and] Nye are all coming here in December," a secret reporter penned to London, referring to Senator Wheeler; Senator Gerald Nye, the influential North Dakota Republican; and Charles Lindbergh, the heroic aviator, anti-Semite, and America First Committee member who opposed the war and US aid to Britain.[25]

But fortunes can turn quickly. In late November, after months of failing to attract an elite leader from the ranks of politics or business to head IADA's Boston branch, BSC struck paydirt. They had finally zeroed in on someone who possessed the intellect, motivation, and organizational skills to helm the Boston branch. Her name was Frances Sweeney.

Marvelously Militant

"Frances Sweeney, a publicity agent . . . [who is] . . . marvelously militant for our cause has agreed to take on the job," the BSC cutout wrote to London in November. She was "a stalwart" who "felt it was [her] patriotic duty to go to town on this to help the Irish themselves and the country as well." The cutout described initiating talks with Sweeney in early fall 1941. It took some time to coax her into a leadership role, but when she was finally onboard, she proved an immediate boon. Almost from day one, fortunes began to turn in IADA's favor, and at the street level—the very combat zone where Moran would need to be engaged.[26]

Characterizing Sweeney as an unsuspecting British operative in violation of the Foreign Agents Registration Act may be an unpopular position. Over the past twenty years, Sweeney was resurrected from obscurity and is now lauded for her anti-Fascist and civil rights activities during World War II. In 2001 historian, First Amendment defender, and public intellectual Nat Hentoff dedicated a new edition of his memoir *Boston Boy* to Sweeney. In her own time, many knew her as "Boston's leader in the fight against intolerance."[27]

We can feel confident in the sincerity of Sweeney's views. "A Fascist is anyone who hates the common man," Sweeney once told a friend. Her conviction was driven by faith. Anti-Fascists like Sweeney were a minority among American Catholics by 1939, but they were not extinct. Sweeney and other Catholic anti-Fascists, no less than the Christian Front, believed they were following authentic Catholic theological imperatives. One lodestar was Pope Pius XI's encyclical *Non Abbiamo Bisogno* (1931), which highlighted the "statolatry" of Fascism and Nazism and presented Fascism as opposed to Catholic Action. The Catholic left argued that obsessive anti-Communism elided the message of *Non Abbiamo Bisogno* and blinded Catholics to the injustices of Fascism and Nazism.[28]

Sweeney's convictions were also driven by experience. She had grown up in an Irish Bostonian family that rejected the clannishness associated with that group. According to one source, her "earliest memory as a child was of her father single-handedly beating some Bostonians who were mauling and torturing a helpless Chinese person on a streetcar." When she was born in 1907, her father James had just left his job as a bartender to take a technical job with the city, handling weights and measures. In this role, he was in contact with many in government service and politics, while maintaining connections to the working class. Frances's mother also worked, as a bookkeeper. James Sweeney was consumed with politics of the proletarian sort.[29]

The Sweeneys were also, it is fair to say, one of the few Catholic families in 1930s Boston that read *New Masses*. A Marxist intellectual journal linked to the CPUSA, *New Masses* was decidedly unusual bedtime reading, perhaps especially for a young woman whom one friend described as "cheerful, bright, energetic, and as Irish as Paddy's shillelagh." Anti-Communism rose dramatically among Boston Irish Catholics in the 1920s, becoming a defining characteristic. But James regularly brought home copies and shared them with his children, and Frances read them, especially once she was in high school.[30]

In addition to reading, events pushed Frances Sweeney toward leftism and eventually Catholic anti-Fascism. Like Moran, Sweeney experienced a transformative job loss during the Great Depression. After graduating from Mount St. Joseph Academy in 1925, Sweeney started working at a Boston insurance company. She moved up from typist to stenographer and was placed in the brokerage department. It was on the brokerage floor where fortunes were made and lost. As a young woman, she was able to observe the raw emotion underlying the profit motive. Then, in 1937, she suddenly was without a job.[31]

This was no ordinary bout of unemployment. Sweeney had many older colleagues who paid the way for their families, breadwinners in an era when few women joined her mother in the workforce. She witnessed the terror of these freshly laid-off friends, the terror and the hardship. Sweeney went looking for work with someone who felt viscerally the injustice of finding oneself on capitalism's cutting-room floor. In fall 1938 she discovered that Granville Hicks was hiring. The editor of *New Masses* and a famously public

CPUSA member since 1934, Hicks was looking for a secretary to assist him while he was a visiting professor at Harvard. Sweeney wanted the job, and she may have fudged a few details to get it. At one point she wrote, "I am 26 years old, college trained, and widely read. I may not be too bright by your standards, but I am eager to learn the kind of knowledge you have." Sweeney was plenty bright, but she was also about thirty years old at the time, not twenty-six. It is also not clear that she was college-trained, although she may have been. But certainly she was, as she pointed out, "familiar with [Hicks's] magazine articles and writings" and was "not afraid of hard work, nor of long hours."

In another note, Sweeney described her tale of leftist epiphany. "We always had the *New Masses* around the house—but they never jolted me very much," she wrote. Then, in high school, she "realized one day that they were nearer right in their thinking than what I was led to believe." She told Hicks that when the forces of the Great Depression overwhelmed her brokerage house, the New Deal was not enough to rescue her or her coworkers. The system was rotten to the core. Even the massive intervention of the New Deal amounted to "do-nothing policies" in the face of the working person's plight.

"I saw a man . . . die," she wrote, "drop over me while he was dictating his last few letters on the job before his transfer."

> He was a man who married late in life because his economic standing would not allow it sooner. A man, who had five children because his church did not believe in birth control. There he was—a man who never earned enough to save—buffeted by two systems—religious and economic. He was just one of many white-collared workers who suffer from Insecurity, which breaks men's spirits.

The trauma triggered a reaction in her own body. "I got choked up—couldn't get my breath—and was taken to the hospital with heart trouble." While recovering, Sweeney learned "that all the older men in my office with good paying positions had been dismissed." She and her coworkers were victims of a kind of predation. "There was Insecurity reaching in after me again."

Sweeney did not return to the brokerage after her hospital visit. Instead she took a moral stand in solidarity with fellow workers:

> I wrote in and resigned my position—it was better doing that than being in a constant state of doubt. I told them that I would probably meet more intelligent people at the Five and Dime Store where I would perhaps

end up; that my soul was suffering from permanent shudders because of their tactics toward their employees. It was ghastly to think of those men who have lost their jobs at the age of 37 to 50 after years of work for one concern.

"I do hope that I am going to be bright enough to do your mail for you," Sweeney added. She got the job.[32]

Hicks must have been mightily impressed, wary as he was of employing a Catholic. Hicks's presence at Harvard had provoked high dudgeon among Catholics. Father Coughlin wrote that crimson, the school color, "took on new significance with the advent of the Red Hicks." Coughlin made sure *Social Justice* readers knew that Hicks was the first confessed Communist to join the Harvard faculty. Sweeney's personal connections also gave Hicks pause. Her uncle was Father J. Hugh O'Donnell, vice president of the University of Notre Dame and an energetic anti-Communist. But Sweeney showed that her faith meant something different than Coughlin's. For Sweeney, Catholicism was a reason to pursue a more universal kind of justice. And Catholicism was a worldview open to criticism. Her observation that her colleague was "buffeted" not only by capitalism but also by the Catholic prohibition on contraception marked her as a radical within the Church community.[33]

Working for Hicks was a defining experience. Sweeney would forever be considered a Communist sympathizer connected to the CPUSA. But in her career as a writer and activist she was less a Communist than an anti-Fascist. There were also anti-Fascist influences in her life, such as Gaetano Salvemini, who, like Hicks, was visiting at Harvard in 1938, while Sweeney was there. Historian Stephen H. Norwood has called Salvemini "the leading Italian spokesperson for anti-Fascism in the United States during the 1930s." Salvemini also had a reputation for inspiring women to take up the cause of international anti-Fascism. Sweeney read Salvemini voraciously and admired his thought.[34]

Salvemini had seen the perils of Fascism early on, when Mussolini forced him out of his position at the University of Florence in 1925. Unlike many anti-Fascists, he did not have to wait for 1935, when activists began following the banner of the Soviet Popular Front. Salvemini was a socialist but not a Stalinist, and he was an anti-Fascist first. Sweeney followed him in this regard. He also vocally opposed the Catholic Church's compromises with Fascism. In his 1936 book *Under the Axe of Fascism*, he implied that *Quadragesimo Anno*, Pope Pius XI's landmark 1931 encyclical on labor, paved the way for Mussolini, blessing with holy water his integration of workers and corporations into the state. The key point for Sweeney was that Salvemini criticized the hierarchy—even the highest-ranking clerics. In Salvemini, she saw that one could resist Church doctrine and still be a faithful Catholic.[35]

Sweeney took that lesson into her work for IADA. Salvemini's ideas buttressed her faith even as she went on to contest the teachings of Coughlin and Ahern, not to mention the official line of Cardinal O'Connell. And she kept IADA going even when, its work barely begun, its purpose seemed to dissolve in a hail of Japanese bombs. The day after the assault on Pearl Harbor, the United States officially joined the war against Japan, meaning that war with Germany, Japan's ally, was soon to follow. The British no longer needed to fight the propaganda war in the United States. But Sweeney, who had no idea that she was working for the British, did not see matters this way. "I think it is a good time to lay the bases of groundwork now," she wrote to her cutout in the days after Pearl Harbor. Sweeney also was committed to the anti-Fascist cause at home, and she knew that Moran would not disappear simply because the United States had entered the war—he had already upset her event hours after Pearl Harbor. Material interest may have also played a role in Sweeney's tenacity: according to one source, she took the IADA job shortly after her father had died, to help the family make ends meet. The cutout forwarded Sweeney's message to BSC, which agreed that IADA should continue to fight Fascism in Boston, the Christian Front specifically.[36]

Indeed, the front looked more popular than ever after the US entry into the war. Moran counted some of his biggest cash collections, and recorded some of his highest turnouts, after Pearl Harbor. On December 9 the American Jewish Committee's Henry Levy sent a report of the post–Pearl Harbor Christian Front meeting to the radio commentator Walter Winchell. Winchell was shocked to read that the front had just secured its "largest audience since the organization showed Nazi propaganda pictures," a reference to the *Sieg im Westen* screenings. Winchell shipped Levy's report to Clyde Tolson, the associate director of the FBI in Washington. Winchell, who commanded huge coast-to-coast audiences, would hammer away at Moran and the Christian Front over the airwaves for the next month.[37]

Moran had responded to Pearl Harbor with a complete lack of moderation, but it seemed that the more reckless his statements were, the more his audience appreciated him. On the morning of December 8, he composed a circular letter stating the front's "position on the war fearlessly and without equivocation." The letter opened with the kind of patriotic sentiments one might expect in the immediate aftermath of a national tragedy. "Our territory has been invaded and our fellow-citizens killed without warning," Moran wrote. "We shall do everything within our power to aid our country in every possible way." What came next, however, was red meat for the Christian Front's base. "We do not accept Mr. Roosevelt's statement that he was seeking peace," Moran continued. "Were it not for the unwarranted interference of Mr. Roosevelt in foreign affairs that were none of his business, and his refusal to grant the Orient the same right of self-determination that we ourselves have demanded in our Monroe Doctrine, the Japanese government would have had no incentive to attack us." As for Germany, Pearl Harbor had nothing to do with it. Moran vowed that while the Christian Front would not oppose the war against Japan, "it would not support war against Germany nor any American war of aggression."

Even as Moran suggested that war with Japan was justified now that the United States had been attacked, he argued that Roosevelt should be held responsible, morally and legally. "When the war is over we will demand an accounting," Moran insisted, before closing the letter with a textual shout in capital letters:

> WHEN THIS WAR IS CONCLUDED, WE SHALL DO EVERY-
> THING IN OUR POWER TO FORCE THE IMPEACHMENT OF
> PRESIDENT ROOSEVELT AND HIS CO-CONSPIRATORS
> [AND] DEMAND THEIR TRIAL UNDER CONSTITUTIONAL
> LAW ON CRIMINAL CHARGES. MAY GOD GRANT US
> STRENGTH AND VICTORY IN BOTH FIGHTS FOR AMER-
> ICAN FREEDOM AND JUSTICE![38]

That evening, Moran read the same statement at a meeting of the Christian Front, receiving a standing ovation from an overflowing crowd. When "the plate was passed," $75 ($1,320.00 in 2020 dollars) came back, one of the front's largest collections ever. With his audience traumatized by the Pearl Harbor attack, Moran invoked religion, but not as a comfort. "Moran particularly condemned the US government for declaring war on the Feast of the

Immaculate Conception," an FBI informant reported. The feast, which is dedicated to the Queen of Peace, is celebrated annually on December 8.[39]

Three days later, December 11, Hitler declared war on the United States, after which Congress replied with a unanimous declaration of war against Germany. Moran's response was that "President Roosevelt is guilty of murder." He told the *New York Post* as much for its December 26 story "US Fascists Keep Up Work Unhindered." Moran reluctantly agreed that Congress was within its rights, given Hitler's declaration. "We must support our government in what now becomes a justified war," he lamented in a postcard to a correspondent. But he continued to press the case that America's war with Germany was a product of Jewish and British fifth columnists. He warned of "an internal enemy far more treacherous and dangerous than the external one," concluding, "we congratulate our Jewish and pro-British warmongers. Presumably they are happy. We are not."[40]

Sweeney raced to counter Moran, bringing to her project an energy at least equal to his own. "We have about ten girls who are magnificent workers, and a Roll Call list of about 400," she wrote in a December 10 letter to one of her supporters, the influential Harvard philosopher and public intellectual Ralph Barton Perry. The membership list reflected the extraordinarily fast development of an organization whose local incarnation was born less than a month earlier. Among the members were Boston power players. These included a number of Irish leaders, such as P. A. O'Donnell, whose department store, E. T. Slattery, was perhaps the most high-end in the city. Another major recruit was surgeon Frank Lahey, founder of the world-renowned Lahey Clinic. Bernard Rothwell, owner of Bay State Milling and "a man of considerable wealth," became IADA's honorary chair.

Rothwell "was frightened by our clerics' reaction to Mr. Roosevelt," Sweeney wrote in her letter to Perry. Sweeney, too, recognized that faith was a battlefield in Boston. She knew that Moran used his stage at Hibernian Hall as if it were a sanctuary; if IADA was to compete with the Christian Front, it would have to do so as a limb of the Mystical Body. That meant Sweeney needed not only professors and doctors and business leaders on her side, but also a Roman Catholic priest.[41]

Her target was Father John Louis Bonn, a Jesuit and a professor at Boston College. A masterful preacher, respected scholar, author, and teacher, Bonn founded the college's theater department. Through his summer acting workshops, he encountered many Jewish Bostonians. The workshop "was a landmark in my life, a milestone, a crucial point," Leonard Nimoy said of Bonn's program. "It gave my life a direction." Nimoy, of stage and *Star Trek* fame, grew up in Boston's West End, the son of Eastern European Jewish immigrants. The workshops constituted a landmark in Bonn's life as well. His perspective was not that of an academic priest sealed in a Catholic milieu. As a priest working outside the Catholic community, he was open to the Jewish people around him and to a theology that acknowledged the place of Jews in society.[42]

In October 1941 Bonn made headlines when, at a Sunday morning Communion breakfast, he "denounced racial hatred against Jews." Bonn unleashed a blistering attack on prejudiced Catholics. "Christ was a Jew, the Twelve Apostles were Jews, and the Virgin Mary was a Jew," he noted. "As followers of Christ, we cannot persecute the Jews." To do so was a violation of the Church itself, he argued. "Those who take part in speaking against the Jews are taking part in persecution of the church, and you are the church." Boston's Coughlinites hit back immediately. One correspondent wrote to Bonn, "I have worked for them"—Jews, that is—"and dealed [*sic*] with them and any priest that strikes up for the Jews should go work like a slave and then you would know what you are talking about." Another asked sarcastically, "Was God the Father a Jew?"[43]

Bonn's theology and forthright talk stunned Sweeney, and as soon as she was on board with IADA, she tried to recruit him. Sweeney's original letter of outreach is nowhere to be found, and the same is true of Bonn's reply. But the cutout made a copy of the reply and placed it in the SOE's secret files. From the copy, we can glean that Sweeney revealed to Bonn her plans to get the Christian Front shut down. What Sweeney did not know was that Bonn was already suspicious of IADA. He replied that, before Sweeney was installed in the organization, he had been approached twice informally about joining. He then asked Sweeney to forgive his "bluntness":

> I regret very much that it is impossible for me to lend my name to the Irish-American Defense Association much less ally myself with any group organized to suppress freedom of speech and of the press in America. Perhaps I misunderstand the aims of your organization . . . I feel Father Coughlin is quite wrong at the moment. I know that anti-Semitism is sinful. I am deeply opposed to Mr. Moran and all his works, yet I would defend to my life his American right to speak and to publish, nor shall I ever join a group that would deprive any man or any

group of that right. Furthermore, I shall attack such un-American attitudes with as great vigor as I attack anti-Semitism.[44]

Sweeney was disconsolate. On her own, she had stumbled upon the Tillich question: How to stop a Christian Front whose support for Fascism and
anti-Semitism was a product of interpretations of doctrine licensed by a clerical officer class? Only an ordained Catholic could provide an effective coun-
tervailing argument to Moran's prostitution of the Roman Catholic religion,
and now her best potential spokesman had turned her down. Evidently
Sweeney thought Bonn had mistaken her intentions. "It grieves me to put it
so bluntly that our clerics are fallible," she wrote to Perry, the Harvard professor. "They often have inadequate information" and "they possess prejudices
which they do not overcome." Turned down by Father Bonn, Sweeney decided to take the situation into her own hands. "This battle must be fought
by liberal Catholics themselves," she wrote. She would abandon her effort to
establish an institutional face for IADA. The struggle against Moran's Fascist and anti-Semitic movement was, as even Bonn agreed, a religious imperative. But it would be one for the laity to accomplish.[45]

Exposing Moran

In 1963 former CIA director Allen Dulles gave a speech outlining the quali-
ties of a good spy. Inquisitiveness, perceptiveness about people, ability to
work under difficult conditions, attention to detail, and skill in expressing
ideas not only clearly but interestingly—these were his top qualifications.
In the fall of 1941, a younger Dulles moved into an office in Rockefeller
Center, one floor above BSC, to take a job running the New York office of
the Coordinator of Information. Dulles didn't know it, but his perfect spy
was working for the British agents downstairs. Neither, of course, did the
spy herself.[46]

Sweeney was inconspicuous and well connected. She knew her community, from the back streets to the newsroom floors and the halls of power. It
was her skill and strategy that won BSC its greatest success in Boston. Sweeney's plan was to use the press to expose Moran's pro-Nazi propaganda activities and thereby put pressure on faith and civic leaders to take a stand against
him. Such designs were perfect for BSC. Sweeney aimed, essentially, to distance herself from events by making the papers her go-between. She would
plant the story, while her own operation would stay under the radar of the

FBI and Massachusetts officials. To carry out such a scheme required knowledge of local politics and media and access to the discrete assistance of trusting partners. Sweeney coordinated all the pieces.

One of those pieces was the *Herald-Traveler*. "As for affairs here in Boston," Sweeney wrote in the days after Pearl Harbor, "we seem to have been adopted by the *Boston Herald-Traveler*." This was just the kind of hometown champion that served Sweeney and BSC best. It was the same paper that had written up Hitler in spring 1940, provoking Herbert Scholz's ire. But the *Herald-Traveler* had also "been extremely anti-Roosevelt on his domestic policies," Sweeney explained, and had expressed pro-Coughlin views. These past positions were excellent camouflage. The *Herald-Traveler* could go after Moran and the Christian Front from the perspective of fellow FDR critics. No one could claim that the paper's criticisms of Moran reflected mere partisan feuding or the same-old opinions, easily ignored. Instead, those criticisms would stand out as principled, which they were.[47]

Sweeney arranged to take advantage of the *Herald-Traveler*'s support when the economist Leo Cherne came to speak in Boston. Cherne was a pro-business New Dealer close to FDR. An animated speaker, Cherne was scheduled to address the Advertising Club of Boston on December 16. Sweeney arranged a luncheon after the speech at Boston's Hotel Statler, and William G. Gavin, the publisher of the *Herald-Traveler*, agreed to attend with Boston Mayor Maurice Tobin as his guest. Sweeney persuaded Cherne to make some light remarks at the luncheon on "morale" and to discuss the Christian Front threat. Thanks to Sweeney's deft orchestration, the mayor would hear all about the Christian Front.[48]

The press would too, hopefully. Sweeney used her associates to get other newspeople in the room at the Statler, in addition to Gavin. She asked Professor Perry to call his contacts in the media and persuade them to attend the Cherne event. "They will never suspect that we are going to reach behind you to eventually snap them in so we can do this Coughlinite job from within," she told Perry. Her objective was not to snap the press into line but to snap Moran's organization in two.[49]

After Cherne's talk, Sweeney's machinations moved into high gear. "Tonight or tomorrow," she told IADA members, like a general addressing their troops before battle, "the paper will 'expose Francis P. Moran' for selling Flanders Hall books of that vile Nazi agent, George Sylvester Viereck." Sweeney developed a range of publicity operations to brighten the media spotlight on

Moran. "We have a magnificent letter from Governor Saltonstall commending and urging Boston newspapers to expose all . . . who preach racial and religious intolerance." There would be another letter "from the Administrator of the Committee of Public Safety for the State urging the same thing." Sweeney also planned to petition "our Irish Catholic Mayor Tobin" for a likeminded letter.

The IADA members themselves would be tasked with holding Moran's feet to the fire in person, producing a good story for the *Herald-Traveler*. The plan was for "a group of young Liberals" to infiltrate the upcoming January 5 Christian Front meeting and "try to pin Moran down into telling his Jew program during the question period."

> Then the paper will throw up its hands in horror at his answers; and our "Republican" publisher will rush with his Republican governor's letter to our great Republican Cardinal [O'Connell] and assume that he will want to do something about such terrible, un-Christian actions. That way . . . we figure that we might be able to shame him [O'Connell] into urging our clergy to urge people to stop buying the books and to stay away from the meetings.

Sweeney had gamed out all the steps, figuring how to get even the cardinal to condemn Moran. She also thought that a story on Moran's anti-Semitism and Nazi propaganda would motivate the state's federal politicians. "The Congressmen around here are only all too glad to play along with the paper, as they have been severely harassed by this group," Sweeney assured. For added measure, she arranged for Rothwell, the businessman and IADA honorary chair, to release a statement to the press comparing the Christian Front to the Nazis and insinuating similarities between Moran and Hitler.[50]

On January 2, 1942, the *Herald-Traveler* ran a front-page story on the Viereck books. Readers learned that Moran and the Christian Front had not only been selling Nazi propaganda published by an unlicensed foreign agent before the declaration of war but were continuing to do so even after the United States and the Nazis commenced formal hostilities. Speaking to the *Herald-Traveler*, Richard Cunningham, the commander of the American Legion in Massachusetts, described the sales as "outrageous" and "demanded vigorously that . . . sales be stopped without delay." Cunningham provided the key quote, encapsulating the perspective that Sweeney and BSC hoped would penetrate boundaries of partisanship, ideology, and religion. "Sales of propaganda books of an enemy seeking to destroy us is not only disloyal,"

Cunningham said, "but indefensible from any American point of view." The story provided some of the worst publicity Moran had ever received, and at an especially fragile moment. The Christian Front had been thriving in the wake of the war declarations, but such popularity was obviously precarious— it could wash away any time in a wave of patriotic condemnation. Later that day, when asked by a friend how he was doing, Moran responded, "I'm being persecuted by the Jews."[51]

Boston would have the weekend of January 2–4 to digest the report that Moran and the Christian Front were knowingly distributing enemy propaganda. Meanwhile, Sweeney was preparing her "group of young Liberals" to attend the Monday meeting where they would demand that Moran answer to the charges in the papers. Everything was coming together perfectly. The press would be paying close attention on January 5, keeping the story going and Moran on his heels. Civic leaders would be unable to turn a blind eye; Governor Saltonstall was on the record condemning the very acts the papers were exposing, and Mayor Tobin had already been warned about the Christian Front at the December 17 luncheon. He would feel immense pressure to come out forcefully, assuming Sweeney's compatriots managed to provoke Moran into saying something untoward. All that remained was to see the plan through.

But the IADA members never got the chance to play their part in Swee- ney's strategy. When the night of January 5 arrived, it was not young liberals who took down Moran, it was the Boston Police. "Acting on a tip that various student groups and 'patriotic organizations' planned to 'start something' at the Christian Front meeting," more than twenty police officers took stations about the hall to discourage an outbreak," the *Herald-Traveler* reported. But the po- lice were not just there for crowd control. Officers mounted the stage at Hi- bernian Hall as Moran brought out some of the Viereck books, then confis- cated the books. According to the *Herald*, the morning sister paper of the *Herald-Traveler*, "The seizure followed issuance of an order from Police Com- missioner Joseph Timilty instructing the department to confiscate all such publications wherever found on sale or offered free." Viereck's books were "banned in Boston," via a general order from Timilty "read at the noon roll call to all police officers." When Moran protested that the officers had "exceeded their authority," they repeated to him Timilty's order. That same evening, Moran placed a phone call to Timilty, who told the Christian Front boss "that his activities were un-American in time of war and that if he defied the general order he would be arrested promptly."[52]

Evidence suggests that Moran kept his cool as the seizure was underway. After hauling away the books, two officers of the Police Radical Squad returned to the stage at Hibernian and gave Moran a receipt for his property. "Keep the books and read them," he wisecracked. "You may learn something."[53] Members of the crowd wanted to know the officers' names. A plant at the meeting from the Jewish Community Relations Council wrote that Moran "said they were Benjamin Goodman and William Goldston," which "evoked considerable shouting and booing." There was no booing from British intelligence. Someone, presumably the cutout or another BSC operative, snipped the book-seizure story from one of the many papers covering it, pasted it to a sheet of stationery reading "Boston Chapter Irish American Defense Association," and mailed it to SOE headquarters in London. The British intelligence archive positively bulges with such clippings, a signal of the importance BSC assigned to the book seizure.[54]

It is impossible to say with certainty whether Sweeney directly sought police involvement or else Commissioner Timilty acted on his own. One source from the period, a draft of an exposé of Moran and the Christian Front, suggests that Sweeney leaned on the commissioner. Donald Grant, a graduate student at Harvard, wrote that "an investigation of Moran was begun at the instigation of a group of Boston Catholics of Irish descent—members of the American Irish Defense Association. It was carried out by an Irish Catholic—Boston Police Commissioner Joseph F. Timilty." It is not entirely clear whether Grant was claiming that IADA had tipped off the police, or whether he was suggesting that IADA had instead fostered a circumstance to which the police felt obliged to respond. Certainly he was struck by the unlikelihood of it all, given the tightness of the Boston Irish community. In any case, these lines appear only in the draft, which is archived by the Jewish Community Relations Council of Greater Boston. The published story, which appeared in the *Nation* on March 15, 1942, omits any suggestion of a causal relationship between IADA and the police crackdown.[55]

Another writer who connected IADA to the police action was Isabel Currier, a liberal Catholic, novelist, and friend of Sweeney's. Writing in *Commonweal* in 1944, Currier offered that Sweeney's "public service was to interest the Boston *Herald-Traveler* in launching a newspaper crusade against the

Christian Front—within three days, the Boston Police Commissioner had demanded that Francis P. Moran disband his organization." Elsewhere Currier wrote that the disclosure of Moran's propaganda activities "forced Commissioner Timilty to order the Front to disband." Like Grant's draft, Currier's published writings leave the Sweeney-Timilty relationship ambiguous. There is no doubt that the exposure Sweeney engineered influenced police action, but the question remains whether Sweeney tipped off the police to the distribution of contraband at the meeting. If she did, then Father Bonn was right to fear that IADA, no matter how laudable its goals, was abetting censorship.[56]

While British intelligence and liberal Catholics were gleeful over the book confiscations, the FBI and the Massachusetts attorney general's office were both were blindsided by Timilty's move. The FBI had been pursuing its own investigation in light of Levy's report, which had been forwarded to the bureau by Walter Winchell. Special Agent J. W. Coulter interviewed Levy, who explained that he was "hoping . . . to bring pressure to bear to have Moran taken into protective custody during the present emergency." The idea of custodial detention was to keep investigative targets under wraps while compiling evidence, and after Pearl Harbor, the FBI and other federal law enforcers were empowered to take in a range of possible suspects without charges. The specific authority came under the Alien Enemy Control Program, which was put in place by presidential proclamation. This program would become the basis for Japanese American internment after Roosevelt's Executive Order 9066. Levy's position was that because of Moran's anti-Semitism, he should not be "left at large," while America was at war. But Peterson disagreed. "Levy was advised," Peterson wrote to Hoover on January 2, "that Moran is a citizen of the United States and as such still is entitled to the right of free speech as long as that does not violate any of the existing statutes concerning national defense." Peterson, who was legally and constitutionally correct, must have been appalled by the book seizure. But Hoover may have been more sympathetic and at least was not deterred by the unexpected moves of the BPD. Within two weeks of receiving Peterson's letter, Hoover opened a custodial detention investigation into Moran under the auspices of the Alien Enemy Control Program.[57]

As for state officials, Massachusetts Attorney General Robert Bushnell was incensed by Timilty's raid. Bushnell was a long-time prosecutor with a penchant for rooting out financial corruption in state government. He was also no stranger to police raids. Known as a "racket-buster," he had ordered numerous such raids on gambling syndicates.[58] But in those cases, police were breaking up illegal activity. What laws had Moran and the Christian Front broken? Bushnell had an investigator, Dennis McCadden, look into that question, and he came back with a sobering report. "To my knowledge," McCadden wrote to Bushnell, "there is no state statute under which Moran can be prosecuted for anything that he said or did . . . nor can he be prosecuted for the sale of the Flanders Hall books." McCadden's opinion was that Timilty was eager "to win for himself nationwide publicity in curbing a person who had been publicized by Mr. Walter Winchell as being inimical to the welfare of the country."[59]

Indeed, Timilty seemed more interested in giving out quotes than assuring due process or establishing proper grounds for investigation and prosecution. Quizzed by reporters about his authority to seize the books, Timilty unloaded with patriotic pronouncements. "Un-American acts," Timilty warned, "would not be tolerated by this department—the distribution of such enemy propaganda is plainly an act of disloyalty." But was it illegal? "America is at war," Timilty thundered.[60]

To the extent that Timilty believed he had specific legal authority, he was relying on the Viereck indictment. But this was itself problematic, for multiple reasons. For one thing, it was not the job of the Boston Police to enforce federal laws. As McCadden put it, Timilty "did not have any evidence," either at the time of the raid or subsequently "to substantiate a violation of any state law or statute." For another, at the time of the raid, Viereck only had been charged. His federal trial was not scheduled to start for another month. In other words, no determination had yet been made as to the legality of Viereck's actions or the status of his pamphlets as contraband. It seemed to Bushnell that, because no ruling had yet established that Moran's books were forbidden, the police were obligated to leave him be. Until a judge stated otherwise, his book sales were protected by the First Amendment.[61]

In the press, Bushnell "announced he would back the Police Commissioner 'to the limit.'" But in fact the attorney general was enraged. He sounded off during a visit with Peterson at the FBI's Boston office. Bushnell was of the "opinion that Timilty had acted precipitously . . . and that the Police Department did not unearth any evidence that would sustain the complaint against Moran for violation of any state law." Worse still, Bushnell told Peterson, "The source of information is [now] closed." No doubt this was upsetting to Peterson as well. Hoover had been riding him for months to figure out a way to shut Moran down. But now Moran could be expected to clam up. "Utterances or acts of a seditious nature . . . have been ended by the action of the police," Bushnell lamented.[62]

Both Bushnell and Timilty saw the situation clearly. Bushnell had ample reason to believe Moran would never be successfully prosecuted for distributing Viereck's books. And Timilty understood correctly that the raid would make him a hero. In April *Life* magazine ran a ten-page full-photo feature praising Timilty for the "virtual disappearance" of the Christian Front in Boston. "Following complaints from the Irish-American Defense Association, . . . Boston Police . . . descended on Moran's headquarters," the piece read. "What Boston did to abate the nuisance of Moran can be done by any other city in the land," *Life* stressed, oblivious to the unusual factors at play, including Sweeney's genius-level publicity campaign and BSC's bankrolling of IADA. Timilty was so chuffed that he wrote a letter to the editor of *Life* thanking the magazine. Had he been more gracious, he would have deferred to Sweeney, but instead he took full credit for "the cessation of the activities and meetings of the so-called Christian Front in this city."[63]

The celebration was premature. The police had taken the Christian Front down, but they had not knocked Moran out. His next opportunity would come thanks to Commissioner Timilty, the very man gloating over Moran's ruin.

CHAPTER 11

Underground

ON JANUARY 7, 1942, TWO DAYS AFTER THE POLICE RAID ON HIBER-
nian Hall, Moran and Commissioner Timilty sat down for a one-on-one interview at police headquarters. "How and where did you get the books?"
Timilty asked. "Flanders Hall Publishing Company," Moran replied. "I purchased them after a trip—the company was going out of business, and the
books were to be destroyed." "Who did you receive this tip from?" "I have
forgotten now. It came to me indirectly."[1]

Commissioner Timilty did not press the point. The interview, which lasted
ninety minutes, hardly seems like an interrogation. Moran was not under arrest, he did not have a lawyer in the room, and there is no stenographer's
record. What we know of the interview comes from an unsigned seven-page
statement generated by the two men together.

By reputation, Joseph Timilty was severe in his treatment of Moran.[2] That
was certainly the image he hoped to project, but reality looked different.
When Timilty and Moran were in a room together, they acted less like cop
and suspect and more like friends. They nearly were. At the very least, they
were similarly creatures of Boston Irish politics. Both were acolytes of James
Michael Curley, the mayor, governor, member of congress, and political boss
who became Moran's business partner in the effort to acquire a radio station.
Timilty's father "Diamond" Jim, meanwhile, had been a powerful local pol
and union leader in Curley's camp. In 1936, when Curley needed a pliable
police commissioner, he chose Diamond Jim's son Joe.[3]

After so many had dithered—and some had worked diligently—it was the Boston Police who finally got to Moran. The Boston Police, whose ranks were full of fronters: card-carrying members, Coughlinites, men who recognized themselves in Moran's vision of a just world. Yet, if no one saw police intervention coming, there was a logic to it. Among all the investigators and spooks in Boston, only the police could have moved so recklessly. Reporters, spies, and activists had to be more careful. Joe Timilty—prompted by Sweeney and equally unaware that he was doing MI6's dirty work—could follow his impulse.

The commissioner did not really know what he was getting into with Moran. Timilty's intelligence on Moran appears to have been meager. Their conversation was unfocused, shifting around politics, theology, and law and never drilling into possible crimes. Timilty asked virtually no follow-up questions when he had the opportunity. The statement the men agreed to is a dissembling and circuitous piece of work.

The greater part of the document consists of Timilty confronting Moran with his own quotes, though only after February 1941, when the Radical Squad restarted surveillance of Christian Front meetings. In other words, the extent of Timilty's evidence was Moran's public statements. During the conversation, Moran was occasionally evasive but mostly acknowledged and defended his firmly held, well-known positions. Many of the questions just filled time. "Do you have a shortwave radio set in your home?" Timilty asked. "Yes," Moran responded, "a receiver." There were no further questions on that subject, no efforts to probe Moran's communications, learn who was feeding him tips, whom he may have been working for.

On and on it went. "On June 30, 1941, you said you hoped Hitler would wipe out the entire British Empire," Timilty pointed out. "The remark is true," Moran responded. He had no qualms with the British people, he said, but "the Empire itself is a curse to the world as a whole, and has always been America's worst enemy." Regarding his "Heil Hitler" salute after the Axis invasion of the Soviet Union, Moran reminded Timilty that the United States was not at war when he made that gesture. He only "wanted to salute the man" for being "the first to challenge the power of that murderous dictator [Stalin]."

Moran frequently got the better of Timilty. For instance, Timilty pressed Moran on his August 18 statement to the effect that draftees "have the perfect right to desert" from the US Army. Desertion, of course, is unlawful, but Moran explained that the right he had in mind was a moral one, sanctioned by Catholic doctrine. If US soldiers "believed they were being forced to train and fight in an unjust war on foreign soil for which they have no concern," Moran said, then "they have a moral right to refuse and if necessary to desert." A devout Catholic, Timilty was not about to argue with tenets of just war theory embraced by Saint Augustine himself. When confronted with other past statements, Moran would simply say that he never said any such thing—that statements attributed to him were "positively untrue and stupid."[4]

Attorney General Robert Bushnell was right about Timilty. The commissioner had a nose for publicity and smelled an opportunity in the story of Moran's books. But publicity is all that Timilty wanted. He betrayed no interest in a serious investigation of Moran. For evidence of Timilty's insouciance, one need look no further than the interview and resulting statement. The document had no legal meaning, but it would have its intended effects. The statement would placate politicians grumbling about accountability: here were the police working dutifully to bring a stop to disloyal talk. Timilty, in particular, would look like an engaged and community-minded officer. And by giving a statement to the overmatched Timilty, Moran would escape pressure to speak with more capable law enforcers. As Bushnell himself lamented, the Boston Police had spoiled every prosecutor's chance at Moran, at least for the time being.

Moran seems to have appreciated this, too. He knew that Timilty had nothing important on him, which meant Moran was in a good position to win a deal in his own favor. A man like Timilty—a political appointee with mayoral aspirations—was easily played. Moran could offer Timilty good publicity in exchange for something far more important: protection. Moran had secrets, and it was best that the police and the courts not begin prying. If he gave Timilty a media win, the police would effectively exonerate him by declaring his case closed. So Moran agreed to almost everything Timilty wanted. The Christian Front would voluntarily shutter its office in Copley Square, turn over all of its books, and cease meetings. Moran was not worried about state charges—even Timilty must have suspected the Commonwealth would gain no traction in court, which explained why the deal appealed to him. But even if Moran could beat a state charge, it was important to prevent a trial that might uncover his intrigues with Scholz. For Moran, it made perfect sense to give up the trappings of the Christian Front if he could stay out of jail.

Stay out of jail and continue working. Significantly, Moran was also allowed to keep the Christian Front's membership cards, a key to his network and therefore his influence. When asked to turn them over, he refused. "The Christian Front in Massachusetts is a one-man affair, and I am the one man," Moran explained to the *Boston Globe*. This must have been tough for observers of the front to swallow. The *Herald-Traveler*, whose journalists knew better than most the scale of Moran's effort, made sure to note the odd claim. Moran promised that his "one-man group would disappear when he retired from it," the paper reported. This was an early sign that shutting down the front did not mean shutting down Moran.[5]

As he walked out of police headquarters, Moran announced to the press, "We are in perfect agreement." Timilty, meanwhile, played up his role as a determined yet merciful patriot and public servant. "I told him straight from the shoulder, that if he does not cooperate in our effort to promote unity with our allies, I will take steps to have him put away for the duration of the war," Timilty said. But Timilty also emphasized "that he intends to cooperate— that he is sincere."[6] If Timilty had known anything about Moran, the commissioner would have realized that there was nothing trustworthy about him. Moran did have sincere beliefs, but honesty was only useful inasmuch as it realized those beliefs. For Moran, truth and falsehood were both means to more important ends. "Even the Devil told the truth at times," he once told an FBI informant.[7]

The Friday Group

While Timilty was gloating, Moran was composing a final letter to his followers, a letter marked by solemnity but also defiance. He recognized the gravity of the situation and was prepared to make a strategic retreat. But he had no intention of retiring.

"The Christian Front of America is hereby officially disbanded," Moran wrote in his circular of January 9, 1942. The rest of the letter offered a moral and legal defense of the group and looked forward to the eventual continuation of its work. "We have committed no crime nor broken any law of the city, the state, or the nation," Moran assured. The front had not been sanctioned; the Viereck books were not "seized" but rather were turned over willingly. Moran made clear that he hoped for the victory "of our country against all its enemies"—"all" implying not just the Germans and Japanese but also Jews, Soviets, and Communists of every stripe, and maybe the British too. "At the termination of the war," he promised, "if we are permitted to resume our activities without official objection, those who accept our principles will rejoin us voluntarily."

What Moran well understood was that these principles would outlast any police pressure or media glare. The public apparatus of the Christian Front was only a tool for articulating, spreading, and enacting an idea. The religious and anti-Semitic urges that animated the Christian Front had not disbanded. Indeed, something very much like the front persisted without Moran. In a late 1942 report, the Office of Strategic Services, the wartime US intelligence agency, concluded that the front had metastasized. The Christian Front "continues to act in Irish associations by controlling key positions," the report held. The same report suggested that while Moran had ceded public leadership, in his stead Father Edward Lodge Curran was carrying on frontlike meetings.[8]

Not only were others perpetuating the front's mission, but so was Moran. He took his work underground, as he said he would. While police were swarming Hibernian Hall, Moran issued a warning: "If they are foolish enough not to lock me up, I'll continue to work personally." He even repeated that warning to Timilty. He told the commissioner straight to his face that he had no plans to quit.[9] Moran had been considering going to ground since at least April 1941, while the New York sedition trial was playing out. At that time, he bemoaned what he called the "censorship" of newspapers that refused to report on the front in a manner he deemed responsible. "Despite these restrictions," he told his followers, "the Christian Front will go on, even undercover if necessary."[10]

That is precisely what happened. Shortly after the police interview, Moran began holding small weekly meetings with stalwart supporters in private homes. They called themselves the Friday Group. The Friday Group was every bit a remnant cell of the Christian Front. There were differences, to be sure: the group had to stay out of public view, and it could not align with Father Coughlin, who was himself under suspicion. In April 1942 *Social Justice* was shut down by US Attorney General Biddle under the Espionage Act. But in most every other respect, the Friday Group was an incarnation of the Christian Front. Surrounded by likeminded admirers who similarly were feeling the sting of public approbation, Moran used the Friday Group as a forum in which to continue developing his political views. The Friday group was an advanced workshop in anti-Semitism and, increasingly, revolution. From underground, Moran was elaborating a more extreme form of the

Boston Christian Front, the kernel of a political force that might one day prove more potent than the original organization had been.

The FBI infiltrated the Friday Group shortly after its first meeting. With Hoover breathing down Peterson's neck, the bureau's Boston field office did not want to miss out on Moran's next move. The FBI's informant, codenamed T-1, was a perfect fit for Moran. She worked at the Catholic information Center in downtown Boston and was a reserve member of the US Navy. Hailing from the Alsace region of France, she spoke both French and German fluently and would discuss sensitive matters with Moran in German.[11]

By May 1942 T-1 had insinuated herself into the Friday Group so thoroughly that Moran and his inner circle began to take her into his confidence. One evening "the men openly discussed before me how they were carrying on sabotage," she reported. She was referring to efforts to disrupt labor unions operating at the Boston waterfront. Moran's cadre "talked of rubber cement, something about sulfuric acid, placing the acid on tires, and putting oil in loads of fish." Labor sabotage was a new avenue for Moran, probably connected to his suspicions that Communists were infiltrating waterfront unions. Later in the evening, as the group sat back with glasses of beer, T-1 raised a toast. "I said 'Heil Hitler' to Moran, and he just grinned." Moran made no comment, instead turning to his latest grievances against Boston Mayor Maurice Tobin. The mayor was trying to spy on him, Moran said, to see if the front was still holding meetings. "On the other hand," he mentioned with satisfaction, "the Boston Police are our friends and we can depend on them."[12] It is fair to say that Timilty made a different impression on Moran than on *Life* magazine.

T-1 found one meeting of twenty-six Friday Group members in Roxbury so boring that she nearly fell asleep—that is, until a woman in the group started talking about revolution. The woman, a nurse, argued that soldiers should mutiny. "It's no worse to be shot while trying to cause revolution here than it was to be shot across the ocean," she claimed. Moran picked up the theme. "The revolution to come has to be started by men in arms," he explained. "It will come, perhaps, in a year." Moran felt that he and his fellow true believers would be well positioned. "We have the police, most of the Catholic clergy, and the majority of the Armed Forces with us," he said. "They will all be ready when the time comes to strike." Moran's Christian Front had been an intellectual foil to Cassidy's revolutionaries. Now, from the metaphorical bunker, Moran was adopting Cassidy's outlook.

Before he dismissed his gathering of would-be Catholic revolutionaries, Moran gave an update on his own work. "I have played it safe," he told his friends. "The authorities have nothing on me." In a way, he seemed liberated. "I will go on with my work of influencing the Army, Navy, clergy and police . . . and of collecting the names and addresses of all Communists in the country." In his mind, Moran had the future all figured out, a future in which his vision of law and justice would predominate within the institutions that really mattered, and the enemy would be firmly under his control.[13]

Alongside the FBI, Arthur Derounian was following the erstwhile Christian Front boss after he formally shuttered his outfit. The undercover journalist did not know about the Friday Group, but he was one of the few who had always understood that Moran was a hazard, regardless of his organizational infrastructure. Moran had a dangerous mind and thus could foment significant strife on his own—he might even more trouble than when he was operating in public. Derounian had followed the New York front as well and recognized that it had come in two flavors: the public organization that held raucous meetings in Brooklyn and gave statements to the press, and the subterranean branch that collected guns and bombs and meant to violently take down the government.

On November 12, 1942, Derounian visited Moran at his new home in West Roxbury. "There was a large picture of Christ on the vestibule wall; there was a statue of Christ on the piano; and a still larger picture of Christ on the living room wall." Their conversation began with small talk. "He told me about ex-governor Curley, and praised him to the heights," Derounian wrote. Moran seemed grateful to Curley. "He knows every legal trick in the books," Moran said. The conversation eventually turned to revolution. "He sees the revolution starting in the Army," Derounian noted. "He sees a tremendous amount of discontent in the Army." Moran forcefully argued that it was his constitutional right to speak of revolution. "Revolution by bullets, not ballots, is the only way to clean house, and get back to the Constitution," Moran thought.

When Derounian asked about the Christian Front, Moran seemed more cautious. "I have no association with anybody," he said, "whatever I do now, I do alone." He explained that he had stopped communicating with Father Coughlin and did not attend anyone's meetings. Occasionally, he admitted, small groups came to meet without him. But Moran was adamant that, in spite of his own revolutionary talk, these people were not planning anything untoward. "I control them all, and I've told them to lay low," he said. "You have to be careful."

Derounian concluded that "Moran is laying low, playing a lone hand, still apparently in charge of subversive forces, but he is not showing his hand except to those he trusts." Where others saw Moran fading, the typically clear-eyed Derounian saw bad tidings. "Someday, a lot of bloodshed and misery" was going to come to Boston, he wrote. "These are hard words, but no one who knows the Fascist can visit Boston and remain impervious to the burning Fascist fever that has enveloped the entire city." Derounian had a flair for drama, and his statement was to an extent hyperbolic. Clearly there were anti-Fascists making an impact in Boston, but with Timilty taking all the credit for shuttering the Christian Front, the likes of Sweeney and IADA were consigned to obscurity. Perhaps Derounian did not realize there were forces aligned against Moran. Or maybe he did realize but believed these forces too weak to make a difference. One way or another, something about the interaction with Moran left Derounian more frightened than ever. "Someday Boston shall come to flame: Jew, Protestant, and Catholic alike will be scorched."[14]

Abiding Anti-Fascism

As Moran moved underground, opponents continued to pay attention. One of these was a new player in the drama. John Franklin Carter was a State Department official close to the Oval Office, who operated as a kind of private detective for President Roosevelt on the international scene. He was astute, liberal, and globalist, a fine journalist who wrote a popular syndicated column under the pen name of Jay Franklin. He was also, according to one scholar, almost certainly a controlled agent of Soviet Military Intelligence, the GRU.[15]

For some reason Carter, who rarely investigated domestic issues, was deeply interested in the situation in Boston. On January 26, after Moran was let off the hook, Carter wrote to Roosevelt, "Moran might not kill anybody himself, but he might easily incite somebody else to have a try at assassination." Carter informed Roosevelt that Boston Congressman and House Majority Leader John McCormack believed "Moran should be taken in front of a couple of doctors and put away for the duration" lest he "incite some weak minded, fanatical person." It is reasonable to speculate that Carter was doing the GRU's bidding, trying to get rid of Moran once and for all. "Francis P. Moran is a thoroughly dangerous man," Carter concluded.[16]

But while McCormack agreed that Moran was a nuisance, he did not share the view that Moran should be imprisoned. The majority leader referred to Moran as a "dough" man, presumably implying a small mind. McCormack's and Moran's families knew each other, which may have been in Moran's favor. Moran's mother Bridget "was the counsellor of the neighborhood," McCormack recalled of his South Boston home. "Everyone would come to her with their troubles." And McCormack's brother, the spirited and towering saloonkeeper Edward "Knocko" McCormack, served as a political foot soldier for Moran's friend James Michael Curley.[17]

McCormack would not, ultimately, sign off on actions against Moran, and Roosevelt remained unmoved. The Carter episode was another lucky break for Moran. Either his arch enemy, the Soviets, were after him, or an extremely well-connected and influential official was. One way or the other, Moran was fortunate to escape yet again.

If Soviet espionage could not bring Moran down, perhaps American activism could. Specifically, IADA. With the United States in the war, Moran apparently suppressed, and isolationists chastened amid an atmosphere of patriotism, BSC pulled the plug on IADA, dramatically cutting its staff. By March OSS determined "that the work of the organization has been done entirely by Ms. Sweeney." That was not entirely true—Sweeney was able to retain a longtime friend, Gus Gazulis, to conduct street-level investigations. But her actions after the front went underground do suggest that she was suddenly operating largely on her own. IADA was finally the American anti-Fascist organization it purported to be.[18]

Early during Moran's underground phase, Sweeney attended a number of speeches by Father Curran—speeches arranged by Moran and attended by his followers. On January 31, 1942, Curran spoke to a crowd of more than 1,200 in the Boston neighborhood of Hyde Park. "Present in the audience were faces familiar to anyone who had attended Christian Front meetings sponsored by Francis P. Moran," an observer from the Jewish Community Relations council wrote.[19] Moran brought Curran back in February, this time at the Hotel Bradford in downtown Boston. Some 3,000 listeners attended, packing what was said to be the largest ballroom in New England. Sweeney was one of the throng. "I cannot emphasize strongly enough the tremendous hold Curran has on his audience at all times," she reported. She described Curran's method as "wedge-driving," an attempt to turn the Allies against each other. And so it was. "Nazism is the enemy abroad," Curran thundered, "but Communism is the enemy at home!" Americans nervous about alliance with the Soviet Union would not have been heartened.[20]

Curran took care to operate within the boundaries of publicly acceptable discourse. His speeches were laden with isolationism and nationalism but not overt anti-Semitism. Anti-Semitism was very much implied, but Curran the lawyer knew how to play it safe. In some ways he was a throwback to Moran's earlier, more cautiously anti-Semitic days. This ensured that Curran would not run into too much opposition, whether from the public or the Church. If Curran went overboard, Cardinal O'Connell might ask him to stay out of Boston, and Curran would have to comply. Whatever O'Connell's opinion of the British and the war, he did not want to deal with the repercussions of forthright priestly anti-Semitism in his archdiocese.[21]

Curran was so popular that Moran arranged another engagement, this time for March 17, a date pregnant with meaning in the local Irish American community. The seventeenth was both St. Patrick's Day and, in Boston, Evacuation Day—the anniversary of the date in 1776 when British troops departed the city after an eleven-month occupation. Word of Curran's address broke a week before the event, and Sweeney organized a public campaign urging the sponsor, the South Boston Citizens Association, to withdraw Curran's invitation. Reverends Donald Lothrop and Walton Cole both lodged protests. Standing in front of Boston City Hall, Cole argued that Father Curran was a Fascist. IADA released an open letter to Mayor Tobin, petitioning him to "exercise executive power to prevent Edward Lodge Curran, associate of the police-closed Christian Front, from speaking." The Non-Sectarian Anti-Nazi League asked Attorney General Francis Biddle to investigate. Methodist Bishop G. Bromley Oxnam called out Curran for his "anti-Semitic emphasis" and pleaded with Boston officials to cancel the event.[22]

But Moran made sure the speech would stay on the calendar. Mayor Tobin was out of town, and one of Moran's former lieutenants in the Christian Front, William B. Gallagher, got the acting mayor to serve as master of ceremonies. Other political figures also backed Curran and Moran. City Councilor Joseph Scannell described Curran as a "Christian and patriotic person who respects the attitudes and beliefs of all."[23] For Moran, Curran's speech was more than an address to supporters. It was also a chance to take a swing at Sweeney. Little did she know, but Moran had something planned for her. Friday Group members had suggested picketing the IADA office on St. Patrick's Day, but Moran held them back. He wanted them at Father Curran's speech.

Despite the swell of controversy surrounding the speech, as Curran's words proved to be anodyne calls for unity. The real drama occurred before Curran took the stage. As the audience was filing the auditorium at South Boston High School—with more crowds outside to listen to the speech on loud-speakers—one of Moran's plants recognized his target: Frances Sweeney. The fronter came up to Sweeney and started harassing her, calling her a Jew. An FBI agent who was present called on police to intervene. When the man was taken away, Sweeney took a seat near the front row. Now she was marked. As confidential informant T-1 explained, Moran had coached the Friday Group beforehand, instructing them to "crowd out Jews" from in front of the stage. "M. told us just what to do," she said.[24]

An eyewitness told the *Evening American* newspaper what happened next. "John J. Hughes, who described himself as a friend of William Gallagher, chairman of the event, asked Ms. Sweeney to leave. She refused. Hughes lifted her out of her seat by the collar of her coat and escorted her down the aisle amidst cries of 'Put Her out.'" Gallagher claimed that Sweeney had taken a seat at the press table to which she was not entitled, but of course the operation against her had been planned. When it came to the constitutional values of citizen assembly and protest, Moran was an absolutist only in his own case.[25]

Sweeney was undeterred by Moran's actions. Indeed, his continued operations emboldened her. Like Derounian, she realized that Moran's danger-ousness would only mount while he was beyond the public eye. With the United States in the war, she shifted her focus from isolationism to anti-Semitism and became more invested in activism on behalf of Boston's Jewish community in the face of continuing bigotry from Moran and his followers. It is precisely because she was herself a Catholic that she felt the need to work on behalf of Jews. "She took her Catholic faith seriously when it proclaimed that anti-Semitism was anti-Christian," a friend wrote.[26]

Sweeney was not one to mince words about the sources of anti-Semitism in her hometown. As she told an agent from the American Jewish Committee, "I am forced in this Boston situation to generalize sharply on racial and religious grounds." The "racial and religious bigotry involved comes directly from the Irish Catholic community." That meant that Moran was still her enemy. "The Christian Front, though officially dissolved continues in undercover organizations," she wrote, with "many members active."[27] In the year to come, she would have her work cut out for her, protecting Boston's Jews from Irish Catholics under Moran's spell.

Conclusion

"WHY DON'T THE JEWS DOUBLE UP THEIR FISTS AND FIGHT IT OUT with me, instead of knifing us in the back?" It was the summer of 1943, and Moran was itching for a confrontation with the Jews of Boston. "I hit hard, and hit it on the button," he told confidential informant T-1. From his position behind the scenes, Moran was growing ever more resentful, his anti-Semitism slipping into exterminationism. It was at this point that he began to talk about "eliminating the Jews." Moran asked T-1 to use her military connections to infiltrate army camps and radicalize soldiers. "Instead of uncontrolled riots and anarchy," Moran explained, "it would be preferable to have men trained in military discipline in order to take over and get rid of the Jews."[1]

Moran had gone over the edge. This was no longer religious anti-Judaism or even religious anti-Semitism mediated by Mystical Body theology and Catholic human rights. Nor could exterminating Jews could ever be camouflaged as Catholic Action. This was pure Nazism, without compromises. The Nazification of Francis Moran began under Herbert Scholz's tutelage, but it flowered after the consul had departed, leaving Moran to navigate alone a city and country increasingly hostile to his views. At least officially. While it is true that the police had technically come down on Moran, Bostonians—and many of their civic leaders—remained in his camp. Those authorities who did oppose Moran preferred to steer clear of him rather than provoke his large band of supporters. For every liberal and anti-Fascist activist willing to go public, there were dozens of former fronters and sympathetic Irish Catholics. And, perhaps most importantly, the Boston Police were more firmly on Moran's side than ever. Commissioner Timilty had done what was best for Commissioner Timilty and moved on. Now that the front was disbanded, he could be happily oblivious to its continued influence in Boston and his police force.

Moran and his followers could no longer get away with public statements in favor of Hitler, but they could exercise their rage toward the Jews around them. Moran did not have to be out front in order to stoke that rage. He still commanded his most ardent supporters and could orchestrate events from underground. In early 1943 he organized several speeches by Father Curran, which were stage-managed by former fronters under Moran's direction. Meanwhile, satisfied that the front was no more, BSC pulled back from its counterprogramming. The FBI's Boston office was in disarray in 1942 and 1943 and cut resources from its investigation of Moran.

It was under these circumstances that Boston experienced an outbreak of anti-Semitism. The "anti-Jewish violence in Boston" became "pervasive," according to historian Stephen H. Norwood. To use Derounian's more evocative language, Boston had "come to flame." The violence was perpetrated largely by Irish Catholic gangs. Some of the perpetrators were former fronters but many were not. They were ordinary fans of Father Coughlin living in neighborhoods steeped in the anti-Semitism that the front disseminated with the aid of clerics like Father Curran. Police abetted crimes against Jews, sometimes by turning a blind eye, sometimes by arresting Jewish Bostonians for defending themselves, and sometimes by directly participating in beatings of Jews.[2]

Historians usually put the beginning of Boston's surging Irish-on-Jewish violence in the fall of 1943.[3] In fact there was rising hostility throughout the year. What changed in the fall was the publicity surrounding the persecution of Boston's Jews. For most of the year, anyone who was not a victim or perpetrator or in close contact with them would have had little sense of what was going on. As far as newspaper editors were concerned, the shuttering of the front was a strong final chapter in the story. Police complicity helped to ensure that the press missed the denouement, because many crimes were never logged through official channels. It would take concentrated investigative journalism, not beat reporting, to break open the story of Boston's anti-Semitic violence. Local Jewish leaders might have alerted the media on their own, but they chose to stay quiet. With so much violence coming their way—state violence, perpetuated by the police and by private citizens protected by the police—many in the Jewish community feared that speaking out would result in still worse consequences.

It is unclear what civic leaders knew about the violence and for how long they knew it. What we do know is that high-ranking authorities evinced little concern until investigative journalists held their feet to the fire. Frances Sweeney was a key figure in exposing the systemic nature of the violence, both bearing witness to it and speaking to other journalists for their stories. The reporting that eventually came out shook authorities and private citizens, demonstrating as it did that the Christian Front remained influential in Boston. Moran had become that much more dangerous underground, and so had his followers and their fellow travelers, left to act on what he had taught. The anti-Semitic sentiments of the police and Irish Catholic civilians were no doubt genuine, but it is also reasonable to wonder if there would have been such a crisis had not Timilty not behaved so rashly, pushing Moran out of sight and martyring him in the eyes of the public.

By the end of 1943, the violence died down and with it Moran's career as an agitator. It was with Moran's departure from public life that the erasure of the Christian Front—from both daily life and historical memory—began. When Timilty tried to accomplish that erasure on his own, he only inflamed the front's militancy. He was understood by Irish Catholic Bostonians to be taking on the role of the Spanish, Mexican, and Russian leftists whose persecution of Christians had inspired the Christian Front idea in the first place. Had Boston's Irish Catholics known that Timilty was in fact an unwitting tool of a British intelligence campaign, they would have been that much angrier. It was, in the last analysis, Sweeney and her liberal associates who ended the front's year of terror, with law enforcement dragged grudgingly along.

The Anti-Semitic Crisis of 1943

"All the Jewish boys were pretty badly hurt," Sweeney wrote to a friend in March 1943. "Eight Jewish boys were set upon by pre-arranged signal as they were leaving Hecht House in Dorchester." Hecht House was Boston's first Jewish community center. It had opened half a century earlier and moved to Dorchester in 1942. The relocation was an indication of a changing city. The local Jewish population, numbering nearly 90,000 and amounting to around

12 percent of the city, was moving to Dorchester, Roxbury, and Mattapan, diversifying these heavily Irish neighborhoods and making Dorchester in particular the geographic heart of Boston Jewry. By the 1960s Boston's Jews would move en masse into the near suburbs of Brookline and Newton, an exodus explained in part by white flight—Dorchester, Roxbury, and Mattapan were increasingly enclaves for African Americans and immigrants of color—but also by the experience of living cheek by jowl with an Irish Catholic community harboring a critical mass of extreme anti-Semites.[4]

Arthur Derounian recorded the gruesome details of the Hecht House attack. One of the Jewish boys was stopped by five attackers, "all Irish Catholics." One asked the boy "if he didn't think Hitler was the greatest person in the world." Then, "when the Jewish boy refused to answer, a boy stepped up and punched him in the face." Each of the five attackers asked the same question and then punched the boy in the face again. Sweeney observed the court proceedings against the Hecht House attackers and found that "mothers are not letting their children go to court to identify their assailants because of fear of reprisals." She noted that "one Irish boy—6'1"—when he was leaving the Dorchester courtroom, threatened the Jewish lad who had identified him."[5]

The Hecht House attack occurred on March 16, 1943, the eve of St. Patrick's Day and the same night Father Curran spoke at a gala event in Boston. Curran was again present at the invitation of the South Boston Citizens' Association, led by Moran's colleague William Gallagher. This time there were no protests, perhaps because Curran was not scheduled to speak. Instead, the isolationist New York congressman Hamilton Fish was the advertised speaker, but he backed out at the last minute. Curran, who was attending the event as a guest, took the lectern in Fish's stead. The last-minute cancellation, and Curran's convenient readiness to address the crowd, may have been a setup—a scheme concocted by Gallagher and Moran for avoiding opposition. During his speech, Curran thanked the South Boston Citizens' Association "for the courage with which they beat back the protests of the Red groups and their pale political allies who sought to keep me out of Boston last year."[6]

"I spoke with social workers at Hecht House who said [the attack] was distinctly the result of Curran," Sweeney wrote. The result of Curran and the result of the Christian Front in its afterlife. Behind the veil of a South Boston neighborhood association, former fronters were continuing to focus the attention of Irish Catholics on the front's violent ideology. With Gallagher as the point man, Moran operated behind closed doors. After the speech,

Sweeney followed Curran to the lobby of the Hotel Gardner in Boston's Fenway district. There was Moran, waiting for the priest. As soon as he spotted Moran, Curran "broke away from his escorts . . . shook [Moran's] hand and pounded him on the shoulder and said, 'My God, I'm glad to see you.'" Moran stayed at the hotel until after midnight, meeting privately with Curran.

The Hecht House affray may have been set off by Curran's speech, but the evening of anti-Semitic and anti-Communist oratory was only a catalyst, bringing together reactive energies that were already coursing through the city. After the speech, Sweeney wrote to her friend that she had noticed "about five riots a month in that area." In Brookline, which Sweeney called "the wealthiest township in the US," two hundred Irish and Jewish students engaged in what the local police chief called "strictly a racial riot." She observed that "Jewish children were beaten severely."[7]

Isadore Muchnick, a city councilor from Dorchester and Harvard-educated lawyer, noticed the same trend Sweeney did. Speaking with Arthur Derounian in April 1943, Muchnick described both violence against Jews and the worrisome prospect of escalation. He had learned from sources around town that Jewish men were responding to the onslaught by joining auxiliary police forces and patrolling neighborhoods with "heavy sticks." At the same time, "Catholics are also serving as auxiliary policemen carrying big sticks." Muchnick feared that "if the attacks keep on, someone, sometime, is going to get killed."

That spring, Sweeney arranged a meeting with the local chapter of the Anti-Defamation League. She suggested that she and other Catholics contact priests of the Boston Archdiocese with a view toward extracting public acknowledgment and condemnation of violence. But the ADL opposed Sweeney's plan, suggesting that it should be "big time Catholics"—lay Catholics—not priests who spoke out. Whereas Sweeney and Derounian, like Tillich, understood that the priesthood was a pillar of Catholic anti-Semitism, it appears that the ADL either did not recognize this or was nervous about a project targeting clerics. Derounian, who was familiar with Sweeney's outreach to the ADL, noted that "nothing was done about the matter."[8]

Another witness to the rising tide of Catholic-on-Jewish violence was Isadore Zack. An officer in the US Army Counter Intelligence Corps (CIC), Zack was assigned to work domestic intelligence in Boston—a sign that, well after the United States had joined the fighting in Europe, the army still considered the city a front in the war. Zack's CIC report was written in the fall, when the crisis was at a high point, but made clear that matters had been getting worse for some time. He was shaken by "the smashing of windows in synagogues, fifteen or more street fights within two weeks and other occurrences of like character which forced one police official to say that the situation had 'reached a boiling point.'" That police statement was for Zack's ears only: the police were not talking openly about the wave of assaults.

Indeed, the volatile "situation was not known to the general public," Zack wrote. He tallied a range of incidents that had not made it into the papers, including "window-smashing at one synagogue and three Jewish stores, numerous awnings slashed at Jewish stores, five individual assaults, one Jewish victim beaten by police without provocation, and an attack by seven Christian boys on two Jewish boys on October 9, 1943." In the absence of police reports, there was less for the papers to go on. Such incidents "had been underway for more than a year without any interference from civic authorities," Zack noted. This was hardly a surprising outcome given Moran's influence in the BPD.

But it was not just a lack of police interest that kept the violence out of the headlines. As Zack explained, "the Boston press ignored what was going on, in keeping with the wishes of Jewish leaders who were afraid publicity would make matters worse."[9] One example of these cowed community eminences was Rabbi Joseph S. Shubow, who shut down an effort to bring police bias to light. In the early fall of 1943, police arrested four Jewish boys in Dorchester, leading to an outraged response from a local politician named Berman, who was aiming for a spot on the Boston City Council. Available sources do not make clear why the boys were arrested, but Berman was up in arms because whenever Irish Catholics beat up Jewish boys, the BPD arrested the Jews. Berman wanted to come forward with his complaint, but, according to an FBI informant, "Rabbi Shubow was of the opinion that the matter should be hushed." Such acquiescence was strategic, if not wise. Shubow was known as an "Americanist" rabbi—he focused on the integration of Jews into US society and was therefore not inclined to rock any boats. He worried that publicizing the plight of the Jewish boys would "do more harm" than good in a city that was already unwelcoming.

Despite the wishes of Shubow and others in the Jewish community, Boston's anti-Semitic violence eventually did break into the news. If the Boston papers were no longer focused on the men, women, and politics of the Christian Front, a liberal New York paper, *PM*, was. Early in October 1943, a *PM* writer appeared at the FBI's Boston field office. The reporter, whose name is redacted in the FBI files, "had no constructive information," according to Special Agent James Mahan. "He merely wanted to know why the entire group (the Christian Front) could not be apprehended."[10]

A couple of weeks later, on October 18, *PM* published a story headlined "Christian Front Hoodlums Terrorize Boston Jews." The author was Arnold Beichman, a journalist who was deeply concerned about issues of racism and anti-Semitism. It may well have been Beichman who visited the Boston FBI. The *PM* article relied on affidavits and other court records describing numerous unsettling incidents. The affidavits described beating after beating, as well as gang violence. In one case, a group of about fifteen youths shattered the windows of synagogue and then stood at the foot of the synagogue screaming, "Let's kill all the Jews!" Beichman reported gangs on Blue Hill Avenue, Dorchester's main thoroughfare, shouting, "They'll be no more Jews on Jew Hill Avenue when the war is over!" Frances Sweeney is quoted in the article saying, "These are not just assaults on Jewish children, they are a manifestation that the Christian Front still thrives and is encouraged in Boston."[11]

The very day Beichman's article was published, Massachusetts Governor Leverett Saltonstall held a press conference in his office. Beichman attended and was introduced to the governor as the author of the *PM* article. Saltonstall shared Beichman's liberalism and was usually good-natured and evenhanded, but on that day he exploded, demanding that Beichman "get right out of this office." The governor insisted that the article was not telling the truth and falsely accused him of complicity in "terrorism." For added measure, Saltonstall commanded his bodyguard to escort Beichman out of the building. *PM* counterpunched the following day, with a story occupying its entire front page and headlined, "A Challenge to Gov. Saltonstall: Stamp out Terrorism against Boston Jews or Disprove It." The story of Boston's anti-Semitic violence—and the governor's refusal to combat it—went national.[12]

Although Saltonstall lashed out at Beichman, he was in fact "extremely disturbed" by the contents of the *PM* article, as he told Commissioner Timilty. Saltonstall was particularly discouraged by Beichman's reports that the BPD was involved the attacks. "The whole matter concerns very much the good name of the people of our city and our state," the governor wrote to the commissioner who had not quite shut down the Christian Front.[13]

In classic style Timilty shielded his officers. He advised Saltonstall that police had "no tangible evidence" concerning "unwarranted attacks and beatings being inflicted upon many innocent Jewish boys and girls." He acknowledged that he had received "periodic complaints of alleged anti-Semitic activity taking place in the Roxbury and Dorchester districts," but "each case has been thoroughly investigated." Nevertheless, he went ahead and "assigned twenty-five additional officers" to Roxbury and Dorchester. It was another knee-jerk move from Timilty, evidencing an unwillingness to engage thoughtfully with the facts of the crisis. Officers were operating on both sides of the law—putting more of them on the street might prevent some violence and lead to arrests of some wrongdoers, but adding officers could just as easily amplify the problems of police brutality and unjust arrests.

Timilty was not trying to protect only his men. He was also guarding his reputation as the undertaker of the Christian Front. The commissioner seemed personally offended by the suggestion that Moran and the front still held sway in Boston. "As no doubt you are aware, I caused the offices of this organization to be raided and closed in Boston," Timilty reminded the governor. "As Police Commissioner I have used active and successful means to silence the Christian Front and have thereby terminated a sore spot of anti-Semitism in this city." Showing the same reckless sense of invincibility that had him tangling with Moran in the first place, Timilty grew flippant with the governor. "It should be remembered that the City of Boston is not an outpost of the Kingdom of Heaven and nobody can make it one," he wrote.[14]

Perhaps Timilty was feeling defensive because his bargain with Moran was backfiring. By the time Timilty responded to Saltonstall, many Boston papers were talking about the role of the Christian Front in instigating anti-Semitic violence.[15] Timilty suddenly looked as irresponsible as he had in fact been. Worse still, from the perspective of the commissioner's ego, Moran had played him for a fool. Moran had promised to shut down the front, and he had, but only in name. There was an obvious loophole in the deal Timilty had bragged about. Exploiting that loophole, Moran was inspiring, perhaps coordinating, a wave of crime and violence that was swallowing the police department and threatening to swallow Saltonstall, too. Evidently Timilty felt comfortable mouthing off at the governor, but it must be recalled that, at this time, the police commissioner was a gubernatorial appointee. The quirky rules of state politics ensured that when Saltonstall had a headache, Timilty had a toothache.

Like the police, the FBI proved unable to contend with the news of Moran's ongoing activity. The problem in the bureau's case was not ignorance. Agents knew a great deal about Moran: confidential informant T-1's reports were substantial, and often chilling, ensuring that the FBI did not share Tim-ilty's delusion that he had shut Moran down. Throughout 1943 Boston's field office received reports of Moran's increasingly violent agitation, his urging of genocide, and roles of former fronters in whipping up anti-Semitic sentiment in Boston.

The problem for the FBI was primarily one of leadership. The Boston field office had been in shambles since March 1942, when Virgil Peterson abruptly resigned. Within three weeks, Peterson had cleared out of Boston and moved to Chicago to take over the Chicago Crime Commission. It was a well-paying job monitoring street crime, gambling, and the rackets and a sensible career move for Peterson, a classically minded cop who had helped catch the noto-rious gangster John Dillinger. As Bostonian and one-time FBI counterintel-ligence chief William C. Sullivan wrote of the World War II–era FBI, "Dealing with Nazism, Fascism, Communism, and espionage were not at all the same as catching bank robbers and kidnappers." Peterson could attest to that. Initially he was replaced by Special Agent Carl Hennrich, but by Au-gust 1943 Hennrich was out, replaced by Edward Soucy, an expert in espio-nage cases. The Moran investigation fumbled and stumbled amid the shakeup. By the time Soucy was installed, the anti-Semitic crisis was smoldering and about to hit the newspapers.[16]

FBI leadership was a problem on the national level as well, thanks to Hoover's erratic behavior. The director's approach to the Moran investigation kept shifting, catching the Boston office off guard. On the day the Beichman story was released, Hoover wrote Soucy a long letter demanding to know why Boston agents had been so ineffective in developing sedition charges— charges that the Justice Department had previously taken off the table. "The subject appears . . . very active, and perhaps a dangerous person," Hoover noted, yet the Boston FBI seemed to be doing its best not to get Moran off the streets. "A sedition charge cannot be made merely through receiving and setting forth general reports on the subject's meetings supplied by confiden-tial informants," Hoover wrote. "Information must be developed . . . con-cerning the recipients of the subject's statements . . . with particular refer-ence to . . . the Armed Forces or . . . the Selective Service Act." T-1's reports, whatever their merits, could not prove that Moran was sowing sedition in the armed forces. Hoover wanted evidence he could use in court, but "the Bu-reau's requests along these lines . . . have been constantly disregarded," he fumed.[17]

Following on decisions made at the Justice Department, Hoover had previously told Peterson to build a case for custodial detention rather than sedition. However, by the time he wrote to Soucy, Hoover seemed to have forgotten his own orders. Soucy must have been startled by the unacknowledged about-face; evidently he took Hoover's latest lashing to mean that T-1 was no longer needed. Instead of coaching her on how to develop evidence material to a sedition charge, Soucy appears to have relieved her of her duties. At the high-water mark of the crisis, T-1 went silent, severing the FBI's connection to Moran's inner circle and to Moran himself.

Blowback

Sweeney, Beichman, and a number of other journalists and activists, as well as some modern historians, have blamed Moran for the wave of police and gang violence that engulfed South Boston in 1943. There is no documented evidence that Moran directed any crimes—except for Gallagher's manhandling and forceful removal of Sweeney from Curran's speech—but it is not unreasonable to assume that he planned some of the abuses that occurred and sanctioned others.

Yet the question of whether and to what extent Moran was personally involved in the brutal, police-abetted anti-Semitic violence of 1943 misses the larger context in two ways. First, Moran did not have to personally arrange every assault. He was an ideological and spiritual leader, not a general. His role had always been to inspire a movement. Second, if we focus inordinately on what Moran did, we run the risk of ignoring the intelligence and law enforcement actions that created the conditions in which he became so much more dangerous. BSC's covert operation enabled the self-serving Timilty to act on his worst instincts, and after the raid had forced Moran underground, the mercurial and disorganized FBI foundered. The bureau continued to collect information on Moran but did nothing with it, then kneecapped its own efforts by abandoning its top informant. There was no attempt by either the FBI or the police to connect Moran's underground activities to the violence in Boston. In other words, Moran's enemies forced him underground and then allowed his anti-Semitism to fester there.

Moran was harder to contain when he was far from the Hibernian Hall stage. For one thing, it became more difficult to collect information on his activities. Instead of speaking publicly, where he was easily accessible to the police, the press, and opposition activists, he now met privately with his inner circle, where he was beyond most surveillance. Indeed, that circle shrank while he was underground, making surveillance harder still. Shortly after the papers began pointing to the Christian Front as an instigator of the violence, he dissolved the Friday Group—its last gathering came at an October 30 celebration of Father Coughlin's birthday, where William Gallagher asked, "Who is Walter Winchell?" eliciting "a cry of Jew, Jew, Jew." Thereafter Moran kept only two or three supporters around him. Like other ideological leaders who have been pushed underground, Moran was "both literally and figuratively outside the boundaries of the law and the norms governing civic life."[18]

Unsurprisingly, Moran was further radicalized in these circumstances. "I am persecuted night and day by the Jews," he told T-1 in one of their last conversations. He had in mind a specific instance: at one point in summer 1943, his wife Nora told T-1 that she had "found a little kike packing up a pile of Francis's books" outside their cellar.[19] But it was not just a burglary that upset Moran. No longer speaking to the public—and now surrounded exclusively by his die-hard supporters, individuals as radical and conspiratorial in their thinking as he was—Moran saw no need for restraint. Indeed, he may have felt pressure to become more extreme, so as to outflank his lieutenants and retain ideological leadership.

It is also important to keep in mind that, as the public face of the Christian Front, Moran had played something of a moderating role in Boston. He was no Floyd Carridi or John Cassidy. He did not get into fistfights or plan terrorist attacks. He delivered lectures, arranged speeches, wrote letters, and showed films. He sermonized and explicated the theology of the Mystical Body. He rarely sanctioned heckling by his supporters, much less violence. He even made a spectacle of turning the other cheek, as when he instructed enraged audience members not to throw the infiltrator Maurice Goldsmith out of a Christin Front meeting. When Moran came under the wing of the Nazi Scholz, he still did not explicitly urge or condone abuses of Jews. But once Moran was underground, all bets were off. He could no longer manipulate his followers as masterfully as he once did, turning the heat up and down as he wished. He became a symbolic figure more than an operational one. Freshly and acutely aggrieved by the injustice Moran had suffered at the hands of the police and perceived left-wingers like Sweeney, and inclined to believe that their sorrows were products of Jewish conspiracies, Christian Front members and fellow travelers diffused into Boston's neighborhoods and did what their hearts told them was right.

In this atmosphere, any attempt at accountability for Moran or his followers would inspire only further gripes. The *PM* stories did not help on this score. According to a November 4 report from FBI Special Agent Mahan, remnant fronters were decrying *PM* for promoting and participating in an "anti-Catholic movement in Boston." This is exactly the sort of reaction Moran would have had. He had not spent the past few years preaching to empty chairs. He had educated a large chunk of Irish Catholic Boston, taught them to think as he did.[20]

Moran seems to have understood his own success better than law enforcement did. By summer 1943, he was describing himself to T-1 "as a tough guy and a gang leader." This is not precisely an admission that he was coordinating the violence that was suffusing Dorchester and other parts of Boston, but he was certainly taking credit for it. And rightly so. Sociologists who study gangs have shown how they can emerge from organizations that "splinter" under "external pressures" such as "law enforcement and neighborhood dynamics." The resulting subgroups of fractured organizations then take on "a life of their own." Moran did not have to provide detailed instructions for every act of violence. He had been training anti-Semites since 1939; they had the tools—physical and intellectual—to strike out on their own. Frequently protected by police, inspired in proximate terms by the likes of Father Curran, and drawing deeply from the well of grievances Moran had filled over a period of years, atomized fronters fostered a hundred mini cells across Boston and brought the fire that Derounian had foreseen.[21]

Final Days

In the last weeks of 1943, with the media and authorities now paying attention, the anti-Semitic crisis waned. At about the same time, Moran's chief law-enforcement protector lost his job: Timilty was relieved from his post after Governor Saltonstall blocked his reappointment as commissioner. Saltonstall had had enough of Timilty, in particular the commissioner's poor handling of the crisis, for which he refused any responsibility. Timilty would go on to run for mayor and lose, his departure from the civic scene bringing to an end what one scholar called the Tammany-style "Diamond Jim and Joe Timilty political dynasty."[22] In fact, others of Diamond Jim's descendants would go on to careers in Massachusetts politics, but the Timilty name became far less prominent, receding as another local dynasty, that of the Kennedys, was taking off.

As for the FBI, Peterson, a more passive protector of Moran, was long gone. But there was not much Soucy could do clean up the messy investigation he inherited. With Hoover having set aside custodial detention in favor of old-fashioned indictment, arrest, and trial, it was now essential that confidential informant T-1 testify against Moran in court—but doing so would mean revealing herself. On November 2, 1943, Soucy explained to Hoover that he had bad news from T-1. She still was "willing to assist" the bureau, but she "expressed unwillingness to appear in court in the event of prosecution." Derounian had once described Moran as "crafty," and so he was. But he was lucky too.[23]

Moran had dodged justice again, and his most brilliant disappearing act was just around the corner: on or about November 3, he joined the army. Not only that, but he aimed to obtain a battlefield role, indicating to his draft board that he was seeking entry with A-1 status, meaning he would be eligible for full combat duty. This reflected an apparent change of heart. In January, he had "advised T-1 that he would accept limited service, or that he would like to be classified as a conscientious objector."[24] It is tantalizing to think that Scholz directed Moran to join the army in a combat role and thereby wind up overseas, but there is no evidence to this effect. Publicly, Moran disavowed patriotism as the reason for his decision not to claim conscientious objector status. The issue, he said, was that he needed an army salary to support his wife and new baby. Announcing his enlistment, he told the *Herald* that he had lost thirty-six private-sector jobs in the previous year because the War Department was out to get him. "I have demanded from the War Department . . . to give me the reason for their action," he said. "Every Communist can get a job when he wants it—even in the White House." Speaking to the *Herald* again on December 3, he repeated the claim, saying he had been "bounced from thirty-six jobs in private industry during the past year because of his activities."[25]

In Washington Hoover learned of Moran's army future while reading his morning newspaper. Livid, Hoover telegrammed Soucy on November 5 saying, "IMPERATIVE REMAINING INVESTIGATION BE COMPLETED." A few days later, November 10, Hoover and Assistant Attorney General Tom C.

Clark agreed that Moran would not be assigned to any militarily sensitive duties, nor would he be on the front lines. Evidently they petitioned the army on the matter, because Moran would never see combat.[26]

Moran was slated to report for duty on December 23. Just before he set off, he met with seventy-five of his closest friends back at Hibernian Hall to deliver what amounted to his "last lecture" before entering the US Army. "If killed in the service of his country, he asked his friends not to consider him a hero." At the very bottom of his draft card, in the space for his signature, he had his draft board type, "I am absolutely and unequivocally opposed to dictatorial regimentation." The draft board let the declaration go through, mainly because they thought it was a statement against Hitler. In Moran's mind, it was a statement against FDR. His friends lavished him with a final cash donation.[27]

In Europe Scholz rolled from one stroke of good fortune to the next. He had arrived in Budapest on December 1, 1941, and stayed exactly one year. Then he was transferred to the consulate in Turin, Italy. At the same time, he was appointed to the RSHA, the Reich Main Security Office. In Turin he continued the role he had performed in Boston, with his diplomatic work as a cover for espionage. Sometime prior to spring 1944, Scholz was transferred to Milan as consul general, maintaining his connection to the RSHA. In this new role, he tangled, through intermediaries, with US spymaster Allen Dulles. In 1944 Turin, Milan, and Genoa experienced violent uprisings of factory workers, which stopped war production and caused headaches for the Waffen SS, the main military force in northern Italy. Many of these strikes were sparked by agents working for Dulles, who was then an OSS operative headquartered in Bern, Switzerland. Scholz, however, managed to tamp down the worker unrest.[28]

Scholz's success caught the attention of Karl Wolff, a high-ranking SS officer and Germany's supreme commander in Italy. Soon Scholz was petitioning Wolff for a promotion. For Scholz, this was a long time coming. He had occupied the same SS rank for ten years, perhaps preferring not to make any requests lest someone dredge up his past association with the disgraced Ernst Röhm. But by spring 1944, Scholz was convinced his time had come. It did not matter to him that the tide of the war had decidedly turned. At this point Allied armies controlled the south of Italy, and Mussolini's puppet Salò Republic was barely hanging on. Some of the grittiest fighting of the war was taking place within earshot of Scholz's consulate. Scholz must have understood that a promotion would not secure much career advancement, given that all Nazi careers would likely soon end. Yet he still wished for recognition within an ideological system he held dear. For Scholz, it was important to be known as a superior Nazi, and Wolff agreed that he deserved the distinction. "*Standartenführer* Scholz is the type of leader who in his overall habits represents the straight line of the SS," Wolff wrote to Berlin. He also noted Scholz's exemplary work as "a voluntary cooperator with Amt VI," the Nazi party's Foreign Intelligence Service.[29]

Scholz got his promotion to *Oberführer*—a rank equivalent to brigadier general—on May 21, just in time for D-Day. Less than a year later, on April 29, 1945, Wolff negotiated the surrender of all German forces in Italy. Hitler committed suicide the next day. As an English-speaking aide-de-camp to Wolff, Scholz may have taken part in the surrender talks, which were hashed out with Dulles. And as Oberführer, he would soon be in the Allies occupiers' sights. According to rules promulgated on May 8, Scholz's rank made him subject to automatic arrest. Somehow, he managed initially to squirm out of the Allies' grip, and for about six weeks after the surrender, no one knew his whereabouts. He was captured in civilian clothes by members of the US Army Counter Intelligence Corps but was not placed in custody. Instead, and in keeping with his silver-spoon style, he repaired to the picturesque Tuscan thermal resort town of Montecatini, where he took a room in the grand Hotel Valentini.

The Caserta-based CIC agents suspected that Scholz was a spy but were unsure what to do with him. They also were uncertain about his rank, and Scholz was not about to answer questions honestly when lying better suited his purposes. So CIC asked for guidance from the State Department. The State Department responded that Scholz had sent weekly reports to Himmler from the Boston Consulate, that he had "a signed photo of Himmler in his home," and that he was an ardent Nazi. Concerning his rank, all the State Department had on file was that he was a Standartenführer. The State Department also mentioned that his wife, Lilo, was "the daughter of Georg von Schnitzler of IG Farben" and was herself "a dangerous Nazi."[30]

The mystery of Scholz was not yet fully explained, but CIC had enough information to be worried and placed Scholz in protective custody. In practical terms, though, nothing changed. In July CIC decided to transfer Scholz to Verona for interrogation, but he claimed he could not be moved because "he was suffering from a weak heart." A US Army medical officer confirmed that Scholz "suffered from severe heart disease," and he was left to ride out his stay in the Hotel Valentini. But Scholz was not sick. He had always been healthy and active and in his Boston days was an avid tennis player.

Scholz had outsmarted CIC, but Captain James Jesus Angleton was not so easily tricked. Angleton, who would later become the CIA's counterintelligence guru, was the leader of Secret Counter Intelligence Unit Z, a special Allied outfit in Italy that decoded Ultra intelligence—German radio communications intercepted by the British. In October he sent CIC a secret message noting that "either by feigned or actual heart ailment, subject has been able to postpone systematic interrogations." Angleton wanted a crack at Scholz, whom he pinpointed as a principal figure in Germany's recovery of the "Ciano Diaries," the personal papers of Galeazzo Ciano—Mussolini's foreign minister and son-in-law. Apparently, while in the Milan Consulate, Scholz facilitated the work of Hildegarde Beetz, an RSHA plant who acted as Ciano's secretary and knew where he had secreted his papers. Angleton wanted Scholz questioned vigorously. "Arrange . . . to interrogate subject on the details of his activities in Italy, which are dubious, to say the least," he wrote.[31]

Yet Scholz soon outfoxed even Angleton, proving that Moran had learned from the slipperiest of fishes. Scholz's scheme was a brilliant one. During interrogation by a Secret Counter Intelligence unit, Scholz asserted that he was stateless. As a refugee, he would have certain protections after the war, while being able to avoid German, Italian, and American laws that could hamper his movement. He also procured a letter of recommendation from Maurilio Cardinal Fossati of Turin. Fossati assured any Allied military authorities that Scholz always carried out his consular duties "with the highest humanitarian and Christian spirit."[32]

Scholz's last deception was to convince American interrogators that he was still a Standartenführer. "Scholz does admit that he was a very ambitious and convinced Nazi," his interrogator noted, but his long standing at the rank of Standartenführer seemed to suggest that he had grown disillusioned with Nazism and stopped trying to advance. "Subject in the opinion of this interrogator has changed his attitudes and beliefs," the duped American agent wrote. With trickery, charisma, and fluent English, Scholz was slipping the nets of US intelligence. But the army did not simply let him go, instead demurring on plans for his repatriation. Scholz would have to bide his time a bit longer.[33]

Then, suddenly, one more hurdle emerged. It was O. John Rogge, a name Scholz might have recognized from his time in the United States. Rogge was a high-ranking prosecutor in the Justice Department. It was he who, violating obvious ethical norms, had taken the meeting with Catholic hierarchs trying to get the New York Christian Front sedition case downgraded or thrown out—although it must be noted that Rogge resisted the entreaties of the clergy. During the war Rogge used the Smith Act to prosecute the Great Sedition Trial involving Joseph McWilliams—"Joe McNazi"—and twenty-nine other alleged Nazi spies. The case dragged through the US District Court of the District of Columbia court for more than two years, and by early 1946, Rogge worried that he was going to lose. The news of Scholz's capture in Italy seemed to provide an opportunity, though. Rogge thought Scholz might know something that could revive his faltering case. *PM* agreed, opining that an interrogation of Scholz "might prove sensationally useful to Rogge." In an astonishing turn, Chief Justice Bolitha J. Laws of the district court suspended proceedings and allowed Rogge to travel to Europe and interview Scholz.[34]

On April 4, 1946, Rogge interrogated Scholz at a US Army Camp in Oberursel, Germany. Scholz was his charming self, and Rogge's performance was abysmal. The prosecutor focused on uncovering Nazi funding of the defendants in his trial, not on Scholz's espionage. In other words, Rogge was asking Scholz the right questions from the standpoint of his own case, but he was allowing the SS man to get away once more. Scholz insisted he had nothing to share and that questions about money should be directed to Heribert von Strempel. To the extent that he was asked about his time in Boston, Scholz was often vague and misleading and downplayed his activities and his role.

Strangely, one thing Scholz did not lie about was his relationship with Moran. Scholz was candid with Rogge about his "secret meetings" with the leader of the Christian Front in Boston. This was the first substantial disclosure of their work together, but it meant little to Rogge. He was fixated on the money trail, which he saw as the best path to victory in the McWilliams case. Had he been willing to pay attention to the news coming from Scholz, Rogge might have realized that he had a real American Nazi spy on his hands, in the form of Moran. Instead Rogge returned to the United States with nothing to show in the context of the trial he would soon lose and which would become known to history as one of the Justice Department's major debacles. Inexplicably, Rogge shelved his information about Moran for another fifteen years.

When Rogge finally published his revelations about Scholz and Moran in 1961, hardly anyone noticed. The war was long since over, the denazification process had petered out unceremoniously, and American policymakers were preoccupied with a Cold War in which Berlin had been the key flashpoint for more than a decade. Maintaining alliance with West Germany was more important than justice for former Nazis, many of whom were now employed in the West German government. The public was in much the same place as official Washington, fearful of the Soviets and eager for reconciliation, especially after so many years of costly and tense occupation in the German capital. Americans also were not as cognizant of Nazi crimes as they would later become. Indeed, the word "Holocaust" had not yet been applied to the Nazi Final Solution. The first American book in the twentieth century to be titled *Holocaust* was not published until 1959, and it concerned not the Nazi atrocities but rather the calamitous 1942 fire at Boston's Cocoanut Grove nightclub, which took nearly five hundred lives. The hunting of ex-Nazis and their collaborators would come later. In 1946 the public would have been aghast at Moran's spying. Fifteen years later, there were other matters to worry about, and Rogge's blind spot became one more reason the Christian Front fell from the minds of postwar Americans.[35]

After the interrogation, Rogge made no recommendation to the US Army regarding Scholz. So Scholz came forward with a recommendation of his own. He argued to Allied intelligence authorities that he had been questioned by the special assistant to the attorney general of the United States and had been exonerated. Rogge's ineptitude became Scholz's passport out of detention. In December 1946 he was moved to a displaced persons camp in Darmstadt. He was no longer Herbert W. Scholz, ex-SS general, diplomat, and spy. He was Doctor Herbert W. Scholz, refugee. And he was inching closer to freedom.[36]

Back in Boston, Frances Sweeney was busy with journalistic activities. In 1943 she started an anti-Fascist and human rights–oriented monthly newspaper called the *Boston City Reporter*. Sweeney headquartered the paper in the same office as IADA. She also collaborated with William Gavin, her friend from the *Herald* and *Herald-Traveler*, to produce a weekly column called Rumor Clinic. *Life* magazine ran a photographic, multipage article on Sweeney's Rumor Clinic, which helped galvanize support for her style of investigative reporting. Throughout 1943 she tracked down the origin of divisive rumors and analyzed disinformation. Much rumor tracking was connected to Catholic-Jewish relations and anti-Semitism. Sweeney's view was that by bringing disinformation to light, truthful reporting could gain the upper hand.[37]

It is unclear if BSC was still supporting Sweeney clandestinely. The SOE documents stop recording IADA activity in late January 1942, and shortly thereafter the Office of Strategic Services found that IADA was essentially a one-woman operation. Yet somehow Sweeney maintained her perch in the high-rent Little Building through early 1944, suggesting that IADA was still taking in funds. Still, her public image was defined more by her journalistic projects than by IADA. In November 1943 Special Agent Mahan of the Boston FBI field office reported that IADA was still involved in advocacy, but he suspected a connection to the Communist Party, not British intelligence. Isadore Zack of CIC thought that Sweeney was working in some unknown capacity for partisans of the Irish Free State, which had dissolved in 1937. "God help military intelligence!" Sweeney wrote to her friend, the Harvard psychologist Gordon Allport, after the superintendent at the Little Building informed her that Zack had been making inquiries. "Izzy Zack spends all his time chasing Commies and me."[38]

The heart of Sweeney's concerns in this period remained Catholic anti-Semitism. Through 1943 and 1944, she moved IADA closer to Jewish organizations such as the American Jewish Committee and the Anti-Defamation League. She continued to believe, like Tillich, that the only antidote to Christian Front anti-Semitism was public clerical philo-Semitism. She renewed her effort to find a priestly champion for her cause until tragedy struck "one rainy night in April, 1944," as Nat Hentoff put it. Sweeney was walking home when she had an "attack." She "fell to the ground, into the gutter and could neither move nor speak." Passersby thought her a swooning drunkard. "She came back for a while, but the slender troublemaker with deep blue eyes died in June."[39]

Few knew it, but Sweeney had recently engaged. Her fiancé, James Bottis, mourned her with poignant words. "It just doesn't seem right that one who could see so much evil around her, and spared neither time nor courage to fight it, should suddenly be taken away," Bottis wrote to Allport. "To those of us who are left behind, her deeds should be a challenge to carry on the good work she started."[40]

Epilogue

"A LITTLE FLOWER BLOOMS ON THE HEATHER." THOSE WERE THE first words that former Chancellor Heinrich Brüning saw as he opened a curious letter retrieved from his mailbox at Harvard University's Lowell House in January 1947. The line was from a popular German love song of 1930, and the letter contained a tiny pressed flower.[1]

Scholz was writing from a special displaced persons camp for former SS officers at the town of Schwäbisch Hall, northeast of Stuttgart, in the US occupation zone. During the war the site had been a concentration camp where the SS imprisoned mainly Polish Jews. The camp's commandant, August Walling, devised unique styles of torture, such as forcing inmates to stand for hours between two tight rows of barbed wire. Following the liberation of the camps, Schwäbisch Hall housed about a thousand ex-SS. For a time the prize prisoner was *SS-Obersturmbannführer* Joachim Peiper, instigator of the 1944 Malmedy massacre, in which German soldiers murdered eighty-four American prisoners of war.[2]

Scholz had evaded US intelligence, but now he was facing real hardship. The winter of 1946–1947 was one of the most disastrous in Germany's history. By January Scholz was suffering the cold and hunger. It is unclear if he had either money or a plan to get out of the camp and make a new life for himself. In need of help, he turned to Brüning. Making no mention of his earlier intimidation campaign against the former chancellor, Scholz appealed to Brüning as a German and a human being. In the letter Scholz warmly recalled their first face-to-face meeting at Glatz (now Kłodzko, Poland) in 1933 and the beautiful mountains of the Glatzer Bergland. But times had most certainly changed.

Brüning responded graciously. "I gave the order to the CERA [a Christian emergency aid organization] to send you food packets," he wrote. "Please write me what you need in terms of clothing and . . . I will try to put something together and send it to you."[3] Perhaps Brüning was moved by the words of this man he knew, felt the tug at his heartstrings. But it seems more likely that Brüning was simply meeting the minimal duty of his conscience. In his files there is a handwritten gloss scribbled across the top of Scholz's letter of supplication. Almost indecipherable, the last few words of the gloss appear to read "as the other Nazis." Brüning received a constant stream of such letters, begging his support. The note suggests that he was treating Scholz as he did the rest. But if Brüning was offering no special care, he was also not turning down his erstwhile tormenter. Given the dire postwar circumstances in Germany, what Brüning did may have saved Scholz's life.[4]

Scholz was adept at saving his life. Shortly after he arranged for his care packages from Brüning, an opportunity for self-preservation presented itself, and Scholz grasped it greedily. The previous year, in his conversation with Rogge, he had given away Heribert von Strempel, telling the assistant attorney general that it was not himself but Strempel who knew the money trail leading to US Nazi spies. The next victim of Scholz's betrayal would be his wife's father, Georg von Schnitzler. The Nazis had been perfecting the backstabbing arts since the Night of the Long Knives, if not before, and Scholz was an impeccable Nazi.

In spring 1947 authorities in the US occupation zone were drawing up indictments against the leaders of IG Farben, who were tried as part of the military tribunal at Nuremburg. "One of the three super directors of the I.G. Farben works" was Schnitzler. He was arrested in April 1945 at his country estate. At the time of his arrest, Schnitzler was "dressed in fine Scottish tweeds, a cashmere sweater, and English leather wing-tip shoes" and was found in a room "with a Renoir painting from the Louvre hanging on the wall." Speaking cheerfully in English, he told the arresting officers that he was looking forward to visiting Wilmington, Delaware, to see "his friends, the DuPonts." Instead he was jailed at Nuremburg facing a possible death sentence. When Scholz learned of the upcoming trial, he saw the possibility of turning state's evidence.[5]

In March 1947 Scholz offered himself to the Americans as a witness against Schnitzler. We do not know what testimony Scholz gave, because his witness file at the US National Archives is entirely empty. But whatever he said seems to have had the desired result. Schnitzler was convicted and sentenced to five years in Landsberg Prison, where Adolf Hitler was held in 1924 after the Beer Hall Putsch, and Scholz wandered out of Schwäbisch Hall.[6]

The trail after 1947 traverses the globe. In 1948, having proven his disloyalty to the Schnitzlers, Scholz and Lilo divorced. Scholz then returned to Italy and took a boat from Genoa to Buenos Aires. He was following one of the classic "ratlines" of high-ranking Nazis and other Fascists escaping Europe after the war. They would travel through Spain and Italy, where letters of reference from Catholic clergy were especially handy in securing passage — Cardinal Fossati's letter was likely Scholz's passport. The family source indicates that, in Argentina, Scholz connected with associates of the Krupp family, and after a short time headed to Bolivia to buy a copper mine. He settled in Cochabamba, where he married an émigré Yugoslav countess and managed his mining concern. When business proved poor, he moved to Coquimbo, in the Chilean Iron Belt, where he briefly took a job with Bethlehem Steel. Dissatisfied with Bethlehem Steel, he bought his own iron ore mine, which immediately lost money.[7]

A decade after Scholz's departure from Europe, the situation in Germany had cooled off. Denazification efforts—vigorous and punitive in US hands; vigorous but less punitive in British and Soviet hands; and neither vigorous nor punitive in French hands—had died down and passed from the Allies to the Germans, who were concerned with reconciliation and rebuilding. In 1958 Scholz was able to obtain a pension from the new German government. He argued for his pension on the sole grounds that he had been an employee of the Ministry of Foreign Affairs. Diplomatic cover also allowed him to return to Germany with his wife and two newest children, as the government allowed that he had been merely a civil servant who went along with the times rather than an ideological Nazi. Scholz settled near Munich, where he bought a villa overlooking picturesque Lake Starnberg, playground of the Wittelsbachs, the Bavarian royal family. He lived quietly the rest of his days and died at Lake Starnberg in the summer of 1985. His death notice described him as "Dr. Herbert W. Scholz, Consul and Diplomat."[8]

Scholz's finest Boston recruit spent his postwar years searching for definition and finding little. Moran mustered out of the US Army as a private in August 1945 and was happy to accept his final paycheck and repair to his home on LaGrange Street in West Roxbury. He "did not intend to resume his former activities," he told the *Herald-Traveler*.[9] Boston had tempered in his absence, a sign both of what his presence had caused—even while he was underground—and of an apparently reduced appetite for ideological anti-Semitism. Army Counter Intelligence Corps officer Isadore Zack noted some street violence in Boston in an early 1945 report, covering the first year of Moran's enlistment. But Zack counted such abuses as the result of juvenile delinquency. "The leadership of Christian Front and pro-Fascist elements in this area is not of great significance or influence," Zack reported.[10] After Moran left, his followers did not continue his mission.

As soon as he left the Army, Moran was contacted by a lawyer representing Tyler Kent.[11] Kent was the cipher clerk and alleged spy at the US embassy in London whom the British in 1940 secretly tried and then imprisoned for the duration of World War II, after the Roosevelt administration agreed to waive his diplomatic immunity. Kent was in the process of suing the US government, contending that the waiver of diplomatic immunity had violated his "sovereign rights." Moran, too, believed he had been stripped of his rights and forced by the White House into a kind of penal situation. In Moran's case this was not an actual prison but rather the army's 620th Engineer General Service Company, a now-infamous labor battalion comprising "any man who seemed dangerously disloyal," as the army put it. These included a large number of Japanese Americans as well as some provably disloyal Americans, such as Private Dale H. Maple, a Harvard student recruited by Scholz in 1940 who became the first American soldier in World War II convicted of a crime tantamount to treason. The job of the 620th was mainly to construct barracks, roads, and latrines in environments where "no support for subversion existed." The men wore the blue fatigues of prisoners of war and were not issued arms.[12]

"There are others," Moran wrote to Kent's lawyer, "who were incarcerated (there is no other word for it) in the same damnable organization in which I spent most of my 'Army career.'" Moran was willing to "cooperate in any way" with the case, especially if Kent's story led to a congressional inquiry. The lawyer scribbled a note at the bottom of Moran's letter, summarizing Moran's claim that he had suffered official retribution in light of his political advocacy:

> Because he opposed Franklin Roosevelt's treason in plotting to put this
> country into a war that was none of our affair, and staged rallies in Boston

in opposition thereto, the above Francis P. Moran, when in the Army, was put in a labor battalion like a Georgia chain gang and forced to dig ditches in 140° heat with armed guards standing over him.

But while Moran was eager to assist, he wanted to do so privately. "I should prefer a minimum of publicity so far as I am personally concerned," he wrote. Experience had not changed Moran's views or relieved his sense of grievance. But the activist in him was no more. He would live the rest of his life quietly, without engaging in either public speaking or underground meddling. He was through with politics and through with Catholicism in the public square.[13]

Moran's final appearance at a community event came on March 15, 1946, at a speech by Father Curran in Boston. Moran showed up "looking very pale and worn." He did not speak with Curran, though he was "observed to have many friends and admirers around him." At this point, the Christian Front in Boston belonged largely to Curran, but it was a shell of its former self. Curran's talks were popular, always garnering at least five hundred listeners, and he kept strictly to the Christian Front's ideological positions. However, as a New Yorker, there was only so much Curran could do to keep the front alive in Boston. Whereas Moran at his height had been holding at least two meetings each week, Curran was showing up barely once a month. And while Curran drew crowds, the wider community was losing its taste for front-style religious appeals. In the aftermath of the war, Catholics began to understand the Nazi death camps as a moral problem for Christianity. Meanwhile Catholic Action and Mystical Body theology appeared suspect, given their attachments to anti-Semitism and Catholic anti-Judaism. The Church never explicitly disavowed these doctrines, but their prevalence in priestly oratory waned after the war, and in time they largely vanished from Catholic discourse.[14]

"I am in the taxi business now," Moran told a group of friends in January 1947. The group had been infiltrated by Gus Gazulis, erstwhile helper to Frances Sweeney. "I've been laying low for quite a while now," Moran said. "A lot of my friends have been getting after me to start up again." He expressed a vague concern with "what's going on with the Jews" and promised to be patient. "Next time we'll really go to town on these Goddamn kikes," he said. But there would be no next time.[15]

Moran entered the public sphere in 1936 with a tiny newspaper bit concerning a violent episode. In 1948 he bowed out of the public sphere in the same way. "Former Christian Front Leader Held Up in Cab," the headline read. "One of the passengers put a knife to his back and demanded his money." All fourteen dollars he had on him. Moran came through the ordeal unscathed; it was the last time his name would appear in a Boston newspaper until the day of his obituary.[16]

Hoover continued to keep tabs on Moran after his discharge. In July 1948 the FBI director took receipt of a copy of Moran's Army personnel file and found it unremarkable. An FBI agent's report indicated that "subject has made no attempts to reactivate the Christian Front and has shown no interest in his former activities." On May 11, 1949, the FBI marked CASE CLOSED across Moran's file. Moran ended his career as a reference clerk at the Boston Public Library and died in West Roxbury in 1971.[17]

Among Nazi agents of influence who went undetected in the United States, Moran arguably did the most damage. He did damage not only in connection to US national security, but also in terms of Jewish-Christian relations. He managed to do his work in the face of investigations from five US agencies: the FBI, Office of Strategic Service, Counter Intelligence Corps, Military Intelligence Division, and Office of Naval Intelligence. All deployed resources against him and had him under surveillance at one time or another. Nor could the British or the Soviets effectuate his removal from the scene. By clandestinely taking direction from Scholz, he certainly broke the Foreign Agents Registration Act, the law specifically designed to root out and prosecute Nazi spies. The author of that law, Representative John W. McCormack, would go on to shield Moran when John Franklin Carter tried to get Roosevelt to recognize the danger the Christian Front leader posed. Even when John Rogge found out that Moran was a spy, nothing came of it. Moran evaded the long arm of the law, by dint of both skill and luck. He was so elusive that he managed to escape even historical memory.

But if Moran faded into the background, his influence lingered. The Christian Front idea, as interpreted by John Cassidy, has remained a marginal one. The United States today is home to revolutionary militias, but they are less motivated by Christian doctrines than by a political philosophy that equates governance with tyranny. Moran's version of the Christian Front, however, is now in some ways mainstream. The notion of a Christian right is commonly associated with Evangelical Protestants and developments of the 1970s and 1980s, as conservative politicians and activists wedded their grievances over abortion and school prayer to the free-market impulses of the Republican Party. But the roots of this movement run deeper—backward in history past Joe McCarthy and the John Birch Society to the likes of Moran, Coughlin, and Elizabeth Dilling. Their style of anti-Semitism is not very prominent today, but other elements of their project are. They interlaced Christianity and patriotism in an effort to assert Christian nationalism; they introduced Americans to the idea that Christians abhor Communism and that liberals are merely Communists without the guts to say so. They were not out of their heads—Communists in Europe and in Mexico really were persecuting Christians. But in the American context, these and other right-wing Christians were the paranoid fringe. And so, with the exception of Coughlin, they have largely been ignored, even as their views seeped into the public and reinforced opinions that were already to be found there.

Indeed, it is not only Moran's Christian-imbued patriotism and anti-Communism that live with us still, but also his techniques for exploiting America's reverence for free speech. Moran, like Coughlin and others in their circle, made many false claims of censorship and some truthful ones. His removal from the public sphere is a cautionary tale in an age when Americans are grappling with difficult questions about whether and how to police public discourse in an effort to protect vulnerable groups. The trouble is that the policing tends to manufacture a sense of victimhood. Thus did the martyrdom of Moran and the Christian Front lead to an explosion of anti-Semitic violence in Boston in 1943. Likewise today, voices ejected from the public sphere—albeit usually by private institutions rather than police—become icons of grievance, rallying points for violent individuals.

There is also a very direct way in which the Christian Front remains with us in the realm of constitutional rights. The source is one of Moran's immediate successors, Reverend Arthur Terminiello. Terminiello was every bit a fronter. On July 13, 1945, while Moran was finishing his tour of duty, Terminiello gave a speech in Boston, where he was introduced by William Gallagher, Moran's colleague from his underground phase. The priest received "a rising ovation" after being hailed as "a Boston boy, a laborer in the vineyard of the South, a former student at Boston College, [and] a resident of Malden," a suburb north of Boston. He proceeded to follow "the Old Christian Front line" and argued that "the enemies of Christ are all around us." Tagged as "a native Fascist" by the press, Terminiello has been viewed as a crazed, inconsequential figure in American history.[18]

In fact Terminiello was a man of consequence. In the late 1940s he took to the Supreme Court a case that to this day has deep significance for speech rights and Christian-Jewish relations. On a five-four vote, *Terminiello v. City of Chicago* upheld the right to engage in public anti-Semitic speech. Terminiello was keeping the Christian Front ethos strikingly alive and well. As commentators noted during the 2016 election cycle, the Terminiello decision protected anti-Semitic chanting during political rallies held by Donald Trump. The Supreme Court decision equally protected anti-Semitic speech at the deadly 2017 Unite the Right rally in Charlottesville, Virginia. The 2016–2017 news accounts on Terminiello barely indicated that he was a Roman Catholic priest, and none mentioned his Christian Front connections.[19]

Terminiello, it must be remembered, was not just a supporter of rights in the abstract. He had a vision for the world, a vision that he shared with Moran and Coughlin and the Christian Front. Untold numbers of our contemporaries share something like that vision, and in this respect the Charlottesville episode was not just an oblique reflection of the front's image in history. It was also a resuscitation of the front's politics, a politics that was once widespread in America. As the sight of American Nazis streamed across television and the internet in 2017, many citizens were aghast. Had this country not expended immense blood and treasure to bring an end to Nazism? Indeed it had—but not enthusiastically. After the war, the people of the United States revised the history of America's role in the conflict, reclaiming the war as the great vehicle of democratic heroism, a purely ideological contest between freedom-lovers and totalitarians. That perspective was both comforting and expedient during the Cold War, but in fact the war with the Axis had been a fraught contest between not only ideological but also geopolitical competitors, and one in which domestic political priorities played a large part. Americans learned to forget that their own people were deeply conflicted, with tens of millions opposing US participation whether because they were antiwar or pro-Fascist or both. In the rush to establish America's new place in the world as an unassailable force for the moral good, the values of the internal opposition were suppressed until the great bulk of society forgot that those values ever existed. But they did not go away. They lay dormant, mutated, found new expression, and reappeared. It is not in the nature of ideas simply to die.

· · ·

The Christian Front left a baleful imprint on the United States, but its long-term impact on Catholicism was more sanguine. Coughlin, Moran, and the front showed the world one aspect of what Catholicism was capable of. They did so alongside a transnational cohort of Catholics who celebrated Franco and found avenues of compromise with Mussolini and Hitler. Yet such compromise—and the particular visions of human rights and Catholic doctrine on which compromise was based—fostered a specifically Catholic opposition. By emphasizing that in Catholicism which was alienating and cruel, the Christian Front inspired its own rejection by others of the faithful and eventually by the institutions of the Church itself.

In our story, that opposition is represented by Frances Sweeney, who prosecuted, per Isabel Currier, "a one-woman crusade against anti-Semitism." Fortunately for the city of Boston and for the wider world, Currier was engaged in understandable hyperbole in the wake of her friend's death at the young age of forty. Sweeney's crusade in fact was joined by many others, although she does stand out for her energy, skill, tenacity, and willingness to not just express but also realize her convictions. "If I die," she said, "I'll die fighting, because if I don't fight, I'll surely die." "Her fight against the bigots of Boston is an epic of freedom," one admirer wrote. In 1946, Bernard J. Sheil, Auxiliary Bishop of Chicago, posthumously awarded Sweeney the Pope Leo XIII Medal "for outstanding service to society by a Catholic."[20]

To adequately appreciate Sweeney's work, we must reflect not only on her goals but also on her methods. She was a thoroughly modern activist, cognizant of the rhythms of both mass media and elected officials and shrewd in linking the two through investigative reporting. Having come of age in the era of Progressive muckraking, she understood how journalistic exposure could motivate accountability, and she used this approach to her advantage. By comparison, Cassidy and Moran were members of the oldest guard. This is not to say that their techniques were fruitless: violence and rhetoric, activist tools since time immemorial, can also achieve a great deal. Sweeney found a different and more complicated niche, and she occupied it with aplomb.

Sweeney's and others' investigations of the anti-Semitic crisis of 1943 forced immediate action by the city of Boston and state of Massachusetts. More enduringly, the revelations induced the state to take seriously its culture of violent anti-Semitism and to seek lasting solutions. Media reports and resulting outrage led to the creation of the Governor's Committee for Racial and Religious Understanding. The committee, a group of officials, judges, and Christian and Jewish clergy, developed protocols for preventing employment discrimination and produced educational materials for public school students and police, teaching comity across boundaries of faith. The committee eventually spawned the Massachusetts Fair Employment Practice Commission, a nondiscrimination enforcement body.[21]

Through it all, Sweeney was motivated by a forward-looking Catholicism. She believed that Catholicism could accommodate change—how else could she have been both a believer and a nonconformist? Anti-Semitism was antithetical to the Gospel's promotion of the law of love, she argued, simultaneously stepping out in front of her church and its theology and demanding that Catholicism live up to the best of what it had always been. As the historian John Connelly put it, "Hitler could—and did—claim to be doing a service to Christianity by persecuting Jews, and Christianity did not have a language with which to oppose him." Sweeney helped to provide the language of opposition that so many Christians lacked at the time. Her Catholic anti-Fascism was grounded in a sense of human solidarity that militated against Coughlin's and Moran's parochial sense of human rights.[22]

Indeed, Sweeny uttered some of the first words in a language that her church would soon adopt. As Augustin Cardinal Bea wrote to Pope John XXIII in 1962, after the dust had settled over the war and the institutions that abetted and tolerated the Holocaust finally began to look inward, "The appalling crimes of National Socialism against six million Jews" would require "a purification of spirit and conscience." For Catholics, this meant above all a reconsideration of the deicide, the age-old wellspring of anti-Judaism within the community of the Church and the soil in which religious anti-Semitism eventually took root.[23]

In October 1965 the Second Vatican Council issued *Nostrae Aetate*, a declaration concerning Catholic relations with non-Christian religions. The declaration contravened the deicide and condemned anti-Semitism. The church of Francis Moran was being displaced by the church of Frances Sweeney. While it was an incomplete corrective, *Nostrae Aetate* at least showed Catholics that their church was not static—that a lever could be stuck under the heavy weight of its history and that weight moved through the concerted efforts of the laity and the hierarchy.[24]

Yet, as we are cognizant of the possibility of reform, we must also note the historical reality of retrenchment. Universalism does not always overcome parochialism. The lever does not always lift the weight. The gains in solidarity made at Vatican II, in the state of Massachusetts, and in the United States broadly after World War II came at the expense of forgetting the Christian

Front. The front, similarly situated organizations, and the people who breathed life into them on the basis of their own passionately held principles were conveniently overlooked or deliberately placed out of view—by the Church, by government authorities, and by historians inclined to disregard the political efficacy of the fringe. But that does not mean their principles no longer attracted adherents. Rather, it means that when those principles reappear in the mouths of citizens, they seem shocking, unrecognizable. We are left to cope anew.

NOTES

Introduction

1. "Christian Front: Why It Has Been Created, Its Fundamental Principles, Its Objectives, Its Plan of Action, To Whom It Appeals," flyer, Avedis (Arthur) Derounian papers, drawer G2, folder: Christian Front 2, Mardigian Library, National Association for Armenian Studies and Research, Belmont, MA.

2. On Judeo-Bolshevism see, for example, Paul Hanebrink, *A Specter Haunting Europe: The Myth of Judeo-Bolshevism* (Cambridge, MA: Harvard University Press, 2018).

3. Rick Perlstein, "I Thought I Understood the American Right. Trump Proved Me Wrong," *New York Times Magazine*, April 11, 2017.

4. Steve Rosswurm, *The FBI and the Catholic Church, 1935–1962* (Amherst: University of Massachusetts Press, 2009), 13.

5. St. Thomas Aquinas, "Of Sedition," in *The Political Ideas of St. Thomas Aquinas: Representative Selections*, ed. Dino Bigongiari (New York: Hafner Press, 1969), 93.

6. On Dilling see, for example, Leo P. Ribuffo, *The Old Christian Right: The Protestant Far Right from the Great Depression to the Cold War* (Philadelphia: Temple University Press, 1983); on Pelley see Scott Beekman, *William Dudley Pelley: A Life in Right-Wing Extremism and the Occult* (Syracuse, NY: Syracuse University Press, 2005); on Deatherage see Charles R. Gallagher, S. J., "Adopting the Swastika: George E. Deatherage and the American Nationalist Confederation, 1937–1942," in *Christianity, Antisemitism, and Ethnonationalism in the Era of the Two World Wars*, ed. Kevin Spicer and Rebecca Carter-Chand (Montreal: McGill-Queen's University Press, forthcoming).

7. Sandrine Sanos, *The Aesthetics of Hate: Far-Right Intellectuals, Antisemitism, and Gender in 1930s France* (Stanford, CA: Stanford University Press, 2013), 21.

8. "Cumulative Report on John F. Cassidy," December 5, 1941, CRC 2, box 52, file 1, Christian Front, 1941, Community Relations Committee Papers, Jewish Federation

Council of Greater Los Angeles, Special Collections and Archives, Oviatt Library, California State University, Northridge.

9. Pius XI, *Non Abbiamo Bisogno*, encyclical, June 29, 1931, http://www.vatican.va /content/pius-xi/en/encyclicals/documents/hf_p-xi_enc_29061931_non-abbiamo -bisogno.html.

10. William Issel, "'The Priesthood of the Layman': Catholic Action in the Archdiocese of San Francisco," in *Empowering the People of God: Catholic Action before and after Vatican II*, ed. Jeremy Bonner, Christopher D. Denny, and Mary Beth Fraser Connolly (New York: Fordham University Press, 2014), 76; "Comment," *America* 62, no. 18 (February 1940), 478.

11. Timothy R. Gabrielli, *One in Christ: Virgil Michel, Louis-Marie Chauvet, and Mystical Body Theology* (Collegeville, MN: Liturgical Press, 2017), ch. 3; Charles E. Curran, *Catholic Social Teaching, 1891–Present: A Historical, Theological, and Ethical Analysis* (Washington, DC: Georgetown University Press, 2002), 103.

12. Paul Tillich, "Catholicism and Anti-Judaism," Paul Tillich papers, 1894–1974, bMS 649/62 (6), 8, Andover-Harvard Theological Library, Harvard Divinity School, Cambridge, MA.

13. House Judiciary Committee Holds Hearing on Constitutional Grounds for Impeachment, December 4, 2019, CQ Transcriptions, CQ-Roll Call, Inc., 65.

14. Special Counsel Robert S. Mueller, III, *Report on the Investigation into Russian Interference in the 2016 Presidential Election* (Washington, DC: U.S. Government Printing Office, 2019), Appendix D, 1.

15. Oscar Handlin, "A Twenty Year Retrospect of American Jewish Historiography," *American Jewish Historical Quarterly* 65, no. 4 (1976): 295–309, 309.

1. The Idea of a Christian Front

1. J. Edgar Hoover to Francis Biddle, August 5, 1936, "Memorandum for the Attorney General," Father Charles E. Coughlin FBI file 62–41602–2X. An unofficial copy of this correspondence can be found at https://www.reddit.com/r/conspiracy/comments/6y5tk6 /the_plot_by_father_coughlin_which_attempted_to. An archival copy of this same correspondence, with names redacted, can be found in Father Charles E. Coughlin's FBI file, folder 1, section 1, communications, 1936–1942, Walter P. Reuther Library, Archives of Labor and Urban Affairs, Wayne State University, Detroit. I am grateful to Kristen Chinery at the Reuther Library for verifying the contents of the Coughlin phone call.

2. Hoover to Biddle, August 5, 1936; Athan G. Theoharis and John Stuart Cox, *The Boss: J. Edgar Hoover and the Great American Inquisition* (Philadelphia: Temple University Press, 1988), 150; Thomas W. Dawsy to J. Edgar Hoover, Memorandum for the Director, August 8, 1936, Father Charles E. Coughlin FBI file 62–41602–2X. The arrest of Pascual Diaz, archbishop of Mexico City, occurred on March 9, 1935.

3. Albert Fried, *FDR and His Enemies* (New York: St. Martin's Press, 1999), 62–63; "Johnson Sees Coughlin a Hitler," *Daily Boston Globe*, March 31, 1935, 1; "Income Defended by Father Coughlin," *Daily Boston Globe*, April 1, 1935, 1.

4. William E. Dodd, "Coughlin—The Nazi Hero," April 24, 1939, radio address over station CKLW in Windsor, Ontario, Canada, published transcript, David M. Rubenstein Rare Book and Manuscript Library, Duke University, Durham, NC.

5. Arnold Lunn quoted in Edward Lodge Curran, "For the *Commonweal*," *Social Justice*, August 1, 1938, 12–13.

6. Arnold Lunn to "My Dear Merry Del Val" [Alfonso Merry del Val y Zulueta], April 9, 1938, Arnold Lunn papers, box 3, folder 20, Booth Family Center for Special Collections, Georgetown University Library, Washington, DC.

7. Paul Urban Foster, "A Bonny Fighter," *Blackfriars* 21, no. 248 (November 1940): 661–664, 661.

8. Henry Simpson Lunn quoted in Mary Lago, *India's Prisoner: A Biography of Edward John Thompson, 1886–1946* (Columbia: University of Missouri Press, 2001), 1.

9. Arnold Lunn quoted in Patrick Allitt, *Catholic Converts: British and American Intellectuals Turn to Rome* (Ithaca, NY: Cornell University Press, 1997), 224.

10. Arnold Lunn, *Spain and the Christian Front* (New York: Paulist Press, 1937), 8, 17.

11. Ronald Knox and Arnold Lunn, *Difficulties: Being a Correspondence about the Catholic Religion between Ronald Knox and Arnold Lunn*, 3rd ed. (London: Eyre and Spottiswoode, 1958), 29, 99.

12. Knox and Lunn, *Difficulties*, 21; Richard Hofstadter, *The Paranoid Style in American Politics and Other Essays* (New York: Vintage Books, 2008), 70; Henry S. Lunn, "Introduction," in *United Christian Front: A Discussion on the Hellenic Travelers' Club Cruise, February–March, 1938* (Cambridge: W. Heffer and Sons, 1938), 3.

13. "Arnold Lunn Will Lecture in Library," *Boston College Heights*, December 10, 1937, 3; "Loyalists Pictured Pro-Soviet by Lunn," *Daily Boston Globe*, December 14, 1937, 10; "Lunn Assails Spanish 'Reds,'" *Boston College Heights*, December 17, 1937, 1, 3. Lunn may have felt on safer ground discussing links between Communism and terrorism because the Jesuit Edmund A. Walsh was proposing such a connection at that time. See Charles R. Gallagher, "The Roman Catholic Church and Modern Terrorism: Ideology, Human Rights, and the Hermeneutic of Discontinuity," *Socialist History* 43, no. 3 (2013), 51.

14. Arnold Lunn, *Spanish Rehearsal* (New York: Sheed and Ward, 1937), 189.

15. Rupert Hart-Davis, *Hugh Walpole: A Biography* (London: Macmillan, 1952), 356.

16. Henry S. Lunn, "Preface," in *United Christian Front: A Discussion on the Hellenic Travellers' Club Cruise, February–March, 1938* (Cambridge: W. Heffer and Sons, 1938), viii.

17. W. R. Inge, "The psychology of revolutions" in *United Christian Front: A Discussion on the Hellenic Travelers' Club Cruise, February–March, 1938* (Cambridge: W. Heffer and Sons, 1938), 47.

18. "A United Christian Front," *The Times*, July 26, 1937, 8; Lunn, *Spanish Rehearsal*, 180–183.

19. Lord Dickinson, P. C., K. B. N., "An United Christian Front," [no date], proof and draft copies of "A United Christian Front An Experiment and its Results," Willoughby

Hyett Dickinson papers, box 48, file United Christian Front, 1936–1939, F/DCK/048/002, London Metropolitan Archives, London.

20. Martin D'Arcy, *Communism and Christianity* (New York: Devin-Adair, 1957), 119; H. J. A. Sire, *Father Martin D'Arcy: Philosopher of Christian Love* (Leominster, Herefordshire: Gracewing, 1997), 81.

21. Martin C. D'Arcy, "A United Christian Front," in *United Christian Front: A Discussion on the Hellenic Travellers' Club Cruise, February–March, 1938* (Cambridge: W. Heffer and Sons, 1938), 162–169.

22. A. W. Brian Simpson, *In the Highest Degree Odious: Detention without Trial in Wartime Britain* (New York: Oxford University Press, 1994), 431.

23. Archibald Maule Ramsay to Paschal Robinson, September 21, 1937, Archivio Storico Della Segreteria di Stato, Sezione Per i Rapporti con gli Stati, Inghilterra, posizione 277, fascicolo 126, Vatican City.

24. Letter Number 4023/37, October 6, 1937, [unsigned draft], Archivio Storico Della Segreteria di Stato, Sezione Per i Rapporti con gli Stati, Inghilterra, posizione 277, fascicolo 126, Vatican City.

25. Pius XI, *Ingravescentibus malis* [Encyclical on the Rosary], September 29, 1937, sec. 6, http://w2.vatican.va/content/pius-xi/en/encyclicals/documents/hf_p-xi_enc_29091937_ingravescentibus-malis.html.

26. Paschal Robinson to Giuseppe Pizzardo, letter number 2070, [undated], Archivio Storico Della Segreteria di Stato, Sezione Per i Rapporti con gli Stati, Inghilterra, posizione 277, fascicolo 126, Vatican City.

27. Z. Aradi, "Cardinal Pacelli Urges United Christian Front to Fight Foes of Church," *The Guardian* [Little Rock, AR], June 3, 1938, http://arc.stparchive.com/Archive/ARC/ARC06031938p05.php. On the position of papal legate *a latere* see John-Peter Pham, *Heirs of the Fisherman: Behind the Scenes of Papal Death and Succession* (New York: Oxford University Press, 2004), 338. On the controversy surrounding Pacelli's Budapest address, see Deborah S. Cornelius, *Hungary in World War II: Caught in the Cauldron* (New York: Fordham University Press, 2011), 65–72.

28. C. Smith [Coughlin secretary] to Frank A. Hall, March 16, 1938, National Catholic Welfare Conference, press department, National Catholic News Service papers, box 14, Rev. Chas E. Coughlin file, American Catholic History Research Center and University Archives, Catholic University of America, Washington, DC.

29. Charles Coughlin, "From the Tower," *Social Justice*, vol. 1A, no. 10, June 20, 1938, 1; Tom W. Smith, "The Religious Right and Anti-Semitism," *Review of Religious Research* 40, no. 3 (March 1999): 244–258, 244; Patricia Erens, *The Jew in American Cinema* (Bloomington: Indiana University Press, 1984), 331. Gene Fein claims that Coughlin's first use of the term "Christian Front" was on June 27, 1938, in the context of a coupon offered to potential *Social Justice* subscribers. However, this appears to be incorrect. Gene Fein, "For Christ and Country: The Anti-Semitic Anticommunism of Christian Front Street Meetings in New York City," *U. S. Catholic Historian* 22, no. 4 (Fall 2004): 37–56, 39.

30. Arnold Lunn never disassociated himself from certain claims that Jews were hostile to the Catholic Church, but in the wake of Kristallnacht, in November 1938, he did publicly condemn the "persecution of the Jews," a statement that placed him at odds with Nazi claims of a Judeo-Bolshevist conspiracy. Ulrike Ehret, *The Catholic Right, Political Catholicism, and Radicalism* (Manchester: Manchester University Press, 2012), 77n17.

31. Coughlin, "From the Tower," 5; Arnold Lunn, "Train to New Orleans," diary entry, December 5, 1938, Arnold Lunn papers, box 3, folder 20, Booth Family Center for Special Collections, Georgetown University Library, Washington, DC.

2. Soldiers for the Body of Christ

1. LIBRARY (codename) to news department, "Father Coughlin: activities," April 19, 1938, FO 371/21547/A 3336, pp. 208, 209, British National Archives, Kew, Richmond.

2. Martin E. Marty and Shimon Gibson, "Tillich, Paul Johannes," in *Encyclopaedia Judaica*, ed. Michael Berenbaum and Fred Skolnik, 2nd ed., 22 vols. (Detroit: Macmillan Reference USA, 2007), vol. 19, 724.

3. Paul Tillich, "Catholicism and Anti-Judaism," Paul Tillich papers, 1894–1974, bMS 649/62 (6), 2–3, 7–8, Andover-Harvard Theological Library, Harvard Divinity School, Cambridge, MA. Emphasis in original. On Nazism as a pagan heresy, see Giuliana Chamedes, *A Twentieth-Century Crusade: The Vatican's Battle to Remake Christian Europe* (Cambridge, MA: Harvard University Press, 2019), 168.

4. "Noted Author Will Speak at Bible Meeting," *Buffalo Courier-Express*, August 21, 1937, 16; "2000 Attend Rally to Denounce Reds," *New York Times*, October 31, 1938, 10.

5. United States Congress, Senate, Committee on the Judiciary, Subcommittee on Hearings, Nomination of Felix Frankfurter, January 11 and 12, 1939 (Washington, DC: Committee on the Judiciary, 1939), 86; Zoll quoted in Lori A. Ringhand, "Aliens on the Bench: Lessons in Identity, Race and Politics from the First 'Modern' Supreme Court Confirmation Hearing to Today," *Michigan State Law Review* 2010, no. 3 (Fall 2010): 795–835, 797.

6. "Preliminary Study on Irish-American Attitudes on Aid to Britain," December 1940 to January 1941, Foreign Nationalities Branch Files, U.S. Office of Strategic Services (Bethesda, MD: University Publications of America, 1988), microfiche, INT-161R-21, 77; "2000 Attend Rally."

7. Edward Lodge Curran, "Edward Lodge Curran Replies to Roosevelt on Sunday Broadcast," *Social Justice*, July 31, 1939, 1; "Boston and Father Curran," April 7, 1942, Foreign Nationalities Branch Files, U.S. Office of Strategic Services (Bethesda, MD: University Publications of America, 1988), microfiche INT-161R-11, 1.

8. Pro-American Rally poster, drawer G2, Christian Front file, Avedis (Arthur) Derounian papers, Mardigian Library, National Association for Armenian Studies and Research, Belmont, MA (hereafter Derounian papers, NAASR); Carol V. R. George, *God's Salesman: Norman Vincent Peale and the Power of Positive Thinking* (New York: Oxford University Press, 1993), 171.

9. "O'Connor and Kuhn at Rally of Fascists," *Daily Worker*, October 31, 1938, 1.

10. "Conclude C.E. Convention," *The Saratogian* [Saratoga Springs, NY], May 13, 1939, 3.

11. Rick Perlstein, "I Thought I Understood the American Right. Trump Proved Me Wrong," *New York Times Magazine*, August 29, 2017, 3.

12. Charles Tull, *Father Coughlin and the New Deal* (Syracuse, NY: Syracuse University Press, 1965), 197. For more on the November 20, 1938, speech, see John Corrigan and Lynn S. Neal, *Religious Intolerance in America: A Documentary History* (Chapel Hill: University of North Carolina Press, 2010), 167.

13. Father Charles Coughlin, "Persecution—Jewish and Christian," broadcast transcript, November 30, 1938, Manuscript Collections: United States Conference of Catholic Bishops, box 16, folder 1, Libraries of the Catholic University of America, Washington, DC, available online at American Catholic History Classroom, https://cuomeka.wrlc.org/items/show/571; Charles Henry Whittier, "The Reverend Charles E. Coughlin," in *American Orators of the Twentieth Century: Critical Studies and Sources*, ed. Bernard K. Duffy and Halford R. Ryan (New York: Greenwood Press, 1987), 78.

14. Coughlin, "Persecution—Jewish and Christian," 12, 14.

15. Gene Fein, "For Christ and Country: The Anti-Semitic Anticommunism of Christian Front Street Meetings in New York City," *U.S. Catholic Historian* 22, no. 4 (2004), 53.

16. "Catholic Groups Urge Ban of WMCA for Barring Fr. Coughlin from Air," Samuel Dickstein papers, box 16, file 8, Charles E. Coughlin file, Jacob Rader Marcus Center of the American Jewish Archives, Cincinnati, OH.

17. Richard Gid Powers, *G-Men: Hoover's FBI in American Popular Culture* (Carbondale: Southern Illinois University Press, 1983), 41.

18. P. E. Foxworth, "Re: John F. Cassidy," Memorandum for the file, January 14, 1940, 1, Christian Front FBI file, 1137495-000–65–HQ–4279, Section 6, released through United States Freedom of Information Act (hereafter USFOIA). On the integration of heroic FBI characters into popular comic strips, see Claire Bond Potter, *War on Crime: Bandits, G-Men, and the Politics of Mass Culture* (New Brunswick, NJ: Rutgers University Press, 1998), 126.

19. Powers, *G-Men*, 142; Foxworth, Memorandum for the file, January 14, 1940, 2.

20. Athan G. Theoharis and John Stuart Cox, *The Boss: J. Edgar Hoover and the Great American Inquisition* (Philadelphia: Temple University Press, 1988), 48; "Revolt Nipped, Says FBI Chief; 18 Men Caught," *Buffalo Courier-Express*, January 15, 1940, 2; Report, Peter J. Wacks, "Klaus Ernecke—Subversive Activities," November 1, 1939, 22, Christian Front FBI file, 1137495-000–65–HQ–4279, Section 1, released through USFOIA.

21. "Catholic Groups Urge Ban," Samuel Dickstein papers.

22. Unsigned report concerning street corner meetings in Flatbush and Brooklyn, November 10, 1938, *American Civil Liberties Union Archives: The Roger Baldwin Years, 1917–1950: A Microfilm Edition* (Wilmington, DE: Scholarly Resources, 1996), Series I,

reel 172, Christian Front Meetings file; for Carridi on makeshift bludgeons, see Geoffrey Sutton Smith, "A Social and Diplomatic History of American Extremism, 1933–1941" (PhD diss., University of California, Santa Barbara, 1969), 550.

23. Report, Jack Fuller, Secretary, Flatbush Non-Sectarian Committee Against Bigotry, "Speech by Mr. Carridy [sic] under the auspices of the Christian-American Committee against Communism, November 11, 1938 at Flatbush Avenue and Albermarle Road, Brooklyn," [3], in Ben Primer, *American Civil Liberties Union Archives*, Series I, reel 172, Christian Front Meetings file, John F. Cassidy subfile.

24. On Carridi's arrest see *Jewish Frontier*, vol. 7, 1940, 8; Fein, "Christ and Country," 40; *Spain in Arms*, publicity poster, drawer G2, Christian Front file 2, Derounian papers, NAASR.

25. All quotes taken from Report of May 3, 1939, Christian Front meeting, drawer G2, folder "Christian Front," Derounian papers, NAASR.

26. Report, *Golgotha*, moving picture sponsored by the Christian Front, drawer G2, Christian Front file, Derounian papers, NAASR.

27. Father Brophy gave the keynote speech in support of McWilliams on July 16, 1940, at the Great Christian Rally on 149th Street in New York. "Great Christian Rally," poster, July 16, 1940, CRC 2, box 51, file 24, Christian Front, June–July 1940, Community Relations Committee Papers, Jewish Federation Council of Greater Los Angeles, Special Collections and Archives, Oviatt Library, California State University, Northridge.

28. Walter Ogden interview with Peter J. Wacks, report, "Subversive Activities," December 1, 1939, 9, Christian Front FBI file, 1137495-000–65–HQ–4279, Section 2, released through USFOIA; "Fascists Get Suspended Sentence Here," *Daily Worker*, September 1, 1939, 5.

29. Walter D. Ogden to [name redacted], [date redacted], letter written on Christian Front letterhead, Nahum Greenberg papers, RG-486, box 7, volume 26, George Deatherage file, YIVO Institute for Jewish Research, New York; "The Christian Front, The Committee for American Action, The Country Gentlemen, the Sports Clubs," report, [name redacted], January 17, 1940, 1, Christian Front FBI file, 1137495-000–65–HQ–4279, Section 8, released through USFOIA.

30. Daniel J. McInerney, review of *American Swastika* by Charles Higham, *Shofar* 4, no. 1 (Fall 1985): 65–67, 66; "Police Balk at Quiz on Affiliations," *Rochester Times-Union*, February 14, 1940, 2; Unsigned and undated memorandum [2], Archives of the American Jewish Committee, record group 347.1 29, EXO-29, box 8, Charles Coughlin file, YIVO Institute for Jewish Research, New York; Ogden interview with Wacks, December 1, 1939.

31. On secret society bans, see John Tracy Ellis, *The Life of James Cardinal Gibbons: Archbishop of Baltimore, 1834–1921*, 2 vols. (Milwaukee, WI: Brace, 1952), vol. 1, 440; "The Christian Front: Why It Has Been Created, Its Fundamental Principles, Its Objectives, Its Plan of Action, To Whom It Appeals," pamphlet, drawer G2, Christian Front file, Derounian papers, NAASR.

32. Father Charles Coughlin, "Units of Militant Christian Front Are Being Formed in Middlewest," *Social Justice*, July 31, 1939, 3; Peter J. Wacks, report, December 1, 1939, Claus Gunther Ernecke and aliases, Christian Front FBI file, 1137495-000–65–HQ–4279, Section 2, released through USFOIA; "Coughlin Rally," Philadelphia, July 14, 1939, typescript, box 281, Christian Front file, Cassidy 1938–1940, Non-Sectarian Anti-Nazi League to Champion Human Rights papers, Rare Book and Manuscript Library, Columbia University, New York (hereafter NSANL papers).

33. Dorothy Thompson, "Coughlin and the Christian Front," undated newspaper clipping contained in letter, Mrs. Wm. Reuben to "Dear Mr. Hoover," January 20, 1940, Christian Front FBI file, 1137495-000–65–HQ–4279, Section 6, released through USFOIA; Cassidy quotes, handwritten on index card, July 14, 1939, Series II: Investigative Files, 1928–1974, Subseries II.1: General, 1928–1974, box 281, Christian Front file, Cassidy 1938–1940, NSANL papers.

34. All quotes from Charles E. Coughlin, "The Popular Front vs. the Christian Front," July 30, 1939 (Royal Oak, MI: C. E. Coughlin, 1939), Department of Special Collections, Shields Library, University of California, Davis.

35. Patrick W. Carey, *Catholics in America: A History* (Westport, CT: Praeger, 2004), 112.

36. J. Bluett, "Mystical Body: A Bibliography, 1890–1940," *Theological Studies* 3, no. 2 (May 1942): 261–289.

37. Sally Dwyer McNulty, *Common Threads: A Cultural History of Clothing in American Catholicism* (Chapel Hill: University of North Carolina Press, 2014), 129.

38. Eric Voegelin, "Growth of the Race Idea" (1940), in *Published Essays: 1940–1952*, ed. Ellis Sandoz (Columbia: University of Missouri Press, 2000), 33.

39. John F. Noll, "A Christian vs. an Anti-Christian Front," *Social Justice* 2a, no. 6 (1938), 3.

40. Voegelin, "Growth of the Race Idea," 35; "For Christ and Country," letter to George C. Marshall, [September 7, 1939], addendum to report of Peter J. Wacks, "Claus G. Ernecke—SUBVERSIVE ACTIVITIES, September 20, 1939, 10, Christian Front FBI file, 1137495-000–65–HQ–4279, Section 1, released through USFOIA.

41. Fulton J. Sheen, *The Mystical Body of Christ: A Timeless Portrait of the Church from a Beloved Catholic Evangelist* (New York: Sheed and Ward, 1935; repr. Notre Dame, IN: Christian Classics, 2015), 298; Coughlin, "The Popular Front vs. the Christian Front."

42. Mary Christine Athans, *The Coughlin-Fahey Connection: Father Charles E. Coughlin, Father Denis Fahey, C.S.Sp., and Religious Anti-Semitism in the United States, 1938–1954* (New York: Peter Lang, 1991), 128.

43. Gene Fein sees the Christian Front as anchored in anti-Communist anti-Semitism. See Fein, "Christ and Country," 44.

44. "City Council Recorded Against Radio Ban on Father Coughlin," *Lowell Sun*, December 6, 1939, 4. The "platoon" language also appears in Charles Coughlin to Hiram W. Johnson, July, 1938, Hiram W. Johnson papers, BANC MSS C-B 581, box 3, Charles Coughlin file, Bancroft Library, University of California, Berkeley.

45. Memorandum, seventh district, borough of Manhattan, affidavit of Sam Pearl [copy], September 25, 1939, Anti-Semitic and Extremist Collection, box 53, Christian Front 2 file, American Jewish Committee Archives, New York.

46. The pope's definition was contained in a 1929 letter XI to the Spanish Cardinal Pedro Segura y Sáenz of Toledo. An English translation of the letter appears in Luigi Civardi, *A Manual of Catholic Action*, trans. C. C. Martindale (New York: Sheed and Ward, 1943), 254; Sheen, *Mystical Body of Christ*, 281.

47. B. F. Duncan, *Crusade or Conspiracy: Catholics and the Anti-Communist Struggle in Australia* (Sydney: University of New South Wales Press, 2000), 12. Although Duncan's study is regionally focused, it captures Catholic Action's global impulse toward anti-Communism.

48. Stephen Anderl and Mary Ruth, *The Technique of the Catholic Action Cell*, 4th ed. (La Crosse, WI: St. Rose Convent, 1946), 40.

49. Daniel J. Lord, S. J., *The Sacrament of Catholic Action* (St. Louis: The Queen's Work, 1936), 5, 39.

50. "Pledge of Recruits in the Christian Front," included in addendum to report, E. J. Connelley, William Gerald Bishop, with aliases–Subversive Activity, January 18, 1940, 77, 78, Christian Front FBI file, 1137495-000–65–HQ–4279, Section 7, released through USFOIA.

51. Peter J. Wacks, file number 61–537, Claus G. Ernecke, subversive activities, September 6, 1939, 2, Christian Front FBI file 1137495-000–65–HQ–4279, Section 1, released through USFOIA. Upon re-interview, Fischer indicated that he was "quite sure that Ernecke had never made such a proposition to him." Ernecke only "requested various information pertaining to [the gun's] use and operation." Ernecke's admission appears in Peter J. Wacks to J. Edgar Hoover, September 20, 1939, file number 61–537, Claus G. Ernecke; the Christian Front, subversive activities, 3, FBI file 1137495-000–65–HQ–4279, Section 1, released through USFOIA.

52. Wacks to Hoover, September 20, 1939, 1.

3. Terror in the Name of Christ

1. Statement of Alexander Saul, in C. A. Grill, report, William Gerald Bishop—Subversive Activities, January 18, 1940, 5, Christian Front FBI file, 1137495-000–65–HQ–4279, Section 6, released through US Freedom of Information Act (hereafter USFOIA).

2. P. E. Foxworth to FBI Director, October 14, 1939, Re: Claus G. Ernecke—Subversive Activities, Christian Front FBI file, 1137495-000–65–HQ–4279, Section 1, released through USFOIA.

3. P. E. Foxworth to Director, October 25, 1939, 5, Christian Front FBI file, 1137495-000–65–HQ–4279, Section 1, released through USFOIA; Peter J. Wacks, report, Ernecke with aliases, November 1, 1939, 16, Christian Front FBI file, 1137495-000–65–HQ–4279, Section 1, released through USFOIA.

4. Coughlin quoted in "Units of Militant Christian Front Are Being Formed in Middlewest," *Social Justice*, July 31, 1939, 3; Wacks report, November 1, 1939; Peter J. Wacks, report, Claus G. Ernecke—Subversive Activities, October 2, 1939, 7, Christian Front FBI file, 1137495-000–65-HQ-421137495-000–65-HQ–4279, Section 1, released through USFOIA.

5. Report, Christian Front meeting, September 20, 1939, Nostrand Avenue and Sterling Place, Records of the Non-Sectarian Anti-Nazi League to Champion Human Rights, investigative files, general, Christian Front, John Cassidy, 29 December 1938–1940, Non-Sectarian Anti-Nazi League to Champion Human Rights papers, Rare Book and Manuscript Library, Columbia University, New York; Christian Front Application Form, [n.d.], CRC 2, box 51, file 14, Christian Front, December, 1939, Community Relations Committee Papers, Jewish Federation Council of Greater Los Angeles, Special Collections and Archives, Oviatt Library, California State University, Northridge, CA (hereafter CSUN); Albert Parry, "Cassidy Urged to Imitate Hitler's Methods," *The Hour* 28 (January 1940), 5.

6. "How Christian Front and Nazi Salutes Differ," New York World-Telegram and Sun Newspaper Photograph Collection, Christian Front File, news clipping affixed to back of photo, June 26, 1940, Library of Congress, Prints and Photographs Division, Washington DC.

7. Wacks report, November 1, 1939, 23; transposed copy of letter from Cassidy to Bishop contained in report, E. J. Connelley, William Gerald Bishop with aliases, January 18, 1940, 90, Christian Front FBI file, 1137495-000–65-HQ–4279, Section 7, released through USFOIA.

8. "Mass meeting to expose smear Coughlin campaign," Star O' Munster Hall, 401 East 138 Street, Tuesday, December 19, 1939, report, drawer G2, folder "Christian Front," Avedis (Arthur) Derounian papers, Mardigian Library, National Association for Armenian Studies and Research, Belmont, MA (hereafter Derounian papers, NAASR); Jewish War Veterans Confidential Report, December 1939, CRC 2, box 51, file 14, Christian Front, December 1939, Community Relations Committee Papers, Jewish Federation Council of Greater Los Angeles, CSUN.

9. Martin Blinkhorn, *Fascism and the Right in Europe, 1919–1945* (New York: Longman, 2000), 102; David Schoenbaum quoted in Dave Renton, *Fascism: Theory and Practice* (London: Pluto Press, 1999), 38.

10. Report, Peter J. Wacks, Claus Gunther-Ernecke and aliases, December 1, 1939, 15, Christian Front FBI file, 1137495-000–65-HQ–4279, Section 2, released through USFOIA.

11. Warren Grover, *Nazis in Newark* (New Brunswick, NJ: Transaction Publishers, 2003), 281, 315.

12. Wacks report, December 1, 1939, 17.

13. Peter J. Wacks, report, Claus Gunther Ernecke with aliases, December 19, 1939, 3, 5, Christian Front FBI file, 1137495-000–65-HQ–4279, Section 2, released through USFOIA.

14. P. E. Foxworth to the Director, December 16, 1939, 1, Christian Front FBI file, 1137495-000–65–HQ–4279, Section 3, released through USFOIA.

15. E. A. Tamm, Memorandum for the Director, January 4, 1940, Christian Front FBI file, 1137495-000–65–HQ–4279, Section 3, released through USFOIA.

16. John Albert Viebrock, [report title redacted], January 22, 1940, statement on the meeting at home of Macklin Boettger, attached to, J. W. Coulter, report, William Gerald Bishop, January 27, 1940, 7, Christian Front FBI file, 1137495-000–65–HQ–4279, Section 9, released through USFOIA.

17. A. Rosen, Memorandum for Mr. E. A. Tamm, January 12, 1940, 4, Christian Front FBI file, 1137495-000–65–HQ–4279, Section 4, released through USFOIA. Between January 4 and January 18, 1940, the United States was transitioning between attorneys general. Hoover refused to proceed unless Holtzaff approved the warrants.

18. United Press report, quoted in Charles R. Gallagher, *Vatican Secret Diplomacy: Joseph P. Hurley and Pope Pius XII* (New Haven: Yale University Press, 2008), 68; E. J. Connelley to J. Edgar Hoover, "Memo for the Director," January 20, 1940, 3, Christian Front FBI file, 1137495-000–65–HQ–4279, Section 10, released through USFOIA; "New Type Ammunition Found in Christian Front Raid," *Buffalo Evening News,* January 19, 1940, 1; "The Three Inch Stokes Mortar," excerpted from Bruce N. Canfield, *U.S. Infantry Weapons of the First World War* (Lincoln, RI: Andrew Mowbray Publishers, 2000), posted on "Doughboy Center," http://www.worldwar1.com/dbc /smortar.htm.

19. E. J. Connelly, report, "Subversive Activity, Seditious Conspiracy, Theft of Government Property," January 18, 1940, 9, Christian Front FBI file, 1137495-000–65– HQ–4279, Section 7, released through USFOIA; E. J. Connelley, Memo for the Director, January 20, 1940, 7, Christian Front FBI file, 1137495-000–65–HQ–4279, Section 10, released through USFOIA; "The Christian Front Arrests," *Irish-American Advocate* [New York], January 27, 1940, 7; "Heavy Bail Is Set in Cases of 'Terrorists,'" *Schenectady Gazette,* January 18, 1940, 7.

20. "New Arrests Slated in Terror Plot," [n.d.], newspaper clipping, CRC 2, box 51, file 18, Christian Front, January 1940, Community Relations Committee Papers, Jewish Federation Council of Greater Los Angeles, CSUN; Roosevelt to Robert H. Jackson, June 26, 1940, "Memorandum for the Attorney General," Franklin D. Roosevelt, Papers as President, Official File, folder 3893, Christian Front 1940, Franklin D. Roosevelt Library, Hyde Park, NY.

21. Jan Hoffman, "Lawyer's 50 Year Journey to the Bar: Christian Rightist from Long Ago Says It's Justice, Finally," *New York Times,* May 31, 1995.

22. "Public Feels Revolt Story Is Fantastic," *Paris Herald Tribune,* January 17, 1940, newspaper clipping, Caroline Drayton Phillips Papers, 1939 diary, MC 560, box 5, Schlesinger Library, Radcliffe Institute, Harvard University, Cambridge, MA; "Gang Planned Death of 14 Congressmen," *San Francisco Examiner,* January 15, 1940, newspaper clipping, CRC 2, box 51, file 18, Christian Front, January 1940, Community Relations Committee Papers, Jewish Federation Council of Greater Los Angeles, CSUN.

23. "Playful Plot Meeting Barred at Front Trial," *Daily News* [New York], April 17, 1940, 1. For William Bishop's view of how the attack on New York would proceed, see J. W. Coulter, report, William Gerald Bishop, January 27, 1940, 17, Christian Front FBI file, 1137495-000–65–HQ–4279, Section 9, released through USFOIA. Bishop indicated that "the Customs House could be taken . . . and that 2000 men could grab the armories and easily hold the city through the means of barricades."

24. Morris Ernst to Arthur Hayes Sulzberger, [unsigned copy of typewritten letter], February 6, 1940, folder 27.5, loose correspondence re Michael Joseph Bierne (Christian Front), January–March, 1940; and "from M. Sheehy, re Ryan case," n.d., typewritten draft letter, folder 45.3, correspondence January 1940–April 1940; both in Morris Ernst papers, Harry Ransom Center, University of Texas, Austin.

25. Maurice S. Sheehy to J. Edgar Hoover, [copy], January 22, 1940, Christian Front FBI file, 1137495-000–65–HQ–4279, Section 11, released through USFOIA.

26. Edward F. Brophy to the editor, *America Magazine*, February 2, 1940, America Magazine archives, box 11, folder 35, "Christian Front material," GTMGamms 60, Booth Family Center for Special Collections, Georgetown University Library, Washington, DC; "The Hypnotized," *Commonweal* 31, no. 4, January 26, 1940, 293; "Hypnotized Men," *Time* 35, January 22, 1940, 19; "Mayor Laughs at Plot," *Daily News*, January 15, 1940, 3. The quoted language from *America* is from a January 27, 1940, article, unavailable in the archive, which Brophy in turn quotes in his letter to the editor.

27. Donald Warren, *Radio Priest: Charles Coughlin, the Father of Hate Radio* (New York: Free Press, 1996), 192.

28. Rick Perlstein, "I Thought I Understood the American Right. Trump Proved Me Wrong," *New York Times Magazine*, August 29, 2017, 2.

29. John A. Viebrock, supplementary statement, January 22, 1940, attached to J.W. Coulter, report, William Gerald Bishop, January 27, 1940, 5, Christian Front FBI file, 1137495-000–65–HQ–4279, Section 9, released through USFOIA.

30. Peter J. Wacks, report, Claus G. Ernecke, Subversive Activities, October 2, 1939, 11, Christian Front FBI file, 1137495-000–65–HQ–4279, Section 1, released through USFOIA.

31. Memorandum for Governor Lehman, Major General William N. Haskell to Herbert H. Lehman, January 26, 1940, Governor Herbert H. Lehman Central Subject and Correspondence Files, box 1, roll 1 (microfilm), Christian Front case, microfilm series number 13682_53, New York State Archives, Albany, NY.

32. E. J. Connelley, report, William Gerald Bishop: Subversive Activity, Seditious Conspiracy, January 18, 1940, 89, Christian Front FBI file, 1137495-000–65–HQ–4279, Section 7, released through USFOIA.

33. Herbert Cox to J. E. Hoover, January 15, 1940, Christian Front FBI file, 1137495-000–65–HQ–4279, Section 4, released through USFOIA.

34. E. A. Tamm, Memorandum for the Director, January 24, 1940, 1, 2, Christian Front FBI file, 1137495-000–65–HQ–4279, Section 10, released through USFOIA.

35. A. Rosen, Memorandum for Mr. E. A. Tamm, January 14, 1940, 4:05 A.M., Christian Front FBI file, 1137495-000–65–HQ–4279, Section 4, released through USFOIA.

36. "The Christian Front," Memorandum for the Director prepared by Mr. E. A. Tamm, January 17, 1940, Christian Front FBI file, 1137495-000–65–HQ–4279, Section 8, released through USFOIA; "'Front' Defense Accuses Soviet Provocateurs of Drafting U.S. Case," *Telegram*, May 5, 1940, newspaper clipping, Walter N. Thayer papers, chronological file, box 21, Christian Front file, Herbert Hoover Presidential Library, West Branch, IA (hereafter Thayer papers, Hoover Library).

37. Memorandum from M. R., "Seventeen Christian Fronters Prosecution," February 20, 1940, Gardner Jackson papers, General Correspondence, box 14, Christian Front file, Franklin Delano Roosevelt Library, Hyde Park, NY; "Mistrial Plea Is Denied 17 in Plot Case," Associated Press report appearing in the *Eagle* [Brooklyn], April 4, 1940, newspaper clipping, Thayer papers, Hoover Library.

38. On the payments to Healy, see Foxworth to FBI Director, Claus G. Ernecke: Subversive Activities, October 14, 1939, 1, Section 1; Fred J. Cook, *The FBI Nobody Knows* (New York: Macmillan, 1964), 254–256.

39. "The Christian Front," report, 16, Earl R. Browder papers, box 9, correspondence subject file, Christian Front, 1938–1940, Special Collections Research Center, Syracuse University, Syracuse, NY (hereafter Browder papers, Syracuse).

40. "Missing Defendant in Plot Ends His Life; Ernecke Found Hanged in Brooklyn House," *New York Times*, April 14, 1940, 1; "Christian Front Suspect Kidnapped, Attorney Fears," *Washington Post*, April 13, 1940, x5. Without specifying evidence, Albert Kahn claimed Ernecke "had been proven to be a Nazi agent." Albert E. Kahn and Michael Sayers, *Plot against the Peace: A Warning to the Nation* (New York: Dial Press, 1945), 183.

41. "The Christian Front," Browder papers, Syracuse, 16.

42. Louis B. Nichols to Clyde Tolson, "Memorandum for Mr. Tolson," July 5, 1940, FBI file of Eleanor Roosevelt, cross references, enclosure 12 of 14, 13. This record is also at FBI Records: The Vault, Eleanor Roosevelt Part 28 of 40, https://vault.fbi.gov /Eleanor%20Roosevelt. Leo J. Titus, *Titus: A North American Family History* (Baltimore, MD: Gateway Press, 2004), 224.

43. J. Edgar Hoover to Robert H. Jackson, "Memorandum for the Attorney General," July 25, 1940, Robert H. Jackson papers, box 39, folder 4, Attorney General files, subversive activities & investigations, Christian Front, sedition, Manuscript Division, Library of Congress, Washington, DC; Leonard Dinnerstein, *Anti-Semitism in America* (New York: Oxford University Press, 1995), 121.

44. "Provocateurs Blamed for Sedition Charge," *New York Sun*, April 5, 1940, chronological file, box 21, Christian Front file; and "'Front' Attorney Charges Red Plot," miscellaneous news clipping; both in Thayer papers, Hoover Library.

45. Maurice Rosenblatt to "Dear Mr. Jackson," February 20, 1940, Gardner Jackson papers, Box 14, Christian Front file, Franklin Delano Roosevelt Library, Hyde Park, NY.

Arthur Miller's novel *Focus*, which concentrates on Christian Front activity in Brooklyn from 1944 to 1946, is a good example of the continuing local influence of the front, years after the trial. Arthur Miller, *Focus* (New York: Reynal and Hitchcock, 1945; New York: Arbor House, 1984).

46. "'Front' Trial Jury Carefully Chosen," *New York Times*, April 5, 1940, 8; Arthur Derounian, Christian Front rally, Prospect Hall, Brooklyn, February 4, 1940, drawer G2, Christian Front file, Derounian papers, NAASR.

47. Derounian, Christian Front rally, Prospect Hall, Brooklyn, February 4, 1940.

48. Arthur Derounian, report on Christian Civil Liberties Committee meeting at Queens Community Center, March 14, 1940, drawer G2, Christian Front, folder 2, Derounian papers, NAASR, emphasis original; Edward F. Brophy, *The Christian Front: Its Justification and Need* ([Place of publication not identified], [Christian Front], 1940), 12, 45.

49. Derounian, Christian Front rally, Prospect Hall, Brooklyn, February 4, 1940. Derounian's comments must be qualified by his apparent anti-Catholicism. For example, in his report from Prospect Hall, he noted that liberals "are fighting the Pope himself— by far the most powerful dictator in the whole world: Stalin and Hitler are puppets by comparison."

50. Report, Christian Front meeting, March 11, 1940, Jewish Community Relations Council of Greater Boston, I-123, box 44, folder 5, Wyner Family Jewish Heritage Center at New England Historic Genealogical Society, Boston (hereafter JHC).

51. [Maurice Goldsmith], "Report of Christian Front Meeting Held Monday Evening, February 12, 1940 at Hibernian Hall, Dudley St., Roxbury, Mass.," Jewish Community Relations Council of Greater Boston, I-123, box 44, folder 5, JHC.

52. "Provocateurs Blamed for Sedition Charge."

53. "The Christian Front," Browder papers, Syracuse, 15; Joshua Zeitz, "Communist! Fascist! New York Jews and Catholics Fight the Cold War," in *Jews, Catholics, and the Burden of History*, ed. Eli Lederhendler (New York: Oxford University Press, 2005), 95; Larry Ceplair, *Anti-Communism in Twentieth-Century America: A Critical History* (Santa Barbara, CA: Praeger, 2011), 36.

54. Victoria Munro, *Hate Crime in the Media: A History* (Santa Barbara, CA: Praeger, 2014), 165; Stephen M. Feldman, *Free Expression and Democracy in America: A History* (Chicago: University of Chicago Press, 2008), 423; Philip Jenkins, *Hoods and Shirts: The Extreme Right in Pennsylvania, 1925–1950* (Chapel Hill: University of North Carolina Press, 1997); Philip Jenkins, "Home-Grown Terror," *American Heritage*, September 1995, 46, https://www.americanheritage.com/home-grown-terror; Philip Jenkins, "Forgetting American Terror: The Christian Front," *Patheos, The Anxious Bench Blog*, March 6, 2017, https://www.patheos.com/blogs/anxiousbench/2017/03/forgetting -american-terror-christian-front. Feldman is typical of the many historians who argue that, by virtue of the indictment and trial, the Christian Front was "suppressed."

55. Stephen H. Norwood, "Marauding Youth and the Christian Front: Antisemitic Violence in Boston and New York during World War II," *American Jewish History* 91, no. 2 (2003): 233–267.

56. Investigation of Un-American Propaganda Activities in the United States, Hearings before the Special Committee on Un-American Activities, House of Representatives, 76th Congress, vol. 5, statement of George Deatherage, 3472; Peter J. Wacks, report, Claus Gunther Ernecke: Subversive Activities, December 1, 1939, 11, Christian Front FBI file, 1137495-000–65–HQ–4279, Section 2, released through USFOIA.

4. What's the Matter with Me?

1.   A. Rosen to E. A. Tamm, memorandum, January 18, 1940, Christian Front FBI file, 1137495-000–65–HQ–4279, Section 6, released through United States Freedom of Information Act (hereafter USFOIA); "FBI Seeks Christian Front Head," Boston *Herald-Traveler,* January 18, 1940, Francis P. Moran file, Boston *Herald-Traveler* clippings morgue, Pickering Educational Resources Library, Boston University, Boston (hereafter Boston *Herald-Traveler* clippings morgue).

2.   Rosen to Tamm, January 18, 1940.

3.   "FBI Seeks Christian Front Head"; V. W. Peterson to J. Edgar Hoover, January 23, 1940, Christian Front FBI file, 1137495-000–65–HQ–4279, Section 8, released through USFOIA.

4.   "Attack Expulsion of T.J. Stevenson," *Boston Herald,* July 20, 1936, 8.

5.   Father Ronald Coyne, "Bridget Agnes Traynor Moran," http://celticowboy.com/ma2.htm, accessed August 13, 2013. The webpage has since been taken down. Copy in possession of the author.

6.   Arthur Crew Inman, *The Inman Diary: A Public and Private Confession,* ed. Daniel Aaron, 2 vols. (Cambridge, MA: Harvard University Press, 1985), vol. 1, 549.

7.   Coyne, "Bridget Agnes Traynor Moran"; "Francis Patrick 'Frank' Moran," http://celticowboy.com/ma2.htm, accessed August 7, 2013; Nancy Moran, taped interview with Bridget Agnes Traynor Moran, n.d., http://celticowboy.com/ma2.htm, accessed August 7, 2013. These webpages have since been taken down. Copies in possession of the author.

8.   "Dies Group Calls N. E. 'Front' Chief," Boston *Herald-Traveler,* March 21, 1940, Christian Front–Boston file, Boston *Herald-Traveler* clippings morgue; Damien Murray, *Irish Nationalists in Boston: Catholicism and Conflict, 1900–1928* (Washington, DC: Catholic University of America Press, 2018), 12–13.

9.   Anthony M. Carrozzo, *Refounding in the Franciscan Tradition, Spirit and Life: A Journal of Contemporary Franciscanism* (St. Bonaventure, NY: Franciscan Institute, 1994), 94; Michael Daly, *The Book of Mychal: The Surprising Life and Heroic Death of Father Mychal Judge* (New York: St. Martin's Press, 2002), 24.

10. Andrew McKenzie, *Doves and Demons: An Irish American's Legacy* (Bloomington, IN: Authorhouse, 2012), 48; Kenneth Himes, interview with author, November 15, 2016, Boston College, Chestnut Hill, MA.

11. Kenneth Himes, interview, November 15, 2016. For discussion of anti-Communism and the cult of Mary, see Thomas A. Kselman and Steven Avella, "Marian Piety and

the Cold War in the United States," *Catholic Historical Review* 72, no. 3 (1986): 403–424. There is also a connection between Mary and Mystical Body theology. Pope Pius X wrote in 1904, "In a spiritual and mystical fashion, all we who are united to Christ . . . have issued from the womb of Mary like a body united to its head." Pius X, "Ad diem illum laetissmum," encyclical, February 2, 1904, http://www.vatican.va/content/pius-x /en/encyclicals/documents/hf_p-x_enc_02021904_ad-diem-illum-laetissimum.html.

12. Joseph M. White, "In Search of Holy Name Province, Order of Friars Minor," *U.S. Catholic Historian* 22, no. 1 (Winter 2004): 113–125, 118.

13. Kenneth Himes, interview, November 15, 2016; Daly, *Book of Mychal*, 24; Richard S. Levy, *Antisemitism: A Historical Encyclopedia of Prejudice and Persecution* (Santa Barbara, CA: ABC-CLIO, 2005), vol. 1, 407.

14. Fulton J. Sheen, "The Reality of Sin," address delivered on March 9, 1941, in *War and Guilt* (Washington, DC: National Council of Catholic Men, 1953), 115–122, American Catholic History Research Center, digital collections, https://cuislandora.wrlc.org /islandora/object/cuislandora:36868#page/120/mode/1up. The "friendly affection" was observed by a fellow former student: Kenneth Himes, interview, November 15, 2016.

15. Report card of Francis Patrick Moran, 1923–1925, St. Joseph's Seraphic Seminary, Callicoon, NY, Archives of the Franciscan Fathers of the Holy Name Province, New York.

16. Paul Tillich, "Catholicism and Anti-Judaism," Paul Tillich papers, 1894–1974, bMS 649/62 (6), 7, Andover-Harvard Theological Library, Harvard Divinity School, Cambridge, MA.

17. Report card of Francis Patrick Moran; Daly, *Book of Mychal*, 24.

18. Charles Hathaway Trout, "Boston during the Great Depression: 1929–1940" (PhD diss., Columbia University, 1972), 347; Francis P. Moran employment history, recounted in W. J. West, report, William Gerald Bishop: Subversive Activities, February 29, 1940, 1, 2, Francis P. Moran FBI file, 1224676-0-097–HQ–827, Section 1, released through USFOIA.

19. "Convention Committee," *Jewish War Veteran*, vol. 7 (1940), 4; Richard N. Blaustein, interview, October 18, 1939, in W. J. West, report, William Gerald Bishop, et al., February 24, 1940, 3, Francis Moran FBI file, 1224676-0-097–HQ–827, Section 1, released through USFOIA; West, report, William Gerald Bishop: Subversive Activities, 2.

20. An example of Catholics arguing that their relatively high numbers of war deaths indicated a patriotism lacked by Jews is Frederick J. Zwierlein, *Talks to Men and Women on the World of Today* (Rochester, NY: Art Print Shop, 1946), 30–35.

21. West, report William Gerald Bishop, February 29, 1940, 2; Report, Christian Front Meeting, December 2, 1940, [3], box 44 (Christian Front Meetings, Propaganda, Moran), folder 5, American Jewish Historical Society, Boston.

22. "Francis Patrick 'Frank' Moran," Celticowboy.com.

23. "Clergy Applaud Father Coughlin," *Social Justice*, May 24, 1937, 14; Bishop Duffy quoted in George Q. Flynn, *Roosevelt and Romanism: Catholics and American Diplomacy, 1937–1945* (Westport, CT: Greenwood Press, 1976), 142; James F. Mahan, File No. 100-2374, Francis P. Moran Custodial Detention Inquiry, June 5, 1943, 27, Francis P. Moran FBI file 1224676-0-097–HQ–827, Section 3, released through USFOIA. The reference to "Father Duffy" likely reflects confusion between Bishop John Duffy and Father Francis Duffy, the famous World War I chaplain. While Bishop Duffy was a Coughlin collaborator, Father Duffy was a pluralist and in key respects the antithesis of Coughlin.

24. Michael C. Connolly, "Splitting the Vote in Massachusetts: Father Charles E. Coughlin, the Union Party, and Political Divisions in the 1936 Presidential and Senate Elections," *Historical Journal of Massachusetts* 43, no. 2 (2015), 101, 103.

25. Report from confidential informant, name redacted, April 3, 1943, 27, attached to Mahan, Moran Custodial Detention Inquiry.

26. Coughlin quoted in M. J. Heale, *American Anticommunism: Combating the Enemy Within, 1830–1970* (Baltimore: Johns Hopkins University Press, 1990), 108, 113.

27. Charles E. Coughlin, "The Myth of Social Security," *Social Justice*, November 9, 1936, 8; Report from confidential informant, 28.

28. Edward C. Blackorby, *Prairie Rebel: The Public Life of William Lemke* (Lincoln: University of Nebraska Press, 1963), 229.

29. "Sybil Holmes, First Woman Ever Elected State Senator," *Boston Daily Globe*, November 5, 1936, 16; "Senator Holmes Warns Long Group," *Boston Daily Globe*, July 10, 1938, B18.

30. "Gleam of Lanterns," *Boston Daily Globe*, April 19, 1938, 1. Tobin retained his paranoid view into the 1950s. See Harold W. Chase, *Security and Liberty: The Problem of Native Communists, 1947–1955* (Garden City, NY: Doubleday, 1955), 56.

31. "Explains Communist Policy," *Boston Daily Globe*, October 1, 1937, 1; "Working for World Revolution," *Social Justice*, October 25, 1937, 1; Marsh quoted in "Professional Patriots," *Boston Daily Globe*, August 14, 1938, B1.

32. Investigation of Communist Propaganda: Hearings Before a Special Committee to Investigate Communist Activities in the United States of the House of Representatives, Seventy-first Congress, second session, pursuant to H. Res. 220 (Washington, DC: US GPO, 1930).

33. "Charges Nazi Propaganda," *Boston Daily Globe*, October 14, 1937; "Pro-Nazi Writer Stops Show by Toting Pistol to Red Quiz," *Boston Daily Globe*, October 28, 1937, 9; "Brandeis Is Called 'Invisible Power,'" *Boston Daily Globe*, October 26, 1937; O. John Rogge, *The Official German Report: Nazi Penetration, 1924–1942* (New York: Thomas Yoseloff, 1961), 314; John Earl Haynes, Harvey Klehr, and Alexander Vassiliev, *Spies: The Rise and Fall of the KGB in America* (New Haven: Yale University Press, 2009), 160.

34. "Boston 'Front' Absolved from Part in Plot," *Boston Daily Globe*, January 16, 1940, Christian Front file, *Boston Herald-Traveler* clippings morgue; West, report, William Gerald Bishop, et al., 1; pistol-licensing quotes from unsigned memorandum, July 15, 1940, Jewish Community Relations Council of Greater Boston, I-123, box 56, folder 15, Wyner Family Jewish Heritage Center at New England Historic Genealogical Society, Boston.

35. *Special Commission to Investigate the Activities within this Commonwealth of Communistic, Fascistic and Other Subversive Organizations, So-Called* (Boston: Wright and Potter Printing Company, 1938), 41.

36. Untitled report, June 13 and 14, 1939, drawer G1, folder "Boston correspondence, data," Avedis (Arthur) Derounian papers, Mardigian Library, National Association for Armenian Studies and Research, Belmont, MA. There was also an active Committee for the Defense of American Constitutional Rights in Philadelphia. "Group Here to Aid 17 Jailed in 'Front,'" *Philadelphia Inquirer*, January 20, 1940, 2.

37. "Dear Friend," n.d. [copy], attached to N. D. Valentine, report, William Gerald Bishop, March 23, 1940, 7, Francis P. Moran FBI file 1224676-0-097–HQ–827, Section 1, released through USFOIA; Richard R. Gaillardetz and Catherine E. Clifford, *Keys to the Council: Unlocking the Teaching of Vatican II* (Collegeville, MN: Liturgical Press, 2012), 71.

38. N. D. Valentine, report, William Gerald Bishop, 5; James M. O'Toole, "Prelates and Politicos: Catholics and Politics in Massachusetts, 1900 to 1970," in *Catholic Boston: Studies in Religion and Community, 1870–1970*, ed. Robert E. Sullivan and James M. O'Toole (Boston, MA: Roman Catholic Archbishop of Boston, 1985), 37; *Special Commission to Investigate the Activities*, 448.

39. Dale Maharidge, *Someplace Like America: Tales from the New Great Depression*, updated ed. (Berkeley: University of California Press, 2013), 203.

40. "Censorship Laid to Radio Chain," *Boston Herald*, January 28, 1939, 12.

41. "Citizen Board Feared Wedge for Snoopers," *Boston Daily Globe*, March 25, 1939, 1.

42. Report, F. C. Leonard, William Gerald Bishop: Subversive Activity, February 12, 1940, 2, Moran FBI file 1224676-0-097–HQ–827, Section 1, released through USFOIA.

5. A Rather Bold Agitator

1. "Rally in Boston Attracts 12,000," *Social Justice*, September 18, 1939, 4. Attendance numbers for the September 8 Boston Arena rally vary widely. The *Globe* reported an attendance figure of 8,000, while Eugene Smith indicated to the FBI that the Boston Police Department told him they estimated 10,000. "Cash-Carry Policy Means U.S. in War—Fr. Coughlin," *Daily Boston Globe*, September 9, 1939, 1; Eugene B. Smith, "The Christian Front in Boston," attached to P. P. Schneider, report, William Gerald Bishop, et al., February 8, 1940, 7, Francis P. Moran FBI file, Section 1, released through the United States Freedom of Information Act (hereafter USFOIA).

2. Boake Carter, obituary, *Syracuse Herald-Journal*, November 17, 1944, 18; Irving E. Fang, *Those Radio Commentators!* (Ames: Iowa State University Press, 1977), 111; Kathy M. Newman, *Radio Active: Advertising and Consumer Activism, 1935–1947* (Berkeley: University of California Press, 2004), 47, 86; "Great Pro-American Mass Meeting on Behalf of Free Speech and Americanism," poster, drawer G2, folder "Christian Front 2," Avedis (Arthur) Derounian papers, Mardigian Library, National Association for Armenian Studies and Research, Belmont, MA.

3. "Press Is Freer Than Radio, Says Carter," *Daily Boston Globe*, October 25, 1939, 5.

4. "500 Picket Station WAAB," *Boston Herald*, October 9, 1939, 20; "Father Coughlin Radio Talks to Continue," *Boston Herald*, October 25, 1939, 7.

5. Veneration of Father Coughlin is an underexplored relic of this time period. Anthony J. Sciolino is one of the few who has considered Coughlin's role as a schismatic figure. See Sciolino, *The Holocaust, the Church, and the Law of Unintended Consequences: How Christian Anti-Judaism Spawned Nazi Anti-Semitism, a Judge's Verdict* (Bloomington, IN: iUniverse, 2012), 138.

6. Eugene Bernard Smith, "Father Coughlin Comes to Boston," unpublished manuscript, attached to P. P. Schneider, report William Gerald Bishop, et al., 4 (emphasis original). Smith, who must have misheard Keating's introduction, refers to the priest repeatedly in his notes as "Healy."

7. Peter J. Wacks, report, Claus Gunther Ernecke: Subversive Activities, December 1, 1939, 5, Christian Front FBI file, 1137495-000-65–HQ–4279, Section 2, released through USFOIA.

8. "Check on Arms in Boston," *Brooklyn Eagle*, January 20, 1940, 2.

9. J. D. Noble, Jr., report, John F. Cassidy: Sedition, January 30, 1940, 6, Christian Front FBI file, 1137495-000–65–HQ–4279, Section 11, released through USFOIA.

10. "Revolt Plot Investigations Are Started," *Richmond Times Dispatch*, January 16, 1940, 1.

11. "City Council Recorded against Radio Band on Father Coughlin," *Lowell Sun*, December 6, 1939, 1; Edward M. Kirby to J. Edgar Hoover, "Dear Mister Hoover," January 18, 1940, Christian Front FBI file, 1137495-000–65–HQ–4279, Section 5, released through USFOIA.

12. Union for Democratic Action, New England section, press release, n.d., Jewish Community Relations Council of Greater Boston, I-123, box 46, folder 1, Wyner Family Jewish Heritage Center at New England Historic Genealogical Society, Boston (hereafter JHC); Unsigned report, "Francis P. Moran," July 31, 1941, 8, 9, Francis P. Moran FBI file, 1224676-0-097–HQ–827, Section 1, released through USFOIA; "List of Curran Activities," n.d., 2, Jewish Community Relations Council of Greater Boston, I-123, box 46, folder 1, JHC. On attendance figures see W. J. West, report, William Gerald Bishop: Subversive Activity, February 24, 1940, 19, Francis P. Moran FBI file, 1224676-0-097–HQ–827, Section 1, released through USFOIA.

13. Report on Christian Front meeting held Wednesday, November 9, 1939, unsigned, 3, Jewish Community Relations Council of Greater Boston, I-123, box 44, folder 5, JHC.

14. Thomas Feeney, the Lynn resident who approached the FBI, was the father of Leonard Feeney, who would become one of the foremost Jew-baiters of the 1950s. Dismissed from the Jesuits in 1953 and later excommunicated at the personal direction of Pope Pius XII, Father Feeney wrote essays and delivered open-air sermons on Boston Common interpreting the dogma *extra Ecclesiam nulla salus* (outside the Church there is no salvation) as an anti-Semitic exhortation. Spencer Blakeslee has referred to Father Feeney as "Boston's homegrown version of Coughlin." Feeney's extremism motivated the Catholic Church to reexamine its position on Jews and influenced the reforms of the Second Vatican Council. In his final days, Feeney repented and was reconciled with the Roman Catholic Church. Spencer Blakeslee, *The Death of American Antisemitism* (Westport, CT: Praeger, 2000), 93.

15. Edward L. Boyle, report, William Gerald Bishop, February 10, 1940, 4, Francis P. Moran FBI file, 1224676-0-097-HQ–827, Section 1, released through USFOIA.

16. Michelle M. Nickerson, *Mothers of Conservatism: Women and the Postwar Right* (Princeton, NJ: Princeton University Press, 2012), 23.

17. Boyle, report, February 10, 1940; Glen Jeansonne, *Women of the Far Right: The Mothers' Movement and World War II* (Chicago: University of Chicago Press, 1996), 33; the confidential informant's report is from August 12, 1941, attached to J. H. Foley, report, Francis P. Moran: Internal Security G, November 18, 1941, 42, Francis P. Moran FBI file, 1224676-0-097-HQ–827, Section 1; Marie M. Ballem to "The Editor," February 1, 1940, America Magazine archives, box 11, folder 35, "Christian Front material," GTMGamms60, Booth Family Center for Special Collections, Georgetown University Library, Washington, DC.

18. "Report of August 6, 1941," attached to J. H. Foley, report, Francis P. Moran: Internal Security G, November 18, 1941, 37, Francis P. Moran FBI file, 1224676-0-097-HQ–827, Section 1, released through USFOIA.

19. Christian Front meeting, report, March 3, 1941, Jewish Community Relations Council of Greater Boston, I-123, Box 44, folder 4, JHC.

20. On Christian Front street-fighting in New York, see James Wechsler, "The Coughlin Terror," *The Nation* 149, September 22, 1939, 96.

21. Report on Christian Front Meeting, November 9, 1939.

22. Garrison Nelson, *John William McCormack: A Political Biography* (New York: Bloomsbury, 2017), 235; memo from B. W. for Mr. Hall, September 28, 1939, 1, National Catholic Welfare Conference Press Department, National Catholic News Service Collection, box 14, Rev. Chas. E. Coughlin file, 1930–1942, American Catholic History Research Center and University Archives, Catholic University of America, Washington, DC.

23. W. J. West, report, William Gerald Bishop, with aliases, et al., February 29, 1940, 4, Francis P. Moran FBI file, 1224676-0-097-HQ–827, Section 1, released through USFOIA.

24. Michael Stenton, *Radio London and Resistance in Occupied Europe: British Political Warfare 1939–1943* (New York: Oxford University Press, 2000), 9–10.

25. Report on Christian Front Meeting, November 9, 1939.

26. Benjamin Kravitz quoted in West, report, February 24, 1940, 21; "Duff Cooper Faces Hecklers," *Boston Herald*, November 28, 1939, 8; "Duff Cooper Heckled during Boston Address," *Daily Boston Globe*, November 29, 1939, 1; Duff Cooper, *Old Men Forget: The Autobiography of Duff Cooper (Viscount Norwich)* (New York: Dutton, 1954), 272.

27. Douglas Martin, "Rev. Donald G. Lothrop, 96, Boat-Rocking Minister, Dies," obituary, *New York Times*, March 5, 2002.

28. Eugene B. Smith, "The Christian Front in Boston," contained in P. P. Schneider, report William Gerald Bishop, et al., 9, Francis P. Moran FBI file, 1224676-0-097–HQ–827, Section 1.

29. "N. E. Leader Says 'Front' against Force," *Daily Boston Globe*, January 15, 1940, 1.

30. "Saboteur Arrests in Boston Likely," *New York Times*, January 16, 1940, 3; Thomas A. K. Reilly, O. P., "End of the World? Not Yet!" *America* 12, no. 23 (1915), 556; Christopher Carstens and Douglas Martis, *Mystical Body, Mystical Voice: Encountering Christ in the Words of the Mass* (Chicago: Liturgy Training Publications, 2011), 65.

31. Henry W. Levy to Frank N. Trager, January 18, 1940, Jewish Community Relations Council of Greater Boston, I-123, box 44, folder 3, JHC.

32. "Boston Minister Appears at Meeting to Denounce Christian Front," Religious News Service, bulletin, January 20, 1940, Jewish Community Relations Council of Greater Boston, I-123, box 44, folder 1, JHC; "Christian Front Leader, Minister Clash at Meeting," *Daily Boston Globe*, January 19, 1940, 1; W. J. West, report, William Gerald Bishop: Subversive Activity, 30.

33. Chas E. Coughlin to Mr. Frank Moran, December 19, 1939, Jewish Community Relations Council of Greater Boston, I-123, box 44, folder 4, JHC.

34. West, report, February 24, 1940, 30.

35. Henry W. Levy to Frank N. Trager, February 14, 1940, Jewish Community Relations Council of Greater Boston, I-123, box 44, folder 3, JHC; David Cesarani, *The Jewish Chronicle and Anglo-Jewry, 1841–1991* (Cambridge: Cambridge University Press, 1994), 151; "Report of Christian Front Meeting Held Monday Evening, February 12, 1940 at Hibernian Hall, Dudley St., Roxbury, Mass.," n.a., Jewish Community Relations Council of Greater Boston, I-123, box 44, folder 5, JHC.

36. "Report of Christian Front Meeting," February 12, 1940.

37. J. Edgar Hoover to SAC, Boston, [copy], March 8, 1940, Francis P. Moran FBI file, 1224676-0-097–HQ–827, Section 1, released through USFOIA; Report, Christian Front meeting, March 11, 1940, Jewish Community Relations Council of Greater Boston, I-123, box 44, folder 5, JHC.

38. "To All Real Americans," newsletter, March 11, 1940, Jewish Community Relations Council of Greater Boston, I-123, box 44, folder 5, JHC.

39. "To Americans Who Vote," newsletter, June 17, 1940, Jewish Community Relations Council of Greater Boston, I-123, box 44, folder 5, JHC.

40. "Boston Man Called before Dies Group," *Daily Boston Globe*, March 22, 1940, 10. On Moran's plight at this time, see "Christian Front Report, July 15, 1940," Jewish Community Relations Council of Greater Boston, I-123, box 44, folder 5, JHC.

41. Report, Christian Front meeting July 1, 1940, Hibernian Hall, Jewish Community Relations Council of Greater Boston, I-123, box 44, folder 5, JHC. On Nazi natalist policies, see Amy Beth Carney, *Marriage and Fatherhood in the Nazi SS* (Toronto: University of Toronto Press, 2018), 112.

42. "Radio Priest Rounds Out 50 Years of Work for Tolerance," news release, Religious News Service, July 18, 1946, Michael J. Ahern papers, box 2, folder 12, "Radio Show and Tolerance," New England Province Archive, Jesuit Archives & Research Center, St. Louis, Missouri (hereafter JARC); M. J. Ahern, S. J., "The Harvard Seminar on Religious Intolerance," *Missionary* 44, no. 2 (1930): 1, in box 2, folder 4, "articles of interest, by and about, 1923–1951," Ahern papers, JARC.

43. Donna L. Halper, *Boston Radio: 1920–2010* (Charleston, SC: Arcadia, 2011), 125; Luther Conant, Jr., "Your Boston," *Boston Evening Transcript*, October 29, 1940, 8.

44. "Last Week's Broadcast," *Boston Pilot*, January 20, 1940, 1.

45. "Fistfights Prevented at Meeting," *Boston Post*, July 30, 1938, 1.

46. "Last Week's Broadcast."

47. Michael J. Ahern, "Some Observations on Our Recent Controversy," typewritten manuscript, box 2, folder "Radio Show, Reactions and Controversy, 1940," Ahern papers, JARC; "Last Week's Broadcast."

48. "Christian Front report," July 15, 1940, Jewish Community Relations Council of Greater Boston, I-123, box 44, folder 5, JHC.

49. Henry W. Levy to Louis E. Kirstein—F. Frank Vorenberg, July 30, 1940, Jewish Community Relations Council of Greater Boston, I-123, box 26, folder 1, JHC; Conant, "Your Boston."

50. Francis P. Moran to William Cardinal O'Connell, [copy], July 17, 1940, Cardinal William Henry O'Connell general files, Christian Front file, Archives of the Archdiocese of Boston, Braintree, MA (hereafter AAB).

51. "Dear Jerry to F. L. P.," n.d., Cardinal William Henry O'Connell general files, Christian Front file, AAB; Moran to O'Connell, July 17, 1940.

6. A Nazi in Boston

1. "New German Consul Named," *Christian Science Monitor*, November 10, 1938, 10.

2. Special Agent W. J. West, File Memorandum, Dr. Herbert Scholz, German Consulate, Espionage, June 12, 1940, Scholz FBI file, 65–HQ–4414, Section 1, released through United States Freedom of Information Act (hereafter USFOIA).

3. File Memorandum, Dr. Herbert Scholz, June 12, 1940.

4. Steven Casey, *Cautious Crusade: Franklin D. Roosevelt, American Public Opinion, and the War against Nazi Germany* (New York: Oxford University Press, 2004), 13;

James Clement Dunn quoted in British Embassy Washington to the American Department, Foreign Office, London, March 10, 1939, FO / 371, America—General, file 105, British National Archives, Kew, Richmond.

5. Francis L. Burwitz to Luther Conant Jr., August 12, 1940, [copy], Jewish Community Relations Council of Greater Boston, I-123, box 168, folder 1, Wyner Family Jewish Heritage Center at New England Historic Genealogical Society, Boston.

6. British Embassy Washington to the American Department, Foreign Office, London, March 10, 1939.

7. "La Guardia Denies Aid to Coughlinites," *New York Times*, July 21, 1939, 5; "Francis P. Moran, Director of the Christian Front, Boston, 108 Massachusetts Ave., Boston, Oct. 11, 1940," drawer A3, folder, "Moran, Francis P.," Avedis (Arthur) Derounian papers, Mardigian Library, National Association for Armenian Studies and Research, Belmont, MA.

8. John Franklin Carter, *The Catoctin Conversation* (New York: Scribner's Sons, 1947), 15.

9. *Adreßbuch der Direktoren und Aufsichtsräte* (Berlin: Finanz-Verlag, 1925), 1524; *Biographisches Handbuch des deutschen Auswärtigen Dienstes, 1871–1945* (Paderborn: Ferdinand Schöningh, 2012), 160.

10. Hans-Jürgen Döscher, *Das Auswärtie Amt im Dritten Reich* (Munich: Siedler Verlag, 1987), 47n43; Adolf Hitler, *Mein Kampf* (New York: Reynal and Hitchcock, 1939), 508.

11. On Hess, see David Luhrssen, *Hammer of the Gods: The Thule Society and the Birth of Nazism* (Washington, DC: Potomac Books, 2012), 124. On Himmler, see Clifton Wilcox, *The Rise of the Nazi SS* (Bloomington, IN: Xlibris Press, 2016), 5; Alan Bullock, *Hitler: A Study in Tyranny*, rev. ed. (New York: Harper and Row, 1962), 63.

12. Herbert Scholz, "Lebenslauf" [resume], in "Sachverhalt—Urteil—Beurteilung in der Külpeschen Logik" (PhD diss., Universität Leipzig, 1932), [47].

13. On the "core" of the SA, see Patrick Moreau, "Strasserism in Germany: In Search of an Anti-Western Alliance with Stalin's USSR and Putin's Russia," in *Entangled Far Rights: A Russian-European Intellectual Romance in the Twentieth Century*, ed. Marlene Laruelle (Pittsburgh, PA: University of Pittsburgh Press, 2018), 249n17; Daniel Siemens, *Stormtroopers: A New History of Hitler's Brown Shirts* (New Haven: Yale University Press, 2017), 32; the description of Röhm appears in H. R. Knickerbocker, *Is Tomorrow Hitler's? 200 Questions on the Battle of Mankind* (New York: Reynal and Hitchcock, 1941), 33; the "strong arm" passage is from Hanna Samir Kassab, *The Power of Emotion in Politics, Philosophy, and Ideology* (New York: Palgrave Macmillan, 2016), 157; Röhm quoted in Guido Enderis, "Nazi Troops Held Anti-Red Bulwark," *New York Times*, December 10, 1933, E3.

14. Hermann Beck, *The Fateful Alliance: German Conservatives and Nazis in 1933: The Machtergreifung in a New Light* (New York: Berghahn Books, 2008), 311.

15. "Goebbels, Joseph," *The Simon and Schuster Encyclopedia of World War II*, ed. Thomas Parrish (New York: Simon and Schuster, 1978), 237; Siemens, *Stormtroopers*, 39 (Goebbels passage), 89.

16. Secret cable 650 from State Department to CASERTA, July 7, 1945, Herbert Scholz FBI file, 65–HQ–4414, Section 2, released through USFOIA. On Germanization, see Eric C. Steinhart, *The Holocaust and the Germanization of the Ukraine* (New York: Cambridge University Press, 2015), 46; and Gregor Joseph Kranjc, *To Walk with the Devil: Slovene Collaboration and Axis Occupation, 1941–1945* (Toronto: University of Toronto Press, 2013), 59. For discussion of the diplomatic role of the SA, see Siemens, *Stormtroopers.*

17. Scholz, "Lebenslauf" [resume], [47]; George R. Leaman, "Contextual Misreadings: The U.S. Reception of Heidegger's Political Thought" (PhD diss., University of Massachusetts, Amherst, 1991), 92.

18. "Henri Bergson," in *Philosophisches Wörterbuch*, ed. Werner Schingnitz and Joachim Schondorff (Stuttgart: Alfred Kröner Verlag, 1943), 55; "Edmund Husserl," in *Philosophisches Wörterbuch*, 248; Yvonne Sherratt, *Hitler's Philosophers* (New Haven: Yale University Press, 2013), 74.

19. "Oswald Külpe," in Leonard Zusne, *Biographical Dictionary of Psychology* (Westport, CT: Greenwood Press, 1984), 240; "Külpe, Oswald," in *International Encyclopedia of the Social Sciences*, ed. David L. Sills (New York: Macmillan, 1968), vol. 8, 467–468. Külpe was born in the heavily Jewish Latvian town of Kandava. See *The Encyclopedia of Jewish Life Before and During the Holocaust*, ed. Shmuel Spector and Geoffrey Wigoder (Jerusalem: Yad Vashem and New York: New York University Press, 2001), 594; Scholz, "Sachverhalt—Urteil—Beurteilung," 29, 43; "Oswald Külpe," in *Philosophisches Wörterbuch*, 324.

20. Ruth Dwight diary, transcription, from Antony Taquey, email to author, June 15, 2017.

21. Dietrich Orlow, "Relations between the Nazis and French and Dutch Fascists, January 1933–August 1934," in *The Impact of Nazism: New Perspectives on the Third Reich and Its Legacy*, ed. Alan E. Steinweis and Daniel E. Rogers (Lincoln: University of Nebraska Press, 2003), 42; Döscher, *Das Auswärtie Amt im Dritten Reich*, 47n43; Ricky W. Law, "Knowledge Is Power: The Interwar German and Japanese Mass Media in the Making of the Axis" (PhD diss., University of North Carolina at Chapel Hill, 2012), 222n66; Ricky W. Law, *Transnational Nazism: Ideology and Culture in German-Japanese Relations, 1919–1936* (Cambridge: Cambridge University Press, 2019), 280.

22. Robert Deam Tobin, *Peripheral Desires: The German Discovery of Sex*, Haney Foundation Series (Philadelphia: University of Pennsylvania Press, 2015), 80.

23. Eleanor Hancock, "'Only the Real, the True, the Masculine Held Its Value': Ernst Röhm, Masculinity, and Male Homosexuality," *Journal of the History of Sexuality* 8, no. 4 (1998): 616–641, 626; Ellic Howe, *Astrology: A Recent History Including the Untold Story of Its Role in World War II* (New York: Walker, 1968), 112; letter to Gauleitung München, May 26, 1933, box VBS1, archive number 1110002439, Bundesarchiv, Berlin. I am grateful to Bernhard Knorn, S. J., of the Philosophisch-Theologisch Hochschule Sankt Georgen, Frankfurt am Main, for his assistance in translating these documents.

24. Arnold Krammer, review of *The Men around Hitler: The Nazi Elite and Its Collaborators*, by Alfred D. Low, *German Studies Review* 21, no. 3 (1998), 619; Ernst Hanfstaengl, *Hitler: The Missing Years* (London: Eyre and Spottiswoode, 1957), 218.

25. Notice, Reichsführer SS to SS-Sturmbannführer Scholz, June 26, 1933, box VBS286, archive number 6400040668, Bundesarchiv, Berlin; J. A. Cloake, *Germany, 1918–1945* (Oxford: Oxford University Press, 1997), 49; Bruce Campbell, *The SA Generals and the Rise of Nazism* (Lexington: University of Kentucky Press, 2004), 120.

26. Peter Longerich, *Heinrich Himmler*, trans. Jeremy Noakes and Lesley Sharpe (Oxford: Oxford University Press, 2012), 392; "German agents" passage from Hiroaki Kuromiya and Andrzej Pepłoński, "Stalin, Espionage, and Counterespionage," in *Stalin and Europe: Imitation and Domination*, ed. Timothy Snyder and Ray Brandon (Oxford: Oxford University Press, 2014), 80; High Command of the SS registered letter from name indecipherable, January 9, 1934, box R9361/111, archive number 18350, Bundesarchiv, Berlin.

27. Dietrich Orlow, *The Nazi Party 1919–1945: A Complete History* (New York: Enigma Books, 2008), 261, 262n258; George C. Browder, *Hitler's Enforcers: The Gestapo and the SS Security Service in the Nazi Revolution* (New York: Oxford University Press, 1996), 203; Richard Deacon, *British Secret Service* (London: Grafton Books, 1991), 278; Curt Riess, *Total Espionage* (New York: G. P. Putnam's Sons, 1941), 87.

28. Volume 36, 1938 Jul 2–Dec 30, William R. Castle Diaries MS AM 2021, Houghton Library, Harvard College Library, Cambridge, MA; Curt Riess, *The Nazis Go Underground* (Garden City, NY: Doubleday, Doran, 1944), 163; Curriculum vitae, Liselotte von Schnitzler, n.d., inventory R9361/111, archive number 183540, Bundesarchiv, Berlin.

29. B. Bernstein to Lucius D. Clay, Report, Headquarters, U.S. Group Control Council, Finance Division, [copy], Foreign Office, German Section, FO 935/49, Restricted Report on IG Farbenindustrie, September 12, 1945, 1, National Archives, Kew, Richmond.

30. Riess, *The Nazis Go Underground*, 164; Bella Fromm, *Blood and Banquets: A Berlin Social Diary* (New York: Citadel Press, Kensington Publishing Group, 2002), 200; George Abell and Evelyn Gordon, *Let Them Eat Caviar* (New York: Dodge, 1937), 134. Fromm's reportage has been disputed but also has been used by many contemporary historians.

31. Amy Carney, *Marriage and Fatherhood in the Nazi SS* (Toronto: University of Toronto Press, 2018), 24; Lisa Pine, *Nazi Family Policy, 1933–1945* (New York: Berg, 1999), 44.

32. Family tree of Liselotte von Schnitzler, inventory R9361/111, archive number, 183540, Bundesarchiv, Berlin; Der Reichsführer SS to SS-Obersturmbannführer Dr. Scholz, March 26, 1934, inventory R9361/111, archive number, 183540, Bundesarchiv, Berlin.

33. Röhm to Reichsführer SS, June 1934, Herbert W. Scholz, SS personnel file, [microfilm], RG 226, roll 105, National Archives and Records Administration,

Archives II, College Park, MD (hereafter NARA); Himmler [initials], to *Oberste SA Führung*, June 14, 1934, box VBS286, archive number 6400040668, Bundesarchiv, Berlin.

34. Paul Maracin, *Night of the Long Knives: Forty-Eight Hours That Changed the History of the World* (New York: Rowman and Littlefield, 2007), 111.

35. Zachary Shore, *What Hitler Knew: The Battle for Information in Nazi Foreign Policy* (Oxford: Oxford University Press, 2003), 31.

36. Helen Lombard, *Washington Waltz: Diplomatic People and Policies* (New York: Alfred A. Knopf, 1941), 54; Fromm, *Blood and Banquets*, 200; Riess, *The Nazis Go Underground*, 164; Memo to the SA-Führer, July 27, 1934, copy from the Riechsführung SS, Subject: Dissolution of the Ministry, Herbert W. Scholz, SS personnel file, [microfilm], RG 226, roll 105, NARA.

37. Sylvia F. Porter, "Farben Is the State, and Hitler Its Puppet in the Nazi New Order," *New York Post*, March 24, 1942, 4; Adam LeBor and Roger Boyes, *Seduced by Hitler: The Choices of a Nation and the Ethics of Survival* (Naperville, IL: Source Books, 2001), 134; Memo to the SA-Führer, July 27, 1934.

38. Dodd, *Through Embassy Eyes*, 151; Roberts, *House That Hitler Built*, 113; SS Chief Amt 3 to SS-Oberabschnitt Ost, August 22, 1934, Herbert W. Scholz, SS personnel file, [microfilm], RG 226, roll 105, NARA.

39. "Nazis Shun Cross at Church Rally," *New York Times*, September 22, 1934, 18.

40. Pacelli quoted in Frank J. Coppa, *Controversial Concordats: The Vatican's Relations with Napoleon, Mussolini, and Hitler* (Washington, DC: Catholic University of America Press, 1999), 171.

7. Hitler's Spymaster on Beacon Hill

1. L. K. Cook to H. H. Clegg, June 4, 1940, Herbert W. Scholz FBI file, 65–HQ–4414, Section 1, released through United States Freedom of Information Act (hereafter USFOIA).

2. John Edgar Hoover to Special Agent in Charge, Boston, June 12, 1940, Herbert W. Scholz FBI file, 65–HQ–4414, Section 1, released through USFOIA; "Activities of German Consular Officers in the United States," June 26, 1940, General Records of the Department of State, RG 59, 862.20211/6–2640, box 5589, National Archives and Records Administration, Archives II, College Park, MD (hereafter NARA).

3. D. J. Harkins to Captain Nixon, memorandum, June 26, 1940, 1, Herbert W. Scholz FBI file, 65–HQ–4414, Section 1, released through USFOIA.

4. Jeffrey M. Dorwart, *Conflict of Duty: The U.S. Navy's Intelligence Dilemma, 1919–1945* (Annapolis, MD: Naval Institute Press, 1983), 117; D. J. Harkins to Captain Nixon, June 26, 1940 in Scholz FBI file, 65–HQ–4414, Section 1, has handwritten note on top, "Rec. from Lt. Rhea Whitley, ONI, 6–27–41"; Commander Daniel J. Harkins papers, unpublished autobiography, [n.d.], box 1, folder 2, Naval History and Heritage Command, Archives Branch, Washington Navy Yard, DC, 4. Harkins spoke fluent German and visited Germany often for work before taking his intelligence position. He claimed

he once accepted "an invitation to have luncheon alone with Hitler," but the engagement was cancelled. In late 1938 a union leader testifying before the House Un-American Activities Committee accused Harkins of being a Nazi spy, on the basis of a wisecrack that Harkins made during a speech to the American Legion in Boston.

5. Sumner Welles to Adolph Berle, July 5, 1940, General Records of the Department of State, RG 59, 862.20211/6–2640, box 5589, NARA; Christopher Vasey, *Nazi Intelligence Operations in Non-Occupied Territories: Espionage Efforts in the United States, Britain, South America and Southern Africa* (Jefferson, NC: McFarland, 2016), 19. On Nazi espionage in the United States, see Raymond J. Batvinis, *The Origins of FBI Counterintelligence* (Lawrence: University Press of Kansas, 1997); Raymond J. Batvinis, *Hoover's Secret War against Axis Spies: FBI Counterespionage during World War II* (Lawrence: University Press of Kansas, 2014); Steven J. Ross, *Hitler in Los Angeles: How Jews Foiled Nazi Plots against Hollywood and America* (London: Bloomsbury, 2017); Laura B. Rosenzweig, *Hollywood's Spies: The Undercover Surveillance of Nazis in Los Angeles* (New York: NYU Press, 2017); Charles R. Gallagher, "Adopting the Swastika: George E. Deatherage and the American Nationalist Confederation, 1937–1942," in *Christianity, Antisemitism, and Ethnonationalism in the Era of the Two World Wars*, ed. Kevin Spicer and Rebecca Carter-Chand (Montreal: McGill-Queen's University Press, forthcoming).

6. Reports on Interrogation of German Prisoners-of-War Made by Members of the Department of State Special Interrogation Mission (September 1945 to September 1946) headed by DeWitt C. Poole [microform] (Washington, DC: The National Archives, National Archives and Records Service, General Services Administration, 1953), reel 1, Heribert von Strempel file, 1.

7. O. John Rogge, *The Official German Report: Nazi Penetration, 1924–1942* (New York: Thomas Yoseloff, 1961), 313; Christof Mauch, *The Shadow War against Hitler: The Covert Operations of America's Wartime Secret Intelligence Service*, trans. Jeremiah M. Riemer (New York: Columbia University Press, 1999), 45.

8. Kenneth Stow, *Jewish Dogs: An Image and Its Interpreters: Continuity in the Catholic-Jewish Encounter* (Stanford, CA: Stanford University Press, 2006), 205n12. On religious, as distinct from racial, anti-Semitism, see Philippe Burrin, *Nazi Anti-Semitism: From Prejudice to the Holocaust* (New York: New Press, 2004), 23; William I. Brustein, *Roots of Hate: Anti-Semitism in Europe before the Holocaust* (Cambridge: Cambridge University Press, 2003), 49.

9. Charles E. Coughlin, "The National Union for Social Justice" (radio broadcast), November 11, 1934, transcribed in *A Series of Lectures on Social Justice* (Royal Oak, MI: Radio League of the Little Flower, 1935; repr. New York: Da Capo Press, 1971), 18; Coughlin quoted in Erik Barnouw, *A History of Broadcasting in the United States: The Golden Web, 1933 to 1953* (New York: Oxford University Press, 1978), 45.

10. "Fr. Coughlin Wars on Liberty League," *Daily Boston Globe*, October 29, 1934, 3; "Coughlin Criticizes Cardinal O'Connell," *New York Times*, December 10, 1934, 3. Samuel Moyn dates the birth of formal human rights discourse to 1940. Samuel Moyn,

The Last Utopia: Human Rights in History (Cambridge, MA: Belknap Press of Harvard University Press, 2010), 44.

11. Report, Christian Front meeting July 1, 1940, Hibernian Hall, Jewish Community Relations Council of Greater Boston, I-123, box 44, folder 5, Wyner Family Jewish Heritage Center at New England Historic Genealogical Society, Boston (hereafter JHC).

12. "Christian Front Report," July 15, 1940, Jewish Community Relations Council of Greater Boston, I-123, box 44, folder 5, JHC.

13. Richard Walter Thomas, *Life for Us Is What We Make It: Building Black Community in Detroit, 1915–1945* (Bloomington: Indiana University Press, 1992), 169.

14. Memorandum of telephone call, Walter Mendelsohn to CTF (Coordinating Task Force), April 30, 1940, reel 23 of 23, Series B: General Office File, part 18: special subjects, 1940–1955, Jews 1940–1941, papers of the National Association for the Advancement of Colored People (hereafter NAACP papers), microfilm reproduced from the Library of Congress.

15. A. Clayton Powell to "Dear Walter" [Walter White], April 26, 1940, reel 23 of 23, Series B: General Office File, part 18: special subjects, 1940–1955, Jews 1940–1941, NAACP papers.

16. Alec Marsh, review of *The Coming American Fascism*, by Lawrence Dennis, *Callaloo* 31, no. 4 (2008): 1362; Edward A. Soucy to J. Edgar Hoover, re: United States vs. Gerald B. Winrod, July 22, 1943, 11, Francis P. Moran FBI file, 1224676-0-097–HQ–827, Section 4, released through USFOIA.

17. William Leonard, "The Failure of Catholic Interracialism in Boston before Busing," in *Boston's Histories: Essays in Honor of Thomas H. O'Connor*, ed. James M. O'Toole and David Quigley (Boston: Northeastern University Press, 2004), 229.

18. James Chappel, *Catholic Modern: The Challenge of Totalitarianism and the Remaking of the Church* (Cambridge, MA: Harvard University Press, 2018), 62; Kevin P. Spicer, *Hitler's Priests: Catholic Clergy and National Socialism* (DeKalb: Northern Illinois University Press, 2008), 271.

19. Richard Steigmann-Gall, *The Holy Reich: Nazi Conceptions of Christianity, 1919–1945* (New York: Cambridge University Press, 2003), 95.

20. Chappel, *Catholic Modern*, 63.

21. "Francis P. Moran, Director of the Christian Front, Boston, 108 Massachusetts Ave., Boston, Oct. 11, 1940," drawer A3, folder "Moran, Francis P.," Avedis (Arthur) Derounian papers, Mardigian Library, National Association for Armenian Studies and Research, Belmont, MA.

22. John Roy Carlson [Arthur Derounian], "Anti-Semitism Under Full Steam in Boston," *New York Post*, December 29, 1943.

23. For English-language discussion of the Führer's Order of September 1939 and the original German-language text, see German Ministry of Foreign Affairs, "Foreign Pro-

paganda and Warfare: The 'Führer's Order,'" https://www.auswaertiges-amt.de/en/aamt/politiscal-archive/-/215212.

24. "Let Us Be Realistic," *Boston Herald-Traveler*, May 28, 1940 [copy], CRC 2, box 133, file 17, Community Relations Conference, Boston, 1940, Community Relations Committee Papers, Jewish Federation Council of Greater Los Angeles, Special Collections and Archives, Oviatt Library, California State University, Northridge, CA (hereafter CSUN).

25. Kurt Bohme to City Editor of the *Boston Herald-Traveler*, May 31, 1940, [copy], CRC 2, box 133, file 17, Community Relations Conference, Boston, 1940, Community Relations Committee Papers, Jewish Federation Council of Greater Los Angeles, CSUN; "Nazi Consul's Ouster Urged in City Council Resolution," *Boston Evening Transcript*, June 10, 1940, [copy], CRC 2, box 133, file 17, Community Relations Conference, Boston, 1940, Community Relations Committee Papers, Jewish Federation Council of Greater Los Angeles, CSUN; "Traveler v. Führer" *Time* 35, no. 25 (June 1940), 60. Sullivan's defense of a free press was ironic given that he was simultaneously calling for bookstores to ban John P. Marquand's novel *H. M. Pulham, Esquire*, which scandalously depicted adultery. Neil Miller, *Banned in Boston: The Watch and Ward Society's Crusade against Books, Burlesque, and the Social Evil* (Boston: Beacon Press, 2010), 179.

26. Francis P. Moran, Director, to City Editor, *Boston Herald-Traveler*, June 5, 1940, Jewish Community Relations Council of Greater Boston, I-123, Boston, box 168, folder 1, JHC.

27. Henry W. Levy to Louis E. Kirstein, memorandum, June 17, 1940, Jewish Community Relations Council of Greater Boston, I-123, box 168, folder 1, JHC; "YD Veterans Urge President to Give Allies Aid They Need," *Boston Herald*, June 8, 1940, 1; "100,000 See YD Parade," *Boston Herald*, June 9, 1940, 1.

8. Rifles and Rhetoric

1. "Brüning on the Rise of the Nazis to Power," undated, typewritten interview, 9, Heinrich Brüning Personal Archive and Brüning Family Archive, box 18, folder 7, "Interview," HUGFP, Harvard University Archives, Cambridge, MA (hereafter Brüning Archive, Harvard).

2. William L. Patch Jr., *Heinrich Bruning and the Dissolution of the Weimar Republic* (Cambridge: Cambridge University Press, 1998), 312; Klemens von Klemperer, *German Resistance against Hitler: The Search for Allies Abroad* (Oxford: Clarendon Press, 1992), 55; Peer Oliver Volkmann, *Heinrich Brüning (1885–1970): Nationalist ohne Heimat* (Dusseldorf: Droste, 2007), 326–327.

3. Dr. Herbert Scholz to Heinrich Brüning, October 17, 1939, box 36, folder 5, "Dr. Herbert Scholz," Brüning Archive, Harvard.

4. "Brüning on the Rise of the Nazis to Power," 23, 29; Choate, Hall & Stewart to "Dear Mr. Consul," April 25, 1940, unsigned letter, box 36, folder 5, "Dr. Herbert Scholz," Brüning Archive, Harvard.

5. J. Edgar Hoover to Adolf A. Berle Jr., December 18, 1939, R 59, General Records of the Department of State, Decimal File, box C309, file 862.20211, Trott, Adam von/9, National Archives and Records Administration, Archives II, College Park, MD (hereafter NARA).

6. "Virgil Peterson, 84, Chicago Crime Expert," obituary, *New York Times*, March 2, 1989.

7. Roger Moorhouse, *The Devils' Alliance: Hitler's Pact with Stalin, 1939–41* (London: Bodley Head, 2014), 119.

8. George Johnson Armstrong to Scholz, November 19, 1940 [typewritten copy], George Johnson Armstrong file, Home Office, HO 144/21558, UK National Archives, Kew, Richmond; "Easy Money Armstrong—Traitor," *The Express*, undated news clipping, George Johnson Armstrong file, news cuttings after execution, Home Office, HO 144/21558, UK National Archives, Kew.

9. Jonathan N. Brown, "'A Valuable Man in the Right Place': The Untold Story of Fritz Fenthol and the Belmonte Letter," *Journal of Intelligence History* 20, no. 2 (2020); Memorandum re Fritz Fenthol, August 6, 1941, 32–35, Record Group 59, State Department Central Files 1940-44, Confidential File, 250/34/21/5, Box C280, 862.20211 Fenthol, Fritz/36, NARA; Memo, John Edgar Hoover to Mr. Frederick B. Lyon, May 23, 1946, Scholz FBI file, 65–HQ–4414, section 2, released through United States Freedom of Information Act (hereafter USFOIA). Curiously, after his trip to Boston, Fenthol traveled to Washington, DC, and spent the entire of day of August 7, 1940, visiting the National Catholic Welfare Conference, the organizational hub of the American Catholic bishops. Fenthol would later be implicated in British intelligence's Belmonte letter ruse. I am grateful to Jonathan N. Brown of Sam Houston State University for sharing information on Fenthol's trip to Boston.

10. Robert A. Miller, *A True Story of an American Nazi Spy: William Curtis Colepaugh* (Bloomington, IN: Trafford, 2013), 40; David Kahn, *Hitler's Spies: German Military Intelligence in World War II* (New York: Macmillan, 1978), 8; Barbara Klaw, "The American Boy Who Became a German Spy," *New York Post*, January 2, 1945, 4. Miller mistakenly refers to Scholz as Dr. Herman Shultz.

11. Confidential report, G-2/10101–2031, October 23, 1940, "bogus birth certificates," RG 319 Army Staff, Office of the Chief of Staff for Intelligence, Intelligence and Investigative Dossiers, Personal Name File 1939–1976, container 692, Scholz, Herbert W., NARA.

12. Christopher Vasey, *Nazi Intelligence Operations in Non-Occupied Territories: Espionage Efforts in the United States, Britain, South America and Southern Africa* (Jefferson, NC: McFarland, 2016), 32.

13. Memo, Christian Front Meeting, August 26, 1940, Hibernian Hall, 2, Jewish Community Relations Council of Greater Boston, I-123, box 44, folder 5, Wyner Family Jewish Heritage Center at New England Historic Genealogical Society, Boston (hereafter JHC).

14. "Sen. Lundeen Bests Army's Marksmen," *Philadelphia Inquirer*, May 10, 1940, 7; Ray Bearse, *Sporting Arms of the World* (New York: Outdoor Life / Harper and Row, 1976), 28, 29.

15. Alton Frye, *Nazi Germany and the American Hemisphere* (New Haven, CT: Yale University Press, 1967), 161.

16. Ian V. Hogg, *The Complete Illustrated Encyclopedia of the World's Firearms* (New York: A and W, 1978), 202.

17. Peter Duffy, *Double Agent: The First Hero of World War II and How the FBI Outwitted and Destroyed a Nazi Spy Ring* (New York: Scribner, 2014), 216, 259. See also the FBI information video "USA Homefront: German Agents, Duquesne Spy Ring," Footage Farm, RI 2/2 250096, https://www.youtube.com/watch?v=I9OWfd—DNG.

18. Memo, Christian Front Meeting, August 26, 1940; Report, Moran—Christian Front—Hibernian Hall, September 9, 1940, Jewish Community Relations Council of Greater Boston, I-123, box 44, folder 5, JHC.

19. Moran circular letter, "Fellow Serfs!" September 26, 1940, Jewish Community Relations Council of Greater Boston, I-123, box 44, folder 5, JHC.

20. Report, May 24, [1940], Jewish Community Relations Council of Greater Boston, I-123, box 44, folder 5, JHC.

21. Report, The Christian Front, May 16, 1941, Anti-Semitic and Extremist Collection, box 53, folder "Christian Front 2," American Jewish Committee Archives, New York.

22. Report, Christian Front Meeting, August 12, 1940, Hibernian Hall, Roxbury, MA, Jewish Community Relations Council of Greater Boston, I-123, box 44, folder 5, JHC.

23. Moran circular letter, "To American [word obscured]," September 9, 1940, Francis P. Moran FBI file, 1224676-0-097–HQ–827, Section 1, released through USFOIA.

24. "Reports of Confidential Informant," name redacted, "Report dated June 23, 1941," 26, contained in report, J.H. Foley, November 18, 1941, Francis P. Moran, Francis P. Moran FBI file, 1224676-0-097–HQ–827, Section 1, released through USFOIA.

25. Report, "CF Boston," October 7, 1940, Jewish Community Relations Council of Greater Boston, I-123, box 44, folder 5, JHC.

26. Moran circular letter, "To the American Congress," October 21, 1940, papers of the Non-Sectarian Anti-Nazi League to Champion Human Rights, series 1, correspondence, 1917–1975, box 8, folder "investigative files: General: Christian Front—Moran," Rare Book and Manuscript Library, Columbia University, New York.

27. Report of October 4, 1941, name redacted, contained in report, J. H. Foley, November 18, 1941, 54. Francis P. Moran FBI file 1224676-0-097–HQ–827, Section 1, released through USFOIA; Report, "from ADL," October 21, 1940, Jewish Community Relations Council of Greater Boston, I-123, box 44, folder 5, JHC.

28. Christian Front report, February 17, 1941, addendum, "My Observations for What They Are Worth," Jewish Community Relations Council of Greater Boston, I-123, box 44, folder 5, JHC.

29. Report, "First Annual Banquet and Ball in Honor of Father Coughlin's Birthday," Hotel Westminster, October 24, 1940, 1, Jewish Community Relations Council of Greater Boston, I-123, box 44, folder 5, JHC; "A Tribute to Father Coughlin: Read by a Priest at a Birthday Party," *Social Justice*, November 4, 1940, 19; "Conversations with Francis Moran," attached to letter, Edward A. Soucy to FBI Director, December 29, 1943, 12, Francis P. Moran FBI File, 1224676-0-097–HQ–827, Section 4, released through USFOIA.

30. Report, "First Annual Banquet and Ball in Honor of Father Coughlin's Birthday," 3–4; for the 1940 definition of Catholic fortitude, see *The Catechism of the Council of Trent*, http://www.saintsbooks.net/books/The%20Roman%20Catechism.pdf, 138.

31. "Christian Front Report," October 28, 1940, 3, Jewish Community Relations Council of Greater Boston, I-123, box 44, folder 5, JHC; Monthly Intelligence Summary, December 1–31 1940, Headquarters, Fifth Corps, Fort Hayes, Columbus, OH, reel 29 of 34, item 141, in *U.S. Military Intelligence Reports: Surveillance of Radicals in the United States, 1917–1941* [microform] (Frederick, MD: University Publications of America, 1984).

32. Christian Front circular, "To Christian Americans," December 9, 1940, Boston Jewish Community Relations Council papers, box 44, folder 4, JHC.

9. Kissing Hitler

1. "U.S. Uses First Force to Win Bloodless Victory in Battle of the Atlantic," *Life*, April 14, 1941, 23.

2. "Scholtz [sic], Dr. Herbert," CONFIDENTIAL list of visits to Captain of the Pauline Friederich, n.d., RG 319, Office of the Chief of Staff for Intelligence, G-2, Records of the Investigative Records Repository, Intelligence and Investigative Dossiers, Personal Name File, container 692, Scholz, Gerda L., HE058865 through Schott, Lisa, GE007964, National Archives and Records Administration, Archives II, College Park, MD (hereafter NARA).

3. U.S. vs. Kurt Walter Laufer, et al., indictment, 3, RG 21, District Courts of the United States, USDC, MA Criminal, Criminal Case Files, 15305–15354, container 232; and United States of America vs. Ernest R. Heitzman, et al., 1, Case Record 15348, USDC, MA Criminal, Criminal Case Files, container 232; both in U.S. National Archives at Boston, Waltham, MA; "Recall," *Greenfield Recorder-Gazette* [MA], April 3, 1941, 8.

4. "To Our Fellow Americans: The Christian Front of America," n.d., Jewish Community Relations Council of Greater Boston, I-123, box 44, folder 4, Wyner Family Jewish Heritage Center at New England Historic Genealogical Society, Boston (hereafter JHC).

5. "Nazi Naval Attaché Faces U.S. Eviction," *New York Daily News*, April 5, 1941, 7.

6. Index card, "German Consuls, Propaganda by," CONFIDENTIAL, received by G2 on June 24, 1941, from informant 1-ND, Army Staff, RG 319, Office of the Chief of Staff

for Intelligence, G-2, Records of the Investigative Records Repository, Intelligence and Investigative Dossiers, Personal Name File, Scholz, Herbert W., NARA.

7. "Isolationists Cheer Marshall, Heckle Shattuck in Debate," *Boston Herald*, January 16, 1941, 1; on Marshall's biography, see Lisa L. Ossian, *The Home Fronts of Iowa, 1939–1945* (Columbia: University of Missouri Press, 2009), 12; on Shattuck's reputation as a hawk, see Porter Sargent, *Getting US into War* (Boston: P. Sargent, 1941), 531; Henry W. Levy to Joseph Roos, January 17, 1941, CRC 2, box 133, file 18, Community Relations Conference, Boston, January–May 1941, Community Relations Committee Papers, Jewish Federation Council of Greater Los Angeles, Special Collections and Archives, Oviatt Library, California State University, Northridge, CA.

8. Lt. Col. A. R. Bolling, "UnAmerican Groups," CONFIDENTIAL, Monthly Intelligence Summary #9, reports for April 1–April 30, 1941, *U.S. Military Intelligence Reports: Surveillance of Radicals in the United States, 1917–1941* [microform] (Frederick, MD: University Publications of America, 1984), reel 24, item #532. On Moriarty and his possible involvement in Moran's visit to Camp Edwards, see George A. Moriarty FBI File, FOIPA No. 0980262-000, Department of Justice, Internet Archive, https://archive.org/stream/MORIARTYGeorgeAndrewsBoston1002012/MORIARTY%2C%20George%20Andrews%20-%20Boston%20100-2012_djvu.txt; Christian Front Report, March 10, 1941, unsigned, Jewish Community Relations Council of Greater Boston, I-123, box 44, folder 5, JHC.

9. "Furloughs for Jews during Passover," *Daily Boston Globe*, March 29, 1941, 13.

10. Christian Front Report, March 10, 1941, 2, unsigned, Jewish Community Relations Council of Greater Boston, I-123, box 44, folder 5, JHC.

11. War Department, MID, CONFIDENTIAL, April 17, 1941, Christian Front weekly meeting, *U.S. Military Intelligence Reports: Surveillance of Radicals in the United States, 1917–1941* [microform] (Frederick, MD: University Publications of America, 1984), reel 24, item #541.

12. Christian Front Meeting, April 15, 1941, Jewish Community Relations Council of Greater Boston, I-123, box 44, folder 5, JHC; War Department, MID, April 17, 1941, 4.

13. "Current Criticisms Not Based on Facts, Globe Writer Told," *Daily Boston Globe*, November 24, 1940, B1; "'Fatigue Duty' at Camp Edwards Is Dispensed With," *Daily Boston Globe*, March 5, 1941, 6; Headquarters First Corps Area, Office of the Assistant Chief Of Staff, G-2, Monthly Intelligence Summary No. 9, April 1–April 30, 1941, *U.S. Military Intelligence Reports: Surveillance of Radicals in the United States, 1917–1941* [microform] (Frederick, MD: University Publications of America, 1984), reel 24, item #563.

14. Rolf Giesen, *Nazi Propaganda Films: A History and Filmography* (Jefferson, NC: McFarland, 2003), 70.

15. Manvell quoted in Philip M. Taylor, *Munitions of the Mind: A History of Propaganda from the Ancient World to the Present Era*, 3rd ed. (Manchester: Manchester

University Press, 2003), 244; Matthew C. Gunter, *The Capra Touch: A Study of the Director's Hollywood Classics and War Documentaries, 1934–1945* (Jefferson, NC: McFarland, 2011), 125.

16. Report of the Christian Front Meeting, June 2, 1941, 3, Jewish Community Relations Council of Greater Boston, I-123, box 44, folder 5, JHC.

17. "Christian Front Audience Sees Nazi Film, Opposes US Draft," *FBIS Daily Reports of Shortwave Radio Broadcasts*, FBIS-FRB-41, September 17, 1941. An archive of the Foreign Broadcast Information Service (FBIS) reports is available at https://www.readex.com /products/foreign-broadcast-information-service-fbis-daily-reports-1941-1996.

18. "Showing of Nazi Propaganda Film Is Un-American Declares State Commander of VFW," June 3, 1941, press release, [copy], statement issued by Edward A. O'Brien, commander of the Massachusetts department of the Veterans of Foreign Wars, box 44, folder 3, JHC; "Text of President's Speech of Defiance to Axis Powers," *Washington Post*, May 28, 1941, 1; Veterans Urge Bay State Ban on Nazi Blitz Films," *Daily Boston Globe*, June 4, 1941, 1.

19. "Veterans Urge Bay State Ban"; Memo to F. Frank Vorneberg, Ben W. Solekman and David N. Watemaker, June 4, 1941, Jewish Community Relations Council of Greater Boston, I-123, box 44, folder 3, JHC; "Veterans Refuse Bid to Nazi Blitz Film," *Daily Boston Globe*, June 5, 1941, 9.

20. "Veterans Refuse Bid to Nazi Blitz Film."

21. Christopher Peter Latimer, *Civil Liberties and the State: A Documentary and Reference Guide* (Santa Barbara, CA: Greenwood, 2011), 133–134.

22. Monthly Intelligence Summary, June 1–30, 1941, Christian Front, U.S. Military Intelligence Reports: Surveillance of Radicals in the United States, 1917–1941 [microform] (Frederick, MD: University Publications of America, 1984), Military Intelligence Division, G-2, reel 24, item #563. On Hoover's interpretation of the Smith Act as an exclusively anti-Communist law, see Arthur J. Sabin, *In Calmer Times: The Supreme Court and Red Monday* (Philadelphia: University of Pennsylvania Press, 1999), 12; George W. Spicer, *The Supreme Court and Fundamental Freedoms* (New York: Appleton-Century-Crofts, 1959), 156.

23. John Edgar Hoover to Special Agent in Charge, Boston, December 31, 1941, 2, Francis P. Moran FBI file, 1224676-0-097–HQ–827, Section 1, released through United States Freedom of Information Act (hereafter USFOIA).

24. D. D. Terry to J. Edgar Hoover, June 24, 1941, Francis P. Moran FBI file, 1224676-0-097–HQ–827. Section 1, released through USFOIA; Athan G. Theoharis and John Stuart Cox, *The Boss: J. Edgar Hoover and the Great American Inquisition* (Philadelphia: Temple University Press, 1988), 136.

25. John Edgar Hoover, Memorandum for the Assistant to the Attorney General Mister Matthew F. Maguire, [copy], September 10, 1941, Francis P. Moran FBI file, 1224676-0-097–HQ–827, Section 1, released through USFOIA; Thomas Sakmyster, "Nazi Documentaries of Intimidation: 'Feldzug in Polen' (1940), 'Feuertaufe' (1940) and 'Sieg im

Westen' (1941)," *Historical Journal of Film, Radio and Television* 16, no. 4 (September 1996): 485–514, 498.

26. Leon M. Birkhead, [copy], telegram to Secretary of State, June 5, 1941, contained in report, J. H. Foley, Francis P. Moran: Internal Security–G, November 18, 1941, Francis P. Moran FBI file, 1224676-0-097–HQ–827, Section 1, released through USFOIA; "Acts to Restrict Axis Propaganda," *New York Times*, June 23, 1941, 13.

27. "Acts to Restrict Axis Propaganda."

28. John Edgar Hoover to Special Agent in Charge, Boston, Special Inquiry State Department, August 1, 1941, Francis P. Moran FBI file, 1224676-0-097–HQ–827, Section 1, released through USFOIA.

29. "Veterans Refuse Bid to Nazi Blitz Film"; Anthony Slide, *The International Film Industry: A Historical Dictionary* (New York: Greenwood Press, 1989), 358; Hoover to Maguire, September 10, 1941.

30. Report, J. W. Coulter, Francis P. Moran: Internal Security–G, January 23, 1942, 24–31, Francis P. Moran FBI file, 1224676-0-097–HQ–827, Section 1, released through USFOIA.

31. "Report of August 6, 1941," confidential informant with name redacted, Francis P. Moran FBI file, 1224676-0-097–HQ–827, Section 1, released through USFOIA; John Edgar Hoover to Special Agent in charge, Boston, December 31, 1941, Francis P. Moran FBI file, 1224676-0-097–HQ–827, Section 1, released through USFOIA; "Police Officers in School at Harvard Begin Course," *Christian Science Monitor*, November 24, 1941, 5.

32. "Closing of German and Italian Consulates in the United States," *Department of State Bulletin*, vol. 4, June 21, 1941, 743.

33. "Consulate Closing Huge 'Joke,'" *Boston Herald*, June 17, 1941, 1.

34. Christian Front circular letter, "To Honest Roosevelt Supporters," July 23, 1941, box 44, folder 4, July 23, 1941, JHC.

35. Report, Christian Front Meeting, O'Connell Hall, June 23, 1941, 1, Jewish Community Relations Council of Greater Boston, I-123, box 44, folder 5, JHC.

36. File card attached to report of June 23, 1941 Christian Front meeting, "6/30/41, Sent to: ADL office, V. W. Peterson, Col. Bolling," Boston Jewish Community Relations Council papers, box 44, folder 5, "Christian Front meetings, propaganda, Moran," JHC.

37. Report, J. H. Foley, November 18, 1941, Francis P. Moran, Internal Security–G, November 18, 1941, 40, Francis P. Moran FBI file, 1224676-0-097–HQ–827, Section 1, released through USFOIA.

38. Report of Confidential Informant T-1, SAC James F. Mahan, August 23, 1942, contained in report, J. W. Coulter, Francis P. Moran, Internal Security–G, November 18, 1941, 21, Francis P. Moran FBI file, 1224676-0-097–HQ–827, Section 3, released through USFOIA; "Nazi Consulate Ordered to Stop Burning Papers," *Daily Boston Globe*, June 26, 1941, 1.

39. Report dated July 9, 1941, from confidential informant with name redacted, contained in J. H. Foley report, November 18, 1941, 29, 39, Francis P. Moran FBI file, 1224676-0-097–HQ–827, Section 1; "U.S. Guns Defective, Christian Fronter Says," *Boston Herald-Traveler*, August 5, 1941, 3, *Boston Herald-Traveler* clippings morgue, Pickering Educational Resources Library, Boston University.

40. "Report on Investigations in Europe," by O. John Rogge, Special Assistant to the Attorney General, September 17, 1946, 144, Tom C. Clark papers, box 117, Supreme Court file, Harry S. Truman Presidential Library, Independence, MO.

41. Reports on Interrogation of German Prisoners-of-War Made by Members of the Department of State Special Interrogation Mission (September 1945 to September 1946) headed by DeWitt C. Poole [microform] (Washington, DC: National Archives and Records Service, 1953), reel 1, Heribert von Strempel file, 6.

42. Peterson (Virgil W. Peterson) to Director (J. Edgar Hoover), telegram, November 15, 1941, Francis P. Moran FBI file, 1224676-0-097–HQ–827, Section 1, released through USFOIA.

43. Confidential informant with name redacted, report, September 2, 1941, contained in J. H. Foley, report, November 18, 1941, 48, Francis P. Moran FBI file, 1224676-0-097–HQ–827, Section 1, released through USFOIA.

44. Report, Meeting of the Christian Front, October 20, 1941, Jewish Community Relations Council of Greater Boston, I-123, box 44, folder 5, JHC.

45. Report, Meeting of the Christian Front, October 27, 1941, Hibernian Hall, Jewish Community Relations Council of Greater Boston, I-123, box 44, folder 5, JHC; Confidential informant with name redacted, report of October 31, 1941, contained in J. H. Foley, report, November 18, 1941, 62, Francis P. Moran FBI file, 1224676-0-097–HQ–827, Section 1.

46. Report, Meeting of the Christian Front, October 27, 1941, 2, JHC.

47. Roger Griffin, "The 'Holy Storm': 'Clerical Fascism' through the Lens of Modernism," *Totalitarian Movements and Political Religions* 8, no. 2 (June 2007): 213–227, 220; Francis P. Moran, transcription of Thanksgiving Day postcard to Christian Front members, November 27, 1941, attached to report, J. W. Coulter, Francis P. Moran: Internal Security–G, January 23, 1942, 2, Francis P. Moran FBI file, 1224676-0-097–HQ–827, Section 1, released through USFOIA. On Nazi mysticism, see Eric Kurlander, *Hitler's Monsters: A Supernatural History of the Third Reich* (New Haven, CT: Yale University Press, 2017), 121.

10. Questions of the Most Delicate Kind

1. "Defense Group of Boston Irish Backs President," *Christian Science Monitor*, November 12, 1941, 5; Report, Christian Front meeting, Hibernian Hall, December 1, 1941, Walton E. Cole papers, box 1, folder 12, "The Christian Front, August 19, 1939–December 22, 1941," 1, Special Collections, Honnold/Mudd Library, Claremont Colleges, Claremont, CA.

2. "Dreadful Symbol," letter to the editor, *Daily Boston Globe*, December 12, 1941, 26; "Irish Defense Association Urges Unity," *Boston Herald*, December 8, 1941, 28.

3. Isabel Currier, "Monument Of, For, and By the Living," *Common Ground* 9, no. 1 (September 1948): 33–41, 35.

4. "Senator Wheeler of Montana Exposes the 'American Irish Defense' Group in the Senate of the United States," *The Advocate*, November 22, 1941, 1; Report, Christian Front Meeting, December 1, 1941; "Irish Neutrality Lien Repudiates Committee for American Defense," *The Advocate*, October 18, 1941, 5; "No More 'Committees,'" letter to the editor, *Daily Boston Globe*, December 12, 1941, 26.

5. "Wheeler Blasts Irish-American War Propaganda," *Chicago Tribune*, November 11, 1941, 17. Wheeler quoted on Lend-Lease in Robert Dallek, *Franklin D. Roosevelt and American Foreign Policy, 1932–1945* (New York: Oxford University Press, 1995), 259. On British "mentoring" of US intelligence agencies, see Jay Jakub, *Spies and Saboteurs: Anglo-American Collaboration and Rivalry in Human Intelligence Collection and Special Operations, 1940–45* (London: Palgrave Macmillan, 1999).

6. Declaration of the Committee for Irish American Defense, n.d., Christopher Temple Emmet papers, box 13, subject file, American Irish Defense, Hoover Institution Archives. Thomas E. Mahl, *Desperate Deception: British Covert Operations in the United States, 1939–1944* (Washington, DC: Brassey's, 1998), 40.

7. Charles C. Kolb, review of William S. Stephenson, ed., *British Security Coordination: The Secret History of British Intelligence in the Americas 1940–1945* (New York: Fromm International, 1998), H-Diplo, December 1999, https://networks.h-net.org/node /28443/reviews/30102/kolb-stephenson-british-security-coordination-secret-history -british; Nigel West, "Introduction," in William S. Stephenson, ed., *British Security Coordination: The Secret History of British Intelligence in the Americas, 1940–1945* (New York: Fromm International, 1999), xii.

8. West, "Introduction," xv. See also Timothy J. Naftali, "Intrepid's Last Deception: Documenting the Career of Sir William Stephenson," *Intelligence and National Security* 8, no. 3 (July 1993): 72–99.

9. See "Organizing the Irish," n.a., in *British Security Coordination*, ed. Stephenson, 85–87; Eunan O'Halpin, "Intelligence and Anglo-Irish Relations, 1922–1973," in *Intelligence, Statecraft, and International Power: Papers Read before the 27th Irish Conference of Historians Held at Trinity College, Dublin, 19–21 May 2005*, ed. Eunan O'Halpin, Robert Armstrong, and Jane Ohlmeyer (Dublin: Irish Academic Press, 2006), 135; Robert Cole, *Propaganda, Censorship and Irish Neutrality in the Second World War* (Edinburgh: University of Edinburgh Press, 2006), 27.

10. David Ignatius, "Britain's War in America: How Churchill's Agents Secretly Manipulated the U.S. before Pearl Harbor," *Washington Post*, September 17, 1989, C1.

11. Bill Hayden, "'Target' a News Thriller," *Journal News* [Nyack, NY], August 21, 1979, 9.

12. Christopher Andrew, *Secret World: A History of Intelligence* (New Haven: Yale University Press, 2018), 609. On black propaganda, generally, see Nigel West, *Historical*

Dictionary of British Intelligence, 2nd ed. (Lanham, MD: Rowman and Littlefield, 2014), 506.

13. Keith Jeffrey, *MI6: The History of the Secret Intelligence Service, 1909–1949* (London: Bloomsbury, 2010), 453.

14. "Report on Our Journey," n.d., 4, HS 8/118, SOE America, file 122, November 1940–July 1945, miscellanea, secret file, UK National Archives, Kew, Richmond, UK.

15. Campbell Stuart to "My Dear Cadogan," March 17, 1941, Secret, cover letter and report, "Notes on Irish-American Opinion," F.O. 371/273/68, General, 1941, Dominions Intelligence File, 88, UK National Archives, Kew.

16. Stuart to Cadogan," March 17, 1941; "Dr. Agar Calls on Austrians to Fight Nazis," *Boston Herald*, May 26, 1941, 5; "Comments by William Agar on the New England Situation," n.d., SOE America files, No. 61, HS8/56, American Irish Defense Association, 1st Report, October, 1941, UK National Archives, Kew.

17. "Father Ahern Calls Communism and Nazism Two of a Kind," report, July 29, 1941, SOE America files, No. 61, HS8/56, American Irish Defense Association, 1st Report, October 1941, UK National Archives, Kew. Ahern was not the only adherent of a concept described elsewhere as "red fascism," which saw Nazism as having emanated from Communism. See Thomas R. Maddux, "Red Fascism, Brown Bolshevism: The American Image of Totalitarianism in the 1930s," *Historian* 40, no. 2 (November 1977): 85–103.

18. Telegram No. 661, [copy], A.C.C.S. ONLY, cipher telegram from New York, July 23, 1941, SOE America file 122, H58/118, secret, November 1940 to July 1945, MISCELLANEA, UK National Archives, Kew.

19. Telegram No. 661, July 23, 1941. Code name 4800 was an allusion to Stephenson's absolute control of British intelligence in the United States, which then comprised forty-eight states. David Dilks, "Flashes of Intelligence: The Foreign Office, the SIS, and Security before the Second World War," in *The Missing Dimension: Governments and Intelligence Communities in the Twentieth Century*, ed. Christopher M. Andrew and David Dilks (London: Macmillan, 2016), 103; Alexander Cadogan to Campbell Stuart, [copy], March 20, 1941, F.O. 371/273/68, General, 1941, Dominions Intelligence File, 82–89, UK National Archives, Kew. The author would like to thank Christopher Andrew for his assistance in trying to identify U. Christopher Andrew, email to author, September 29, 2016.

20. "Father Ahern Calls Communism and Nazism Two of a Kind," July 29, 1941, footnote; "Comments from William Agar on the New England Situation," n.d., SOE America files, No. 61, HS8/56, American Irish Defense Association, 1st Report, October 1941, 22, UK National Archives, Kew.

21. Alfred E. Smith to Dear Mr. Byrne [copy], September 5, 1941, SOE America files, No. 61, HS8/56, American Irish Defense Association, 1st Report, October 1941, 44, UK National Archives, Kew; Edward Burke to Dear Mr. Byrne, September 2, 1941, SOE America files, No. 61, HS8/56, American Irish Defense Association, 1st Report, Octo-

ber 1941, 43, UK National Archives, Kew; "Activities of Boston Group," n.d., SOE America files, No. 61, HS8/56, American Irish Defense Association, 1st Report, October 1941, 9, UK National Archives, Kew.

22. "England Called Short of Arms," *Christian Science Monitor,* July 18, 1941, 19; "Halifax Sees 100th Hudson Off for Britain," *Washington Post,* July 18, 1941, 11.

23. "Minister" to "Mr. Eden" [draft], November 24, 1941, [all marginalia in Churchill's script], HS 8/118, SOE America Files, 122, secret, miscellanea, November 1940–July 1945, UK National Archives, Kew.

24. "The Irish in Massachusetts," n.d., SOE America files, No. 61, HS8/56, American Irish Defense Association, 1st Report, October 1941, 18, UK National Archives, Kew; James Fisher has noted that a similar "anti-British, isolationist, anti-Communist" ethos helped the Christian Front insinuate itself in labor circles in New York in the 1930s and 1940s. See James T. Fisher, *On the Irish Waterfront: The Crusader, the Movie, and the Soul of the New York Waterfront* (Ithaca, NY: Cornell University Press, 2009), 81.

25. "Irish Situation in Boston," n.d., SOE America files, vol. 63, HS 8/58, American Irish Defence Association, Third and Fourth Report, November 1941, UK National Archives, Kew.

26. "Report on IADA Activities in Boston," November 28, 1941, HS 8/58, SOE America, vol. 63, American Irish Defence Association, Third and Fourth Report, November 1941, UK National Archives, Kew, Richmond, UK; "Irish Situation in Boston."

27. Joseph Nevins, Suren Moodliar, and Eleni Macrakis, *A People's Guide to Greater Boston* (Berkeley: University of California Press, 2020), 110; Nat Hentoff, *Boston Boy: Growing Up with Jazz and Other Rebellious Passions* (New York: Knopf, 1986; Philadelphia: Paul Dry Books, 2001), 77–80; "Boston Tolerance Leader Honored," *New York Post,* February 14, 1945, 18. The Foreign Agents Registration Act required individuals doing political or advocacy work on behalf of foreign entities to report any "disbursements in support of activities" to the federal government. Sweeney, who was paid $30 per week ($550 in 2020 dollars) out of BSC funds, never reported her salary—nor would she have seen any reason to. See Jacob R. Strauss, "The Foreign Agents Registration Act: An Overview," *In Focus* Congressional Research Service, December 1, 2017, https://heinonline.org/HOL/P?h=hein.crs/crsmthmbdvloo01&i=1.

28. Arnold Beichman, "Frances Sweeney Gives Life in Fight on Fascism," *PM,* June 20, 1944, 13; Patrick W. Carey, *Catholics in America: A History* (Westport, CT: Praeger, 2004), 90.

29. Beichman, "Frances Sweeney Gives Life."

30. Frances Sweeney to "My Dear Mr. Hicks," October 3, 1938, Granville Hicks papers, box 60, correspondence, subfile, Frances Sweeney, Special Collections Research Center, Syracuse University, Syracuse, NY (hereafter Frances Sweeney file, SCRC); Francis E. McMahon, "Frances Sweeney Is Dead, but Her Work Must Go On," *New York Post Daily Magazine,* July 1, 1944, 7.

31. Fifteenth Census of the United States, 1930, Sweeney, family #116, 25 Mount Vernon St., Boston, Suffolk County; Sixteenth Census of the United States, 1940, Sweeney, family #26, ward 17, Boston, Suffolk, Massachusetts.

32. Frances Sweeney to "Dear Mr. Hicks," September 3, 1938, Frances Sweeney file, SCRC.

33. "Harvard's Hicks," Social Justice, May 9, 1938, 19.

34. Stephen H. Norwood, "Complicity and Conflict: Columbia University's Response to Fascism, 1933–1937," Modern Judaism 27, no. 3 (October 2007), 267; Arthur Goldberg, "Foe of Mussolini to Talk on Dictatorship March 17," Buffalo Evening News, March 3, 1938, 14; Isabelle Richet, "Marion Cave Rosselli and the Transnational Women's Anti-Fascist Networks," Journal of Women's History 24, no. 3 (Fall 2012): 120–127; Beichman, "Frances Sweeney Gives Life."

35. Carl Levy, Gramsci and the Anarchists (New York: Berg, 1999), 230; Gaetano Salvemini, Under the Axe of Fascism (New York: Viking Press, 1936), 127.

36. Excerpts from letters from Miss Frances Sweeney, secretary, I.A.D.A. Boston chapter, indicating situation in New England, December 30, 1941, [copy], HS 8/58, SOE America vol. 63, American Irish Defence Association, Third and Fourth report, November 1941, 6, UK National Archives, Kew; Isabel Currier, "Monument Of, For, and By the Living," Common Ground 9, no. 1 (Autumn 1948), 35.

37. Henry W. Levy to Walter Winchell, December 8, 1941, 1, addendum to letter, John Edgar Hoover to Mr. V. W. Peterson, December 20, 1941, Francis P. Moran FBI file, 1224676-0-097–HQ–827, Section 1, released through United States Freedom of Information Act (hereafter USFOIA).

38. "To the Sovereign Authority—Our Fellow Citizens," Christian Front circular letter, December 8, 1941, drawer A3, folder "Moran, Francis P.," Avedis (Arthur) Derounian papers, Mardigian Library, National Association for Armenian Studies and Research, Belmont, MA.

39. "Christian Front Wants FDR Impeached after the War," PM, December 9, 1941, 10; Confidential informant, report on Christian Front Meeting, Hibernian Hall, December 8, 1941, 6, 9, attached to report, J. W. Coulter, Francis P. Moran—Internal Security G, January 23, 1942, Francis P. Moran FBI file, 1224676-0-097–HQ–827, Section 1, released through USFOIA; Levy to Winchell, December 8, 1941.

40. Victor Riesel, "U.S. Fascists Keep Up Work Unhindered," New York Post, December 26, 1941, 4; transcribed postcard from Francis P. Moran to Catherine Clancy, December 11, 1941, 3, included in J. W. Coulter, January 23, 1942, report, Francis P. Moran, Internal Security-G, Special Inquiry, Francis P. Moran FBI file, 1224676-0-097–HQ–827,Section 1, released through USFOIA.

41. Frances Sweeney to Ralph Barton Perry, December 10, 1941, records of the American Defense, Harvard Group, box 12, Frances Sweeney file, 1941–1945, Harvard University Archives, Cambridge, MA.

42. "Leonard Nimoy Guest of Honor at Theater Luncheon," *Boston College Colleague*, Boston College, April 1978, https://newspapers.bc.edu/?a=d&d=bccolleague19780401 -01.2.13.

43. "Priest Hits Racial Hatred," *Boston Daily Record*, October 27, 1941, correspondence file, 1928–1949, box 11, folder 1, John Louis Bonn, SJ papers, BC.1986.014, John J. Burns Library, Boston College (hereafter Bonn papers, BC); J. Kelly to John Louis Bonn, SJ, n.d., correspondence file, 1928–1949, Bonn papers, BC; address of 201 Maple St., Lynn, MA, to John Louis Bonn, S. J., October 26, 1941, correspondence file, 1928–1949, Bonn papers, BC.

44. Rev. John Louis Bonn, SJ, to "My Dear Ms. Sweeney," December 9, 1941, [copy], HS 8/60, SOE America, vol. 65, American Irish Defence Association, Sixth Report, January 1942, UK National Archives, Kew.

45. Sweeney to Perry, December 10, 1941.

46. Chas W. Freeman, ed., *Diplomat's Dictionary* (Collingdale, PA: Diane Publishing, 1994), 181; Jennet Conant, *The Irregulars: Roald Dahl and the British Spy Ring in Wartime Washington* (New York: Simon and Schuster, 2008), 141.

47. Excerpts from letters from Miss Frances Sweeney December 30, 1941. The turning point for the *Herald-Traveler*'s editors was the declaration of war. Sweeney saw the newspaper shift from pro-Coughlin to anti-Coughlin almost immediately. It was a bold move. If they kept it up, Sweeney speculated, "they won't have any Irish Catholic readers left."

48. Eric Thomas Chester, *Covert Network: Progressives, the International Rescue Committee, and the CIA* (Armonk, NY: M. E. Sharpe, 1995), 112–113; "Cherne and Hovgard to Address Ad Men," *Boston Herald*, December 14, 1941, 61.

49. Frances Sweeney to Ralph Barton Perry, December 12, 1941.

50. Excerpts from letters from Miss Frances Sweeney, December 30, 1941; "Rothwell Raps 'Front' Action," news release, [copy], December 22, 1941, box 1, folder 12, "Christian Front," Rev. Walton E. Cole papers, Special Collections, Claremont Colleges Library, Claremont, CA.

51. "Nazi Propaganda Sale Scored Here," *Boston Herald-Traveler*, January 2, 1942, 1, Nazi Propaganda file, *Boston Herald-Traveler* clippings morgue, Pickering Educational Resources Library, Boston University, Boston (hereafter *Boston Herald-Traveler* clippings morgue); J. W. Coulter interview with Mr. Frederick W. Lyons in report, J. W. Coulter, January 23, 1942, 26, Francis P. Moran FBI file, 1224676-0-097–HQ–827, Section 1, released through USFOIA.

52. "Police Seize 51 Books at Meeting Here," *Boston Herald-Traveler*, January 6, 1942, 1, Nazi Book Ban file, *Boston Herald-Traveler* clippings morgue; "Police Seize Pamphlets in Roxbury," *Boston Herald*, January 6, 1942, 1; "Moran Protests Pamphlet Ban," *Christian Science Monitor*, January 6, 1942, 2; "Moran Facing Probe by U.S.," *Boston Herald-Traveler*, n.d., Christian Front file, *Boston Herald-Traveler* clippings morgue; "Books by Viereck Banned by Timilty," *Christian Science Monitor*, January 5, 1942, 5.

53. "Christian Front Meeting Scene of Pamphlet Seizure," *Niagara Falls Gazette*, January 6, 1942, 10.

54. Report, Christian Front Meeting, January 5, 1942, Jewish Community Relations Council of Greater Boston, I-123, box 44, folder 5, Wyner Family Jewish Heritage Center at New England Historic Genealogical Society, Boston (hereafter JHC); "Seize Nazi Books at Meeting Here," news clipping, HS 8/60, SOE America files, vol. 65, UK National Archives, Kew. The clipping is one of ten in the archive.

55. Donald Grant, draft article, February 4, 1942, Jewish Community Relations Council of Greater Boston, I-123, box 44, folder 3, JHC; Donald Grant, "Coughlin's New Capital," *The Nation* 154, no. 12 (March 1942): 334–336.

56. "Frances Sweeney," *Commonweal* 40, no. 18 (August 1944), 427; Currier, "Monument Of, For, and By the Living," 36.

57. V. W. Peterson to Director, Federal Bureau of Investigation, Personal and Confidential letter re Henry W. Levy, January 2, 1942, Francis P. Moran FBI file, 1224676-0-097–HQ–827, Section 1, released through USFOIA. On custodial detention, see Mary Elizabeth Basile Chopas, *Searching for Subversives: The Story of Italian Internment in Wartime America* (Chapel Hill: University of North Carolina Press, 2017), 31; "World War II Enemy Alien Control Program Overview," US National Archives, https://www.archives.gov/research/immigration/enemy-aliens/ww2.

58. Murray B. Levin and George Blackwood, *The Compleat Politician: Political Strategy in Massachusetts* (Indianapolis: Bobbs-Merrill, 1962), 57; Eunice Howe interviewed by Eva Moseley, December 6, 1999, Belmont, MA, tape no. 2, side 1, Eunice Howe papers, Schlesinger Library, Radcliffe Institute, Harvard University, Cambridge, MA.

59. Memorandum of a conversation, J. W. Coulter and Dennis J. McCadden, January 8, 1942, contained in J. W. Coulter, report, January 23, 1942, 24.

60. "Seize Nazi Books at Meeting Here: Police Squad Steps into Christian Front Gathering," *Boston Herald-Traveler*, January 6, 1942, German Propaganda Books Distributed by Christian Front file, *Boston Herald-Traveler* clippings morgue.

61. Memorandum of a conversation, Coulter and McCadden.

62. "Mass to Ban Nazi Books," *Boston Herald-Traveler*, n.d., Christian Front file, *Boston Herald-Traveler* clippings morgue; Attorney General Robert T. Bushnell interviewed by J. W. Coulter, January 8, 1942, in J. W. Coulter, report, January 23, 1942, 25.

63. "Voices of Defeat," *Life*, April 13, 1942; Joseph F. Timilty, Police Commissioner, Boston, letter, *Life*, May 4, 1942, 5.

11. Underground

1. Statement of Francis P. Moran, January 7, 1942, Boston Police Headquarters, CRC 2, box 133, file 21, Community Relations Conference: January–February 1942, Community Relations Committee Papers, Jewish Federation Council of Greater Los Angeles, Special Collections and Archives, Oviatt Library, California State University, Northridge, CA.

2. See, for example, Jack Beatty, *The Rascal King: The Life and Times of James Michael Curley, 1874–1958* (Reading, MA: Addison-Wesley, 1993), 450.

3. Robert Sobel, *Coolidge: An American Enigma* (Washington, DC: Regnery, 2014), 137.

4. Statement of Francis P. Moran, January 7, 1942.

5. "Christian Front Leader Offers to Aid War Effort," *Daily Boston Globe*, January 8, 1942, HS 8/60, SOE America file, vol. 60, Irish American Defense Association, Sixth Report, UK National Archives, Kew, Richmond, UK; "Moran Facing Probe by U.S.," *Boston Herald-Traveler*, January 8, 1942, Nazi Propaganda file, Boston *Herald-Traveler* clippings morgue, Pickering Educational Resources Library, Boston University, Boston (hereafter *Boston Herald-Traveler* clippings morgue).

6. Moran quoted in "Christian Front Books under Police Scrutiny," *Daily Boston Globe*, January 7, 1942, 6; Timilty quoted in "Christian Front Records Turned Over to Police," *Boston Herald-Traveler*, January 7, 1942, Nazi Propaganda file, *Boston Herald-Traveler* clippings morgue.

7. Report of October 21, 1941, addendum to J. H. Foley, report, November 18, 1941, 57, Francis P. Moran Internal Security—G, Francis P. Moran FBI file, 1224676-0-097–HQ–827, Section 1, released through United States Freedom of Information Act (hereafter USFOIA).

8. "Developing Situations—The Irish in Boston," report, September 11, 1942, U.S. Office of Strategic Services, Foreign Nationalities Branch Files, microfiche, INT 16IR-9 (Bethesda, MD: University Publications of America, 1988).

9. Statement of Francis P. Moran, January 7, 1942.

10. Report, Christian Front meeting, April 15, 1941, Jewish Community Relations Council of Greater Boston, I-123, box 44, folder 5, Wyner Family Jewish Heritage Center at New England Historic Genealogical Society, Boston (hereafter JHC).

11. Report of Confidential Informant T-1, 13, attached to James F. Mahan, report, Francis P. Moran, custodial detention—G, June 5, 1943, Francis P. Moran FBI file, 1224676-0-097–HQ–827, Section 3, released through USFOIA; J. W. Coulter, report, "Results of Confidential Informant REDACTED set out. REDACTED also set out," 11, February 6, 1943, entry for June 9, 1942, Francis P. Moran FBI file, 1224676-0-097–HQ–827, Section 3, released through USFOIA.

12. Report of Confidential Informant T-1, June 5, 1943, 13.

13. Report of Confidential Informant T-1, July 25, 1942, 20, addendum to J. W. Coulter, report, "Results of Confidential Informant REDACTED set out. REDACTED also set out," February 6, 1943, Francis P. Moran FBI file, 1224676-0-097–HQ–827, Section 3, released through USFOIA.

14. Memorandum of Conversation, Francis Moran, at his home, November 14, 1942, drawer A3, folder Moran, Francis P., Avedis (Arthur) Derounian papers, Mardigian Library, National Association for Armenian Studies and Research, Belmont, MA.

15. Gene A. Coyle, "John Franklin Carter: Journalist, FDR's Secret Investigator, Soviet Agent?" *International Journal of Intelligence and Counterintelligence* 24, no. 1 (December 2010): 148–172.

16. "Report on 'Sedition' among the South Boston Irish," January 26, 1942, FDR Papers as President, President's Secretary's File, Carter, John Franklin, Franklin Delano Roosevelt Presidential Library, http://www.fdrlibrary.marist.edu/_resources/images/psf/psfco217.pdf.

17. WPA Interview with John W. McCormack as Speaker of the House, May 18, 1971, John W. McCormack Papers: Audio Tape Interviews, reel 1, Howard Gottlieb Archival Research Center, Boston University, Boston, MA; Gerard O'Neill, *Rogues and Redeemers: When Politics Was King in Irish Boston* (New York: Crown, 2012), 122–123.

18. Report, "Boston and Father Curran," April 7, 1942, 1, microfiche, INT 16IR-11, Foreign Nationalities Branch Files, U.S. Office of Strategic Services (Bethesda, MD: University Publications of America, 1988).

19. Report on address delivered by Rev. Edward L. Curran of Brooklyn, January 31, 1942, at the Mattapan District Meeting of the Knights of Columbus, Hyde Park High School, Edward Lodge Curran file, Jewish Community Relations Council of Greater Boston, I-123, box 46, folder 1, JHC.

20. Frances Sweeney to Mr. D. C. Poole, March 9, 1942, [cover letter], Report on an address delivered by Rev. Edward Lodge Curran of Brooklyn, microfiche, INT 16IR-6, Foreign Nationalities Branch Files, U.S. Office of Strategic Services (Bethesda, Md: University Publications of America, 1988).

21. Memorandum, Henry W. Levy to William Kirstein, March 11, 1942, Jewish Community Relations Council of Greater Boston, I-123, box 26, folder 1, JHC.

22. "Protest over Father Curran Failed to Shake Committee," *Daily Boston Globe*, March 15, 1942, A1; "Curran Foes Wire Tobin," *Boston Herald*, March 15, 1942, 12; "Anti-Nazi League Protests Christian Front Activity in Boston Evacuation Day Ceremonies," March 15, 1942, Records of the Non-Sectarian Anti-Nazi League to Champion Human Rights, box 777, folder "Christian Front Activity in Boston Evacuation Day," Rare Book and Manuscript Library, Columbia University, New York; "City Will Not Bar Fr. Curran," *Boston Herald*, March 14, 1942, 1.

23. "March 17 Plan Arouses Ire," *Boston Herald*, March 8, 1942, 8; Scannell quoted in "Protest over Father Curran," March 15, 1942.

24. Report, confidential informant T-1, March 18, 1942, attached to J. W. Coulter, report, "Results of Confidential Informant REDACTED set out. REDACTED also set out," February 6, 1943, 2, Francis P. Moran FBI file, 1224676-0-097–HQ–827, Section 3, released through USFOIA.

25. *Evening American* [Boston], March 16, 1942, newspaper clipping, Jewish Community Relations Council of Greater Boston, I-123, box 46, folder 1, JHC.

26. "Dr. McMahon Writes," *New York Post Daily Magazine*, July 1, 1944, 7.

27. "Summary of Christian Front Obstruction to War Effort in Boston," n.d., 1, American Jewish committee, Anti-Semitic and Extremist Collection, box 53, folder Christian Front 2, American Jewish Committee Archives, New York.

Conclusion

1. Conversation with Mrs. Francis P. Moran, July 22, 1943, report of unidentified informant attached to letter, Soucy to FBI Director, December 29, 1943, Francis P. Moran FBI file, 1224676-0-097-HQ-827, Section 4, released through United States Freedom of Information Act (hereafter USFOIA); report of April 3, 1943, attached to James F. Mahan, report, Francis P. Moran, Custodial Detention-G, June 5, 1943, 28, Francis P. Moran FBI file, 1224676-0-097-HQ-827, Section 3, released through USFOIA.

2. Stephen H. Norwood, "Marauding Youth and the Christian Front: Antisemitic Violence in Boston and New York During World War II," *American Jewish History* 91, no. 2 (June 2004): 233–267, 244.

3. John F. Stack, Jr., *International Conflict in an American City: Boston's Irish, Italians, and Jews, 1935–1944* (Westport, CT: Greenwood Press, 1979), 134.

4. "Fran" [Frances Sweeney] to "Dear Tom," March 21, 1943, [copy], 1, drawer G1, Boston Correspondence and Data, Avedis (Arthur) Derounian papers, Mardigian Library, National Association for Armenian Studies and Research, Belmont, MA (hereafter NAASR); Marc Lee Raphael, *The Synagogue in America: A Short History* (New York: New York University Press, 2011), 121.

5. Report, April 12, 1943, drawer G1, folder: Boston Correspondence and Data, Arthur Derounian papers, NAASR, 1–3; "Fran" [Frances Sweeney] to "Dear Tom."

6. "French Tars March Today," *Boston Herald*, March 17, 1943, 12.

7. "Fran" [Frances Sweeney] to "Dear Tom."

8. Report (Derounian), April 12, 1943, 3, 4.

9. Confidential report, Headquarters First Service Command, Office of the Director, Intelligence Division, Racial Disturbances in the Greater Boston Area, October 20, 1943, The Isadore Zack—U.S. Army Counter Intelligence Corps (CIC) Papers, 1942–1997, MC 160, box 2, folder 52: Domestic Intelligence Memos, Milne Special Collections and Archives, University of New Hampshire Library, Durham, NH (hereafter Isadore Zack papers).

10. James F. Mahan, report on Francis P. Moran, November 4, 1943, 15, Francis P. Moran FBI file, 1224676-0-097-HQ-827, Section 4, released through USFOIA. On Shubow's views, see Naomi W. Cohen, "Dual Loyalties: Zionism and Liberalism," in *Envisioning Israel: The Changing Ideals and Images of North American Jews*, ed. Allon Gal (Detroit: Wayne State University Press, 1996), 321n4.

11. Arnold Beichman, "Christian Front Hoodlums Terrorized Boston Jews," *PM*, October 18, 1943, 5. Beichman was a staunch liberal and was anti-Fascist, but he was not a leftist. In 1946 he was fired from *PM* after resisting a leftist takeover of the publication. He then turned toward anti-Communism. Like a number of liberal Jewish intellectuals of

his generation, Beichman followed anti-Communism to neoconservatism. He eventually became a columnist for the *Washington Times* and a fellow at the Hoover Institution.

12. "Gov. Saltonstall Denies Boston Anti-Semitism: Throws Reporter Out," *New York Evening Post*, October 18, 1943, 4; "A Challenge to Gov. Saltonstall: Stamp Out Terrorism against Boston Jews or Disprove It," *PM*, October 19, 1943, 1. A roundup of national coverage appears in Arnold Beichman, "Probe of Boston Assaults Put on Statewide Basis," *PM*, October 21, 1943, 5.

13. Leverett Saltonstall to Joseph Timilty, October 18, 1943, Leverett Saltonstall papers, box 9, folder anti-Semitism, 1943, Massachusetts Historical Association, Boston.

14. Joseph F. Timilty to "My Dear Governor Saltonstall," November 22, 1943, Leverett Saltonstall papers, box 9, folder anti-Semitism, 1943, Massachusetts Historical Society, Boston.

15. John Bond, "Jewish Group Lays Disorders Squarely on Christian Front," *Christian Science Monitor*, October 21, 1943, 1; "Racial Troubles Not 'Kid Stuff,' Schoeberg Says," *Daily Boston Globe*, November 29, 1943, 12; Editorial, *Dorchester Record*, October 7, 1943, 2. The *Boston Herald* of October 21, 1943, was an outlier, arguing that there was no substantial evidence to blame the Christian Front for the anti-Semitic incidents.

16. "Virgil Peterson," typescript, n.d., Virgil Peterson papers, box 2, folder 3, Chicago History Museum Research Center, Chicago; William C. Sullivan, *The Bureau: My Thirty Years in Hoover's FBI* (New York: W. W. Norton, 1979), 17; "FBI Sets Up New Divisions," *Observer Dispatch* [Utica, NY], December 2, 1939.

17. J. Edgar Hoover to SAC, Boston, "personal attention," October 18, 1943, re Francis P. Moran, Francis P. Moran FBI file, 1224676-0-097–HQ–827, Section 3, released through USFOIA.

18. F. L. Welch, Memorandum for Mr. D. M. Ladd, October 30, 1943, Francis P. Moran FBI file, 1224676-0-097–HQ–827, Section 3, released through USFOIA; Jeremy Varon, *Bringing the War Home: The Weather Underground, the Red Army Faction, and Revolutionary Violence in the Sixties and Seventies* (Berkeley: University of California Press, 2004), 152.

19. Conversation with Mrs. Francis P. Moran, July 22, 1943.

20. Mahan, FBI report, November 4, 1943, 13.

21. Moran quoted in conversation with Mrs. Francis P. Moran, July 22, 1943; Deborah Lamm Weisel, "The Evolution of Street Gangs: An Examination of Form and Variation," in *The Modern Gang Reader*, ed. Arlen Egley, Cheryl L. Maxson, Jody Miller, and Malcolm W. Klein (New York: Oxford University Press, 2006), 95–96.

22. George V. Higgins, "Himself," review of *The Rascal King: The Life and Times of James Michael Curley, 1874–1958* by Jack Beatty, *American Scholar* 63, no. 1 (1994): 130–137, 134.

23. Edward A. Soucy to Director, FBI, November 2, 1943, Francis P. Moran Security Matter, Francis P. Moran FBI file, 1224676-0-097–HQ–827, Section 3, released through USFOIA; Arthur Derounian, typewritten memo, Francis Moran, n.d., drawer A3, folder "Moran, Francis P.," Arthur Derounian papers, NASSR.

24. Confidential informant T-1, report of April 3, 1943, attached to James F. Mahan, June 5, 1943, 26, Francis P. Moran FBI file, 1224676-0-097–HQ–827, Section 3, released through USFOIA.

25. "Moran, Ex-Christian Front Head, Fired 36 Times, Blames War Department," *Boston Herald*, November 3, 1943, 10; "Moran Given Army Physical," *Boston Herald*, December 3, 1943, 12.

26. Hoover to Communications Section, November 5, 1943, transmit message to SAC Boston, Francis P. Moran FBI file, 1224676-0-097–HQ–827, Section 3, released through USFOIA; J. Edgar Hoover to Tom C. Clark, November 10, 1943, Memorandum for Assistant Attorney General, Francis P. Moran FBI file, 1224676-0-097–HQ–827, Section 3, released through USFOIA.

27. "Francis P. Moran Slated to Report to Army December 23," *Daily Boston Globe*, December 3, 1943, 24; "F. P. Moran Says He Will Revive the Christian Front," *Boston Herald*, December 18, 1943, 11; Moran draft card, [copy], Francis P. Moran FBI file, 1224676-0-097–HQ–827, Section EBF 55, 1, released through USFOIA.

28. Memo, Scholtz, Hubert [sic], SECRET, SCI to SCI Unit Z, Milan, 31 October, 1945, Herbert W. Scholz FBI file, 65–HQ–4414, Section 2, released through USFOIA. The source indicates that Scholz was sent to Turin under consular cover for "special work." Allen Welsh Dulles, *From Hitler's Doorstep: The Wartime Intelligence Reports of Allen Dulles, 1942–1945*, ed. Neal H. Petersen (University Park: Pennsylvania State University Press, 1996), 81.

29. Karl Wolff to "Lieber Max!" April 10, 1944, Herbert W. Scholz, SS personnel file, [microfilm], RG 226, roll 105, National Archives and Records Administration, Archives II, College Park, MD (hereafter NARA).

30. Caserta to State Department, telegram [copy], Dr. Herbert Scholz, June 21, 1945, Herbert W. Scholz FBI file, 65–HQ–4414, Section 2, released through USFOIA; Memo [copy], Counter Intelligence Corps Detachment Headquarters Fifth Army, German Diplomats Suspected of Connection with GIS, June 29, 1945, Herbert W. Scholz FBI file, 65–HQ–4414, Section 2, released through USFOIA; State Department to Caserta, telegram [copy], July 7, 1945, Dr. Herbert Scholz re: June 21, 1945 telegram, Herbert W. Scholz FBI file, 65–HQ–4414, Section 2, released through USFOIA.

31. C. O. SCI Z Units, [Secret Counter Intelligence Unit Z], James Angleton to SCI Unit 2, Milan, report re Herbert Scholz [secret], October 31, 1945, Herbert W. Scholz FBI file, 65–HQ–4414, Section 2, released through USFOIA. On the Ciano Papers, see Howard Smyth McGaw, "The Ciano Papers: Rose Garden," *Studies in Intelligence* 13, no. 2 (1969): 1–63.

32. M. Fossati, *Arcivescovado di Torino*, bona fides for Dott Herbert Scholtz [sic] [copy], July 12, 1946, RG 319, Records of the Army Staff, Digital IRR Files, file D160 686, NARA. I am grateful to Professor Richard Breitman of American University for assisting in the declassification of Scholz's CIC file.

33. Report, date indecipherable, Intelligence Detachment, Repatriation Center, Ludwigsburg, Germany, RG 319, Records of the Army Staff, Digital IRR Files, file D160 686, NARA.

34. Victor H. Bernstein, "Will Nuremburg Put the Finger on U.S. Fifth Column?" *PM*, April 5, 1946, 2; "U.S. Prosecutor Off to Germany for Sedition Evidence," *Daily Boston Globe*, April 1, 1946, 7.

35. O. John Rogge, *The Official German Report: Nazi Penetration, 1924–1942* (New York: Thomas Yoseloff, 1961), 313–314; Zev Garber and Bruce Zuckerman, "Why Do We Call the Holocaust 'The Holocaust'?: An Inquiry into the Psychology of Labels," *Modern Judaism* 9, no. 2 (1989): 197–211, 201. The incompetent police response to the Cocoanut Grove fire has come to be the best-known known albatross around Timilty's neck and is commonly regarded as the reason Governor Saltonstall let him go. In fact, the anti-Semitic crisis, and Timilty's mishandling of the Christian Front, were both the last straw and the key to the commissioner's removal.

36. Dr. Herbert W. Scholz to G-2 Liaison Detachment, December 30, 1946, RG 319, Records of the Army Staff, Digital IRR Files, file D160 686, NARA.

37. "Boston Rumor Clinic Combats Stories that Harm Morale," *Life*, October 12, 1942, 88.

38. Report, James F. Mahan, Francis P. Moran: Custodial Detention–G, November 4, 1943, 15, Francis P. Moran FBI file, 1224676-0-097–HQ–827, Section 4, released through USFOIA; *Boston City Reporter*, 9th ed., January 1944, [2], drawer G1, "Boston Clippings" folder, Arthur Derounian papers, NAASR; Frances Sweeney to Gordon W. Allport, May 3, 1943, Gordon W. Allport papers, Box 10, Frances Sweeney file, Harvard University Archives, Cambridge, MA.

39. Nat Hentoff, *Boston Boy: Growing Up with Jazz and Other Rebellious Passions* (New York: Knopf, 1986; Philadelphia: Paul Dry Books, 2001), 85.

40. James Bottis to Gordon W. Allport, June 1944, Gordon W. Allport papers, box 10, Frances Sweeney file, Harvard University Archives, Cambridge, MA.

Epilogue

1. Herbert W. Scholz to Heinrich Brüning, [handwritten letter], January 2, 1947, Heinrich Brüning Papers HUG FP 93, box 36, folder 5, Harvard University Archives, Cambridge, MA (hereafter Brüning Papers, HUA).

2. Geoffrey P. Megargee, *The United States Holocaust Memorial Museum Encyclopedia of Camps and Ghettos, 1933–1945*, vol. 1: *Early Camps, Youth Camps, and Concentration Camps and Subcamps under the SS-Business Administration Main Office (WVHA)* (Bloomington: Indiana University Press, in association with the United States Holocaust Memorial Museum, 2009), 1059.

3. [Brüning to Scholz], unsigned copy, January 24, 1947, Brüning Papers, HUA.

4. Scholz to Brüning, January 2, 1947.

5. Helen Kirkpatrick, "Industrial Giant Glad to See Friends," *Syracuse Herald-Journal*, April 11, 1945, 8. Schnitzler visited DuPont on a business trip in 1937.

6. "Scholz, Dr.," Personal Name Files of Defendants and Witnesses in the IG Farben Trial, 1946–1948, Record Group 260, Records of U.S. Occupation Headquarters, World War II, National Archives and Records Administration, Archives II, College Park, MD.

7. Confidential source contemporaneous with events, interview with the author, June 1, 2018.

8. Funeral program, Dr. Herbert W. Scholz, July 10, 1985, from a confidential source contemporaneous with events.

9. Final Payment Roll, Francis P. Moran, Office of Military Personnel, National Personnel Records Center, St. Louis, MO; "Christian Fronter Out of the Army," typewritten news story, Jewish Community Relations Council of Greater Boston, I-123, box 44, folder 3, Wyner Family Jewish Heritage Center at New England Historic Genealogical Society, Boston (hereafter JHC).

10. "Domestic Intelligence Memorandum No. 27," CONFIDENTIAL, January 5, 1945, 3, folder 34, box 2, Isadore Zack papers.

11. Francis P. Moran to Charles Parsons, January 20, 1945, Tyler Gatewood Kent Papers, miscellaneous papers re: *Kent v. United States*, 1944–1946, box 1, folder 11, Manuscripts and Archives, Yale University Library, New Haven, CT.

12. Paul N. Herbert, *Treason in the Rockies: Nazi Sympathizer Dale Maple's POW Escape Plot* (Charleston, SC: History Press, 2016), 21; Paul Higbee, "Suspects in Sturgis," *South Dakota Magazine*, November/December 2000, https://www.southdakotamagazine .com/suspects-in-sturgis; Thomas E. Ricks, "A Pro-Nazi U.S. Army Unit in WWII," *Foreign Policy* (online), February 18, 2011, https://www.foreignpolicy.com/2011/02/18/a-pro -nazi-u-s-army-unit-in-wwii. Maple was set to die by hanging, but his sentence was commuted. John Hammond Moore, *Wacko War: Strange Tales from America, 1941–1945* (Raleigh, NC: Ivy House, 2001), 51–52. The now-dismantled online Moran family history indicated that Francis "guarded Japanese prisoners." More likely he worked alongside Japanese Americans. His army occupational specialty is a mystery because his personnel file was lost in the 1973 National Personnel Records Center fire.

13. Moran to Parsons, January 20, 1945.

14. Report, March 20, 1946, "Invincible Ireland," address by Reverend Edward Lodge Curran, Jewish Community Relations Council of Greater Boston, I-123, box 46, folder 1, JHC.

15. Unsigned Memo, January 1947, with handwritten note from "Gus" to "Dear Arthur," drawer A3, folder "Moran, Francis P.," Avedis (Arthur) Derounian papers, Mardigian Library, National Association for Armenian Studies and Research, Belmont, MA.

16. "Former Christian Front Leader Held Up in Cab," *Herald-Traveler*, March 9, 1948, news clipping, *Boston Herald-Traveler* clippings morgue, Pickering Educational Resources Library, Boston University, Boston.

17. Report, Francis Moran, May 11, 1949, Moran FBI file, 1224676-0-097–HQ–827, Section 5, released through United States Freedom of Information Act; *Polk's Boston City Directory, 1963* (Boston: R. L. Polk, 1963), 1295, available online via the database "U.S., City Directories, 1822–1995," https://www.ancestry.com/search/collections/2469.

18. Report, Friends of the Rev. Arthur W. Terminiello at New England Mutual Hall, Boston, July 13, 1945, 1, Jewish Community Relations Council of Greater Boston, I-123, box 18, folder 5, JHC; John Connelly, *From Enemy to Brother: The Revolution in Catholic Teaching on the Jews, 1933–1945* (Cambridge, MA: Harvard University Press, 2020), 2.

19. Judge Andrew P. Napolitano, "Trump Rally Violence, the First Amendment and 'The Heckler's Veto,'" FoxNews.com, opinion, March 17, 2016, http://www.foxnews.com/opinion/2016/03/17/trump-rally-violence-first-amendment-and-hecklers-veto.html; Emma Green, "Why the Charlottesville Marchers Were Obsessed with Jews," *Atlantic*, August 15, 2017; Alison Frankel, "In the Age of Donald Trump, a Special Duty for Lawyers," Reuters.com, November 11, 2016, https://www.reuters.com/article/us-otc-specialduty-idUSKBN136262.

20. Isabel Currier, "Of, For, and By the Living," *Common Ground* 9, no. 1 (Autumn 1948): 33–41, 38; H. E. Kurland, "Country Lost a Fighter in Death of Frances Sweeney," *New York Post*, July 13, 1944, 23; "Boston Tolerance Leader Honored," *New York Post*, February 14, 1946, 6.

21. "Governor's Committee for Racial and Religious Understanding," public policy pamphlet produced by the Commonwealth of Massachusetts Executive Department, Boston, February 14, 1945, https://archives.lib.state.ma.us/bitstream/handle/2452/782357/ocn814851796.pdf; "About the Commission Against Discrimination," Massachusetts Commission Against Discrimination, https://www.mass.gov/info-details/about-the-commission-against-discrimination.

22. Connelly, *From Enemy to Brother*, 173.

23. Bea quoted in Connelly, *From Enemy to Brother*, 249.

24. Connelly, *From Enemy to Brother*, 297.

ACKNOWLEDGMENTS

I WAS RECENTLY REMINDED OF THE FRENCH PHILOSOPHER SIMONE Weil's words, "Attention is the rarest and purest form of generosity." Weil was expressing her gratitude to a correspondent who had "paid real attention to some pages" she sent for review. To Weil, attention was a moral and spiritual matter.

In this regard, I am deeply grateful to a number of people who inspired, encouraged, and "paid real attention" to the researching and writing of this project. Thanks, first of all, must go to Andrew Kinney at Harvard University Press. His belief in the project, his high standards, his compassion with deadlines in the face of the sudden death of my brother, and his astute insights into the framing of arguments have been invaluable. I am indebted as well to HUP's Simon Waxman for his scrupulous eye, organizational detail, and cheerful good humor while working under deadline. His regard for not only the political history of the case, but also its religious nature, was extraordinary. I also profited from enriching conversations with Boston College colleagues James O'Toole, Devin Pendas, Benjamin Braude, and Heather Cox Richardson. Professors Kevin Kenny, Robin Fleming, and Sarah Gwyneth Ross, who served as chairs of the BC History Department during the research phase of this project, were deeply supportive.

My research was made possible only through the generosity of archivists and librarians. David Sigler of the Special Collections and Archives at the California State University, Northridge, was helpful in navigating the voluminous files of the Jewish Federation Council of Greater Los Angeles. Marc

Mamigonian at the National Association for Armenian Studies and Research facilitated extensive research in the papers of Arthur Derounian, the only journalist to successfully infiltrate the Christian Front. At the Boston Public Library, Aaron Schmidt helped me locate photos of Christian Front activity in Boston. Lindsay Sprechman Murphy, at the Wyner Family Jewish Heritage Center, assisted in my research concerning the Jewish Community Relations Council of Greater Boston. Margaret Sullivan was enormously helpful in accessing records of the Boston Police Department. Anne H. Kenny, at BC's O'Neill Library, was especially diligent in tracking down obscure historical sources and ephemeral publications.

For permission to work on the Christian Front file in the historical archives of the Secretariat of State of the Holy See, I would like to express my sincere gratitude to the Most Reverend Paul Gallagher, the Holy See's secretary for relations with states, and his dedicated team of archivists.

Danielle DuBois Gottwig, at the National Archives and Records Administration, was extremely patient with my multiple requests for declassification of FBI files under the Freedom of Information Act. I would also like to thank the specialists at the Federal Bureau of Investigation Record / Information Dissemination Section, who painstakingly read through thousands of pages of FBI historical files on the Christian Front. Their silent work of civil service is deeply appreciated.

Early on, my research moved from the local to the transnational. Consequently I am appreciative of the financial support provided by the Jack, Joseph and Morton Mandel Center for Advanced Holocaust Studies at the United States Holocaust Memorial Museum, where I had the honor of being the William J. Lowenberg Memorial Fellow on America, the Holocaust, and the Jews in 2016–2017. A research trip to the Bundesarchiv in Berlin in the summer of 2015 was funded by a grant from the Clough Center for the Study of Constitutional Democracy at BC. I am grateful for two grants from BC's Morrissey College of Arts and Sciences, which supported my research in Rome and the purchase of photographs. I am indebted to Gregory Kalscheur, SJ, Dean of the Morrissey College. Two BC students served as research assistants. Sarah Finlaw and Nicholas M. Centrella Jr. brought their intelligence and budding professionalism to the task, as they helped me dig through archives.

A number of scholars arranged talks at which I was able to receive valuable feedback. Retired Brigadier General Kevin T. Ryan and his Defense and

Intelligence Projects series at the Harvard Kennedy School sponsored one such talk. Father Dennis McManus of the Center for Jewish Civilization at Georgetown University brought me to the Georgetown School of Foreign Service. Professor Timothy Johnson kindly invited me to deliver the 2017 Cecile and Gene Usdin Judeo-Christian lecture at Flagler College. Professor Beth Griech-Polelle was instrumental in arranging a Christian Front talk for the 2018 Raphael Lemkin Lecture at Pacific Lutheran University.

Many scholars, writers, and experts of various sorts provided advice, scrutiny, and friendship. David I. Kertzer of Brown University has been a tremendous resource and guide. Peter Eisner was always there when things got stressful. He and his wife Musha welcomed me into their home. At the US Holocaust Memorial Museum, Victoria Barnett, Suzanne Brown-Fleming, Wendy Lower, Michael Gelb, and Benton Arnovitz offered friendship and encouragement. Steven Feldman was an invaluable help in numerous ways. Richard Breitman was instrumental in getting US Army Counter Intelligence Corps files identified and released. Intelligence specialists Christopher Andrew, Rupert Allason (a.k.a. Nigel West), Carol Rollie Flynn, and Joe Wippl assisted along the way. Father Bernhard Knorn, SJ, of the Philosophical-Theological University of Sankt Georgen in Hamburg, spent many hours helping translate SA and SS documents. Historian David T. Courtwright and theologian Harvey Egan, SJ, always had time when I called on them.

Closer to home, my Jesuit community of St. Mary's Hall at Boston College has offered a pleasant residence of study, prayer, and support while finalizing this project. Over the years, my good friends of the Jewish-Catholic Roundtable in Bedford, Massachusetts, provided much support and many clarifying comments. I am grateful to the Jesuit Community at Georgetown University, where I spent my fellowship year in 2016. Gratitude also goes to the Jesuit Community at Loyola Marymount University in Los Angeles for their hospitality during my West Coast research trips. To all who have helped me become a better writer, and a better historian, I am grateful.

INDEX

African Americans, 142, 223
Agar, William, 188–189, 190
Ahearne, David, 56
Ahern, Michael, 2, 114–116, 189, 190
Angleton, James Jesus, 235
anti-Communism: Christian Front and, 33; defined, 3; as ecumenism motivator, 25; Francis Moran and, 86; of Irish Americans, 194; as religious imperative, 41; St. Joseph's and, 79; support for, 87; as theological, 48
Anti-Defamation League (ADL), 160, 176, 179, 224
anti-Fascism, 193–194, 196–197
anti-Judaism, 12, 32, 139–140
anti-Semitism: within Boston, 221; Boston Christian Front and, 142; Communism and, 102; crisis of 1943, 222–229; criticism of, 200; crucifixion and, 80; defined, 32; economic argument regarding, 102; of Francis Moran, 104–105, 139–140; free speech and, 246; John Cassidy's viewpoint regarding, 39; National Conference of Christians and Jews and, 161; prominence of, 116; as racial, 12; religiously imbued, 32–33; as source of violence, 221–222, 225–226, 245; as theological, 32; and the Vatican, 3
Armstrong, George Johnson, 151–153
assimilation, 5–6

Ballem, Marie, 103
baptism, 7, 48
Beer Hall Putsch, 128–129

Berle, Adolf, Jr., 137, 173, 174
Berlin, Isaiah, 31, 32
Biddle, Francis, 171, 218
Bildungsbürgertum, 124–125
Birkhead, Leon, 172–173
Bishop, William, 54, 56, 57, 58–59, 60, 63, 68, 98–99
black propaganda, 186, 191–192
Boettger, Macklin, 54, 58
Bolling, A. R., 168
Bolshevism, 7, 8
bombing, 54, 58–61, 64
Bonn, John Louis, 199–201
Boston: anti-Communism within, 87; anti-Semitic outbreak within, 221; Blue Hill Avenue, 226; Dorchester, 222–223; faith battlefield within, 199–200; IADA within, 192; Irish of, 77–78, 107, 188–189, 194; Jewish communities within, 222–223; Jewish Community Relations Council, 101–102; Little Building, 192; Mattapan, 223; Old South Meeting House, 116; postwar conditions within, 242; racial riots within, 224, 225; Roxbury, 223; violence within, 221–222
Boston Christian Front: accusations against, 110; anti-Semitism within, 142; attendance, 156; closure of, 211–212; FBI and, 112, 173–174; financial support for, 113, 158, 198; Friday Group of, 212–216, 219, 230; heckling by, 166; Jewish presence within, 157; Joseph Timilty role within, 227; Max Bradley within,